T0128739

UNDERSTANDING
THE *GLOBAL SHIFT,*
THE POPULARITY
OF DONALD TRUMP,
BREXIT AND
DISCONTENT
IN THE WEST

RISE OF THE EMERGING ECONOMIES: 1980 TO 2018

ROCKY M. MIRZA: PH.D.

Order this book online at www.trafford.com
or email orders@trafford.com

Most Trafford titles are also available at major online book retailers.

Print information available on the last page.

ISBN: 978-1-4907-9327-6 (sc)
ISBN: 978-1-4907-9328-3 (hc)
ISBN: 978-1-4907-9329-0 (e)

Library of Congress Control Number: 2019931483

Trafford rev. 01/25/2019

www.trafford.com

North America & international
toll-free: 1 888 232 4444 (USA & Canada)
fax: 812 355 4082

CONTENTS

ACKNOWLEDGMENTS

I wish to thank my friend and colleague Dr. Peter Dunnett for proofreading the manuscript and suggesting minor changes. I wish to thank my wife, Penny Mirza, for her unwavering support of the ideas I have expressed in this book.

This book is dedicated to

Candidate and Pres. Donald J. Trump, the only Western leader I have ever admired.

INTRODUCTION

Whites, mixed-race blacks, Hispanics, and Asians rail against President Trump, leaders of Brexit, Brexiteers, and Far Right politicians in Western Europe, with the unified slogan that they are defending American, British, and European values. The values they claim to defend are centuries of military invasions, conquests, colonizations, warmongering, slavery, and subjugation of nonwhites in Africa, Asia, and the New World. The problem today is the same it has been since Portugal began six centuries of Western domination after conquering the West African city of Ceuta in 1415. Those on the Left who rail against President Trump, Brexiteers, and Far Right Western politicians are confused. They have fallen victim to six centuries of Western propaganda, which deliberately lied about Western evils with slogans such as "Christianizing the heathens," "taming the Wild Indian," "civilizing the naked savages," "carrying the white man's burden," "fighting Communism," "bringing democracy," "fighting terrorism," "fighting Islamic extremism," and many more outrageous claims to "civilized" behavior. Where once the Western media, as represented by key outlets such as CNN in the United States, BBC in the UK, and CBC in Canada, was united in defending these so-called Western values against non-Western, Third World, or Communist values in the East, the Western media now has a new target. This new target is primarily President Trump, but to a lesser extent those it refers to as the Far Right and the Brexiteers. President Trump is correct to identify the true opposition to him as the mainstream media, not the American people. What has been called "freedom of the press" has enabled the rise of a very powerful mainstream media in the United States, which influences the behavior of all the other mainstream media in the West. It no longer reports the news but targets politicians it is against. It was evolved as a tool to dictate its own political agenda regardless of the wishes of the electorate. Its only opposition is social media, and at this time, it is still far more influential than social media.

What has given rise to President Trump, Brexiteers, and Far Right Western politicians is not racism or homophobia or nationalism or all the other labels made up by the Western mainstream media. It is what we have named the Global Shift, which this book is all about. This revolutionary phenomenon originating with the Chinese SEZs after 1979 has simultaneously led to the destruction of high-wage manufacturing jobs in the West and the much higher economic growth rates in Third World economies such as China, India, Indonesia, Mexico, and Brazil compared to Western economies such as the United States, Germany, France, Italy, and Britain. This Global Shift, misleadingly referred to as *Globalization*, began modestly in 1965 with the Mexican *maquiladoras* but much more seriously after 1979 with China's SEZs.

President Nixon made a bold move when he decided to engage with China, on China's terms, to get China to help the West win its Cold War with the Soviet Union. President Nixon allowed China to keep its Communist government and independent military because China was, at the time, a very poor country with almost zero probability of ever challenging the United States for hegemony. However, once the Soviet Union collapsed in 1991 and it was clear that China's rate of economic growth would far outpace the United States, U.S. presidents after 1991, George H. W. Bush, Bill Clinton, George W. Bush, and Barack Obama, should have returned to America's Cold War policy of isolating China. Isolating China and other pro-Communist countries after World War II was a key reason to maintaining Western domination of the World. Just look at North Korea compared to South Korea or Taiwan. The U.S. presidents after the fall of the Soviet Union in 1991 did not reverse the Western engagement with China begun by President Nixon because none of them were visionary leaders like President Trump, Brexiteers, and Far Right Western politicians.

Western leaders in the United States and Western Europe after 1991 had their heads buried in the sand. They follow each other like a bunch of sheep. President Nixon had engaged with China not for trade but for political clout against the Soviet Union. But Western leaders after 1991 did not know their history and foolishly assumed that engaging with China was done for economic gains. They saw China as a source of cheap consumer goods with which to bribe their voters. They also saw China as a country where the West could move their dirty polluting factories to win the votes of the environmentalists. They also saw China as a country they could ship their "recycled" wastes and plastics. They also saw China as a way of boosting their own economic growth rates and buy votes with their election promises to increase economic growth. What they did not see was the recent discontents with major sections of their electorates who lost high-paying industrial jobs, whose cities were decimated by the

Global Shift, who incorrectly blamed immigrants rather than the Global Shift for their plight and who saw a heartless establishment, dumbed-down media, Wall Street billionaires, high-wage technocrats, and stupid intellectuals calling them a "basket of deplorables."

When the American empire created the New World Order after the Second World War with a single Western superpower, the United States, replacing several Western empires, the British, French, German, and Italian empires, the United States committed to pay for the bulk of the defense costs. In addition, the United States committed to subsidizing the defense costs of Japan, South Korea, Saudi Arabia, and Canada. These defense commitments were made by the United States to ensure that the member countries of NATO, as well as Japan, South Korea, and Saudi Arabia, will never dare oppose any and all invasions, wars, and regime changes initiated by the United States. The United States was able to pay for these massive defense commitments because its GDP was significantly larger than any other country. Since none of the Western leaders before President Trump were visionaries, nor could ever think outside the box, they collectively regarded this post–World War order as the only norm, never to be challenged or tweaked or reformed. As sheep, they followed each other blindly.

Candidate Trump recognized that in 2017, the United States could no longer afford these costly defense commitments. He recognized that because he was the only Western leader in my lifetime with the ability to think outside the box. The GDP of the United States had fallen relative to many countries during the period from 1946 to 2017. In addition, candidate Trump saw that these costly defense commitments had minimal defense benefits to the United States compared to using those funds to enhance the U.S. military and provide better benefits for its own service people. Candidate Trump campaigned on NATO being obsolete and for Japan, South Korea, and Saudi Arabia paying the full cost of their own defense. He further campaigned on the fact that the United States could no longer afford to police the globe and continue its addiction to warmongering and regime changes by military invasions and creating millions of refugees.

The irony of the undeniably stupid and vicious attacks first on candidate Trump and later on President Trump by all the Western media, Western leaders, Western intellectuals, Western entertainers, and all and sundry is that those attackers suggest that President Trump's ideas will weaken rather than strengthen U.S. leadership of the world. They deny the relative decline of the United States even though China has moved from tenth place in 1980 to second place, as measured by GDP, and many more emerging economies such as India, Brazil, Indonesia, and others are gaining on the United States. They deny the fact that the *American dream* has moved to China. Upward mobility is far greater in China today than in the United States. Chinese today are far more optimistic about their economic future than Americans. Many Americans today, especially uneducated whites and blacks, fear downward mobility. The attackers claim that continued engagement with these emerging economies will enhance the power of the United States even though there is overwhelming evidence to the contrary. The dumbed-down Western media is unable to see that Trump is a smart, independent thinker unlike the Barack Obamas, Emmanuel Macrons, and Justin Trudeaus, whom the media heap undeserved praises on. Somewhat ironically, with the media's foremost choice of "sage" leadership, Obama, gone, Trudeau was initially anointed to succeed. But Macron came along and overthrew Trudeau only because France has a little less of a lightweight economy compared to Canada. Yet that same dumbed-down media now claims that Macron is trying to "make France great again." Wonder where that idea was stolen from? Hypocrisy is a key hallmark of dumb Western leaders, but no one can ever accuse President Trump of hypocrisy. He may be politically incorrect, but political correctness has become the new tool of the other Western leaders to deceive, lie, and embrace six centuries of Western hypocrisy.

One misleading theory used by these protrade demigods is Ricardo's theory of comparative advantage. While this theory proves that trade benefits all who engage in it, the part they are ignorant of is that Ricardo's theory says nothing about how the gains are shared. Engaging with China boosted the annual economic growth of China from 2.5 percent to 10 percent. That engagement boosted the economic growth of the United States from 2.5 percent to 3 percent. When the Global Shift began in China in 1980, the United States had a GDP 12.7 times that of China. In 2015, the U.S. GDP was only 1.6 times that of China. How can anyone deny that China got the lion's share of the gains?

Of course, if the West was only concerned with economic growth, continued engagement with China and other emerging economies would be sensible. But the West has never been content with economic gains. Western leaders today who viciously attack President Trump are no less imperialists today than they were six centuries ago. All of them support, for example, the senseless and costly bombings of the Muslim countries in the Middle East and North Africa. They do so not because of economic gains but despite massive economic costs. Their goal in these bombings, killings, destruction, and creation of millions of refuges is continued Western colonizations and regime changes. Yet they are too stupid to recognize that the United States cannot continue on the path of free trade with China and the emerging economies without losing its economic advantage, which pays for the military cost of empire. They foolishly expect U.S. taxpayers to continue to foot the lion's share of their imperial ambitions while agreeing to free trade where most of the gains go to the emerging economies.

In addition, the G7 leaders have no intention of sharing their imperial ambitions with any of the emerging economies such as China or India. In fact, they kicked out Russia from the G8 to become the G7 when Russia refused to embrace their imperial goals and chastised President Trump for suggesting to bring back Russia. In creating the G20, they made sure that both the EU, as a group, as well as some members of the EU such as Britain, France, Germany, and Italy were members so as to overwhelm the emerging economies and make the G20 less relevant compared to the G7. They even tried to oust Russia from the G20 but were unable to because of opposition from the emerging economies.

We see President Trump as the only visionary and smart Western leader today. President Obama was not only less smart but also no visionary. He was the typical sheep. Only President Trump understands that it was the West engaging with China and other emerging economies that reduced the relative GDP rankings of the United States and its Western allies. While the gains from international trade has benefitted both the West and the emerging economies, far more of the gains went to the emerging economies. Continued engagement will only continue to erode the relative economic, political, and military power of the West. That's good if you favor greater equality and reduced Western dominance. There is no question that I favor this continued erosion of Western domination. Just read my other three books. However, I am not as stupid as the critics of President Trump to deny the truth of what President Trump is saying even though I think it's too late for President Trump to reverse course. Presidents George H. W. Bush, Clinton, and George W. Bush could have reversed course. Perhaps even President Obama may have had a small chance of reversing course. But it's too late for President Trump. However, President Trump is correct in having the United States focus much more on its needs precisely because the Global Shift has weakened the relative economic power of the United States. President Trump is also correct in helping those hurt by the Global Shift by protecting the U.S. market even at the expense of some gains from trade. Those gains have gone to consumers, those benefitting from the Internet and computer technology, and to those in finance, banking, and Wall Street. The gains have come at the expense of those who had relatively high-wage jobs in manufacturing and construction. While the Global Shift has reduced wealth and income inequality between developed and developing economies, it has increased income and wealth inequality in the United States, Britain, and other developed economies. At the same time, increased competition caused by the Global Shift has reduced the power and benefits of unions in the West. President Trump's massive tax cuts will more than pay for the small loss from trade protection. Canada is playing a dangerous game in ramping up a trade war with President Trump. It's no secret that Canadians rub their hands with glee whenever Prime Minister Trudeau and his far too outspoken mouthpiece, Chrystia Freeland, "dump on Trump." But Canada will pay a heavy price for such childish behavior. President Trump's massive tax cuts placed Canada at a significant competitive disadvantage. If Canada loses the "Auto Pact," which predated NAFTA, because of its hypocrisy in pretending that Canada has any more moral values than President Trump, Canada's auto sector is doomed.

In summary, President Trump, Brexiteers, and Far Right leaders have a much better grasp of the disruptions caused by the Global Shift than the critics on the Left. However, neither side has a full understanding. It's the hope that this book will enlighten both sides. Those on the Left, unfortunately, are no less warmongers, racists, or imperialists than those on the Right. The solution to the refugee and immigration crises in the United States and Europe is not taking a few more rather than a few less refugees and illegal migrants. It's stopping the bombings, which destroys the livelihoods of so many. Those on the Left blatantly use the refugees and the illegal migrants to further their own political agendas such as winning elections, continuation of six centuries of Western imperialism, and continuation of their pompous claims that the West knows what is best for those in the developing countries. In my view, they are far more die-hard racists than those on the Right. Those on the Left, who are *not* racists, are used and abused by the Left far more than the Right is using racists to further their cause. As an example, just look at how the mixed-race black leaders today use and abuse the majority of blacks to further their own selfish careers and causes. President Trump will do far more for blacks in the United States than President Obama ever did.

No other Western leader would have had the vision to meet with Pres. Kim Jong-un and begin the most significant peace process of the twenty-first century. This act alone makes President Trump the greatest Western leader of all time, far above addicted warmongers like Winston Churchill, Franklin D. Roosevelt, or Barack Obama. It's President Trump, not President Obama, who deserves the Nobel Peace Prize. I cannot end this introduction without a much-deserved "shout-out" to a basketball legend turned peacemaker, Dennis Rodman.

CHAPTER 1

Understanding the Popularity of Donald Trump and Brexit, China versus the American Empire, East versus West, and Trump versus Xi

When I began writing this book in early 2016, there was no candidate or president Donald Trump, no Brexit, and the so-called Left dismissed the rising popularity of the so-called Far Right and anti-EU sentiments within Europe. But Trump's presidency and Brexit have led me to deal with this reality up front, rather than as an afterthought, because it fits so well into my primary thesis regarding the Global Shift. In my view, the primary reason for the popularity of Donald Trump and Brexit is the Global Shift of good-paying jobs and rapid economic growth to the emerging economies. Many Americans with no more than a high school education worked in factories producing cars and other manufactured goods for wages as high as forty dollars per hour. When many of these jobs moved to Latin America and Asia, most of the displaced American workers could only find service jobs in retail paying as little as ten dollars per hour. Some on the Left have benefitted from the Global Shift by finding high-paying jobs in the high-tech industries that were born with the Internet, the digital age, and the use of personal computers. This so-called digital revolution occurred, by coincidence, at the same time as the Global Shift and complemented each other in many ways.

While both the Global Shift and the digital revolution lowered prices for all consumers, this downward effect on the price of consumer goods, ironically, benefitted the same group of wage earners getting the new high-wage jobs, far more than those losing the old high-wage jobs, since high-income earners can purchase far more consumer goods than low-income consumers in a free enterprise economy, touting the benefits of private property and consumer sovereignty as far more civilized than Communism. Of course, the concern over good-paying jobs was compounded by other factors such as the creation of sixty million refugees by the Western "war on terror," a new propaganda discovered by the West to feed its addiction to warmongering after the demise of Communism following the fall of the Soviet Union. The influx of these refugees into Western Europe, the influx of Latinos into the United States, and the growth of the nonwhite population in the West because of immigrants from their many ex-colonies in Asia and Africa gave those fearful of the loss of high-paying jobs an additional cause for complaint. Many of these other factors can be tied to the Global Shift, though some existed long before the Global Shift. Those on the Right blamed *Globalization*. Those on the Left and the media labeled those on the Right racists and bigots.

We need to begin with the rise of the American empire after the Second World War. The Second World War, like all the other wars waged by the West, had absolutely nothing to do with Adolf Hitler and protecting freedoms. That's pure Western propaganda. The war in Europe was a war between Britain and Germany for worldwide imperial dominance. The war between Japan and the United States was also for imperial dominance but in the Pacific. The Second World War destroyed the three major empires, Britain, Germany, and Japan. Simultaneously, the war produced two superpowers, the United States and Russia. The United States, like the Western European empires of Portugal, Spain, Holland, France, Britain, Italy, and Germany, was addicted to warmongering from its birth. Having secured its dominance in the Americas and Europe, the American empire was determined to defeat the Soviet Union to become the sole superpower and dominate the world in the image of a new Roman empire. It found a useful propaganda in pretending to fight Communism. While the Soviet Union had peacefully spread the populist ideals of Communism to poor Third World ex-colonies of the West, the American empire turned Communism on its head by convincing many that it was evil and that *private property,* not *communal property,* was both godly and civilized. Despite its conversion of the rich countries such as Germany, Japan, Britain, France, Italy, Spain, Canada, South Korea, Australia, and many more, to its cause of fighting the evil Communists, by 1972, the Soviet Union was still a thorn in the side of American dominance. President Nixon came up with what seemed like a brilliant idea at the time. He would exploit the growing rift between the two dominant Communist countries, Russia and China, to wean China to its side and bring down the Soviet Union. That turned out to be a disaster that no one could have predicted. We have likened the visit of President Nixon to China in 1972 to the accidental rediscovery of America by Columbus in 1492. Just as no one foresaw the rise of the American empire resulting from the landing of Columbus in the New World, no one foresaw the economic and military rise of China resulting from President Nixon's visit.

While the Western European empires crumbled from their addiction to warmongering, the Soviet Union crumbled from within. As it turned out, the United States did not need the aid of China to bring down the Soviet Union. But President Nixon's visit led to the creation of a new superpower that would rival the American empire. At the time of Trump's candidacy for president and Brexit in 2016, the Western media did not understand the threat to American/Western dominance posed by the rise of China and the emerging economies in Asia, Latin America, and Africa. But Donald Trump and his supporters saw it without fully understanding it. So did those who supported Brexit and the far right leaders in France, Germany, Austria, and Spain. While the Right understood that the West was in relative decline without fully understanding why, the intellectuals, the elites, and the educated totally missed the emerging Global Shift and called the supporters of President Trump and the Far Right *stupid, racists, ignoramus, homophobes, sexists, religious fanatics,* and a whole host of other demeaning names. The Left outdid itself by being so outspoken in its use of politically incorrect language while accusing those it chastised openly and incessantly of being politically incorrect. It was the most outrageous example of the pot calling the kettle black.

Understanding Why President Trump Is Right in Opposing *Globalization*, while President Xi Is Also Right in Supporting Globalization

As it turned out, it is the mainstream media, the intellectuals, the elites, and the educated, in the West, who deserve to be called *stupid* and even childish. The important question that neither side has asked is why China, along with a host of other emerging economies, a poor, backward country, when president Nixon visited in 1972, could have risen to challenge the world's only superpower, after the fall of the Soviet Union, within four decades of the Global Shift. The Global Shift began in China in 1980, when China created its first SEZ, special economic zone, in the village of Shenzhen, on the border with Hong Kong. How could it challenge the West's superpower, and its allies, Germany, Japan, Britain, France, Italy, Spain, Austria, Canada, Australia, South Korea, and others, within such a short time, four decades? That's the important question that both the Right and the Left, in the West, should have asked. Instead, both sides talk about China's massive economy as if it was normal, when in fact it has been the most abnormal and miraculous occurrence in history. The United States has taken almost three centuries to grow to the size it is today. Britain, Germany, France, and the other American allies took as long as the United States to grow to the size they are today. China took just *four decades* to become as large as the United States. Why is that viewed as normal by all sides? To provide an answer to this very important question ignored by everyone is the reason for this book. Most people today recognize that China is a rising power. No one has bothered to ask why or how such a miraculous rise occurred. But it's not just China but all the emerging economies outside the West, such as India, Brazil, Indonesia, Malaysia, Vietnam, and many more, all previously poor Third World economies. That is why we have devoted two chapters of this book exclusively to China but the remainder of the book to all the emerging economies.

As I said before, the Right in the West instinctively feel that the totally unexpected rise of China and other emerging economies is a threat to Western dominance. They are absolutely correct. But they cannot fully explain why. The Left, which is far more educated but *totally stupid*—yes, you can be simultaneously educated and stupid—takes full advantage of the failure of the Right to rationally explain why the rise of China and the emerging economies is a threat to the West, to scapegoat them as ignorant racists. The Left pound their chests in glee when they attack the Right in every media opportunity they get. The Left has totally abandoned its traditional role of fighting for income and wealth equality, helping the impoverished and disadvantaged, speaking out against warmongering, invasions, and imperialism, and creating a more just society. Instead, their childlike mission today is to hurl insults and abuses to the Right simply because of the personal delight and satisfaction they get from doing that. With their total control of all the mainstream media in every Western country, the Left is on a new mission to be dictatorial, mean, and nasty to any who dare speak any differently than they do. The Left has abandoned any sense of being honest or truthful, and use their total control of a very biased and dumbed-down media to spread egregious lies. They twist every statement by President Trump and those on the Right to find some miniscule way of turning whatever is said on its head, to show how brilliant and smart they are and how stupid their opponents are. They add insult to injury by claiming that it's those they hurl insults at who are evil, misleading, nasty, and insulting. They have absolutely no respect for authority if the representative of that authority, such as President Trump, was democratically voted into power by a majority they loathe, despise, and feel superior to, the "basket of deplorables" as their hero, candidate Hillary Clinton, called them, "the racists, sexists, homophobic, xenophobic, Islamophobic."

I have written extensively on the evils of Western racism against the nonwhite people of the globe and against the First Nations whose lands they stole in the New World and in Australia and New Zealand. I abhor racists. But I refuse to believe that those who support this new Left, and their anointed leaders like Barack Obama, Hillary Clinton, Angela Merkel, Justin Trudeau, and Emmanuel Macron, are any less racist than those on the new Right in the West. If they were, they would have spent their time and energy opposing the invasions and bombing of Afghanistan, Iraq, Syria, and Yemen; they would have opposed Israel and supported the Palestinians; they would have lobbied for the return of at least some of the lands stolen from the First Nations by Canada, Australia, New Zealand, and the United States; and they would have worked hard to reduce economic growth and the ever-growing consumption of junk and speedily updated gadgets like the latest Apple iPhone, by the rich and the middle-class in the West.

The reality is that leaders of the Left in the West are as warmongering imperialists, racists, polluters, pro-growth and consumption addicts, as the leaders of the Right in the West. Both sides care very little for the plight of those in the West who have suffered from the Global Shift, or the blacks in the U.S. ghettoes, or the refugees in Lebanon, Syria, and Turkey, or the First Nations still living in reserves with no running water. Both sides want to continue the six centuries of colonization and warmongering practiced by the West. All they care about is the election of their anointed leaders, not the leaders of the other equally evil side. Neither side has any desire to change the warmongering and lying ways of the West or create a more just society. They thrive on the same propaganda and hypocrisy practiced for six centuries by the British, French, and Americans. The only difference is that the Left today has total and absolute control of every mainstream media in the West and can therefore hurl far more abuse on the Right than the Right can on the Left. And the Left takes great delight in hurling incessant and childish abuse. The Right is forced to use nonmainstream media such as Breitbart, which cannot compete with the likes of CNN, BBC, CBC, the *New York Times,* and many more.

It's Not the Gains from Trade Inherent in Ricardo's Theory of Comparative Advantage, *Stupid; It's the Massive Gains by the Emerging Economies Compared with the Pitiful Gains by the West. This Is Why the West Simultaneously Gains from Globalization* but Loses Its Relative Dominance.

As a professional economist, I totally understand more than most the gains from international trade grounded on the theory of comparative advantage developed by David Ricardo. Many intellectuals defend the views of the Left by pointing to the economic benefits of free international trade and the political and social benefits of international engagements at every level, including capital flows and immigration, in addition to trade. What these intellectuals, journalists and "educated" do-gooders, miss is exactly what they missed during the prior six centuries of Western domination. Western domination did not result purely, or even primarily, from free and voluntary trade or free and voluntary international engagements. It resulted mostly from colonizations, military thefts of lands and resources and propaganda about the *white man's burden,* Christianizing the heathens, and civilizing the barbarians and primitive natives.

Just as these intellectuals confused the evils of imperialism with the benefits of free trade prior to the Global Shift, they are proudly ignorant of the post–Global Shift genuine concerns of those who see the decline of Western domination. While I wholeheartedly support the relative decline of the West because no one should ever be dominated the way the West has dominated Third World countries, I do not subscribe to the view of the Left that this decline is not occurring, and that those who complain about their relative decline in income and opportunities in the West are simple racists and bigots. The West is in *relative* decline. Denying that, as the Left implicitly does, is far more ignorant than denial of global warming, which the Left incessantly accuses the Right of doing. In this book, we will not simply make the point that the West is in relative decline but do much more. We will provide objective data, facts, and analyses of that relative decline. Much more importantly, we will explain how China and the other emerging economies were able to reverse in *four decades* what they could not do in six centuries. The latter is the question that should be asked by both the Left and Right, but not asked by either side. To take the rise of China as normal is to take miracles as normal.

The *abnormal* and totally unexpected rise of China to a size, as measured by GDP, rivaling that of the United States, is the fundamental question that needs to be asked and answered. Only after asking and answering that question can we debunk the implicit myth of the Left that President Trump and his supporters in the United States and Western Europe are total morons in suggesting that the United States and Western Europe need to be made great again, because they have declined. Note that the Left never says that the United States and Western Europe do not deserve to be great. Had they said that, they would have had my total support! The Left fully and wholeheartedly supports the view that the United States and Western Europe deserve to be greater than all others. They simply deny that the United States and Western Europe are no longer great or in relative decline. They therefore see no need for Trump's slogan, "Make America Great Again," and ridicules it by pompously claiming that the United States is greater than ever. They ignore America's growing domestic and foreign debts, expensive lost wars in Afghanistan, Iraq, and Syria, degraded infrastructure, and slower growth than China and India. They firmly believe that America can still afford to police the globe and pay for defending Western Europe, Japan, South Korea, and Saudi Arabia while fighting the Russians and Chinese. While the Right does not have all the answers as to why the United States and Western Europe are in relative decline, it is far ahead of the Left, which is in a dream world of total denial. In this dream world, the Left uses its total control of all the mainstream media, to make the masses across the globe believe that the Right is led by stupid racists and bigots who cannot see the benefits of *Globalization*.

President Nixon's visit to China created a genuine *free-trade* regime, which caused the gradual erosion of a prior Western engineered global system that favored the West at the expense of the Third World.

Unlike the many wars fought before by the Western empires to steal by colonization rather than trade, the recent wars waged by the West in Afghanistan, Iraq, Syria, Yemen, and North Africa have far greater military costs than what can be stolen. Where once gains from colonization and theft of lands and resources exceeded the military costs, the American invasion of Iraq, for example, cost far more than paying for the oil through free trade. Since the fifteenth century, Western empires opted for colonization and theft over free trade whenever they had the military advantage, because the benefits from colonization exceeded the benefits from trade. Had these Western empires followed David Ricardo's theory of comparative advantage, the gains from trade would have been shared far more equally between the East and the West. The same Western intellectuals and "educated" and media personnel who vehemently oppose the Trump supporters and the Brexit supporters and the Far Right supporters were the same group who for centuries confused trade with colonization. They even coined the term "slave trade." Trade is a voluntary exchange. How can slavery ever be voluntary?

What the so-called Left is totally missing is that the Global Shift, inadvertently created by President Nixon's visit to China, has ended the six centuries of Western colonization paraded by the same misguided intellectuals now on the Left, as trade. Now that we have trade as opposed to colonization, the gains from trade are going much more to the emerging economies than to the Western developed economies. What matters is not whether the West gains or loses from this new era of trade replacing colonizations but why the West is gaining far less than the East. What matters most to both the Left and the Right, in the West, is Western dominance in military and economic strength, media domination, domination of so-called international institutions such as the UN, IMF, WTO, financial markets, the reserve currency, propaganda, pretend democracy and freedoms, cultural domination, and meting out of severe punishment to those deemed to have committed acts much less reprehensible that those committed by the West, such as torture and incarceration in Guantanamo or ethnic cleansing of First Nations. It's this relative decline caused by the Global Shift, which the new Right fears and the new Left refuses to acknowledge or believe, is occurring. The evidence that the West is in relative decline is overwhelming. Yet the new Left continues to reject the evidence. Neither the Left nor the Right, in the West, has ever been willing to share the resources of the world, much like Canada and the United States never wanting to share the lands with the First Nations. In the West, it has always been about dominance and getting it all except for a few crumbs like reserves for First Nations on the most useless lands.

In 1972, when President Nixon visited China to court China's help in defeating the Soviet Union, China embraced the idea because of its border dispute with Russia, Chairman Mao's philosophical disagreement with the new direction taken by the new leaders of the Soviet Union, and most importantly, the failure of a stagnant economy to be able to even feed and clothe its massive population. At the time, the greatest genius in the world would never have expected this rapprochement with China to ever threaten continued American/Western domination of the world. In 1972, the GDP of the United States was US$1,225,400 million. By contrast, the GDP of China was US$112,160 million. In other words, the GDP of the United States was eleven times as large as that of China. In addition, five of the closest allies of the United States, working in unison to maintain Western domination, had GDPs larger than China. Japan's GDP was US$303,610 million. Germany's GDP was US$290,122 million. The GDP of France was US$201,850 million. The GDP of the UK was US$160,694 million. The GDP of Italy was US$139,956 million. Other close allies of the United States providing military and economic muscle to maintain Western domination, such as Canada, Australia, Spain, Holland, Sweden, Belgium, Switzerland, Denmark, Austria, Greece, Norway, Finland, Portugal, and South Korea, also had large GDPs.

It took several years after President's Nixon visit for the United States and China to formally begin an open post–Cold War relationship. As a result, it was not until 1980 that China created its first SEZ, and even then, this first SEZ was established in the village of Shenzhen to take advantage mostly of an opening with Hong Kong, not the United States. However, without the blessing of the United States, Hong Kong, as a colony of America's closest ally in Western domination, the UK, would never have dared to open up to China. America would have bombed Hong Kong back to the Stone Age, as it later did to Iraq, Afghanistan, and Libya, and threatened to do to Pakistan if Pakistan had not cooperated with the American-led Western invasion of Afghanistan. If we date the Global Shift as beginning in China in 1980, then the facts clearly show that China benefitted far more than the United States from this new free trade era, which replaced Western colonizations with trade. The argument by the new Left that everyone wins from trade and *Globalization* is irrelevant. As an economist, I wholeheartedly agree with that view, as I totally get David Ricardo's theory that trade must benefit both parties since it's voluntary. But the West's primary goal has never been gains from trade. That has always been a secondary goal. Its primary goal has always been world domination, a goal fully subscribed to by both the Left and the Right. As such, the Left only uses Ricardo's theory as one of many fallacious arguments to denounce those on the new Right as racists and bigots. The Left has not abandoned its long traditional goal of Western domination. However, it now has a new primary goal that is subservient to its other goal of Western domination. That new primary goal is not stopping Western warmongering, invasions, creation of millions of refugees, reduction of income and wealth inequality, protection of the environment by reducing economic growth and ever-increasing consumption of junk, improved democracy, lesser Western propaganda, or greater freedoms. Its new primary goal is using its total control of the mainstream media to find the most ridiculous arguments and the greatest quantity of fake news and distorted facts to hurl disrespectful abuses at the new Right.

While we devote this entire book to explain how the Global Shift has reduced the *relative* dominance of the United States and its Western allies, we can see this if we are objective with this single fact. In 1979, the year before the Global Shift began rather modestly with China opening its economy to the British colony of Hong Kong on its southern border, the GDP of China was US$175,574 million. In that same year, the GDP of the United States was US$2,544,500 million, almost fifteen times that of China. Today the GDP of China is almost as large as that of the United States. While it is true that the U.S.-China post–Cold War trade relationship has benefitted the United States, it has clearly benefitted China far more. US-China free trade has added at best 0.5 percent to U.S. economic growth. At the same time, it has quintupled China's economic growth, increasing China's annual economic growth from under 2 percent to almost 10 percent. To get the full picture of this massive Global Shift from the West to the emerging economies, we need to add the fact that this new free trade era boosted China's growth rate relative to America's allies as well and boosted the growth rate of other emerging economies such as India, relative to the United States and its allies in world domination.

Yet another example of the ignorance of the new Left is their argument that China's current support of *Globalization* is proof of how moronic President Trump's withdrawal from the TPP and criticisms of NAFTA are. In this they are being consistently inconsistent. Since China has gained far more than the United States from the Global Shift, it's consistent to expect China to promote *Globalization* while the United States denounces it. The double failure of the new Left to see the consistency of both the relative decline of the United States and its allies and the switching of places by President Trump and President Xi is consistent but consistently incorrect and stupid—stupid because the new Left has not relinquished its goal of Western domination. If your goal continues to be Western domination, supporting *Globalization* when *Globalization* increase your gains by far less than it increases the gains of the, East is stupid. While the new Right may not be smart enough to understand why the West is in relative decline or understand how to remedy that, at least it is not stupid. The new Left, led by the brightest intellectuals, the educated, the mainstream media journalist, the pundits, the defenders of global warming, the majority of Western leaders, Hollywood moguls and actors, the biggest rock stars and recording artists, the most successful entrepreneurs, and the self-appointed Black leaders, are totally *stupid.* There is no other word that best describes their behavior and analyses.

The evidence is indisputable that the West and America are in relative decline. The evidence is equally indisputable that the relative decline of America and the West is due exclusively to the Global Shift. I applaud this relative decline of the West because Western domination of the world over the last six centuries has brought nothing but warmongering, military invasions and destructions, colonizations and military thefts of lands and resources from the Third World, environmental degradation caused by excessive consumption by relatively rich Western consumers driven by economic growth supported by the same deranged people complaining about global warming, massive use of propaganda, ethnic cleansing, torture and incarcerations in offshore prisons like Guantanamo, forced Western culture and values on others, pretend democracies and freedoms, and stifling of the development of humanity and the human race. Nevertheless, I cannot agree with the new Left that leaders like President Trump are incorrect in stating that our Western leaders have enabled the rise of China and the emerging economies by not understanding that the Global Shift and its implicit internationalization of the world is the cause of that relative decline.

President Trump was on the ball when he told President Xi, during his state visit to China in November 2017, that "I do not blame you for taking advantage of the stupidity of our previous leaders to benefit your people." If you believe in America's superiority over all others, you cannot subscribe to the type of free trade that occurred in the last forty years. That free trade brought minimal gains to the United States and its Western allies and maximal gains to China and the emerging economies. That reduced centuries of inequality between the rich West and the poor Third World. That's a good thing if you favor equality. It's stupid if you contend that it has made America or its Western allies "great," or not reduced their relative power and influence. President Trump is correct when he says that "we need to make America great again." By this, he means restoring American dominance. Where he falls short is not knowing how to do that. Just as it was impossible to turn back the clock on the rise of the American empire accidentally caused by the rediscovery of the New World by Columbus in 1492, I believe that it will be impossible to turn back the clock on the relative rise of the emerging economies accidentally caused by President Nixon's visit to China in 1972. But President Trump and others on the new Right who support him are far more ahead of the curve in understanding the new reality than the new Left and their educated intellectual leaders, because these highly educated and highly successful leaders have their heads buried in the sand and take great pride and ecstatic joy in hurling abuses at the new Right while understanding less than a kindergarten child.

Why It Would Be Difficult, If Not Impossible, for President Trump to Make America Great Again or the New Right to Maintain Western Domination

As we will explain in great detail in the remainder of this book, the world took a revolutionary turn when the United States decided to end its Cold War with China. That decision was made by the United States to destroy the Soviet Union and make America the only superpower in the world. Those on the Right, in the West, understands this. Those on the Left, in the West, also needs to understand that, if they do not. Rapprochement with China was never about the gains from free trade as espoused by Ricardo's theory of comparative advantage, not for the West. While it is true that one of the three reasons for China to agree to rapprochement was trade, China never expected in its wildest dreams to benefit so much. As we will explain in great detail in the book, trade with China is very different from what trade had been throughout human history. Ricardo's theory and all other economic theories assume that trade means that a country will produce goods at home but sell it to a foreign country. It will use the funds provided by that foreign sale to buy goods produced in the host country. What economists today have totally failed to recognize is the difference between that long historical meaning of trade and what we label as the Global Shift. The new type of trade unleashed on the world by President Nixon's visit to China in 1972 is one in which a country such as the United States builds a factory in China to produce goods, not to sell to China, but for Americans. This is a revolution and should not be confused with historical trade or *Globalization*.

This new and revolutionary form of international engagement also explains the massive trade deficits between China and the United States and its allies such as the UK. David Ricardo's theory of comparative advantage would never create such large trade imbalances, since it implies that each of any two trade partners will export the goods it has the comparative advantage for, to buy the goods from the other trade partner with the comparative advantage in the other good. The Global Shift, on the other hand, combines capital outflow from the developed Western country, such as the United States or the UK, to the struggling poverty-stricken Third World economy such as China or India, to build the polluting factories to produce the massive quantities of cheap manufactured goods for the consumption addicted voters living in the same pretend democracies in the developed West. As such, the largely foreign-owned factories in China and India will export most of their output to the United States, UK, and other Western countries. This will be counted as exports by China or India. But the poverty-stricken Chinese or Indians have little income to even buy the cheap goods produced in their own countries by Western-built factories much less the much more expensive goods produced in the West. Of course, these imbalances, implicit in the Global Shift, have naturally lessened as the Global Shift increased the wages and purchasing power of the workers employed by the Western factories in the emerging economies. In addition to this expected decline in trade imbalances, the West will receive profits and dividends from their capital investments in building the factories. These inflows of interest and dividends are not recorded in trade balances but as one of the many other flows making up the current account of the balance of payments. As such, focus should shift from the balance of trade to the balance on current account. Of course, the dumbed-down Western media would never be able to comprehend the difference between the balance of trade and the balance on current account.

While the long-established international trade required cheap water transportation to make it economically feasible, the new type of international trade created by the Global Shift was far more dependent on much cheaper water transportation if it were not to be limited to small land border regions such as China and Hong Kong, or the United States and Mexico. That is why containerization was an essential piece of the Global Shift. Once Western corporations saw the cost advantage of accessing the almost unlimited quantity of cheap labor in Mexico, China, India, Vietnam, Malaysia, Bangladesh, and other poor Third World countries, the Western obsession with entrepreneurial competition to both boost profits and provide the lowest prices for its ever-hungry mass of high-income consumers kicked in. It is a phenomenon never experienced before in the history of mankind. Since economists have not bothered to analyze this new phenomenon, world leaders and the media have misleadingly called it *Globalization*. This is misleading because *Globalization* had been with humanity long before Marco Polo and the Silk Road. To call this new revolutionary form of international engagement *Globalization* is to miss its revolutionary nature. It's also the reason why neither China nor the United States expected rapprochement to ever enable China to become the new superpower to challenge the West after the fall of the Soviet Union.

President Trump and his supporters in the rust belts of America, created by this Global Shift of high-paying manufacturing jobs to China and other emerging economies, understand what has happened. The new Left does not. It is having too much fun hurling undeserved abuses to the new Right to understand anything, much less something that is new to economic theory and analysis. The problems for President Trump and his supporters are insurmountable. We will address these problems under *nine* important, if somewhat overlapping, headings below.

President Trump Needs a Western Boycott of the Global Shift to Succeed

It was extremely easy for the United States to unilaterally open China to the West. It is impossible for the United States to unilaterally close China to the West. When President Nixon visited China in 1972, all the pro-U.S. economies in Asia, Japan, South Korea, Taiwan, Hong Kong, and Singapore were hungry to do business with China. Their economies had done exceptionally well by joining the United States in its goal to defeat the Soviet Union. By supporting the United States in the Cold War, they got access to the U.S.-controlled "international" institutions such as global financial markets and were able to trade with the developed economies as well as access Western capital to develop their infrastructures. But by 1972, while growth rates were still high, they were slowing. China was their new opportunity to prevent their growth from slowing.

After China had created infrastructure at its ports and enhanced containerization, it was ready to expand the Global Shift from the developed economies in Asia to the developed economies in the United States, Canada, Australia, and Western Europe. Western corporations producing manufactured goods with high levels of pollution in China for Western consumers have become the norm. President Trump cannot reverse this unilaterally by the United States. He needs support from all the American Cold War allies, Germany, Japan, Britain, France, Italy, Spain, Austria, Portugal, Canada, South Korea, Australia, Greece, Singapore, and many more. Hong Kong, where China began its Global Shift, is no longer a British colony. It's a part of China. China also claims Taiwan, where China's Global Shift moved to after Hong Kong.

President Trump is not loved by America's Cold War allies. One reason is his rage against the Global Shift and China. Far from supporting President Trump, the current leaders of these Cold War allies in most, if not all countries, think the president's claims that the Global Shift has been bad for the United States is flawed and the thinking of a somewhat mentally deranged moron. They see the Global Shift as a bonanza, touting the benefits of international trade and capital flows, implicit in basic economic theory. In their view, President Trump is a backward, misinformed Neanderthal who is too dumb to understand basic economic theory. They will oppose any attempt made by President Trump to join his quest to roll back the Global Shift. Unfortunately, if

President Trump rolls back the Global Shift in the United States and his Cold War allies do not, the United States will be at a competitive disadvantage. While the Cold War allies will have access to cheap labor in the Third World, the United States will not. American prices will be higher, and American exports will fall. President Trump's policy will fail both because the economy of the United States is smaller than the combined economies of America's Cold War allies and because the United States will decline relative to its Cold War allies because of this competitive disadvantage.

Opposition to President Trump in the United States: Why the Critics of President Trump on the Left and the Right Make It Impossible for America and the West to Reverse Course or Reduce the Relative Decline in Western Dominance

A second reason why President Trump will not succeed in reversing the Global Shift is the strong opposition to his policy in the United States. The democrats in the United States have fallaciously argued that President Trump's election to the presidency is tainted by the fact that he did not win the popular vote. This is a fallacious argument because the reason for America's system, whereby you win the presidency by winning the votes in the electoral college, is to give more weight to states with smaller populations than the more popular states like California. If winning the popular vote was relevant, there would be no need for the electoral college. Democrats are more likely to win the popular vote and still lose because they tend to win more of the electoral votes in more of the popular states like California. We bring up this fallacious argument made by Democrats partly to provide one example of many fallacious arguments used by the new Left because it controls the popular press. More importantly, the fact that President Trump lost the popular vote means that more Americans disagree with his policy of reversing the Global Shift than support it. These are the same Americans who have total control of the mainstream media and use that control to denounce every policy of President Trump. As with all his policies, the mainstream media portrays the president's attempt to reverse the Global Shift as the policy of a mentally deranged ignoramus. The much-touted "most trusted name in news," CNN is nothing more than a dumbed-down mouthpiece for the new Left in the United States.

It matters little that the president's claim that it is the Global Shift, which is responsible for the relative decline of the United States, is correct or not. What matters is that most Americans believe CNN and not the president. The new Left and CNN, the most *untrusted* name in news, truly believe that the United States is not in relative decline. By definition, if the United States is not in relative decline, blaming decline on any reason is nonsensical. The new Left and CNN take great pleasure in making the president seem out of touch with reality. The views of CNN are echoed by all the other sheep, calling themselves independent journalists in all the other media outlets in the United States and in media outlets across the globe where lazy reporters are only happy to repeat almost verbatim what CNN reports. A gullible public takes the CNN message and proudly repeats to all and sundry as if it was their original idea. Within two years of Donald Trump's candidacy, CNN, allied with the BBC and CBC, had made Donald Trump the most dimwitted candidate for the American presidency and the most dimwitted president of any country in the world. That is truly amazing, since there is overwhelming readily available facts to prove that the United States is in relative decline. That is but one example of the disastrous power of America's so-called freedom of the press.

President Trump is not only opposed by the Democrats who won the popular vote but also opposed by many leaders in his own party, the Republican Party, and many of their supporters. While they support the president's slogan, "Make America Great Again," more than Democrats, because they are in less denial that the United States is in relative decline, they oppose President Trump for a variety of other reasons ranging from the president's use of Twitter, the president's refusal to be tougher on the Russian president Vladimir Putin, the president's refusal to use "politically correct" language, the president's tough talk of "draining the swamp" in Washington, personal grudges by the Bush family because candidate Trump defeated their son, by other Republican candidates in the primary who lost to him, by the likes of John McCain for not calling him a war hero, or others he responded to when they attacked him publicly, and the fact that the president has not been a longtime dedicated Republican and used the Republican Party only because an independent candidate has less chance of winning the presidency.

When you combine the larger percentage of Democrats in the United States, as exemplified by the popular vote, with the large minority of Republicans who opposed President Trump because he was never their favorite choice in the Republican primary, you have a large majority of Americans opposing the claim of the president that the Global Shift has made the United States a relatively weaker player on the global stage. When you combine that dislike with every journalist, intellectual, pundit, celebrity, and successful entrepreneur, taking such joy and delight in hurling all manner of abuses at the president and his family as well as making him out to be a moronic ignoramus, you can see why he will fail in his efforts to reverse the Global Shift even in the United States, much less in the countries allied to the United States during the Cold War.

China's Leaders after President Nixon's Visit Were Much Greater Visionaries than American Presidents

Empires decline under poor leaders and rise under competent leaders. The American empire was hit with a double whammy with sixteen years of incompetent leadership by Pres. George W. Bush and Pres. Barack Obama, presidents with absolutely no vision for a future world order. At the same time, China was led by three very competent leaders, Den Xiaoping, 1978–1989; Jiang Zemin, 1989–2002; and Hu Jintao, 2002–2012. Deng Xiaoping is rightly credited with taking advantage of President Nixon's initiative to engage with China and end the Cold War relationship. Deng followed the West by moving China from a centrally planned economy to a mixed economy. China's mixed economy model was different from the Western mixed economies in one respect. While the West used "product type" to determine mixture, China used geography. In the West, products such as education and health care, for example, are produced by central planning in what is called the public sector. Cars and computers, for example, are produced by free enterprise in what is called the private sector. In China, the central planning model was continued in the North, while the South became the free enterprise engine for economic growth and engagement with the West.

What no one, including Deng and Nixon, expected was the subsequent enormous rates of economic growth that the Global Shift will produce in China's mixed economy! We explain in great detail later how this came about. Suffice to say here that China experienced rates of economic growth never experienced before by such a large economy. Japan was the second-closest example, but most of the large developed economies such as the United States, Britain, Germany, and France were far behind. A 3 percent growth rate for those economies was excellent. China, on the other hand, achieved growth rates of 10 percent in the decades after the Global Shift in 1980. With such success exceeding all expectations, it would have been foolish for Deng's successors to not stay the course set by Deng. Both Jiang Zemin and Hu Jintao, therefore, continued Deng's policy and expanded the number of SEZs, pushing northward from Shenzhen. At the Communist Party Congress in 2017, President Xi has announced to the world his country's plan of continued engagement of the West. The new Left, all the Western media, and even some in the new Right, immediately attacked President Trump for allowing President Xi to usurp the God-given and righteous leadership role of the American empire.

The righteous indignation expressed by Western leaders, the Western media, and the new Left, at the refusal of President Trump to maintain America's leadership of ever more *Globalization* instead of relinquishing that role to President Xi, is further proof that the new Left, backed by all the mainstream media and most of the Western leaders, firmly subscribe to America's continued leadership of Western domination. It is simultaneously further proof that the new Left blatantly ignores reality and continues to support the disastrous policies of Presidents George W. Bush and Barack Obama, which caused the relative decline of the West. Finally, it is further proof that the new Left refuses to acknowledge America's relative decline and recognize that continued *Globalization* benefits China's rise, not continued American dominance. President Xi is wise in continuing the policy of his predecessors, since those policies narrowed the gap between China and the United States. But it's equally wise for President Trump to announce a change from the policies of his predecessors since the Global Shift has been a disaster for the United States and Western hegemony.

Once again, the new Left has it totally wrong. It most certainly does not make political sense for President Trump to lead continued *Globalization* as the pundits suggest he should. The dumbest error committed by the new Left, and their minions of educated intellectuals, is their conclusion that President Xi's commitment to continued

Globalization is proof that President Trump is foolish to reject continued *Globalization*. The correct analysis is that President Xi should lead the charge toward ever more *Globalization* since China's continued rise depends on it. It's equally correct for President Trump to reject further *Globalization*, since America's relative demise over the last four decades has been due to President Nixon's decision to engage with China. If you want America to continue to lead the world, and both the new Left and the new Right insist that is what they want, what matters is not the economic gains by everyone from continued *Globalization*. What matters is the undisputed fact that the Global Shift is single-handedly responsible for the steady erosion of the gap between the GDP of the United States and the GDP of China. Combine this fact with the other fact that the GDP gap between America's Cold War allies and emerging economies, other than China, is simultaneously being eroded by the Global Shift. Dominance requires huge differences in GDP between those who dominate and those who are dominated. The fact that *Globalization* benefits all economies is totally irrelevant if your goal is continued U.S./Western domination.

President Nixon cannot be faulted for opening the door with China. He did it to enhance America's lead over the Soviet Union. But by the time Pres. Bill Clinton took office in 1993, the Soviet Union had collapsed, and there was early evidence that China, not the United States, would be the primary beneficiary of President Nixon's rapprochement. By the time Pres. George W. Bush took office in 2000, the evidence that China was gaining more from the Global Shift than America was far more convincing. When President Nixon visited China in 1972, China had the seventh-largest economy in the world, behind the United States, Japan, Germany, France, Britain, and Italy. In 2000, when Pres. George W. Bush took office, China had moved up to sixth place, overtaking Italy. More importantly, as we explained before, the Global Shift only began in China in 1980 with China's first SEZ in Shenzhen. As we stated above, the GDP of the United States in 1980 was *fifteen* times that of China. In 2000, the GDP of the United States was only *eight* times as large. President Clinton and his two successors, Presidents George W. Bush and Barack Obama, had ample evidence and opportunity to end the engagement with China, which was bringing about the demise of American/Western domination of the world. President Nixon had a good idea, but his successors dropped the ball when it was clear that there was no longer a need for China's help in bringing down the Soviet Union, while there was growing evidence that a continuation of international engagement of the West with the emerging economies would erode the historical lead built by the West during the previous six centuries of Western colonizations and warmongering.

In 2000, President Bush had an opportunity to end trade and capital flows between China and the West. The United States still had a firm grip on its Cold War allies, and China's economy had not yet grown to such a massive size. Instead, President Bush did not have the foresight to grasp this opportunity. To be fair, no other Western leader, political or economic advisor, intellectual or entrepreneur, saw this need either. Instead of turning the tide on China's rise, Pres. George W. Bush began America's wars in the Middle East with his invasion of Afghanistan in 2001. These useless and very expensive wars have diverted the relatively small gains to the United States from the Global Shift to expensive warmongering. This has increased the differential gains to China compared to the United States, caused by Presidents Bush and Obama continuing the disastrous policy inspired by President Nixon's visit to China in 1972.

President Bush can be excused to some extent, compared with President Obama. After all, the new Left incessantly beat the same drum that Obama was smart and Bush was dumb. Bush was also hit with 9/11, and the great majority of Western leaders saw this as an opportunity to feed their hunger for warmongering. The West had rested up after the disastrous Vietnam War and was hungry again for another Vietnam; 9/11 provided that opportunity. The West had acknowledged that Vietnam was a disaster, not because it was a useless war but because the West had lost. The invasion of Afghanistan would be different because the West would win this time. We can therefore excuse the lack of vision of a dimwitted president George W. Bush, as labeled by the new Left, and credit him for providing a much-needed opportunity for the West to feed its addiction to warmongering at the expense of accepting the relative rise of China and the emerging economies. No such excuses can be made for the new Left's anointed genius, Barack Obama. As it turned out, President Obama was the biggest disaster for the preservation of American/Western hegemony.

I need to reiterate that I totally abhor American/Western hegemony. But the new Left, which takes great pride in hurling abuses at President Trump and label him as even more dimwitted than Pres. George W. Bush, declares their unquestionable belief in the moral righteousness of American/Western hegemony. The facts clearly show that President Obama's continued warmongering, exceeding that of Pres. George W. Bush, combined with his much greater promotion of *Globalization* than Pres. George W. Bush, caused the relative decline of America more than any other American president. While some of his supporters may have cringed at his penchant for ever more warmongering, all of them fully backed his tireless promotion of *Globalization* and international engagement between East and West. What are the facts? When President Obama took office in 2008, we see that the gap between the GDP of the United States and China had narrowed during the presidency of his predecessor. That would have been a warning for any smart leader. But contrary to the drum beating of the new Left, President Obama had no vision either for America or for his slogans of "Hope and Change," "Main Street not Wall Street," and "Fat Cats of Wall Street." They were popular slogans that rallied his supporters but were never intended to help America or those who voted for him, not even the blacks who turned out in force to vote for their first black president.

President Obama was the quintessential talker who did nothing to change course. He continued and expanded the same disastrous wars began by his predecessor. He continued to support those he labeled the "Fat Cats of Wall Street" over the poor and destitute of Main Street with taxpayer bailouts of Wall Street, using the excuse of the 2008 financial crisis even though the same tax dollars to Main Street, used to purchase American cars and repay mortgages, would have had the same stimulus effect on the economy. But our primary focus here is to prove that President Obama's glorification of *Globalization*, strongly supported by the new Left and all the mainstream media, is the single cause of America's relative decline. In 2008, China and the emerging economies were well on their way to removing American/Western dominance. But they still had a long way to go and would never had made it had President Obama reversed course and dismantled rather than embraced *Globalization*. What America needed in 2008, and even in 2000, was a President Trump, not a George W. Bush and certainly not a President Obama. The sad reality is that it's too late for President Trump to reverse course even if he had the support of the media and the American people. Unfortunately, President Trump has zero support from any mainstream media in the West. He has a large minority support in the United States and an even smaller minority support in the countries of the Western alliance. He faces a brilliant leader in President Xi, smart enough to take advantage of the fact that President Trump has so little support for his vision to make "America great again" by challenging *Globalization*.

While the West continues to celebrate the disastrous pursuit of *Globalization* under President Obama and opposes President Trump, shamelessly using every weapon they have, including branding him a racist, the GDP gap between the West and the emerging economies continues to narrow. Soon there will be no gap, and American hegemony will be a relic of history like the Greek, Roman, and British Empires before. The astounding rise of the emerging economies, caused by the Global Shift and misguided Western leaders, is what we explain in great detail in the remainder of this book. By the time President Trump took office in 2017, China had become the second-largest economy in the world, surpassing all of America's Cold War allies and moving to overtake the United States. In addition, India had overtaken France and was close to overtaking the UK. Other emerging economies like Brazil were also narrowing the gap. Most economists agree that if we use the purchasing power parity, PPP, measure of GDP, instead of exchange rates, in 2017, China already had a larger GDP than the United States.

Multiple Goals by President Trump: Choose Economy or Warmongering and Policing the Globe, *Not Both*

Candidate Trump was on the ball when he said that America could no longer afford to pay for policing the globe and subsidizing the defense of countries such as Canada, Japan, South Korea, Saudi Arabia, and all the countries in NATO. America needs to switch the use of its deficient tax dollars from defending its Cold War allies to rebuilding its collapsing infrastructure and pay down its ballooning debt. Unfortunately, the dumbed-down media made him out to be an ignoramus. The media and the idiots on the new Left as well as the John McCain and Bush idiots in his own party insisted that there had been no decline in America's ability to continue to do all it had done since the end of the Second World War. When candidate Trump said that NATO was obsolete, they mauled him. When candidate Trump said that Japan and South Korea should defend themselves from North Korea, even at the cost of all three acquiring nuclear weapons, they mauled him again.

The tactic of the new Left and their loyal media hacks is never to even try to see the common sense of the vision of candidate Trump for necessary change but to kill his ideas by painting him as totally ignorant of America's traditional role in the world. In reality, what they call traditional role began only after the three leading world empires, Britain, Germany, and Japan, self-destructed during World War II. America took up that post–World War II role because it could afford to. It was the only Allied nation not destroyed by the war. In fact, its economy had grown during the war. It was rich relative to Western Europe, Japan, Saudi Arabia, and South Korea. Its desire to control these countries made it agree to subsidize their defense against the Soviet Union. It could afford to do that then. But it no longer can. Candidate Trump was the only candidate from both the Republican and Democratic parties who saw that and campaigned on it. All of the other candidates were much more stupid than candidate Trump, but the media made candidate Trump look like the only stupid candidate.

Unfortunately, President Trump decided to drop his campaign ideas to switch tax dollars from defending the allies to building America's infrastructure. It is true that he is trying to get the allies to pay more of the cost. That is not a viable alternative. The need is for both the United States and all its allies to reduce their enormous waste of tax dollars on defense, not have them match that of the United States, as a percentage of GDP. They all need to cut back to have more resources for infrastructure and economic growth if they ever hope to reduce the enormous gap between their economic growth rates and those of the emerging economies of China, India, and others.

While the Global Shift is the prime reason for the growth differentials, wasting valuable resources on offensive wars and arms competition with Russia and China only serves to widen those differentials. In addition, candidate Trump promised increased defense spending on the U.S. military at home and on veterans. He wanted to improve America's defense capabilities and take better care of veterans. He not only promised that but also campaigned on *less* defense expenditure for NATO, Saudi Arabia, Germany, Japan, and South Korea and less funds on policing the globe. As president, he is spending on both. That's untenable. But it's what the opposition on both the Left and the Right wants. It's impossible for President Trump to rebuild America's collapsing

infrastructure to boost its economic growth without reducing defense
subsidies to its Cold War allies and abandoning America's post–World
War II lead in costly wars in Afghanistan, Iraq, Syria, Libya, Africa, and
Asia. These wars today bring little or no economic benefit to the United
States. Where once it was cheaper to steal oil and other products, it's
now cheaper to produce it at home or pay for it with trade. The Global
Shift has replaced Western colonization and theft by military force with
trade. During the six centuries of Western colonization and theft, the West
gained far more than the colonies. It's the emerging economies that are
gaining more from the Global Shift. The West cannot afford the defense
expenditures it could when it used what it misleadingly called "defense"
for offensive wars of invasion and theft. America's invasion of Iraq, for
example, cost far more than paying for oil in the international oil market.
President Trump should have stuck to his campaign vision.

The Refugee Crisis, Illegal Mexicans in the United States, Islamophobia, and the Rise of the Nonwhite and Mixed Race Population in the West

President Trump announced his candidacy for the presidency, walking
down an escalator and calling Mexicans rapists and drug lords. It was a
campaign gimmick intended to focus media attention on his candidacy. He
needed that media attention because both parties had anointed candidates.
The Democrats had anointed Hillary Clinton, and the Republicans had
anointed Jeb Bush. Trump was an independent candidate but knew only
too well that an independent candidate stood no chance against a party
candidate. He chose the Republican Party as what he saw as the lesser evil.
But he needed a way for the media to take him seriously and not dismiss
his candidacy. Jeb Bush, Ted Cruz, Marco Rubio, Chris Christie, Rand
Paul, and others had name recognition within the Republican Party. The
outsider, Trump, needed a splash to be taken seriously by the media. He
chose immigration as his key issue because increasing illegal immigration
into the United States from Mexico and further south was a concern to
both parties. The *Economist* had labeled President Obama "Deporter-in-
Chief" because he had deported more Mexicans than any other president.
Illegal immigration was a hot-button issue for Republicans and Democrats

alike. It was an issue that would resonate with both parties and was therefore good for an independent candidate.

However, candidate Trump's choice of "politically incorrect" words was just the excuse the media needed to brand him a racist and jump-start their mission to destroy his candidacy. When they failed, they became even more determined to destroy his presidency. It matters little as to what motivated the so-called independent media to be so vicious in their attacks. What matters was its very determined and relenting efforts to totally destroy his presidency after failing to destroy his candidacy. You do not have to be smart to twist every word uttered by any person to make it seem racist, homophobic, disrespectful of minorities and the disabled, or be stupid and ignorant. The media has decided that its mission is not to provide facts and truths but dissect statements to turn their true meanings on their heads. The journalists have become experts at doing just that to President Trump. They work as an indivisible team across the West, especially in the United States, Canada, and the UK.

President Trump, like Brexit supporters and other so-called Far Right parties in France, Germany, Austria, and other Western countries have taken advantage of a growing concern by whites over the increasing percentage of nonwhites in their countries. The type of nonwhite concern varies among countries. But they have one thing in common. They result from centuries of white invasions and colonizations of nonwhite countries. In the United States, the growing nonwhite concern focuses on illegal immigration from Mexico. This has its roots in the U.S. invasion and conquest of half of what was originally Mexican territory stolen from the First Nations. In the European Union, the growing nonwhite concern focuses on the refugees now flowing from European warmongering in the Middle East and making worse the earlier flows of nonwhites into Europe from the British, French, German, Dutch, Spanish, and Portuguese ex-colonies. In Canada, the growing nonwhite concern focuses on inflows from ex-colonies of Britain, France, and the United States, such as India, Hong Kong, Taiwan, the Philippines, and countries in Africa and the Caribbean. These older inflows are now augmented by flows from China and more recently refugees fleeing Canada's wars in the Middle East and Africa, part of Canada's mission to fight the Western-invented excuse, terrorism. These nonwhite immigrant inflows into Canada combine with the growing demands by First Nations to return some of the lands Canada stole from them.

In all these Western countries, battling the growing de-whiting of their populations, the rising numbers of mixed-race people resulting from many years of intermarriage, and more recently, the Western creation of terrorism confuse and confound people. Confusion caused by mixed-race people is a greater problem in the United States where the white population initially insisted in defining someone of mixed-race *black* even if the percentage of white in the mixing is over 90 percent. Today, these mixed-race blacks have taken over the leadership positions of blacks in the United States and insist on continuing the use of this outdated term, more from ignorance than any sound argument. Unfortunately, it hides the different needs of the nonmixed blacks and the mixed blacks. Mixed blacks have far more economic opportunities, high-income job opportunities, income, wealth, and influence. But they insist on speaking for nonmixed blacks who live in ghettoes, in poverty, with fathers who are incarcerated for selling drugs, facing every form of discrimination, police brutality, and lack of opportunities for advancement except in the armed forces. This ever-changing racial landscape in the West confounds everyone. President Trump and the leaders of Brexit and the Far Right are, in my view, no more racists than other whites. Racism is a very deep-rooted historical problem in the West. It began over six centuries ago with Portugal enslaving Africans. It is part of who whites are and have been for more than six centuries of military invasions and colonization of nonwhite countries. Racism in the West is not an invention of President Trump or leaders of Far Right parties. They just happen to be easy targets for those who are themselves die-hard racists but refuse to look in the mirror.

Today's racism is very different from the days when slavery was reserved for blacks and First Nations, and Asians were only slightly above slaves, being used as indentured servants, and referred to derogatorily as backward "coolies." It has been upgraded in a way that is politically correct and "civilized." For example, the people whose lands were stolen by the United States and Canada are no longer "wild Indians" or "naked savages," but First Nations. Such a glorified name, which acknowledges their prior existence in the stolen lands as nations before the whites stole their lands. But whites refuse to return any of the stolen lands or provide compensation or remove the need for their continued "incarceration" in the reserves they were forced to live in to restrict their movements or provide them with independent nation status. Their ethnic genocide by Canada and the United States has not been recognized by the international community in any way. Canada and the United States are held up as the most civilized protectors of human rights across the globe and publicly chastise countries like China and Russia, which have committed far fewer crimes against humanity than they have. Such hypocrisy is the hallmark of Western "civilization."

The reality is that Western "civilization," with its penchant for racism, warmongering, military invasions, and genocide, is still accepted as superior in every way: more freedoms, more democratic, more racially tolerant, more godly, and more moral. But it's all a self-defined quality based on military and economic domination over the nonwhites in both Western countries and the Third World, largely poor defenseless ex-colonies of Western imperial powers. Their self-determined "civilized" behavior does not stand up to any objective test of what constitutes civilized behavior. President Trump and Far Right leaders are no better or worse than other Western leaders. President Trump is no lesser or greater a racist than Justin Trudeau of Canada, Angela Merkel of Germany, or Emmanuel Macron of France. They all believe in warmongering in the Middle East and Africa today as Portugal did six centuries before. The only difference is that they change the excuse for their invasions and warmongering and colonizations. Portugal's excuse was Christianizing the heathens. Today's excuse is fighting terrorism. Since today's warmongering is mostly in countries where Islam is the religion of the majority of people being bombed and ethnically cleansed by the WMDs of the West, a new form of racism has been added to the previous six centuries' history of racism. This is called Islamophobia. Now religion has been added to skin color to reinforce racial practices, behavior, intolerance, discrimination, and confusion. Modern racism is far more confusing and confounding than the days when it was "civilized" for whites to enslave blacks. That Western definition of "civilized" is still the basis of how the West measures "civilized" today, but it's far more complicated. That is why it's so easy for the *politically correct* leaders like Trudeau and Macron and Merkel to be held up by the equally racist new Left as pillars of Western civilization and the *politically incorrect* President Trump to be the easy target of their own indiscretions and ingrained white supremacy beliefs.

In my view, it's this new outspokenly abusive Left who must now bear responsibility for the continued invasions, bombing, warmongering, destruction, and creation of over sixty million refugees. When candidate Trump expressed his view that the United States could no longer afford to be the policeman of the world, the Left should have embraced that view wholeheartedly if they were not such dedicated warmongers and racists. Instead, they openly and abusively chastised candidate Trump for being an ignoramus with respect to the U.S. historical role of policing the globe. In doing so, they implicitly supported continued bombing of the people of the Middle East and North Africa. In my view, only racists would support such ethnic cleansing of nonwhite people who do not have the planes and bombs to retaliate. *Terrorism* is the dropping of massive Western-made high-tech bombs, using high-tech military jets or drones, on defenseless people who do not have the planes and bombs to retaliate against your cowardly behavior. If an advanced country like China or Russia would use their jets and drones to drop bombs on Canadians, Americans, and Western Europeans, the people of those countries would get a taste of true terrorism. What the West calls terrorism is an excuse invented by the West to justify their terrorism unleashed on Muslims.

More dastardly, the Left used the refugees to prove that they were not racists by supporting the influx of a small percentage of the sixty million into Western countries such as Germany, Canada, and the United States. When you support warmongering to create sixty million refugees, you cannot prove you are not a racist by opening your doors to two million. What of the other fifty-eight million? Moreover, no one wants to be a refugee, not even the ones you welcome into the West. They would much prefer if you had not bombed their homes and destroyed their livelihoods and killed and maimed their family and friends.

Ironically, it's those on the Right, like candidate Trump, who oppose the influx of refugees who implicitly oppose the warmongering, which creates the refugees in the first place. The Left is using and abusing the refugees to feed their own innate racism and gleeful desire to use any evil means to chastise those in the West whom they truly hate with a vengeance. This is most exemplified by mixed-race blacks who are sufficiently educated and prosperous to get air time on news networks such as CNN. When you see these so-called leaders of the black community, notice how relatively white they are in color. Like President Obama, they have little experience of what it's like to live as a poor non-mixed black person in the United States. Yet they are the only ones who get to speak for blacks in America. When candidate Trump makes any effort to reach out to the real black communities and ghettoes who were abandoned by President Obama, these so-called mixed-race black leaders in the media immediately abuse candidate Trump and gleefully continue that abuse of President Trump every chance they get. Just as the new Left only seek to glorify themselves by using the refugees and support continued warmongering, these new mixed-race black leaders only seek to glorify themselves by using blacks and support continued impoverishing, incarcerations, and ghettoes.

A 2017 example of this continuing confusion caused by referring to a mixed-race person in the United States as black occurred when mixed-race Meghan Markle began courting Prince Harry. Many on social media pounced on her because she was a black American. One of the ways she and Prince Harry decided to diffuse racial animosity to the couple was to emphasize that only her mother was black, making her a *mixed-race* American, not a *black* American. Some blacks welcomed the support she can bring to reducing the long history of Western racism. Others, I am sure, will denounce her for not proudly claiming to be black.

The Increasing Concern over Global Warming and Climate Change

Another misguided but effective attack on President Trump by both the new Left and those on the Right who oppose him is the pretend concern over global warming and climate change. Again, President Trump uses politically incorrect language such as "climate change is a hoax," which the smart but lying Left does not. Environmental degradation is an inescapable consequence of human existence and consequent need to degrade the natural environment to feed his needs. Imagine you are the first person on earth surrounded by nature. You cut down one tree to build a shelter from the elements and you degrade the natural environment. As we become more and more greedy for ever more consumption, we degrade the environment more and more. Excessive consumption is the true cause of environmental destruction. Global warming and climate change are aspects of environmental degradation. It can only be rolled back if we stop chasing endless economic growth, which brings about ever more consumption of junk, excessive use of energy, excessive pollution, need to recycle more and more rapidly obsolete gadgets as we chase after new models ever faster, moving the polluting factories we created with our industrial revolution, from the West to poor Third World countries like China, India, Bangladesh, and elsewhere across the far reaches of the globe, blaming China and India for our greed and creations, giving our Western consumers ever cheaper prices and ever higher incomes to feed their insatiable appetites for ever more junk, all in the name of creating employment and growth. India, for example, was a very spiritual country, until we infected it with our "civilized" disease we proudly call consumerism.

Every Western leader from Trudeau to Macron to Gore to Merkel to Schwarzenegger not only supports economic growth but also measures the success of their policies by how much growth they create. The more growth they create, the more successful they claim to be. In like manner, their primary weapon against their rivals is their claim that their rivals will create less growth. How can these leaders be held up as example of environmental protectors? President Trump, like Justin Trudeau, ran his campaign on creating more growth than his opponents. Since greater growth degrades the environment, why does the Left put Trudeau on a pedestal and Trump in the doghouse when it speaks of climate change? The reason is language and deceit, not substance or objectivity. If Justin Trudeau was an environmentalist, he would have returned some of the lands Canada stole from the First Nations because First Nations recognize the sacred nature of their lands and how to live as one with nature instead of chasing after ever more development, pipelines, and industrialization. Prime Minister Trudeau would also have banned the export of Canadian recycled junk, including electronics and plastics, to Third World countries. Canada, the United States, and the EU exported at least half of their recycled junk to China, for example. This helped the poor in China before China moved from Third World economy to emerging economy. But China today creates its own recycled junk from the factories built by the West to manufacture goods for both Western and Chinese consumers. In 2017, China was forced to ban imports of Western junk, but smugglers still illegally import Western junk into China. Leaders in the West, such as Justin Trudeau and Emmanuel Macron, care no more about global pollution than President Trump. But pretending to care win votes.

Among the many reasons why President Trump will fail to convince America's Cold War allies to support his boycott of the Global Shift is their opposing views on climate change. Most of America's Cold War allies believe that global warming can be reduced by reducing the use of fossil fuels such as coal. President Trump has promised his supporters in America's rust belt that he will reverse President Obama's move to phase out the use of coal, which has caused massive unemployment in the coal-producing regions in the United States. Most of the Western leaders firmly believe that moving back to coal is moving back to a dirty and polluting environment. Never mind that they all support companies moving Western factories using coal to Third World countries so that their high-income voters can get ever cheaper manufactured and electronic goods to feed their addiction to the consumption of junk, which is the primary cause of environmental degradation. They truly believe that global warming and climate change can be halted and even reversed by switching from fossil fuels to clean energy. At the same time, they see their shift of dirty polluting factories from their economies to China as solving the environmental concerns of their voters without denying their voting consumers the right to buy cheap manufactured goods produced in China and other emerging economies. The Global Shift is a win-win for them. Their voters get clean energy but do not have to pay the higher price for consumer goods that clean energy brings because their business owners can build polluting factories using fossil fuels in China and other emerging economies and ship the consumer goods to their voters at home, relatively cheaply, using container shipping.

The fact that these leaders of America's Cold War allies are wrong is of no consequence. It's what they believe, and President Trump has zero support from any Western media because the new Left has total control. They are wrong for two reasons. First, the only solution to planetary degradation is the reduction of consumption by high-income consumers. No amount of clean energy and recycling will reduce planetary degradation if these same leaders promote high growth rates to create more high-income jobs to win elections. In fact, the more high-income jobs they create with their clean energy and recycling projects, the greater will consumption of junk increase. Second, the pollution that the Global Shift has moved from developed economies to Third World economies is drifting more and more to all countries in planet Earth. In addition, countries like China and India are beginning to understand that they cannot continue to exchange Western pollution for higher economic growth. Their voters also now demand a cleaner environment. Yes, there are voters in China. China is no more a one-party state than the pretend democracies in the West.

The new Left pretends to be against global warming by honoring the rich and famous, the Leonardo DiCaprios, Al Gores, Justin Trudeaus, Arnold Schwarzeneggers, and David Suzukis, who publicly denounce global warming but privately consume a hundred times as much junk as the average person does, simply because they have a hundred times the average income. In honoring the rich advocates against global warming and climate change, the new Left implicitly buys into the idea that excessive consumption is not the cause of environmental degradation. DiCaprio and Gore's implicit solution to global warming is "consume as much as we do but recycle and switch to green technologies." Get off dirty coal and drive electric cars and you can consume as much as us without destroying the planet. In my view, DiCaprio should stick to acting and Gore should stick to politics. Gore was a half-decent vice president by American standards, and DiCaprio is an amazing actor. The new Left lobbies for more and more growth, which is the essential cause of global warming and planetary degradation, but simultaneously pretends to be against global warming and climate change, by spewing mythical solutions such as green growth, recycling, carbon tax, Paris agreements, Kyoto, and other feel-good propaganda, which only serve to maintain their insatiable appetites for ever more consumption of the latest polluting consumer gadget. They totally ignore the "reduce" and "reuse" parts of the 3Rs and focus exclusively on recycle. They ignore "reduce" and "reuse" because that would reduce consumption, which they fear will reduce job creation. In fact, they shamelessly urge their voters to consume more and more so they can meet the job-creation targets they set during the election campaign. Recycle creates additional jobs in recycling. They even suggest that we can have more high-paying jobs and more consumption, not less, and better save the planet, if only we would embrace green technologies. Those who would dare to suggest that we cannot have more and more and still save the planet are stupid. All of their anointed leaders such as Justin Trudeau and Emmanuel Macron simultaneously preach the inherently *inconsistent* goals of higher economic growth and saving the planet. No Western leader dare ask their voters to sacrifice economic growth to save the environment. They would lose the election if they did. This is why those on the Left pretend that you can have higher growth without degrading the environment. That's an impossible dream, and they know it. That's the real hoax.

Canada's prime minister, Justin Trudeau, was catapulted to rock star status when he attended the Paris summit on climate change in December 2015. President Trump, by contrast, was put in the doghouse by his Cold War allies for announcing his withdrawal from the Paris climate accord in 2017, by which time almost all the other 196 parties had signed up. The reality is that both President Trump and Prime Minister Trudeau got elected by promising higher rates of economic growth than their respective rivals. In the United States, candidate Donald Trump promised massive tax cuts to increase economic growth in the United States more than his Democratic rival. In Canada, candidate Justin Trudeau promised large budget deficits to grow the Canadian economy faster than his Conservative rival who focused on balancing the budget. President Trump followed through with massive tax cuts, and Prime Minister Trudeau followed through with massive budget deficits. In addition, Prime Minister Trudeau used tax dollars to purchase a pipeline to facilitate increased oil production from the dirty tar sands in Alberta because private enterprise decided it was unprofitable. The pipeline became unprofitable because of opposition from the province of British Columbia, the First Nations of Canada, and environmental groups. All of those who opposed the pipeline cited environmental concerns. Yet Prime Minister Trudeau continues to preach like the Macrons, Schwarzeneggers, DiCaprios, and Suzukis that the pipeline is needed to create jobs and increase economic growth, but protecting the environment and going green in no way reduce jobs or economic growth.

As I have said, this standard answer by the new Left is the real hoax about climate change. Let us focus a little more on our anointed rock star against climate change, Canada's Justin Trudeau. The facts show that Canada is far less likely to achieve its carbon dioxide emissions reduction targets set by the Paris Accord, under Prime Minister Trudeau, than the United States, under President Trump. Let us look at another fact. Prior to Justin Trudeau taking office, Canada has been exporting its recycled electronic junk to poor countries like China, causing great environmental damage because almost all the junk sat on the land after the poor had taken whatever it was valuable to recycle. Fast forward to Justin Trudeau's visit to the Philippines on November 18, 2015, for a meeting with the president of the Philippines, Benigno Aquino III, on the margins of the APEC Summit in Manila. The headline read, "Trudeau Mobbed by Shrieking Fans in Manila." What was much less publicized was environmentalists pleading with him to return to Canada the 103 containers of Canadian junk and polluting garbage sitting unloaded in the Port of Manila. Canada had misled the Philippines about the pollution threat of the contents to get approval by the Philippine government. In typically politically correct language, rock star Trudeau promised to take care of the problem, having zero intention of doing so.

When Trudeau returned to the Philippines for the ASEAN Summit in November 2017, a whole two years later, he was reminded by environmentalist of the problem he had conveniently ignored. The 103 containers were still sitting unloaded in the Port of Manila. As usual, he gave the politically correct answer, "He had a Canadian solution," to the problem. What was his Canadian solution? Blame Chronic Incorporated, a private enterprise. He only has the power to use Canadian tax dollars to build planes and bombs to kill people in the Middle East. He could not use Canadian tax dollars to deal with illegal shipping of Canadian garbage such as adult diapers and household trash. But he had the time to display his rock star Playboy image by taking advantage of the fact that a Filipino fast-food chain, *Jollibee,* had opened an outlet in Canada in Winnipeg. He visited an outlet in Manila to pose with fans to protect his rock star image while ordering a meal. Prime Minister Justin Trudeau is no different from other Western leaders pretending to care about the environment and climate change. No wonder he was rightly mocked on Canadian TV by Canadian comedians that he never intended to do anything about the Canadian garbage. All the Western leaders such as Trudeau care about is buying votes in their pretend democracies while using taxpayer dollars to build bombs and planes to destroy poor countries in the Middle East and Africa. They are only different from President Trump in that they take great pride in being able to master the art of lying by taking advantage of political correctness, while President Trump abhors political correctness and prefers to be honestly blunt.

Growing Inequality of Income and Wealth in the West

The free enterprise system, industrialization, and theft from colonizations made Western countries very rich. But it also created huge income and wealth inequality. Under threat of a labor uprising based on the Communist ideals of greater income and wealth equality, the West changed from free enterprise to mixed economies. Income and wealth were redistributed with progressive income taxes, legalizing labor unions and a growing "Communist" sector the West called the public sector.

One of the ironies of the new Global Shift from the West to the emerging economies is that it has simultaneously reduced income and wealth inequality between Western countries and Eastern countries while increasing income and wealth inequalities in the Western countries. This has occurred for several reasons. First, many of the high-paying jobs in manufacturing, the polluting jobs shifted to China and India, have been replaced by low-paying service jobs. At the same time, high-paying service jobs go to younger and technologically savvy workers who benefit from the combination of the Global Shift and the digital revolution. Third, the power of unions has declined. Unions were an important factor in income redistribution from business owners to workers and the staving off of a Communist revolution in the West. In the post–Global Shift era, employers are forcing unions to abandon company pensions, wage increases, and medical and other benefits because they face competition from the emerging economies. At the same time, the tech-savvy workers prefer individual freedom to bargain individual pay and benefits over the union collective bargaining model. Finally, the United States has engaged on a warmongering spree since 9/11, which drains tax dollars from social programs to fighting its invented terrorism. The United States has convinced its Cold War allies to do the same.

This growing income and wealth inequality in the West has attracted many voters to the new Left. The best example of this in the United States was the rise of Bernie Sanders during the last Democratic primary. Had the Democratic Party not rigged the process in favor of Hillary Clinton, Bernie Sanders may very well have won the Democratic primary. While this new Left is as warmongering as all Western leaders, it does favor income and wealth redistribution. As a result, it garners support from those against continued Western imperialism and warmongering. This increases the threat to Trump's presidency from the new Left, even though the new Left will be unable to redistribute income and wealth without abandoning the high costs of continued warmongering and while competing with the emerging economies.

Many of those who support the new Left in the United States and Europe are as confused as those speaking out against racism and Islamophobia. The members of the new Left can be divided into two groups. Those on the new Left who support a leader like Hillary Clinton are typically in a high-income and wealth class, who oppose a leader like Donald Trump because of party affiliation. They support warmongering, regime change, and fighting terrorism. Those on the new Left who support a leader like Bernie Sanders or a movement like Occupy Wall Street are in a low-income and wealth class, who care less about affiliation with a party and more about dealing with poverty and the increasing income and wealth inequality. Many among this group, though not all, recognize that the primary causes of their low-income and wealth status are *Globalization*, the digital revolution, expensive warmongering, and the rollback of both union power and income redistribution policies of the government. That is why the second choice of many of them, after Bernie Sanders, was candidate Trump, not candidate Clinton. Trump's campaign promise to roll back both *Globalization* and America's role of policing the globe and financing regime change and subsidizing NATO and the defense of Germany, Japan, South Korea, and Saudi Arabia resonated with this subgroup of the new Left. This has confused the new Left movement as much as America's invented war on terror has confused nonwhites and Muslims.

Blacks are equally confused as to the cause of growing poverty among the black population. Many blacks support both those in the new Left who do so for the party and for a continuation of President Obama's "war on terror," the Hillary Clinton group. But many also support the Bernie Sanders group because of their focus on more income redistribution and equality of job opportunities. Unfortunately, their mostly mixed-race black leaders are typically in the Hillary Clinton/Obama group. They would have liked to give greater support to candidate Trump but were demonized by their mixed-race, upper-middle-income, and relatively privileged leaders. They fell back on the Black Lives Matter movement, doomed to fail like the Occupy Wall Street movement. Poor blacks cannot improve their dire situation unless they focus on switching tax dollars from useless warmongering to social services. While it is true that some poor blacks will benefit from opportunities in the armed forces, the majority will suffer because these wars are very costly. The Global Shift is here, despite President Trump's efforts, because of the reasons we have outlined above. Western governments can only provide more services for the poor if they redirect tax dollars from warmongering and regime change.

Poor blacks need to seize leadership from well-off blacks who are mostly mixed race, have upper-middle-income jobs, live outside the black ghettoes or black neighborhoods, are successful athletes, movie stars, and pop singers, and imitate the aspirations of whites who support Democrats like Bill Clinton, Hillary Clinton, and Barack Obama. These poor blacks should have learned from the fact that they fought hard to elect the first black American president but got absolutely nothing from him. Once elected, President Obama repeated over and over again how he was *not* a president for blacks but a president for all Americans. He and his family were very determined to be the most *white* president and family to ever occupy the White House, imitating the Camelot image of President Kennedy and First Lady Jackie Kennedy. Only after the repeated police shootings of unarmed blacks did President Obama belatedly pretend to show some concerns for his die-hard poor black supporters. It's totally understandable why the upper-middle-class, mixed-race black leaders would remain defiantly supportive of President Obama and his anointed successor, candidate Hillary Clinton. They benefitted from the Obama presidency as they got some plum jobs in his administration. This enabled them to be more competitive with their upper-middle-income white counterparts. The fact that President Obama carried on and enhanced President Bill Clinton's policy of incarcerating large numbers of black fathers from the black ghettoes, for minor offenses selling illegal drugs, did not affect them. It's the children of the incarcerated fathers who were left to grow up without fathers and reduce even more their chances of escaping the cycle of black poverty.

Poor, non-mixed-race blacks need to take away leadership of blacks from the upper-middle-income, mixed-race blacks, and even the reverends, and join forces with poor whites to lobby hard for America to end its wasteful warmongering and fight of invented terrorism and use those billions of dollars to provide social services and educational opportunities for them. That has a much greater chance of success than movements like Black Lives Matter and Occupy Wall Street. Win or lose, they would have shown their humanity and empathy with the millions of Muslims whose livelihoods are destroyed, whose economies are ruined, who are killed and maimed, whose friends and families are killed and maimed, and who suffer as refugees in Syria, Iraq, Pakistan, Turkey, and elsewhere. Those are the people they need to ally with, not the fat cats of Wall Street, America's rich and powerful, and well-to-do mixed-race blacks. They also have more in common with the millions of Mexicans deported by President Obama. Mixed-race black leaders supported Hillary Clinton's candidacy because President Obama anointed her with the task of preserving his legacy. That legacy is one of warmongering, regime change in Libya and Syria, and protecting and enhancing the privileges of a minority of privileged mixed-race blacks who compete with upper-middle-class whites and who have absolutely nothing in common with poor blacks. They can relate to President Obama because he came from a privileged mixed-race family and was brought up by his white mother and white grandparents in Hawaii. His black experience was as limited as the mixed-race black leaders he promoted.

The Resurgence of Russia under President Putin

The American empire had fought a long and hard Cold War with the Soviet Union to seize world hegemony. After the empires of Britain, Germany, and Japan had self-destructed during the Second World War, the American empire emerged as the dominant Western empire. The American empire demonized Communism to find an excuse to wage the Cold War against the Soviet Union. As I have explained, it was the United States' single-minded determination to bring down what President Reagan labeled the "evil empire" that had previously led President Nixon to forge an alliance with an equally Communist state China to destroy the Soviet Union. That alliance alone should convince anyone that the evil preached incessantly by the West was not Communism but unhindered pursuit of warmongering and invasions by the West and led by the *evil* American empire.

Unfortunately, the new leader of the Soviet Union, Mikhail Gorbachev, was naïve. Gorbachev became the general secretary of the Communist Party of the Soviet Union in 1985. He believed the propaganda in the West that Communism was evil and that the West believed in peace. Nothing could be further from the truth. Western propaganda is unmatched by any non-Western state. The West uses it because it works. Many non-Westerners are as naïve as Gorbachev. Some in Russia today continue to be naïve. As a result of this naivety, Gorbachev began to make overtures to the United States intended to end the Cold War. He became a hero in the West with policies called *glasnost* and *perestroika*. The meaning and intent of those policies are irrelevant. What is relevant is that when a non-Western leader is hailed as a hero in the West, that's a sure sign that the leader has sold out the independence of his/her country and will become a puppet leader. The United States had already made one painful error in allying with China without demanding that China become an economic colony of the United States like Britain, Germany, Japan, Canada, France, Italy, Spain, Portugal, Greece, and South Korea. It will never do it with another state, much less Russia, and certainly not under the leadership of President Reagan. Gorbachev ended the Soviet Union in 1991 in the hopes of not simply ending the Cold War but forging a peaceful relationship between Russia and the West. While the Soviet economy was no longer the same powerful economy it had been under Stalin and Khrushchev, it was not its economic problems that ended the Soviet Union but the power of

Western propaganda. Gorbachev had sold out Russian independence to the West in return for the Nobel Peace Prize.

Prior to the dissolution of the Soviet Union on December 15, 1991, Boris Yeltsin had been elected as the president of Russia in June 1991. He continued as president of the Russian Federation after the dissolution. While the Russian Federation was the largest of the fifteen republics that had made up the Soviet Union, the West lost no time colonizing as many of those other republics as they could, as well as Eastern European countries allied to the Soviet Union by the Warsaw Pact. East Germany was "colonized" by West Germany. The Baltic republics of Lithuania, Latvia, and Estonia, as well as Poland, Hungary, Bulgaria, Croatia, the Czech Republic, Romania, Slovakia, and Slovenia, were "colonized" by the EU. Georgia and Ukraine declared independence but became semicolonies of the West. Ukraine was the next largest republic after Russia.

Yeltsin continued the policy of Gorbachev in engaging with the West. Like Gorbachev, he was misled into thinking that the West would do business with Russia without demanding Russian subservience to Western domination. Unlike China, Russia's expansion of the free enterprise sector of its economy did not increase its economic growth. Instead, economic growth was negative during the Gorbachev and Yeltsin leaderships. Estimates by the World Bank showed that Russia's poverty rate increased from 1.5 percent in the years just before the fall of the Soviet Union in 1991 to almost 50 percent in 1998. This collapse of the economy served to galvanize Russian leaders who had opposed Gorbachev and Yeltsin's subservience to the West. Russia's experience was exactly the opposite of China. China had kept its political system and independence while boosting its economic growth after allying with the West. Russia had lost its political system and independence while destroying its economy after allying with the West. During this transition, Russia's military was severely weakened and threatened both by Western expansion from East Germany and the Baltic to its border and by internal revolt in Chechnya in 1994. China, on the other hand, used its new economic growth to boost its military.

Yeltsin was unable to halt Russia's economic and military decline and faced growing criticism from those opposing the Western inspired reforms begun by Gorbachev. An indication of how far Gorbachev's popularity had sunk was given by the 1996 presidential election. Gorbachev's party scored less than 1 percent of the votes. Yeltsin managed to barely hang on to the presidency against the threat from the opposition Communist Party of the

Russian Federation, only by throwing lots of money from the oligarchs, into the campaign. The oligarchs had been enriched by the reforms and therefore opposed a return to Communism. Even so, Yeltsin fell short on the first ballot and had to ally with the third-place Aleksandr Lebed, a popular ex-general, to defeat the Communist Party in the final ballot. As the Russian economy continued to collapse after the 1996 election, Russia was unable to pay its debts. Tax evasion in Russia was rampant. The Asian financial crisis of 1997 made Russia's financial and economic situation worse as world price for commodities and oil plunged. The Russian ruble plummeted. There was widespread and growing calls for Yeltsin to resign. He was increasingly seen as an incompetent leader who had surrendered Russia's sovereignty to the West and got nothing in return. The Russian people were poorer than under the Soviet Union. The United States even refused to admit Russia into the WTO. It was not until 2012 that Russia was admitted to the WTO. Even China was admitted before Russia. China was admitted in 2001.

Yeltsin attempted to stem the tide of opposition to his presidency by firing his prime minister and his cabinet members in March 1998. The new prime minister secured an IMF bailout in July 1998. When the IMF bailout did not stop the fall in the ruble, Yeltsin changed his prime minister again in September 1998. This did not reduce the demands for Yeltsin to resign. Yeltsin changed his prime minister again in May 1999. His last change was made in August 1999 when he selected Vladimir Putin, a relative unknown, as the new prime minister. After so many trials, Yeltsin had stumbled on the man who would finally lead Russia out of the decline it had suffered at the hands of Gorbachev. Yeltsin decided to resign the presidency of Russia on December 31, 1999, and make Putin the acting president. In the next presidential election in March 2000, Putin won the presidency.

President Putin was fortunate that he took over the presidency after the price of oil was bouncing back. Since oil and other commodity exports account for 80 percent of the total value of exports by Russia, the bounce back of oil and commodity prices helped Putin restore confidence in the Russian ruble and jump-start economic growth. During the first seven years of Putin's presidency, Russia's GDP grew at a staggering 6.7 percent annually. Putin was increasingly seen in Russia as a competent economic and military leader. He had handily won the Second Chechen War, shortly after becoming prime minister in 1999, dealt decisively with the Chechen terrorist attack of 2002, and prevented Georgia from colonizing South Ossetia and Abkhazia in 2008.

The key difference between Putin and Gorbachev, however, was Putin's understanding of Western intentions. He understood clearly that the goal of the West was always total hegemony. It would only cooperate with Russia if Russia agreed to become a subservient colony like Japan and Germany. The West is happy to co-opt more allies willing to help it defeat militarily any and all who oppose its total dominance of the world. Germany and Japan had little choice because their economies had been destroyed by the Second World War. Had they opposed U.S. economic colonization, they would have been doomed to eternal poverty like North Korea. In like manner, after the Korean War, had South Korea opposed U.S. economic colonization, it would have been isolated and impoverished like North Korea. Vladimir Putin also understood that if the leader of a country opposes U.S. economic colonization, the United States will find a way to rally its allies and the world to enable regime change. After the American-led regime changes in Afghanistan, Iraq, Libya, Ukraine, Syria, and Yemen, Putin knew he was next in line. He recognized that he needed to go on the offensive. He intervened in Crimea to prevent a Ukraine handover of Crimea to the West. He supported those in the Ukraine opposed to handing over Ukraine to the West. He intervened militarily in Syria to prevent regime change by the West. In general, he punched way above Russia's economic standing as measured by its GDP. He wrested "man of the year" from President Obama and became the foremost leader on the international stage.

Candidate Trump acknowledged the rise of Putin on the world stage and congratulated his strong leadership of Russia. He wisely suggested that America and Russia should become closer allies and work together in dealing with the problems created by President Obama, such as the rise of ISIS. Unfortunately, the new Left and many in the Republican Party oppose any new idea suggested by candidate Trump. As a result of their fear that Trump's campaign promise might gain traction during his presidency, they concocted a distraction to prevent that reality. With the aid of their total control of the media, candidate Trump's opposing idiots have found a cause in investigating their vocal claims of Russian meddling in the presidential election. The fact that the United States has meddled in the elections and internal affairs of every country in the world is not their concern. The fact that if there was Russian meddling it was the fault of the presidency of Obama to have allowed it is of no concern to them. All these dedicated idiots want is a way of stopping President Trump from carrying out a campaign promise to work with Russia on global problems such as terrorism and North Korea's nuclear program. These idiots are such dedicated warmongers that they would relish the thought of the United States going to war with Russia to remove Vladimir Putin and bring about regime change. That had been the goal of Secretary of State Hillary Clinton and President Obama. One reason for their support of the presidential candidacy of Hillary Clinton was war with Russia. That alone proves how idiotic they are.

One of the ironies of the desire of the new Left and many on the Right to wage war on Russia and demonize Russia's democratically elected leader is that America needs an alliance with Russia today more than at any time since the Second World War. American presidents had been very wise in allying with Russia during the First and Second World War. There was no need for that alliance after the Second World, until now. President Nixon had been wise to ally with China to win the Cold War with Russia. But that alliance with China has led to a threat from China that no one envisaged. We have explained that Presidents George W. Bush and Obama had ample evidence to see that America's continued engagement with China was the primary cause of America's relative decline. Candidate Trump is wise in both ending that economic alliance with China and creating a new military alliance with Russia. Both of these strategies will reduce the relative position of China. Instead, he is attacked on both counts. Keeping the economic alliance with China will only reduce the economic gap between the United States and China. Attacking Russia will not only prevent a military alliance between the United States and Russia but also drive the creation of a military alliance between Russia and China. More on that increasing China-Russia alliance in the next section on the new Silk Road.

China's New Silk Road: One Belt and One Road (OBOR)

In 1823, the United States announced to the world with the Monroe Doctrine that Latin America was its backyard to colonize, and Western European empires were being warned to not challenge the United States. At the time, the dominant European empires, especially France and Britain, were far more powerful than the relatively puny American empire. However, the most dominant empire of the day, Britain, backed the American empire to bond a lasting alliance. At the time, Britain was more interested in its colonizations in Asia, Africa, and the Caribbean than in South America. History has a habit of repeating itself. When China's leader Xi Jinping announced China's plan to build a new Silk Road in 2013, he was making a challenge similar to that of Pres. James Monroe, that Asia was China's backyard and that other empires, including the dominant American empire, should stay out.

China had long been the most powerful country, not just in Asia but in the world. That changed when the British invaded in the nineteenth century. But President Nixon's visit has enabled China to rise again. Just as Pres. James Monroe waited until the American empire had consolidated its own country, the United States, before making his imperial move in 1823, President Xi waited until China was strong enough economically and militarily before making his move in 2013. Just as the United States would become the dominant empire in Latin America after 1823, so too will China become the dominant empire in Asia after 2013. Just as the United States had not contemplated its global status in 1823, China is currently focusing on being the dominant empire in Asia, not in the world. That can come later if the West self-destructs as Germany and Britain self-destructed during the Second World War.

China's decision to dominate Asia by initiating a mammoth infrastructure investment project begins with *seven* subprojects, all emanating from China and linking neighboring countries. The Eurasian Land Bridge will link China to Western Russia via Kazakhstan. China has been linked to Russia from its northern province of Harbin for many years. The Western attempt to isolate Russia only serves to galvanize China's desire to rebuild its long historical trade relationship with Russia. When Alaska was colonized by Russia to fish for sea otters, it was China that provided the market for the otter skins. The new Eurasian Land Bridge is complemented by the China-Mongolia-Russia Corridor, enhancing the importance of the historical link from Northern China to Eastern Russia. It's a two-pronged infrastructure connection emphasizing the importance of the China-Russia relationship and the huge geographical size of Russia.

A second link from Western China will connect Turkey via West and Central Asia. Turkey is another country that the West has attempted to isolate since defeating the Ottoman Empire. Turkey straddles the border of Asia and Europe. The Ottoman Empire had long been the primary adversary of the Western European empires. Its defeat during the First World War had enabled the West to colonize the rich oil producers of Iran, Iraq, and Saudi Arabia. Turkey was isolated both from the West and from its Arab colonies. Unsure of Western intentions, it is playing both the EU and China to keep its options open. China is only too happy to exploit Turkey's dilemma and Western indifference and feet dragging on the question of Turkey's membership in the EU. One of the goals of China's OBOR is to connect China with both the Middle East and Europe.

China's plans for its new Silk Road recognizes the post–old Silk Road dominance of sea transportation over land transportation. While railways and high-speed trains are far more efficient land transportation compared to camel caravans, China recognizes that its defeat by the British was due to the superiority of the British navy. American hegemony added air supremacy. Water transportation of goods for trade is still cheaper than railways and planes. This is why the Maritime Silk Road is as important to China's Belt and Road Initiative as the building of roads and railways through the old overland Silk Road. The Maritime Silk Road complements the new overland Silk Road by adding maritime links from China's coastal areas outward by sea through strategic locations of new container ports in neighboring countries such as Singapore, Pakistan, India, Bangladesh, Myanmar, and the Mediterranean. A second goal of China's OBOR is to link China to Southeast Asia and East Africa. It's the most ambitious transportation project ever envisaged by a world leader. While the earlier Western European empires, Portugal, Spain, Holland, France, and Britain, used their maritime locations to build great ships and strong navies to plunder far from their homes, China's strategy is to harness current technological advances in both water and land transportation to fan out in many directions from its home base into neighboring territories and later push further afield. It's a strategy rooted in the special way it embraced the Global Shift and free enterprise. Free enterprise in China began with its creation of SEZs in its southern and eastern coasts bordering the South China Sea and the East China Sea, pushing initially into Hong Kong and Taiwan, and then further afield, building the world's largest container ports in China. Having used that strategy more successfully than any other country to build an economy now rivaling that of the United States, China is now embarked on its new Silk Road adventure to dominate Asia in the same way that the United States dominated the New World before the Second World War. China's OBOR is a planned US$5 trillion infrastructure project intended to connect China with sixty other countries by rail, road, and sea as well as modern digital communication.

In 2018, China announced its intention to add a Polar Silk Road to its ambitious OBOR project. China released a white paper to explain how its new China's Arctic Policy is to be linked to its ambitious OBOR infrastructure project. China understands that dominating Asia is just a stepping-stone to challenging the West for equal status to the United States as a superpower. It sees incorporation of its presence in the warming Arctic region as early as possible as a strategic move to complementing its new Silk Road initiative. Since the OBOR is primarily an infrastructure project, adding the Arctic will mean building infrastructure, including shipping lanes, in the Arctic, as the Arctic warms up. China's first expedition to the Antarctic was in 1984. It now has four research stations in Antarctica. Once again, the West, especially Canada and the United States, will prove to be short-sighted in their continued efforts to isolate Russia. Russia is the key country bordering the Arctic region. Russia also currently has the dominant military and exploratory force in the Arctic. By continuing their foolish efforts to isolate Russia, Canada and the United States are pushing Russia to allow China to increase its presence in the Arctic. China is not an Arctic nation, but its increasing political, economic, and military alliance with Russia, the largest Arctic nation, is key to China being able to push its Arctic agenda in the form of the Polar Silk Road.

China's National Petroleum Corporation owns 20 percent of Russia's Liquefied Natural Gas plant located on the Yamal Peninsula in the Russian Arctic. In 2016, China used its massive OBOR fund to purchase another 10 percent as part of its pledge to cooperate with Russia in building an ice road in Russia's Arctic. China has stated its intention to purchase most of the liquefied natural gas produced by this plant from Russia, thereby providing Russia a guaranteed customer. In 2013, China was able to secure observer status on the Arctic Council. The Arctic Council is made up of Arctic nations including Russia, the United States, and Canada. During a state visit to Australia in 2014, Pres. Xi Jinping referred to China as an Upcoming Polar Power. China has begun to build stronger political, economic, and tourism relations with Scandinavian countries, since Sweden, Denmark, Norway, Finland, and Iceland are also members of the Arctic Council. These five Nordic countries are all participating in an Arctic Research Centre set up by China in Shanghai. A Chinese mining company has bought some mining rights in resource-rich Greenland, a territory of Denmark. Northern Finland's Lapland region is attracting increasing numbers of Chinese tourists.

China's interests in adding the warming Arctic to its global ambition is meant to ensure its share of the potential mineral, fishing, and other resources, which become more accessible the more the Arctic warms up. In addition, China wants to ensure that it will be able to freely use a relatively ice-free Arctic as a shorter alternative shipping route to the route through the Suez Canal. A shipping route from China to Europe via the Northeast Passage over Northern Russia is expected to be much shorter and quicker. As an example, China to Holland should take twenty-eight days instead of forty-eight days. China's ships have successfully sailed the Northeast Passage since 2013. China is also interested in the Northwest Passage over Northern Canada. This can save shipping time compared with the route through the Panama Canal. As an example, shipping time from Shanghai to New York can save a full week. China did its first test run of the Northwest Passage in 2017, using its ice-breaker research vessel *Xuelong* (*Snow Dragon*). As expected, Canada was not very happy. China had initially purchased the ice-breaker from Ukraine and adapted it to be able to sail to the Canadian Arctic village of Tuktoyaktuk in Canada's Northwest Territory in 1999. The Northwest Territory is land stolen by Canada from the indigenous peoples. It will be interesting to see if the indigenous peoples of the Arctic trust China any more than Canada and the United States, both of whom stole all the lands of the First Nations to create Canada and the United States.

Xuelong made follow-up voyages to the Arctic in 2003, 2008, 2010, and 2012. Chinese scientists used a helicopter on *Xuelong* to fly to the North Pole during the 2010 voyage. During the 2012 voyage, *Xuelong* attempted to sail to the North Pole from Iceland but did not quite make it. *Xuelong* makes annual voyages to take supplies to China's Zhongshan Research Station in Antarctica. China is currently building a second ice-breaker, *Xuelong 2,* which is expected to be completed in 2019. This will be its first fully home-made ice-breaker and is expected to be more advanced than *Xuelong.* China will also want to be able to participate with countries like the United States and Russia in using submarines for military exercises in the Arctic.

President Trump is the only Western leader to recognize that increased *Globalization* will enhance the rise of China and increase the relative decline of the West. However, he will fail to convince his Cold War allies and the Western media. Even if he could, it will be difficult to turn back the clock. In 2017, the U.S. trade deficit rose by 12 percent instead of decreasing. Trade deficits with both China and Mexico also increased. President Trump's Cold War allies and the Western media are committed both to *Globalization* and expensive warmongering. President Trump will fail, and the West will continue to decline relative to the emerging economies. That's good for a new World Order, which will be far more equitable, but bad for both the new Left and the new Right, in the West, because what they have in common is continued Western hegemony.

CHAPTER 2

A Summary of the Magnitude of the Global Shift from the West to the Emerging Economies: 1980–2018

This chapter will provide an overview of the details provided in the next eight chapters dealing with specific countries such as China and India or specific regions such as Latin America and the Caribbean. While those details are essential for a full understanding of the revolution we call the Global Shift, most readers will be anxious to get an overview, which not only is educational in itself but will also motivate the reader to read more. In our view, this Global Shift is as revolutionary as the voyages of discovery by Portugal and Spain during the fifteenth century. Like Portugal's modest discoveries along the West African coast between 1415 and 1490, the Global Shift began modestly along the narrow strip of land on the border of Mexico and the United States, referred to as the maquiladoras, during the 1960s. Just as Portugal's modest discoveries along the West African coast led to a sea route to Asia, and Spain's rediscovery of America led to the birth of the American empire, so too did the Global Shift to China in 1980 led to where we are today, with new emerging economies like China and India challenging the six centuries of Western dominance. There are numerous ways in which we can illustrate with objective data how the economies that were dominant during the nineteenth and twentieth centuries have been challenged by the new emerging economies. Since the challenge we hear the most of today is that of China challenging the United States for first place, it's appropriate to begin there.

How China Rose from Tenth Place in 1979 to Second Place Today

China had been one of the world's most powerful countries until the British invaded with its far superior navy in the 1840s and began the Western colonization of China. In 1820, China's GDP was 33 percent of the World's GDP. By contrast, the GDP of the United States was only 1.8 percent of the world's GDP. The GDP of the UK in 1820 was 5.2 percent of the world's GDP. China experienced more than a century of relative economic decline where the West either raped its natural resources or dismissed it from the global stage. In 1913, China's GDP had fallen to 9 percent of the world's GDP. During the Cold War, China's economy was puny compared to the United States and many of the American allies such as Japan, Germany, France, the UK, and Italy. Nevertheless, President Nixon saw China as a sufficiently important *Communist* country on the other side of the Iron Curtain that he was willing to form an alliance with China to win the Cold War against the Soviet Union. When President Nixon visited China in 1972, China had such a puny economy, compared to the United States, that no one ever expected that allowing Western countries to trade with China could ever create an economy so large that it would even challenge Japan, the West's foremost ally in Asia, much less the United States. How that miracle occurred because of what we call the Global Shift is explained in great detail in chapters 4 and 5 of this book. Here we provide only the basic facts that show that this miracle did occur.

When President Nixon visited China in 1972, the GDP of China was US$112,160 million. By comparison, the GDP of the United States was US$1,225,400 million, eleven times as large. How could allowing China to engage in international trade, which benefits *both* trading partners, according to Ricardo's theory of comparative advantage, ever cause China to close that massive gap between itself and the United States? Everyone would say never. It was not until 1980 that China was able to sort out the new relationship it would have with the United States and implement the laws and regulations needed to set up the first of its special economic zones, SEZs, in Shenzhen. In 1979, the year before China was able to embrace the Global Shift, China's GDP was US$175,574 million. By contrast, the GDP of the United States was US$2,544,450 million, 14.5 times as large. The economic gap between the United States and China had widened during the years between President Nixon's visit in 1972 and the year prior to China being able to take advantage of the negotiated new relationship between the two countries.

China gradually opened up only its southern ports and provinces to international trade and foreign investment. It took a while for the benefits from this new international trade and capital inflows to show up in the form of higher economic growth. As late as 1987, China's GDP represented only 1.6 percent of the world's GDP. Nevertheless, only thirteen years later, China's GDP had risen to US$1,198,480 million in 2000. By contrast, the GDP of the United States had grown to US$9,764,800 million. The U.S. GDP was now only 8 times as large as China compared to 14.5 times as large in 1979. While both economies were benefitting from engaging in international trade and capital flows, China was benefitting far more. China had also moved up in the global ranking of countries by GDP, from tenth place in 1979 to sixth place in 2000. Any half-brained American president or Western leader would have clearly seen that President Nixon's political alliance with China against the Soviet Union had serious negative economic consequences for Western dominance. Moreover, the reason for President Nixon's political alliance with China no longer existed. The dreaded Soviet Union had collapsed in December 1991. The United States and its allies had several years after the end of the Soviet Union to reverse their engagement with China and prevent the narrowing of the economic gap between China and the United States. The fact that they did not is proof to me that Western leaders are dimwitted, think in a narrow tunnel, and seek out only those with poor economic advice. While Ricardo's theory of comparative advantage proves that both partners must benefit from international trade, it says nothing about how equally or unequally the gains will be shared. By 2000, it was crystal clear that most of the gains from international trade between China and the West was going to China. That is not an economic argument against trade, but it is a very significant political and military argument against trade if you want to maintain the political and military dominance you secured from centuries of military invasions, conquests, and colonizations.

While it was possible to reverse President Nixon's political and economic alliance with China as late as 2000, it would be too late to reverse it in 2018, as President Trump is contemplating. Candidate Trump had campaigned on attacking China on currency manipulation and huge trade surpluses with the United States. But even candidate Trump missed the key problem of the West engaging with China. That key problem is the massive economic gains to China compared with the miniscule gains to the West. President Trump is facing great opposition from both Americans and his allies in any effort to roll back Western engagement with China. While President Nixon was able to single-handedly begin Western engagement with China, it would be impossible for President Trump to single-handedly reverse course. There are many reasons for this, but the reasons are similar to one Western European country attempting to prevent all countries from exploring the New World fifty years after Columbus had shown the way.

The narrowing of the economic gap between China and the United States, which took place in the first two decades after China embraced the Global Shift, did not let up. China's sixth place ranking in 2000 was not a major threat to Western dominance both because the U.S. GDP was still eight times as large as China's, and all the other four largest economies, Japan, Germany, the UK, and France, were dedicated American allies. But in 2000, China was just getting started. Another decade later, China's GDP had increased to US$5,878,629 million. This was the decade when the dumbest leaders in the West should have taken notice. The U.S. economy had only grown to US$14,582,400 million in 2010, less than 2.5 times that of China. In addition, all the U.S. allies now had lower GDPs than China. How could that have happened in a single decade? It had taken a century and two devastating world wars between Britain and Germany for the United States to have an economy larger than Britain or Germany. That the West failed to see China creeping up on them, because they had agreed to trade with China, is further proof that the West is led by dummies. Western leaders continue to behave today, exactly the same way as the leaders of Portugal and Spain behaved, after they had ushered in the beginning of Western domination. At that time, it was China's leaders who were dummies for not taking notice. China paid a heavy price and was raped and pillaged by the West. Britain even forced China to buy the opium it produced in its *colony* of India to addict China's citizens. Today, Western leaders suffer from the same myopia that had inflicted the Chinese leaders in the nineteenth century.

In 2017 China's GDP had increased to US$11,795,297 million. With a GDP of US$19,417,144 million in 2017, the GDP of the United States was now only 1.646 times that of China. The gap had narrowed further between 2010 and 2017, from 2.48 times to 1.646 times. The forecast by the IMF for 2020 is a GDP of US$15,066,667 million for China and a GDP of US$22,063,044 million for the United States. This forecast narrows the gap further to a U.S. GDP only 1.464 times that of China. All of the measures we have used so far are based on exchange rates with the U.S. dollar. All estimates of China's GDP using the purchasing parity measure, PPP, puts China's GDP in *2015* higher than that of the United States. Using the PPP measure, China's GDP in 2015 was 19,695,741 million compared with the GDP of the United States of only 18,036,650 million. By contrast, using exchange rates, China's GDP in 2015 fell to

US$11,226,186 million. It will be sometime after 2020 that China will likely overtake the United States as the world's largest economy using exchange rates.

G5 Developed Economies Compared with Five Largest Emerging Economies: 1980–2018

In the post–World War II period, the United States formed an economic alliance with the world's five largest Western economies to run the world's international trade, capital flows, financial markets, banking, and credit. It was called the G5. The members were the United States, Japan, Germany, France, and the UK. Prior to the Global Shift, the total GDP of the G5 countries in 1979 was US$5,429.5 billion. By contrast, the GDP of the five largest Third World economies, which the Global Shift changed to emerging economies, was a paltry US$797.7 billion. This was a mere 14.7 percent of the GDP of the G5. The five economies in the Third World list, from largest to smallest, were Brazil, China, India, Mexico, and Saudi Arabia. Note that in 1979, Brazil's GDP of US$225 billion exceeded that of China's GDP of US$176 billion.

While the Global Shift had begun in China in 1980, it was several years later before it took off in India. But by 2000, the Global Shift had begun to change many Third World economies to emerging economies. In 2000, the GDP of the G5 countries had increased to US$19,898 billion. In that year, the GDP of the five largest emerging economies was US$3, 274 billion. This represented 16.5 percent of the GDP of the G5. It was a modest improvement from 14.7 percent because only China had made significant gains, moving China to overtake Brazil for the number-one spot in the emerging G5. But it was a signal of what was to come as more and more Third World economies embraced the Global Shift in the twenty-first century. In 2000, Saudi Arabia was replaced by Russia because Russia had become an independent emerging Economy after the break-up of the Soviet Union in 1991. Russia's GDP of US$259.7 billion exceeded that of Saudi Arabia's GDP of US$188.4 billion in 2000.

As the Global Shift caused growth rates in the new emerging economies to surpass the growth rates of the G5 economies, the GDP gap lessened. In 2010, the GDP of the G5 economies had increased to

US$28,893 billion. The GDP of the five largest emerging economies had increased to US$12,289 billion. This now represented a whopping 42.5 percent of the GDP of the G5. This was a massive increase over a single decade. It was the same five economies as in 2000, but India had moved up from fourth place in 2000 to third place after China and Brazil. Russia had also moved up from fifth place in 2000 to fourth place in 2010, overtaking Mexico. Just as the Global Shift had significantly increased the GDP of China by 2000, it had now significantly increased the GDP of the five largest emerging economies by 2010.

In 2015, the GDP of the G5 economies had increased to US$31,068 billion. The GDP of the same five largest emerging economies had increased to US$17,727 billion. This represented 57.1 percent of the GDP of the G5. This was another massive narrowing of the GDP gap in five years. While it is not especially surprising that the countries that became the G5 in the 1970s, because they were the largest Western economies, are the same five economies in 2015, it is more surprising that the five largest emerging economies in 2000 are the same in 2015. This will not likely continue into the future. Economic growth rates in Brazil, Russia, and Mexico have slowed, while the Global Shift is gaining momentum in some other emerging economies such as Indonesia. In fact, Indonesia's GDP surpassed that of Mexico in 2017. Replacing Mexico with Indonesia in 2017, the GDP of the five largest emerging economies increased to US$18,972 billion. With a GDP of US$32,598 billion for the G5 economies, the GDP of the five largest emerging economies had increased from 57.1 percent of the GDP of the G5 in 2015 to 58.2 percent in 2017.

In 2017, the share of the world's GDP produced by the G5 was 41.8 percent. The share produced by the five largest emerging economies was 24.3 percent. These ten economies together produced 66.1 percent of the world's GDP. These measures are all based on exchange rates. If we use the PPP measure, the gap between the Western G5 and the emerging G5 disappears. However, per capita GDP in the emerging economies are still much lower than in the West because of the much higher populations of the emerging economies. The IMF forecasts for 2022 are as follows. The GDP of the G5 will increase to US$38,793 billion. The GDP of the five largest emerging economies will increase to US$27,775 billion. This will be 72 percent of the GDP of the G5. These are the same five economies in both categories. The 2022 forecast imply a continued narrowing of the GDP gap between the richest five Western economies and the richest five non-Western economies, as measured by exchange rates.

Western Asian Economies Compared with Emerging Asian Economies: 1980–2018

Just as the American empire first consolidated its dominance of the New World by declaring the Monroe Doctrine in 1823, before competing with Japan in the Asia-Pacific, China is determined to consolidate its dominance of Asia, before competing with the American empire in Latin America and the Caribbean. This is why we now compare the *three* major Asia-Pacific economic colonies of the American empire, Japan, South Korea, and Australia, with the *three* major emerging economies in Asia, China, India, and Indonesia, before and after the Global Shift.

In 1979, the GDP of the three major American *economic colonies* in the Asia-Pacific region had a combined GDP of US$1,221 billion. By comparison, the combined GDP of China, India, and Indonesia was a paltry, US$382 billion, 31 percent of the GDP of the American economic colonies. By 2000, the Global Shift had not yet made a significant impact, especially on India and Indonesia. The combined GDP of China, India, and Indonesia had grown to US$1,823 billion. But the GDP of the three American economic colonies had grown to US$5,579 billion. This represented a modest relative increase for the three emerging Asian economies to 33 percent. It was the following decade that the Global Shift made a huge difference. The combined GDP of the three emerging Asian economies increased to US$11,177 billion in 2010. This was in marked contrast to the relatively modest increase of the combined GDP of the three American economic colonies to US$7,437 billion.

The combined GDP of the three largest emerging economies in Asia had overtaken the combined GDP of the American allies in the Asia-Pacific. After the Second World War, the American empire had carefully manipulated the Japanese people to rebuild the strongest economy in Asia that would be subservient to the American empire, politically and militarily. Prior to the Global Shift, this post–World War II American strategy had successfully contained the rise of China. With an economically strong subservient ally in the Asia-Pacific, the American empire could devote more time, energy, and resources to policing the globe. Australia had always been a reliable ally as a white ex-colony of Britain. The Korean War brought another economically powerful, subservient ally in South Korea. In the period following the Korean War, the American empire owned the three largest economies in the Asia-Pacific, Japan, Australia, and South Korea. The Non-Aligned nations of China, India, and Indonesia had such relatively poor economies that they posed no threat to American dominance in the Asia-Pacific region.

Prior to the Second World War, the American empire had faced off against a fierce competitor, the Japanese empire, in the Asia-Pacific region. In the post–World War II period, the Japanese empire had switched roles from fierce competitor to subservient ally. The American empire had free reign over all of Asia and the Pacific as Japan was aided by Australia and South Korea in doing the bidding of the American empire. But the American empire made an irreversible mistake when President Nixon chose to allow China access to Western investment without subjecting China to the same humiliating subservience as it had imposed on Japan, South Korea, and Australia. The American empire made that mistake because it never expected China to grow its economy from its puny size in 1972, the year President Nixon visited China, to its enormous size today and bring with it other Asian economies that were not puppets of the West. In 1972, the GDP of Japan was US$303,610 million compared with China's GDP of US$112,160 million. India's GDP was US$71,128 million compared with Australia's GDP of US$58,257 million. Indonesia's GDP was US$11, 605 million compared with South Korea's GDP of US$10,735 million. Taiwan and Hong Kong were also subservient allies of the West. The Philippines was also mostly pro-West.

As we saw above, it was not until the first decade of the twenty-first century that the Global Shift changed the economic might of the three largest Asian emerging economies, relative to the three largest subservient Western allies. But the groundwork for that change was planted after President Nixon's 1972 visit to China and especially after China established its first SEZ in Shenzhen in 1980. There was no turning back after the first decade of the twenty-first century. By 2017, the combined GDP of the three largest Asian emerging economies had increased to US$15,270 billion, almost double the combined GDP of US$7,699 billion for the three largest Asian Western economies. Note that the GDP of Japan had fallen from US$5,498 billion in 2010 to US$4,841 billion in 2017.

Some will criticize our decision to compare three staunch subservient allies of the West with the implicit unity of three independent emerging economies. But the Global Shift has not only created new high-income economies in Asia but also dented the single minded, joined at the hip, post–World War II connection between the United States and the three

Asian allies. It was these same three U.S. allies, Japan, Australia, and South Korea, that took advantage of the green light given to them after President Nixon's visit to China, to invest in China, India, and Indonesia. Their economies today are far more integrated than before the Global Shift. For example, today China is the largest export market for Australia, and an FTA between China and Australia came into effect in 2015. This increasing economic integration with China has eroded their political allegiance to the United States. This is why President Obama had to "pivot to Asia." Japan, Australia, and South Korea, as well as Taiwan and Hong Kong, are no longer the assured semicolonial allies of the American empire. The rise of China, as well as India, Indonesia, Pakistan, Vietnam, Malaysia, Bangladesh, and the Philippines, has disrupted the old post–World War II alliance of the rich economies of the Asia-Pacific with the American empire.

On the other side of the coin, China is using its earlier alliance with India and other Third World Asian economies, which it created as a leading member of the Non-Aligned Movement with India, to fight Western imperialism, to forge stronger economic and political alliances in Asia to compete with the American empire in the Asia-Pacific region, as Japan had done before the Second World War. China has the advantage over the American empire because of its strategic geographic location in Asia. China's economy is also growing faster than the United States. China also has fewer commitments to other areas of the globe. The American empire is spread pretty thin in Asia, Europe, Africa, and the Americas. When the American empire had no commitment to Europe, it still found the Japanese empire a formidable rival in the Asia-Pacific region. Now that the American empire is committed to defend all of Europe and fight a rising Russia, it has little chance of winning the Asia-Pacific region against a rising China, no matter how much it pivots.

Why Has the G20 Not Replaced the G7?

The G5 had expanded to the G7 by adding two more of the largest Western economies, Italy and Canada. The G5 and expanded G7 ruled the world's economic, financial, political, technological, racial, cultural, media, propaganda, and military for the entire remainder of the twentieth century following the end of World War II. They did whatever their little hearts desired. They invaded, manipulated, stole, and enriched themselves, at the expense of Third World countries too militarily weak to match their planes and bombs. They doled out aid to those they had bombed and destroyed their homes and livelihoods. They lived high on the horse as they turned millions into refugees and watched as many millions died of hunger, starvation, malnutrition, diseases, and civil wars instigated by them and weapons sold by them to the combatants.

After the Global Shift increased the GDP of many Third World countries, especially that of China, these emerging economies, led by China, began to demand greater inclusion in the decisions made by institutions such as the G7, IMF, WTO, World Bank, UN, international settlements, reserve currencies, and global financial centers. One attempt to respond to these demands was the creation of the G20. Note that the West did not expand the G7 to the G20 as they had earlier expanded the G5 to the G7. The West kept the G7 group of Western economies to ensure that power and control of the globe would be maintained by the West until others are slowly co-opted or marginalized. The G20 group was created in December 1999. It would have to prove itself as a better alternative to the G7. It will be up to the emerging economies to prove their usefulness. In the meantime, the G7 will continue to meet and govern as if nothing has changed.

The G20 includes all the economies in the G7. In addition, the EU was given a special membership, even though four of the G7 members, Germany, France, Italy, and the UK, are EU members. This was clearly an attempt by the West to weight the membership of the G20 in favor of the West. In 2016, the GDP of the EU was US$16,408 billion. This was almost as large as the combined GDP of the ten emerging economies in the G20. Their combined GDP in 2016 was US$20, 868 billion. The combined GDP of the nine Western members of the G20 was US$38,117 billion. But adding the GDP of the EU increases the total to US$54, 525 billion, more than double the combined GDP of the ten emerging economies. Without the EU, the combined GDP of the emerging economies is 54.7 percent of the combined GDP of the nine Western economies. When the GDP of the EU is added, that percentage falls to 38.3 percent. That much higher GDP will enable the Western countries to call the shots in the G20 while continuing to keep the G7 as a powerful force in controlling the world.

Other Western countries included in the G20 are Australia and South Korea. This means that half of the members are the richest

Western economies, the United States, the EU, Japan, Germany, the UK, France, Italy, Canada, Australia, and South Korea. With the inclusion of the EU as a separate member, overlapping with Germany, the UK, France, and Italy, the GDP of the Western members will exceed that of the combined GDP of the emerging economies for the foreseeable future. Together with the continued role of the G7, the West is determined to maintain control of global institutions into the foreseeable future. Their response to the demands of the emerging economies was more symbolic than substantial. The emerging economies will have to take some control. It will not be voluntarily relinquished by the West. The ten emerging economies in the G20, in order of size of GDP in 2017, are China, India, Brazil, Russia, Indonesia, Mexico, Turkey, Saudi Arabia, Argentina, and South Africa.

Although created in December 1999, the first leaders' summit of the G20 was not held until 2008, the year the United States caused the global financial crisis. It's instrumental that the West pretends to seek advice and help from Third World countries only after it has seriously messed up. It's no different from begging for food from First Nations in the New World when faced with starvation but colonizing and stealing as soon as it has acquired dominant military force. The West also has a long history of co-opting Third World leaders by demonizing those who oppose their imperialist goals and anointing those who cooperate with their evil deeds. China's leaders have so far shown their awareness of Western tactics by creating parallel organizations similar to those of the West while cooperating in Western institutions such as the G20, IMF, and the UN. At present, it's a cat-and-mouse game between the West and the emerging economies. China hosted the 2016 G20 summit. Regardless, the West has to relinquish some power if it wants to continue to do business with the emerging Third World.

A good example of this is the recent mistreatment of Russia by the West. Canada lobbied shamelessly to remove Russia from the G8. The G7 had expanded to the G8 when Russia was added in 1997. Russia was unceremoniously dumped from the G8. Canada's ridiculous argument against Russia was that Russia had recently colonized the Crimea. The truth is that the Crimea had been a part of Russia since 1783. More importantly, Canada was able to use the standard Western hypocrisy of morality by totally ignoring the fact that all of Canada is First Nations lands stolen by British and French colonizations. Colonization by the West is "civilized" behavior. It is done to Christianize the heathens, tame the Wild Indians, infect them with diseases like smallpox, incarcerate those not killed in reserves with no running water, enslave many to work on the lands stolen, abuse their children in residential schools, while beating their language and culture out of them, and enslaving Africans to work the stolen lands because you had stolen more than could be worked by the enslaved First Nations.

In 2014, Australia lobbied hard for Russia to be removed from the G20. It used the same insidious argument against Russia as Canada had done, even though Australia is also a country totally built on lands stolen and colonized by the British from the Aboriginal inhabitants. Australia had also become as "civilized" as Canada because it had Christianized the heathens and tamed the wild Aborigines. The leaders of the West have shown remarkable consistency in being equally immoral and hypocritical. Australia made sure that Canada's hypocrisy would be equally matched by its own hypocrisy. The fact that the emerging economies opposed the move by Australia and Russia maintained its membership in the G20 bodes well for the future. It showed that the leaders of the emerging economies were willing to call out the West for hypocritical behavior. The divide-and-rule tactic of Australia failed that time. But the West is never one to give up. In 2017, the West needs the emerging economies because of Brexit, the rise of the Right in Europe, the refugee crisis, and the election of President Trump in the United States. For now, they will play relatively nice and bide their time.

Some will argue that we should use the PPP measure to show that the ten emerging economies are on par with the nine Western economies in the G20. However, that argument can be countered by the fact that the population of the ten emerging economies is much larger, causing their per capita GDP to be much lower than the nine Western economies. While Western countries can use their much higher per capita GDP to build planes and bombs to continue invading and destroying Third World economies, the lower per capita GDP in the ten emerging economies restricts their ability to divert as much resources from poverty alleviation to military grandeur. President Nixon's visit to China in 1972 unleashed a Global Shift that favors the Third World over the West. But the West had a long head start that enabled it to build a huge advantage. The West will never voluntarily share world governance with the Third World. It's not clear whether the Third World will ever be strong enough to wrest their rightful share of world governance.

Some Western leaders like President Trump and the Far Right in Europe are already pushing back against free and open economic engagement with the Third World. In addition, it's unclear if continued free and open economic engagement will continue to favor the Third World over the West. While all trading partners benefit from free trade, how the gains are shared is totally unpredictable and will change over time and fluctuate in favor and against the same partners. Just look at trade in commodities. It favored Canada, Australia, and Russia before the financial crisis in 2008. Since 2008, it has moved against commodity exporters. In addition to how economic gains are shared in the future, political alliances will change. Just as countries like Japan, South Korea, Australia, and Taiwan are developing closer political ties with China to assist their increasing economic ties, some Third World countries may move in the opposite direction, fearing dominance by China. All we can say is that change has come after more than a century of total Western dominance. The future is less predictable than the last century.

Pairwise Comparison of the Western G7 Economies with the Seven Largest Emerging Economies, a New E-7

Western countries have never been willing to share power with the countries of the Third World that they had invaded and colonized by using their superior navies and air forces. In the United States, Canada, and Australia, they had stolen every inch of land from the First Nations and Aboriginal owners even though those original owners had generously reached out to them with food and shelter when they first arrived as beggars. This is why they did not expand their original G5 to add some of the new emerging economies like China, Brazil, and India. In the past, they had expanded their G5 to add two other countries, Italy and Canada, because they were Western allies. They had also expanded temporarily to add Russia when they were sure to be able to co-opt Russia to their side after the fall of the Soviet Union. They had used Russia before to help them win the First and Second World Wars only to discard Russia, as they did with the G8, once Russia could not be manipulated like Japan and Germany. In like manner, the West created the G20 after it caused the 2008 financial crisis, to get assistance from the emerging economies, which had been less devastated by that crisis. As a result of this unchanging history of never sharing power, the emerging economies must create their own rival institutions to compete with Western institutions such as the G7, the IMF, the World Bank, the WTO, the World Economic Forum, the reserve currency, the UN, and the International Court. As we will see in future chapters, the emerging economies are attempting to do that, led by China, India, Brazil, and Russia. Here we will address the possibility of creating an E7 capable of competing with the G7, using a pairwise comparison of the following emerging economies, China, India, Brazil, Russia, Indonesia, Mexico, and Turkey, with each of the G7 countries, the United States, Japan, Germany, the UK, France, Italy, and Canada.

The United States compared to China

China has a much longer history of both "civilized" and imperial behavior than the United States. The United States only became the largest economy in the world after the Second World War. Prior to that war, many countries had large economies and colonies. These included both Western and Eastern countries. In the West, dominant countries included the United States, Britain, France, and Germany. In the East, dominant countries included China, India, Russia, and Turkey. With the largest economy after the Second World War, the United States unilaterally took on leadership of the West while subjugating most of the world. It became the largest imperial power the world had ever known. It was able to do so by building the most powerful air force that it could use, and did use, to bomb countries into submission. At the same time, it created the most powerful propaganda machine to convince the world that it took on the leadership role for the good of all. The American empire's reign can best be seen through the eyes of a well-trained and obedient dog that is a beloved pet of his master. The dog is well cared for as long as he is well behaved and obedient. To many ignorant humans, the master is seen as a good master who takes care of his pet in clean, comfortable surroundings with sufficient food and health care. "What a good dog!" everyone says. "What a good master!" everyone says. No one asks the dog what he wants or prefers. It may just be that the dog prefers to be more of an animal and less of a human pet. The American empire has never given any country free choice. It, and it alone, decides what is best for every country. If you behave like the good dog, you are rewarded. If you disagree with the master, you are punished in the most severe manner.

In 2017, the American empire found itself, to the surprise of its pundits, intellectuals, movie stars, rock stars, media, and most voters, led by a different president, one who does not share the penchant of Western leaders for lies and hypocrisy. He prefers a little honesty, and that drives all the die-hard hypocrites and idiots wild. As an example, in early 2018, President Trump referred to some countries such as Haiti by some rather unhypocritical, some would say colorful, language. "Shit hole" was the term some claimed he used. Others claimed it was "shit house." The hypocrites were up in arms. Americans proclaimed loudly, "That's not who we are." Non-Americans proclaimed loudly, "That's not who America is." Stand aside, hypocrites. That's exactly who America was and is and will continue to be, if no other superpower stands up to it. America never embraced countries like Haiti, to take Haitians into America as refugees or help Haitians with aid because of earthquakes or famine. America *colonized* Haiti as it had colonized all of Latin America and the Caribbean after proclaiming the Monroe doctrine in 1823. Those who chastise President Trump are die-hard imperialists, pretending to be humanitarians.

The new reality is that colonies are no longer valuable. They are liabilities. Haiti, Puerto Rico, Iraq, Afghanistan, Iraq, Libya, and Syria are good recent examples of such liabilities to the United States. President Trump understands that. Other Western leaders do not. They want to continue the Western imperialism begun by Portugal in the fifteenth century. They want the invasions, bombings, and colonizations to continue. They also want and expect the U.S. taxpayers to pay for most of that increasingly expensive cost. They are willing to take a few refugees and color their populations with some nonwhite immigrants if that is what it takes for them to continue to rule the world like a master who takes care of his obedient dog. Like the dog's master, they mistakenly believe that the dog is happier being his pet, instead of a free animal.

In this post–Global Shift environment, where colonies are a liability rather than an asset to be raped and plundered, China has little difficulty in behaving better than the United States. That's because the behavior of the United States is stuck in its recent past of world domination through invasions, bombings, and colonizations. Neither the American media nor the other Western media wants to let go as criticisms of

President Trump abound. All of the these leaders, with the exception of President Trump and some labeled as "Extreme Right," are dedicated to maintaining Western imperialism, no matter what the cost. They are the new evangelists preaching the gospel of Western civilization, making the age-old mistakes of carrying the white man's burden, Christianizing the heathens, taming the wild Indian, bringing freedom and democracy, and using the same hypocrisy and propaganda. The Third World is sick of six centuries of that preaching and hypocrisy. China will have an easy time doing better than the United States, as it simply has to let go, preach less, be less hypocritical, be less pretentious, be less all-knowing and "civilized," and be less of "one-size fits all."

Today, China has the GDP to challenge American domination. In 2018, China's GDP, as measured by PPP, was larger than the United States'. Within a few years, China's GDP will be larger than the United States', even when we use the exchange rate measure. Even if China's annual economic growth falls to an average of 5 percent, it will still be larger than the United States', at an average of 3 percent. China's challenge to the United States begins in Asia because Asia is in China's backyard. But it will move to Africa and Latin America because those areas of the world have long been colonized and subjugated by the West, recently led by the United States. They despise being a good pet, no matter how well the master takes care of them. They are hungry for some freedom to make their own mistakes and develop their own culture and their own political governance. Western democracy, where you buy votes by promising the moon to all voters, where you have no real choice as the system dictates the nature of political parties and candidates, where the media lies and controls the message, where leadership is dumbed down to the lowest common denominator, where a brain-dead talk show host like Oprah Winfrey could become president, where every leader must invade, bomb, and destroy militarily weak countries, where human rights abuses are covered up and glossed over as "civilized," where laws prevail over justice, where income and wealth inequality abounds because of the sanctity of private property, is not a model to be embraced by all. We need to experiment with alternatives.

The West will never learn. They are too full of themselves. Those in the West who claim to be on the Left and claim to be nonracists are the worst culprits. Their embrace of political correctness only serves to deceive. For instance, they will always refer to the original owners of the lands and resources stolen by Canada and the United States as First

Nations and loudly denounce "racial" names such as Indians. But they will never ever honor the meaning of such a politically correct term by returning some small amount of lands and resources to create a single independent First Nations state in Canada or the United States. That would be a grave mistake, they would chant, since we are all Canadians or all Americans. Their self-righteous pomposity has no limits.

Japan Compared to India

India, like China, was a powerful empire before British colonization. During the Western colonizations of China and India, Japan became a powerful empire, overtaking both India and China. But Japan's economy, like that of Britain and Germany, was totally destroyed by the Second World War. Japan, like Germany, agreed to surrender its future political and military sovereignty to the United States in return for economic redevelopment. That choice paid an enormous economic dividend. Japan became the world's second-largest economy, once again overtaking both India and China. But just as the Global Shift has grown China's GDP to a size larger than that of the United States, it is growing India's GDP to a size larger than that of Japan. In 2018, India is the fastest-growing large economy in the world. As late as 2010, three decades after the Global Shift began in China, Japan's GDP was US$5,498 billion, 3.2 times as large as India's GDP of US$1,729 billion. But the Global Shift had arrived in India later than China. By 2017, India's GDP had risen to US$2,454 billion. Japan's GDP of US$4,841 billion in 2017 was slightly less than twice that of India. Using the PPP measure, India's GDP in 2017 was almost twice as large as that of Japan, $9,489 billion for India, compared with $5,420 billion for Japan.

Prior to the Second World War, the Japanese empire was a formidable competitor of the British and American empires in the Asia-Pacific region. India, like China, was a relatively poor Third World country, largely ignored by the West. As a result of the Global Shift, India's GDP is large enough to be the second-largest economy in the E7, just as Japan remains the second-largest economy in the G7. Since Japan chose to be an economic colony of the United States, it has far less independence than India. India never surrendered its political or military independence to the West. It chose to lead a Non-Aligned group, which remained economically too poor to have much say on the world stage. The Global Shift has changed all that. India has an opportunity to work with China to lead the E7 group. It will have a greater say in that group compared with Japan, in the G7, since Japan is little more than a puppet of the American empire. As an economic colony of the American empire, Japan could never provide an alternative to Asia or Africa or Latin America and the Caribbean. Japan was simply an economy with a large GDP standing ready to help fund the colonization and warmongering of the West in the years after the Second World War. Japan was a formidable ally of the West in subjugating the Asia-Pacific region after the Second World War. With its economy shrinking relative to that of China and India, it will play less of a role in supporting American hegemony in the region. Japan surrendered any chance it may have had of competing with the United States for a leadership position in the Asia-Pacific region by agreeing to become an economic colony of the United States in return for postwar reconstruction aid from the United States. India never did that and has therefore maintained its credibility as an independent player in the region and across the globe.

Germany Compared to Brazil

Germany was the state that built an empire in the twentieth century with the ability and power to defeat the British Empire and become the dominant world power. Unfortunately, its leader, Adolf Hitler, decided to invade Russia while fighting the British during the Second World War. Hitler's invasion of Russia destroyed most of its military to the point where it was unable to defeat the British. It self-destructed along with the British, enabling the rise of the American empire. Like Japan, Germany surrendered its political and military independence for U.S. assistance to rebuild its shattered economy. Like Japan, that choice produced a significant economic dividend. Germany became the third-largest economy in the world before the Global Shift.

While the Global Shift created significant growth in Brazil up to 2010, Brazil has experienced great political and economic instability in the last decade. It is growing much less than India and China. As a result, its GDP still lags behind that of Germany. In 2017, Brazil's GDP, as measured by PPP, was $3,216 billion. That was less than Germany's

$4,135 billion. Using exchange rates, Brazil's GDP in 2017 was US$2,141 billion compared with Germany's US$3,423 billion. While economic growth in Brazil rebounded in 2018, at this time, it is unclear whether Brazil will ever overtake Germany. Nevertheless, Brazil will have the third or fourth-largest GDP in a newly created E7. More importantly, Brazil's location in Latin America places it in a strategic geographical location to aid China in replacing U.S. dominance in Latin America and the Caribbean. It will be the equivalent of the G7 having a member in Asia, Japan. With Brazil in the E7, Asia is linked economically with Latin America and the Caribbean. Unlike Japan, which is a subservient economic colony of the United States, Brazil can play an independent role in Latin America and the Caribbean as a member of the E7. This provides the variety of options that the Third World countries have been demanding since they were colonized by the West.

The UK Compared to Russia

This pairwise comparison has some unique features compared with the other six pairs. The UK and Russia had both been imperial powers and developed economies before the Second World War. As great powers, they had both competed and cooperated with each other. At times, the Russian empire was the more powerful. At other times, the British Empire was the more powerful. During the Second World, the British Empire self-destructed, along with Germany, Japan, and Italy. But the Russian empire emerged stronger than ever. Its only surviving competitor was the American empire. Under Josef Stalin, the Russian economy experienced a higher rate of growth than its rival, the U.S. economy. Unfortunately, poor leaders after Nikita Khrushchev caused the Russian economy to stagnate, moving it down from developed economy status to emerging economy status. This was a downgrade compared to all the other E7 economies that upgraded from Third World developing economy status to emerging economy status.

Under the able leadership of Pres. Vladimir Putin, the Global Shift reached Russia, generating high rates of economic growth, until the fall in oil prices, combined with unfair sanctions by the West, which have once again caused the Russian economy to stagnate. Like Brazil, there is a rebound in 2018. Russia will be an important member of a new E7.

It is the largest country in the world with massive economic potential. It is the second-most militarily powerful country in the world after the United States, with the second-largest nuclear arsenal. In the latter regard, it is far ahead of the UK. The UK was the most powerful empire until the rise of Germany. Today it is a "poodle" of the American empire. It shows zero military independence on the world stage, always following American interventions, invasions, and bombing, like an obedient dog. It has economic problems of its own because of its recent decision to renounce its membership in the EU. Those who led the "Brexit" charge are often branded as right-wing extremists like President Trump. As we have said, they are correct in understanding that continued military invasions and Western imperialism no longer pay economic dividends and that the new *Globalization*, which we call the Global Shift, provides more gains to the emerging economies, like Russia, than to developed economies like the UK. While engaging in the Global Shift will enhance the economic growth of both the UK and Russia, it will simultaneously make the Russian economy much larger than that of the UK.

In 2017, the GDP of the UK was US$2,497 billion, making it the fifth-largest economy in the world. By comparison, the GDP of Russia was US$1,561 billion, making it the eleventh largest in the world. However, if we use the PPP measure, the Russian GDP in 2017 was larger than that of the UK. With the PPP measure, the GDP of the UK was $2,905 billion compared to $3,938 billion for Russia. Russia is an important member of BRICS and will likely occupy the third or fourth spot in a new E7. More importantly, it provides the military muscle that the E7 will need to counter the G7. At a meeting in January 2018, hosted by Canada in Vancouver, it was clear that the West was determined to meet without China, Russia, and India but still claimed that they represented the international community. They boldly proclaimed that the entire world was unified against North Korea even though they represented only 10 percent of the world's population and behaved exactly as they had done as Western imperial masters to the great majority of people living in the Third World. They continued to claim to have a God-given right to possess nuclear weapons and deny others, such as North Korea, that right so that they can regime change leaders who do not want to be poodles like leaders of the UK or Canada. An E7 can never do any worse than the G7. At the very least, it will represent a much larger percentage of the international community.

France Compared to Indonesia

Indonesia is the surprise latecomer to emerging economy status. It was not on anyone's radar when analysts such as Jim O'Neill of Goldman Sachs initially shone the spotlight on the four BRIC countries, Brazil, Russia, India, and China. But Indonesia is today competing with India and China for the number-one spot as the fastest-growing large economy. Economic growth peaked at 6.4 percent in 2010, averaging 5 percent thereafter. In 2017, Indonesia's GDP was US$1,021 billion, compared to a GDP of US$2,420 billion for France. France has often switched with the UK for fourth- and fifth-place ranking in the G7. In 2017, it ranked fifth behind the UK. In like manner, Indonesia ranked fifth in the suggested E7, behind Russia. Just as Russia has the potential to overtake the UK's GDP, as measured by exchange rates, Indonesia is on track to overtake France as the seventh-largest economy in the world. Likewise, Indonesia's GDP in 2017 was larger than that of France using the PPP measure, just as Russia's GDP in 2017 was already larger than that of the UK, using the PPP measure. Using the PPP measure, France had a GDP of $2,833 billion in 2017, compared to Indonesia's GDP of $3,257 billion. It is safe to say that France will maintain its fifth-place rank in the G7 and Indonesia will maintain its fifth rank in the suggested E7 into the foreseeable future.

Italy Compared to Mexico

In 2017, Italy had a GDP of US$1,807 billion compared to a GDP of US$987 billion for Mexico. Mexico is the country where we identified the beginning of the Global Shift with the creation of the Border Industrialization Program, BIP, Maquiladoras Program, between the United States and Mexico. Today, President Trump is pushing back against NAFTA and the new economic engagement between Mexico and the United States, which began with the BIP program in 1965. Once again, while the program has benefitted both countries, it has benefitted Mexico far more than the United States, moving Mexico from Third World developing economy status to emerging economy status. In 1965, when the BIP program was initiated, no one would have imagined a poor country like Mexico challenging a developed country like Italy for equal ranking in the global economy. But that is the situation in 2017. Mexico's GDP is very likely to overtake Italy's GDP, as measured by exchange rates, in the foreseeable future. Using the PPP measure, Mexico's GDP in 2017 was already larger than that of Italy. In 2017, Mexico's PPP measure of GDP was $2,406 billion compared to Italy's GDP of $2,303 billion.

Canada Compared to Turkey

Canada is a very proud member of the G7 group, always pushing the warmongering agenda of the American empire to compensate for its economic dependency status with the United States. With the election of President Trump, it has become even more fearful of losing its special dependent economic relationship with the United States. It has tried for more than a century to reduce its economic dependence on the United States, without any success. As a commodity exporter, Canada's fortunes rise and fall, both with the United States, and with international commodity prices. It has the lowest GDP in the G7, with a GDP of US$1,600 million in 2017.

Turkey is what is left of the once great Ottoman Empire. It has reached out to the EU to join that Western club but has been denied membership as of 2018. The Global Shift has been good to Turkey, boosting its economic growth and confirming its status as an emerging economy. In 2017, its GDP was US$794 billion. This entitles it to a last-place position in my suggested E7, comparable to Canada's position in the G7. Using the PPP measure, Turkey's GDP in 2017 exceeded that of Canada. It was $2,082 billion compared to $1,753 billion for Canada. If Turkey can maintain its higher growth rate, it could overtake Canada and have a larger economy even if we use the exchange rate measure.

G7 Compared to E7

The G7 is an elitist and *undemocratic* institution that loudly and incessantly claims to be the voice of the international community. That claim is pure, unadulterated propaganda. It insists on such propaganda because it has the power to do so since it controls the world's media and tolerates zero freedom of the press. The total population of the G7 countries in 2017 was 760 million. That represented only 10.2 percent of the world's population. That makes it *undemocratic.* Of course, the West will dismiss that argument because what the West deems democratic is always trumped by propaganda. Its superior wealth and military power makes it elitist. It uses that wealth and military power to invade, bomb indiscriminately, conquer, and steal. It punishes severely those who are not obedient pets. It uses both military and economic punishments as it has the most powerful military and controls the UN, the WTO, the World Bank, the IMF, the reserve currency, global financial markets, and media propaganda.

The E7 will never replace the G7, but it will provide an alternative choice that is both more democratic and less elitist. In 2017, the total population of the suggested E7 was 3,576 million. That represented 47.4 percent of the world's population. It cannot be deemed to be as elitist as the G7 since its per capita income in 2017 was US$5,803 compared to US$47,375 for the G7 group. In addition, it has yet to develop elitist institutions such as equivalents to the UN, WTO, World Bank, reserve currency, and control of global financial markets. It will also have to increase its military power and per capita incomes to match that of the G7 countries. An E7 will never attempt to become unilateral like the G7. While the Third World has a long history of wanting to share power with the West, the West has an equally long history of never wanting to share power with the Third World. But a newly created E7 will force the West to share power or compete with it. Unlike the poverty-stricken Third World, the E7 countries are richer. That economic clout will enable it to build its military power and force the G7 to take notice. As the irreversible Global Shift continues to narrow the economic and military gap between the G7 and the E7, the West has to share power, as it was forced to share power with the Soviet Union, despite its invention of the Iron Curtain to isolate the Soviet Union. Any war declared by the G7 on the E7 will have to be a Cold War, as with the Soviet Union, since both sides have nukes. Had Russia not developed its own nuclear weapons independently, the West would have long declared a hot war to invade, conquer, and colonize Russia.

In 2017, the combined GDP of the suggested E7 group was US$20,752 billion, compared with the combined GDP of the G7 group of US$36,005 billion. However, if we use the PPP measure, the GDP of the suggested E7 group exceeded that of the G7 group. GDP for the suggested E7 was $47,578 billion compared with $38,766 billion for the G7. But per capita GDP was much less even if we use the PPP measure. Using the latter measure, per capita GDP for the G7 group was $51,000 compared with only $13,305 for the suggested E7 group.

CHAPTER 3

The Global Shift Began with the *Mexican Maquiladoras*

When the voyages of discovery, led by Portugal and Spain, began in the fifteenth century, no one imagined that it would lead to the total domination of the world by the West during the nineteenth and twentieth centuries. In like manner, what we call the Global Shift, and others misleadingly call *Globalization* or outsourcing, is not yet recognized as having the same significance as those voyages of discovery in *reversing* that Western domination during this current century. The twenty-first century will see the relative decline of the West and the resurgence of the historical dominance of the world by China and India, aided by Russia and Third World economies such as Brazil and Indonesia. As I began to write this book in 2016, two of the most significant political events of 2016 were the direct result of this Global Shift. These two events are the phenomenon of Donald Trump in the United States and Brexit in the UK. I explained in the first chapter how the Global Shift produced these two political storms. More details will unfold as the book progresses.

One difference between the rise of the West after the voyages of da Gama and Columbus and the rise of the East after the Global Shift is that in the rise of the West, the largest of the Western empires, the American empire, was the latecomer; while in the rise of the East, the largest of the emerging economies, China, was there almost from the beginning. While the Global Shift began in Mexico, its move to China, after the visit of American president Richard Nixon in 1972, was the key that unlocked its massive potential to change the world. Nixon's visit to China would prove to be as revolutionary as the rediscovery of the New World by Columbus in 1492. But unlike 1492, when it took over four centuries for the United States to lead the Western domination of the world, China will lead the Eastern domination in less than a century after 1972. President Nixon was impeached for Watergate, but history will prove that his visit to China unleashed forces that reversed American dominance just as the first voyage of Columbus gave birth to American dominance.

During the sixteenth century, many in Western Europe, the Middle East, Russia, and China, then the centers of world dominance, dismissed the voyages of Columbus as uneventful. They could never foresee the rise of the American empire. In like manner, today, many in the West, the United States, Germany, Britain, France, Japan, South Korea, and other Western powers, show little understanding of this Global Shift unleashed by President Nixon's 1972 visit to China.

Economics is often a powerful force that can shape events in ways that are the opposite of political forces. This is one reason why the West is unable to comprehend that it will be politically difficult to stop the reversal of dominance from the West to the East. Many Western leaders fear the rise of China and suggest moves to curtail that rise. But these leaders do not understand the economic forces unleashed by the Global Shift. Western consumers have far more economic power than political leaders from both the Right and the Left credit them with. Western consumers were spoiled when Western imperialism stole the lands and resources of the indigenous peoples, as well as the lands and resources of Third World economies, enslaved Africans, and employed others under semislavery conditions to bring them dirt cheap bananas, coffee, tea, spices, and many other consumer goods. In like manner, the Global Shift has brought Western consumers dirt cheap textiles and other consumer products by employing Chinese, Indians, Vietnamese, Bangladeshis, and others in working conditions that are cheap, miserable, dangerous, and extremely polluting to the environment. It will be very difficult for Western politicians, accustomed to "buying votes" in Western pretend democracies, to resist the economic clout of Western consumers.

When Third World immigrants long to migrate to the West, their desire has absolutely nothing to do with freedom or democracy and everything to do with high living standards based on high money incomes and cheap consumer goods. This is how the West won its battle with Communist Russia. The leaders of the West preached the restrictions on freedoms in Communist regimes, but it was the greater availability of consumer goods in the West that won over the voters in the pretend democracies of the West. It's the same with the war on drugs or global warming. American consumers of illegal drugs are single-handedly responsible for America's failed war on drugs. In like manner, Western consumers of ever-increasing quantities of junk, produced both in the West and the emerging economies, are single-handedly responsible for polluting the environment and causing global warming.

Up until the Global Shift, Third World consumers and indigenous peoples were protective of the environment, emphasized spirituality over materialism, and were not infected by the Western consumer bug and credit card madness. But Western leadership insisted that Third World and indigenous peoples could never become as "civilized" as Westerners unless they copied and embraced unquestioningly the Western addiction to the consumption of ever-increasing quantities of gadgets, junk, and the latest electronics. It's therefore no surprise that the middle and upper classes of the emerging economies follow Western consumers like sheep.

The current Global Shift is not the first time that the West engaged with the Third World. It had previously engaged with the Third World by stealing their lands to create large plantations to produce exotic crops such as bananas, coffee, pineapples, and other tropical fruits while creating employment for local workers. We will explain why this did not generate ever-rising incomes in the Third World comparable to the current Global Shift. A second way in which the West had engaged with less developed economies was the creation of branch plants. Canada is a prime example of a *branch plant* economy created by American firms such as GM. This also increased employment opportunities for the host countries. We need to explain why this also did not generate the ever-increasing incomes currently being generated in the less developed economies by the Global Shift.

Historical Context Leading to the U.S.-Mexico Maquiladoras Program

In this chapter, I will explain the origins of the Global Shift with the birth of the U.S.-Mexico Maquiladoras Program. The United States has had a long and turbulent history of a love-hate relationship with its southern neighbor Mexico. As I have documented in my *American Invasions,* the early goal of the United States was to conquer and dominate the New World and expand westward to the Asia-Pacific region. It was not until Britain and Germany self-destructed their economies during the Second World War that the United States turned its attention from the New World to the entire world. It is important that we summarize U.S.-Mexico relations prior to the Maquiladoras Program to fully understand the context and importance of that program. The Maquiladoras Program has to be seen in the context of the United States consolidating its relationship with its southern neighbor within the global context of the United States pursuing its single-minded goal to become the so-called leader of the free world, which we have labeled in our previous books leader of the "unfree" world, or reincarnation of the old Roman Empire. Never in its wildest dreams would the United States ever have imagined that in creating the Maquiladoras Program, it would have set in motion the economic forces that would *reverse* its own dominance of the world, begun accidentally by the fifteenth-century voyages of Christopher Columbus. As the saying goes, "Easy come, easy go."

Mexico was one of the most important colonies in Columbus's New World, long before the relatively unimportant English settlements in North America. The Spanish conquistador Hernan Cortez conquered Mexico from the Aztec Empire in 1521, almost a century before the settlement of the first English colony of Jamestown, Virginia, in 1607. That first English settlement on the Atlantic coast of North America, which morphed into the United States, was tiny compared to the Spanish conquests in South and Central America. The sixteenth-century Spanish colony of New Spain, in South and Central America, was larger in geographical area and more populous than Spain itself. Mexico was by far the largest and most important part of New Spain. By contrast, the seventeenth-century English settlements, which became the USA, were relatively small areas of land and sparsely populated.

Nevertheless, the thirteen English colonies gained their independence from Britain before Mexico achieved its independence from Spain. The Americans fought for and won their independence from Britain during the War of 1775-1783. The independent USA of 1783 had a total area of 342,000 square miles. It was a newer, much smaller, and less populous country than the Spanish colony of Mexico. American independence, therefore, inspired Mexicans to fight for their independence from Spain. Mexico began its war of independence in 1810 and won its independence from Spain in 1821. The United States moved quickly to recognize Mexico as an independent country and establish diplomatic relations. As in the United States before, it was the local-born whites of the European invaders who wanted independence from their respective mother countries to remove the aristocrats of the mother country and replace them with a home-grown white aristocracy. Both the English and Spanish empires had stolen the lands, which became the independent countries of the USA and Mexico, from the First Nations. They had both used superior military force to steal the territory from their original owners. Now the children of the original thieves wanted to govern these First Nations lands.

While the land area stolen from the First Nations by Spain far exceeded the land area stolen by the British before U.S. independence, the independent USA invaded, conquered, and stole ever-increasing quantities of First Nations lands, eventually becoming larger in geographical size than Mexico. (See my *American Invasions.*) It was 1823, only two years after Mexico had won its independence from Spain, that the United States invoked the infamous Monroe Doctrine. While seemingly pompous at the time, given the puny size of the American empire relative to European empires, the United States did succeed in wresting the New World from the European empires. After 1823, the United States was a far greater military threat to Mexico than any European empire.

Unlike the United States, which prospered and grew in military, political, and economic stature, as well as in geographical size, after its independence from Britain, Mexico declined in military, political, and economic stature, as well as in geographical size. Its northern neighbor the USA, far from being a trusted ally against European empires, was its greatest military threat. While the United States had agreed to its border with Mexico by signing the Adams-Onis Treaty in 1828, the United States would hunger for Mexican territory as it simultaneously hungered for Canadian territory and First Nations territory. The United States had an insatiable appetite for wars, invasions, and conquests. Prior to the Second World War, the American obsession with expansion was focused on the New World and the Pacific. Mexico on its southern border and Canada on its northern border were obvious targets. Canada was protected by the powerful British Empire. The Spanish empire had become far too weak to come to the aid of its ex-colony Mexico.

U.S. invasions and conquests of Mexican territory began in Texas. Once the United States had taken the thirteen English colonies from Britain in 1783, it immediately began to invade and conquer First Nations lands that were on its borders. These included the lands that became the added states of Vermont, Kentucky, Tennessee, Ohio, and Louisiana. The rapidly expanding USA invited whites from Europe to populate these stolen lands and imported black slaves from Africa to provide cheap labor for the white immigrants. But some Americans wanted even more lands than what could be quickly stolen from the

First Nations. Those Americans moved into Mexican territory in Texas, beginning immediately after Mexico had secured its independence from Spain in 1821. This was a clear signal to the newly independent country of Mexico that the United States would be its foremost military threat. The Americans who moved into Mexican territory in Texas had no intention of becoming Mexicans. Their goal was to steal Mexican land, import African slaves to work the land, and exercise political independence from the Mexican state. An important example of not accepting jurisdiction by the Mexican government was their insistence on enslaving Africans even after Mexico had abolished slavery in 1829.

Americans in Texas initially declared Texas an independent state in 1835 but knew that they would need the military protection of the United States to secure that independence from Mexico. Just as the thirteen English colonies had sought the military help of France to defeat England in their War of Independence, so would the Texan Americans seek the military help of the United States to fight Mexico for their independence. France had helped the Americans gain independence with the intention of territorial gains in America, at the expense of Britain, but gained no new territory in America. Not so with Texas, for the USA. The Texan American independence movement led to a war between Mexico and the USA in 1846–48. When Mexico lost that war, Texas became another state in an expanded USA. Never content with its ever-expanding territory, the USA also stole California and New Mexico from Mexico. While the USA became ever larger in geographical size, Mexico shrunk to less than half its original geographical size. Where once Mexico had a far more advanced and populous economy than the original USA of 1783, it had become a relatively puny country compared to the United States by 1850. With the Gadsden Purchase of 1854, another thirty thousand square miles of Mexican land became American land. While owned by Mexico, it was poor desert, but the Americans used it to build a transcontinental railway, which would further boost the economy of the USA relative to that of Mexico. The Gadsden Purchase also enabled the United States to steal Arizona from Mexico and the First Nations.

The turnaround in the US-Mexican relationship began when France renewed its efforts to gain territory in the New World. As I mentioned earlier, France had helped the United States gain its independence from Britain in the hope that the United States would become its long-term ally in fighting the British for territory in the New World. But the United

States reneged on that alliance and allied with the British instead. (See my *Rise and Fall of the American Empire.*)

Under Napoleon III, France saw an opportunity to compete with the United States for the half of Mexico that the United States had not yet conquered and stolen. When the United States was embroiled in its civil war, Napoleon III invaded Mexico and imposed a puppet ruler, Maximilian I. But once the U.S. Civil War ended, the United States was militarily powerful enough to challenge France. Ironically, when the United States had begged France to help it fight the British for its independence, the thirteen English colonies that had rebelled were far inferior in military might compared to the French empire at that time. French military help to the rebels was decisive in their defeat of Britain. By the time of Napoleon III's imposition of Maximilian I in 1864, the French empire had declined in military might, while the American empire had increased significantly in military might. When the United States protested the French invasion of Mexico after the end of its civil war in 1865, Napoleon III withdrew his army from Mexico rather than confront the superior military of the United States.

The Beginning of a New U.S.-Mexican Relationship after the U.S. Civil War

When the United States intervened in Mexico after its civil war, it began a new policy of forming an alliance with Mexico rather than conquering it and stealing territory as had been its policy before its civil war. Where once the United States had been the greatest military threat to Mexican independence, the United States had now intervened to prevent French colonization of Mexico. It was this new post–Civil War U.S.-Mexico relationship that eventually led to the Maquiladoras Program. The Mexican people had opposed Spanish, American, and French colonization. The United States now had its back. But this new U.S.-Mexico relationship was strained under the long rule of Gen. Porfirio Diaz, 1876–1910. The United States disliked the fact that General Diaz was not a democrat but liked the fact that he welcomed American investment in Mexico. The United States also disliked the fact that General Diaz objected strongly to U.S. soldiers crossing into

Mexico to pursue and kill the Apaches who fought the Americans for stealing their land in Arizona. But the United States liked the fact that economic stability in Mexico under General Diaz was good for American businesses. Mexico became a safe bet for American investors. A railway connecting Mexico City to El Paso, Texas, was completed in 1884. This gave birth to the economic boom in the border region where the Maquiladoras Program would begin.

Mexico was thrown into chaos by the Mexican Civil War, 1910–1920. The Civil War was caused by popular discontent with the unequal distribution of the economic gains achieved during the long Diaz presidency. In particular, the majority of Mexicans opposed foreign economic imperialism that favored the United States, Britain, France, and a small group of Mexican elites. The Diaz presidency had created large numbers of poor landless peasants and large numbers of urban poor. His industrialization policy, paid for by foreign investors, had not raised incomes for the mass of workers. At the same time, consolidation of land ownership in the hands of large local and foreign plantation landowners created growing numbers of rural poor. Growing discontent of poor Mexicans coincided with an aging Diaz to create the Mexican Revolution of 1910–40.

Popular revolutions are never pro-imperialist. It was natural to expect the United States to intervene to protect its economic interests in Mexico. American interventions, military invasions, and regime changes had been the norm in Latin America since the Monroe Doctrine. In 1913, U.S. ambassador to Mexico Henry Lane Wilson cooperated with Gen. Victoriano Huerta to overthrow the democratically elected government of Francisco Madero. This time, U.S. intervention was to protect its massive business investments in Mexico. U.S. president William Howard Taft boasted that he was protecting $2 billion of U.S. investment in Mexico. In the post–Civil War period, the United States had changed its policy toward Mexico. As I said above, it had switched from conquering Mexican territory to an alliance with Mexico. But the United States had also used that alliance to pursue economic imperialism in Mexico.

The military coup occurred in February 1913. Democratic governments are elected by the majority of voters. They are never pro-imperialist. This is why all foreign governments overthrown by the United States are *democratic* governments, and all governments imposed by the United States are *dictatorships*. Dictators imposed by the United States often fall foul of new U.S. administrations. This occurred in

Mexico when Pres. Woodrow Wilson took over the U.S. presidency from Pres. Howard Taft in March 1913. President Wilson decided to overthrow the U.S.-imposed dictatorship of General Huerta. He ordered the U.S. navy to bomb and occupy the Mexican port of Veracruz in 1914. In 1916, the United States sent ten thousand soldiers under Gen. John Pershing into Mexico. Its primary goal was to capture Mexico's most famous revolutionary leader, Pancho Villa. After a year in Mexico, U.S. forces had failed to capture or kill Villa. However, what saved Mexico from a full-scale invasion and conquest by the United States was the First World War.

Up until the rise of Germany, Britain had been the dominant empire in the world. After the American War of Independence, the British had forged a strong economic and political alliance with its ex-colonies, which had become the independent USA. The British had implicitly supported the Monroe Doctrine to enable its ally, the growing American empire, to dominate the New World. In the meantime, the British received implicit support from the American empire in its pursuit of world domination outside Latin America. When Germany threatened this British domination during the First World War, the British called on its ally for help against Germany. The clincher for the United States supporting Britain was the Zimmerman Telegram of 1917, intercepted by the British and made known to the United States. In that telegram, Germany offered military aid to Mexico against a U.S. invasion.

Pres. Woodrow Wilson made the decision to switch American forces from invading and conquering Mexico to aiding Britain in its war with Germany. He was persuaded both by the long and incessant pleas by the British and the decision of Germany to use its submarines to disrupt U.S. supplies to Britain and its allies. The American empire had been expanding its economic and military prowess by supplying the countries at war with Germany.

Colonies rebel against imperialism but recognize their need to ally with a powerful empire to win independence from another empire. The Americans had allied with the French empire, and the Mexicans had allied with the American empire against Napoleon III. In 1917, the obvious choice for Mexico against the American empire was the German empire. It had not yet exploited Mexico as much as the Spanish, American, British, and French empires had done.

U.S.-Mexico Relationship after World War I

The Mexican Revolution had produced a new Constitution for Mexico in 1917. The new Constitution provided for land reform to improve the lives of the peasants, improve union rights for organized labor to improve wages and working conditions, and have restrictions on foreign investment in Mexico. While the Civil War continued, Venustiano Carranza became the first president under the new constitution. But he was killed by opposing revolutionaries, and Gen. Alvaro Obregon took over the presidency in 1920. President Obregon formed a strong alliance with popular Mexican artists such as Diego Rivera, Jose Clemente Orozco, and David Alfaro Siqueiros to get mass support for the revolution against U.S. intervention in Mexico.

These artists were commissioned by the Mexican state to paint murals on public buildings depicting pre-imperial Mexican culture and glorifying the heroes of the revolution against imperialism. By being widely displayed on public buildings, it was easy for the masses to see and appreciate. It was a wise move by the fledgling revolutionary government since the United States was an ever-present threat after the end of the First World War. With the Russian revolution, the United States had found a new and widely supported reason for continuing its long history of political, economic, and military interventions in Latin America. That new excuse was "fighting Communism." The artists were willing participants since the state financed their work. It was a win-win for both sides. Mexican muralism became internationally recognized as a respectable art form as a result of this cooperation between artists and the Mexican state.

Mexican presidents who followed Obregon continued his policies, which redistributed land to the peasants, reduced the power of the Catholic Church, increased the power of unions, improved the rights of women, provided public education to the masses, nationalized some industries such as oil and railroads, and generally moved Mexico toward a much more mixed economy than the United States. Naturally, the United States painted Mexico as a pro-Communist state, ever watching for an opportunity to invade and conquer it. But the Great Depression and the Second World War intervened, saving Mexico yet again from American conquest. Mexico's economy prospered after the Great Depression. During the Second World War, the United States saw Mexico more as an ally than a potential colonial conquest. U.S. president Franklin Roosevelt introduced his so-called Good Neighbor policy on March 4, 1943, signaling a new relationship between the United States and Latin America.

America was born out of land stolen by military force from the First Nations. Most of the First Nations were killed off. The remainder were imprisoned in reserves. White Europeans were invited to populate the stolen land. African slaves were forcibly brought to work the stolen land. Despite these evils, the founding fathers of this stolen land were able to use powerful propaganda to convince the West that America was a freedom-loving Republic. But to Latin Americans, it was the "Colossus of the North" to be rightly feared and distrusted. It was this latter image of America that President Roosevelt wanted to change with his Good Neighbor policy. Roosevelt's intent was to signal to its neighbors a new military noninterventionist USA. The United States would now be opposed to *armed* intervention. While this was seen as a positive change, Latin Americans were wise to be skeptical. Military nonintervention did not rule out economic, financial, CIA, or propaganda interventions. As it turned out, the American declaration of war on the Japanese empire forced the United States to be a good neighbor with Latin America. The Second World War, more than Roosevelt's Good Neighbor policy, forced the United States to improve its behavior toward Mexico.

The Bracero Program: 1942–1964

By the outbreak of the Second World War, the U.S. economy had largely recovered from the Great Depression. Slavery had been abolished, and white European immigration had dried up. As the U.S. economy boomed from supplying the European warmongers, it encountered labor shortages. At the time, Mexico had ample supplies of cheap labor. The Bracero Program was a way of benefitting both the USA and Mexico. Mexico would supply the much-needed cheap labor to the United States, and the United States would provide employment for Mexicans. It began on August 4, 1942, when the two countries signed the Mexican Farm Labor Agreement. The U.S. labor shortage was most harmful to its farm sector. The program allowed U.S. farmers to bring Mexican workers temporarily into the United States, and the workers were guaranteed a minimum wage of thirty cents per hour. Under the program, an average of two hundred thousand Mexican workers entered the United States each year. With the outbreak of war between the American and Japanese empires, the U.S. labor shortage problem worsened.

It was the ending of the Bracero Program in 1964 that inspired the creation of the Maquiladoras Program a year later. If Mohamed could not go to the mountain, the mountain would have to come to Mohamed. What was not understood at the time was the revolutionary nature of this shift from six centuries of workers moving from their homelands to man the factories of the industrialized West to the West taking the factories to the homelands of the world's teeming millions of poor. The Bracero Program was ended because American workers complained that competition from the Mexican workers was preventing real wages for Americans from rising. While this was true, the substitution of the Bracero Program with the Maquiladoras Program turned out to be the greatest disaster for American workers. As the Maquiladoras Program was imitated throughout Latin America and then in Asia and Africa, American workers faced competition from the world's abundant supply of cheap labor. Never again would Western workers be insulated from competition from the world's teeming millions.

The Maquiladoras Program

The United States had ended the Bracero Program because the Second World War, which had caused the labor shortage in the United States, could no longer be used by U.S. farmers to justify importation of cheap farm labor from Mexico. But ending the program worsened Mexico's excess supply of labor. As a result, the Mexican government initiated the Maquiladoras Program with the United States to alleviate its concern with high unemployment in the border region with its northern neighbor. Initially, the U.S. factories had to be set up within twenty miles of the U.S. border. Using this long but narrow border area to launch the program made good economic sense. It would be relatively easy for the U.S. manufacturing firms on the American side of the border to move production to the Mexican side of the border. Transportation costs both to transport the inputs from the United States to Mexico, and the finished product from Mexico to the United States would be relatively low.

The fact that the U.S. side of the border had been part of Mexico before the U.S. conquest meant that Mexicans who had chosen to stay in the United States after the conquest had relatives and friends on the Mexican side of the border. Close interactions between those living on either side of the border meant that the Mexican workers hired by the U.S. firms in the maquiladoras would be familiar with the U.S. work habits, customs, language, and required skills. This gave an advantage to Mexican cities such as Tijuana and Ciudad Juarez. On the other side of the coin, U.S. managers, reluctant to live in Mexico, could live close to the Mexican border on the U.S. side. They could manage the factories on the Mexican side relatively easier than if they lived in cities far from the Mexican border. This gave an advantage to U.S. cities such as San Diego, McAllen, and El Paso.

A second important factor that made the program economically viable was its specialization on assembly. Many manufactured goods are produced in three relatively separate stages, design, parts, and assembly. Cars, TVs, electronics, clothing, shoes, and many consumer durables are produced this way. The stage requiring the least skilled labor is assembly. This is why the Maquiladoras Program specialized in assembly where it could use cheap, relatively unskilled Mexican workers. If you think this is denigrating Mexican workers, Canada and the United States agreed to an Auto Pact in 1965, where the United States specialized in parts and Canada specialized in assembly. The Maquiladoras Program allowed duty-free imports of parts and materials from the United States into the Mexican side of the border where the U.S. companies would set up factories using Mexican workers to assemble the finished products. Initially, all the assembled products had to be exported to the United States. U.S. importers would pay customs duties only on the value added by the cheap Mexican labor. This is the *key* difference between old-fashioned *Globalization* and the Global Shift. In the case of old-fashioned *Globalization*, American factories sell exports of manufactured goods to Mexicans. In the Global Shift, American factories located in Mexico sell their output of manufactured goods to *Americans*. This important difference had to be explained to economists by candidate Trump during the U.S. presidential campaign in 2016, since economists have their heads buried in the sand, thinking that the Global Shift is simply an evolution of international trade based on Ricardo's theory of comparative advantage. Instead of admitting their error, economists, like other so-called intellectuals, continue to chomp at the bit to take every opportunity to denigrate President Trump.

One commonality between Mexico and China, where the Maquiladoras Program made its greatest transformation of the world's economy, was that both economies were relatively closed economies prior to the Maquiladoras Program. China was a closed economy to the West, because the United States refused to allow any country in the West to trade with any *Communist* country. Mexico was a closed economy because its government was pursuing a policy of import substitution, which required high tariffs on the import of manufactured goods. It was similar to what Canada had done with its National Policy of 1879 to keep out U.S. imports of manufactured goods. As a result of both Mexico and China disengaging from the world economy, their economies had suffered immensely. This was the trigger for both countries to open up in a very limited and selective way by inviting foreign investment into designated "economic zones." In Mexico, it was the narrow but long borderlands with the United States. In China, it was the areas close to Hong Kong and Taiwan.

The Maquiladoras Program was officially launched in 1965 as the Border Industrialization Program. Six border states in Mexico were involved in the program. These border states were Chihuahua, Sonora, Tamaulipas, Coahuila, Nuevo Leon, and Baja California. The continuous devaluation of the Mexican peso after the Maquiladoras Program further enhanced the economic advantage to American firms of hiring Mexican workers, instead of American workers, to assemble consumer durables, which could be sold at much lower prices than similar products assembled by American workers. As the demand for Mexican workers put upward pressure on Mexican wages, the devaluation of the peso offset the cost in U.S. dollars. What the Maquiladoras Program initiated was intense price competition for expenditures by Western consumers on *manufactured* goods. In the past, this kind of price competition had dominated *primary* products such as bananas, sugar, coffee, and raw materials. Intense price competition in food products such as bananas, coffee, and sugar had impoverished farmworkers in Latin America. Likewise, intense price competition in raw materials had led to the substitution of raw materials such as rubber and natural fibers with synthetics.

By the 1960s, a much larger percentage of the income of Western consumers went to manufactured goods, mostly household appliances and cars, compared with food products. Workers in the West had largely moved out of jobs producing primary products to jobs producing manufactured goods. These factory jobs paid relatively high wages to workers with very basic education. If Western entrepreneurs could outsource these high-wage jobs to low-wage countries like Mexico, that would truly be revolutionary. The Maquiladoras Program showed how this could be done.

Canada's Branch Plant Economy Compared with the Maquiladoras

Our primary goal in this book is to explain how the Global Shift is a truly revolutionary phenomenon that will *reverse* the five-century world domination by the West. This cannot be fully explained in a single chapter. That is why we will constantly digress to make comparisons with the prior five centuries of *Globalization* efforts to emphasize and understand the difference between those five centuries and this current half century. We begin these digressions and comparisons with one of the earliest attempts at *Globalization* by the United States, the creation of a "branch plant" of the United States in "British" Canada.

Canada, like Mexico, borders the United States. While Mexico is on its southern border, Canada is on its northern border. Once the United States had secured its independence from the British Empire, it expanded its size by conquering both First Nations lands and Mexican territory. It attempted to conquer Canadian territory as well but failed because Canada was a colony of the powerful British Empire. We saw how the United States abandoned its old strategy of conquering all of Mexico after the Second World War and switched to economic integration with the Bracero and Maquiladora programs. In the case of Canada, the United States abandoned military invasions much earlier. After its second failed military invasion in 1812–14, it switched to economic integration.

Canada, like Mexico, feared U.S. interventions. Canada attempted to counter U.S. interventions by enhancing its relationship with the British Empire and imposing high tariffs on U.S. imports. But the American empire needed markets for its industrial output just like the older Western European empires. These older Western European empires colonized militarily defenseless parts of the globe both to steal their natural resources and to sell their industrial goods. During the era of mercantilism, the Western European empires not only fought each other for these colonies but also used military force to prevent colonies from trading with countries other than the mother country.

The United States, from its beginning, pursued a different imperial strategy. Unlike Britain, France, and Spain, which separated their colonies from the mother country, the United States integrated all conquests into an ever-expanding behemoth it called the United States instead of the American empire. In the case of Canada, two failed military invasions convinced it to pursue what many have called "economic" rather than "political" colonization of Canada. If it could not conquer Canada by military force, because of Canada's defense by the powerful British Empire, it would seek markets for its industrial output by establishing branch plants of U.S. corporations in Canada. Instead of a U.S. corporation such as GM establishing another factory or plant in the United States to produce cars for sale in Canada, GM would establish the plant in Canada and sell the cars produced by GM Canada to Canadians. This marked the beginning of the U.S. branch plant economy in Canada.

While political writers have called these branch plant economies, which expanded from Canada to other parts of the globe, "economic colonization," there is an important difference between this economic colonization and the old-fashioned political colonization. That important difference is the nonuse of military force. We have emphasized that the key difference between colonization and trade is that colonization uses military force and coercion, while trade is voluntarily agreed to by two trading partners. That is why trade is a non-zero-sum game, while colonization is a zero-sum game. We have also explained that it's often difficult to separate trade from colonization and that often what political writers call trade is mostly colonization.

However, if we are to be consistent, we need to agree that the creation of branch plant economies, by both the American empire and the older Western European empires, has more elements of trade and foreign investment than colonization. It can never be purely trade and foreign investment, because there is often enormous economic, financial, political, and military threats made by the more powerful empire. In other words, the host country is threatened if it does not open its economy to such branch plants. Similar threats were made before by the Western empires to get both China and Japan to open their economies to "trade." In any case, the creation of branch plant economies, beginning with Canada, marked an evolution of traditional *Globalization* but was still very different from what we call the Global Shift.

The key difference, which we will elaborate on throughout this text, is that the foreign direct investments by industrialized nations, like the United States, into developing economies, like Canada, targeted the high-income consumers in the host countries. In this way, it was similar to the Western European empires, starting with Britain, colonizing countries like India to sell them textiles. This is why many political writers see branch plant economies as an extension of old-fashioned political imperialism. Some go as far as to say that a branch plant economy is a colonial economy. We disagree with that extreme view.

The current Global Shift of the last half century also uses foreign direct investment to build factories or manufacturing plants in developing economies, since called emerging economies. But it does not target consumers in the host countries. The industrial output is transported to the home country for sale to Western consumers. That important difference is the key to understanding the difference between the current Global Shift and earlier or traditional *Globalization*. It's also why it will be as revolutionary as the birth of the American empire caused by the accidental rediscovery of the New World by Columbus.

In passing, we need to note that old-fashioned imperialism, creation of branch plant economies, and what we call the Global Shift all involved foreign direct investment. What is different in each case is the goal of the direct investment. In the old-fashioned colonialism, the direct investment built infrastructures to enable the imperial power both to *steal* the resources of the colony and to govern the colony. In the branch plant economies and in the Global Shift, the direct investment built the factories to produce industrial goods. In the branch plant economies, the industrial goods were sold to high-income consumers in the *host* countries. In the Global Shift, the industrial goods were shipped across the U.S.-Mexico border and later by sea in containers, from the emerging economies to the *home* countries, for sale to their consumers.

It's somewhat ironic that the origin of branch plant economies, such as in Canada, has to do with the British desire to move the world from its long history of *mercantilism* to free trade based on the theory of comparative advantage developed by one of its most famous economists, David Ricardo. Under mercantilism, the British North American colonies, which later became Canada, had a special economic relationship with the mother country. This special economic relationship was threatened when Britain abolished the Corn Laws in 1846. This act announced to the world that Britain would lead the charge to abolish the old restrictions on international trade, embedded in mercantilism, in favor of free trade based on Ricardo's theory of comparative advantage.

The British North American colonies, far from embracing the abolition of mercantilism, and the imperial restrictions imposed on them by the mother country under mercantilism, felt abandoned and betrayed by the mother country. Colonies do not like to be conquered and colonized any more than First Nations enjoy being forced off their lands and natural hunting and fishing into reserves. But both create dependence after years, decades, and centuries. Just as some First Nations in Canada wish to continue this long period of enforced dependence, many Canadians wanted to continue the long period of enforced dependence imposed on them, under mercantilism, by the mother country. When it was clear that Britain was bent on embracing free trade principles, Canadians urged Britain to negotiate an alternative semidependent status for them with Britain's ex-colony to the south, the USA. This alternative semidependent economic arrangement for Britain's North American colonies was called the Canadian-American Reciprocity Treaty. It came into effect in 1854, eight years after Britain's abolition of the Corn Laws. It had to be negotiated between Britain and the United States since Canada was not yet an independent country.

The purpose of the Reciprocity Treaty was to replace the ex-protected British market for Canadian exports of primary products with a new protected U.S. market. Colonies like those in British North America had been colonized by military force both to supply the mother country with primary products and provide markets for the industrial exports of the mother country. Britain's embrace of free trade after 1846 left all the British colonies vulnerable. The British North American colonies were among the most favored of British colonies, and the mother country was able to use its clout with its ex-colony to the south to bargain a good deal for Canada. This turned out to be an example of short-term gain for long-term pain. It replaced British political imperialism over Canada with American economic imperialism over Canada. It came at an opportune time for the United States since the United States had abandoned its desire to conquer and add Canada to the United States, after two failed military invasions, in favor of economic integration. The Reciprocity Treaty removed the 21 percent import duty previously imposed on imports of primary products from Canada into the United States.

The Reciprocity Treaty, negotiated by Britain because of pressure from Canadians, signaled the gradual weaning of Canada from Britain but simultaneously making Canada increasingly dependent on the rising American empire. It was in many ways replacing British imperialism with American imperialism. The Reciprocity Treaty was the precursor to the branch plant economy and later economic integration policies such as the Auto Pact and the FTA. Canadians would learn and accept that it was impossible to have this close economic integration with the American empire and maintain its political independence.

After Canada became a unified independent country in 1867, it wanted to shed its historical image as "hewers of wood and drawers of water," which had been its historical role, both as a colony of the British Empire and later as an economic colony of the American empire. Canada wanted to imitate the industrial revolution of both its ex-colonial master, Britain, and its neighbor to the south, the American empire. The American empire had already abrogated the Reciprocity Treaty in 1866, a year before Confederation, and this made it easier for the newly independent and unified Canada to switch from its dependence on the U.S. market for its exports of primary products and grow its industrial sector. Historically, all economies have transitioned from developing to developed status by shrinking the percentage of its total economy represented by primary products while simultaneously expanding the percentage represented by manufactured goods.

The policy that Canada used to grow its industrial sector has been called the National Policy. It was implemented by Canada's first prime minister, Sir John A. Macdonald. It was a policy that imposed high tariffs on imports of U.S. manufactured goods and low tariffs on imports of raw materials. This was intended to give Canadian manufacturers the competitive edge they needed to out sell the Americans. The policy began in 1879 and continued through the Great Depression of the 1930s. Canada was not unique in protecting its economy from more advanced industrial economies. David Ricardo's theory of free trade, based on the sound economic principle of comparative advantage, while promoted by the British Empire as superior to the old theory of trade based on Mercantilism, was never fully embraced by other countries, including Canada and the United States.

Unfortunately, for Canada, high tariffs on U.S. manufactured goods, rather than enable the rise of Canadian manufacturing corporations, mostly served to create a *branch plant economy* in Canada, for American manufacturing corporations. The Scots had previously complained about England creating a branch plant economy in Scotland for English manufacturing corporations. Now the term was correctly being applied to Canada with regard to U.S. corporations. U.S. foreign direct investment was building factories in Canada, called branch plants, to produce the same manufactured goods kept out of Canada by the high tariffs under the National Policy. The National Policy had succeeded in expanding Canada's industrial sector relative to its primary sector. In doing so, it had created relatively high-wage industrial jobs for Canada's growing population fed by increased white immigrants from Europe. At the time, Canada had a very racist whites-only immigration policy. The only unintended consequence of the National Policy was the ownership of the factories by American corporations. It was a price Canada was willing to pay both because of the jobs it created in the expanding industrial sector and the tax revenues it provided. At the time, Canada, like most countries, did not have an income tax. Its major source of tax revenues was the duties on imports of manufactured goods.

Auto Pact, FTA, and NAFTA

Economic integration between Canada and the American empire, begun by the Reciprocity Treaty and continued under the *branch plant economy,* was further enhanced by the Auto Pact of 1965 and the FTA of 1988. In like manner, U.S.-Mexico economic integration, begun by the Bracero Program and continued under the Maquiladoras Program, was further enhanced by the creation of NAFTA in 1994. By the time NAFTA was created, what had been two distinct bilateral relationships, U.S.-Mexico and U.S.-Canada, morphed into a single trilateral economic integration of the three North American economies. While this was an important change in the nature of the economic, political, and military integration among the "three amigos," what was more significant, for our purposes, was how the Auto Pact, the FTA, and NAFTA were merging old-fashioned *Globalization* with the new Global Shift. Just as the earlier merging of the evils of imperialism with the benefits of free trade made it easier for Western imperial powers to hide their imperial invasions under the guise of free trade, it will be more difficult for us to disentangle old-fashioned *Globalization* from the modern Global Shift. But in both cases, it is essential that we separate them if we are to understand the consequences. In the past, our failure to separate the evils of Western imperialism from the benefits of free trade gave the West a free ride to use its powerful propaganda machine to portray its warmongering, military invasions, military conquests, and theft of lands and resources as carrying the "white man's burden." In like manner, if we do not separate that old form of *Globalization* from the Global Shift, we will miss the revolutionary nature of the Global Shift in reversing the five centuries of Western dominance.

Let's begin with the Auto Pact since it predated the FTA and NAFTA. First, an important lesson in economic theory that will help us to understand the importance of the Auto Pact to Canada. Consumers foolishly believe that low prices result primarily from competition. While competition can, in some cases, lower prices, the key to low prices is low production cost. Where large firms can achieve much lower production cost by taking advantage of massive economies of scale, a single large firm, a monopoly, or a few large firms, oligopolies, will always trump competition by many small firms in providing the lowest price to consumers. Studies have shown that the cost of producing cars by small firms would be about five times as high as the cost of producing the same cars by large firms.

During the *branch plant* phase of the Canadian economy, Canadians had become accustomed to having the choice of many different types of cars produced by the American branch plants of the three U.S. car manufacturers, GM, Ford, and Chrysler. When Canada decided to get into the business of manufacturing cars, Canada was at a serious cost disadvantage compared to the United States, because the Canadian market was less than 10 percent of the U.S. market. If Canadian car manufacturers were to give Canadian consumers the same variety of cars the U.S. branch plants had given them, the Canadian plants would be much smaller. Since their cost would be much higher, they would be at a competitive disadvantage and not be able to compete with U.S. imports even if the government imposed high tariffs. The only viable solution was to create a single U.S.-Canada car market, which the Auto Pact did. This lowered production cost by further increasing economies of scale, increasing the length of the production runs, and having the United States specialize in parts while Canada specialized in assembly.

The Canada-U.S. Auto Pact of 1965 served to enhance opportunities for both the U.S. car manufacturers in the United States and their branch plants in Canada. Gains were greater in the Canadian branch plants since their size could be increased by much more. While the U.S. plants now had access to a market 10 percent greater, the Canadian plants had access to a market ten or eleven times as large. Up until the Auto Pact, the U.S. branch plants in Canada were very inefficient compared with plants in the United States, primarily because of their much smaller size. But the high tariffs prevented imports of cheaper cars produced by plants in the United States. However, most of the parts used by the Canadian branch plants were produced in the United States. While this helped to moderate the price difference in favor of Canadian consumers, it caused a huge trade deficit for Canada. The Auto Pact significantly increased the value of output of the Canadian auto industry, making it larger than Canada's pulp and paper industry. Canadian exports of cars to the United States increased from 7 percent of total output in 1964 to 60 percent in 1968. Imports of U.S. cars increased from 3 percent of total sales to 40 percent in the same period.

The enhanced efficiency of the U.S.-Canada car industry created by the 1965 Auto Pact enabled it to better face the challenge from the Japanese car makers following the quadrupling of the price of oil in 1973. However, the Auto Pact increased the economic dependency of Canada on the United States, which had begun with the Reciprocity Treaty and the National Policy. While the expansion of Canada's auto sector created many well-paid jobs, they were blue-collar jobs. Administration was reserved for Americans. Sir John A. McDonald's National Policy had intended to promote a Canadian manufacturing sector that was independent of the United States. It had done exactly the opposite, and the Auto Pact signaled the death of any future Canadian manufacturing industry that was totally independent of the United States. It paved the way toward greater rather than lesser economic integration, which culminated in the FTA of 1988. With increased economic dependence on U.S. manufacturing giants came increasing political subservience to the United States and pressured support for U.S. foreign policy. That foreign policy was one of continuous warmongering, military invasions, regime changes, replacement of democracies by U.S.-imposed and supported dictators, and subjecting "international" institutions, such as the UN, the IMF, the WTO, the World Bank, global financial markets, and reserve currencies, to U.S. control.

While a minority of Canadians complain about loss of sovereignty, the majority of Canadians view the higher income produced by the economic integration with the highly developed and technologically advanced U.S. economy an acceptable trade-off. This majority voted in favor of greater economic integration by supporting free trade in most products rather than only in cars and car parts. This was the reason for the FTA of 1988. The intent of the FTA was to phase out barriers to trade between the United States and Canada and reduce barriers to direct foreign investment.

U.S.-Canada Free Trade Agreement of 1988

Before we proceed to discuss the FTA, it's important that we explain the difference between free trade and free capital flows. The reason is that what are called free trade agreements or free trade areas almost always deal with both trade and investments. But in economics, trade is a separate economic theory dealing with trade flows based on the theory of comparative advantage, distinct from foreign investments. Foreign investments are analyzed under capital flows and separated into short-term capital flows and long-term capital flows. Short-term capital flows are affected mostly by interest rate differentials. Long-term capital flows must be analyzed separately for direct investment and portfolio investment. While portfolio investments depend largely on differentials in long-term interest rates, direct investments are affected by many factors such as profit differentials, real estate opportunities, political stability, currency stability, and a whole host of other risks and other considerations.

It's therefore important to understand that FTAs, such as the U.S.-Canada FTA of 1988, deal with both trade and capital flows. As such, they integrate economies not only by increasing trade flows but also by increasing opportunities for short-term capital flows, portfolio investments in private and government bonds, and direct investments in manufacturing, infrastructure, and real estate. Nationalists often oppose FTAs not so much because of trade liberalization but because of the influx of foreign ownership, which comes with the influx of foreign direct investment.

FTAs are never supported by the majority of workers. These workers have not been convinced by David Ricardo's proof that free trade never creates unemployment. Ricardo's theory of comparative advantage proves that lower-paying jobs lost because of an FTA are fully replaced by higher-paying jobs, for the economy as a whole. Of course, some workers can gain at the expense of some workers who lose, mostly because of retraining or labor mobility issues. The majority of Canadian workers opposed the U.S.-Canada FTA because they feared the loss of manufacturing jobs to the United States. U.S. productivity in manufacturing was significantly higher than productivity in Canada's manufacturing sector. Since money wages in Canada's manufacturing sector was not lower than money wages in the U.S. manufacturing sector, the United States had a wage cost advantage. This scared Canadian workers, despite Ricardo's theory that free trade is based on comparative rather than absolute advantage.

In addition to opposition from Canadian workers, because of fear of unemployment, Canadian Nationalists also opposed the U.S.-Canada FTA, both because of the reduction in Canadian sovereignty caused by further economic integration with the American empire and the increased influx of U.S. direct investment, which had begun under Sir John's National Policy and made Canada a *branch plant* economy of the American empire. We have also explained that the Auto Pact enhanced the domination of Canada's car manufacturing by the three U.S. auto giants, GM, Ford, and Chrysler. While Canadian Nationalism predated the 1988 U.S.-Canada FTA, many die-hard Nationalists came out in force to oppose this agreement. The Conservative government, led by Brian Mulroney, made the proposed FTA with the United States an important issue in the 1988 election. The Nationalists backed the Liberal party in opposing the FTA. They argued that this agreement would effectively make Canada the fifty-first State of the Union. The loss of the election was a severe blow to Canada's Nationalists. Despite the fact that the majority of Canadians voted against the FTA, under Canada's plurality system, the voters who opposed the FTA split their votes with the Liberal and NDP parties, enabling a plurality for the Conservative party with only 43 percent of the votes.

The intent of the U.S.-Canada FTA was to gradually eliminate barriers to trade in both goods and services between Canada and the United States. As a result of the FTA, and the later NAFTA, Canada's exports increased steadily, eventually doubling as a percentage of Canada's GDP. In addition, the FTA was designed to reduce barriers to capital flows between the two countries. This was expected to increase the already significant U.S. foreign direct investments, FDI, in Canada, and expand the U.S. *branch plant* economy in Canada. U.S. corporations in Canada would have to serve two masters, the laws of the United States and the laws of Canada. While Canadian workers opposed the reduction in trade barriers because of the productivity argument we explained above, they embraced the enhanced FDI part of the agreement, since that would increase employment of Canadian workers by large U.S. corporations. These U.S. corporations would very likely afford higher wages and benefits than small Canadian corporations. In general, Canadian workers care far less about loss of sovereignty than Canadian Nationalists.

NAFTA: The American Empire Replaces Political Union with Economic Union

As we have documented at great length in our *American Invasions,* the United States had invaded both Canada and Mexico with the intention of adding those lands to its ever-expanding Union. Two military invasions of Canada had failed because of Canada's defense by the then powerful British Empire. But military invasions of Mexico had succeeded in adding half of Mexican territory to the Union. The First World War led the United States to belatedly support the allies against Germany when the British leaked a telegram implying Germany's support of Mexico against American imperialism in Mexico. This saved Mexico from further American conquests. As we have explained above, the United States changed its policy of military invasions and conquests of Mexican territory to economic integration, as it had done earlier in Canada. This economic integration with Mexico began with the Bracero Program and continued with the Maquiladoras Program. These programs were separate and independent of the programs used to integrate with Canada. The integration programs with Canada were the Reciprocity Treaty, the creation of *branch plants,* the Auto Pact, and the FTA. NAFTA was the first attempt to unify the Canadian and Mexican economic integration programs.

There is no question that Canada's economy benefitted immensely from its economic colonization by the United States. Mexico's economy also benefitted from the Bracero and Maquiladoras Programs, but not to the same extent as Canada, since the economic colonization of the half of Mexico not conquered by the United States had been far less. In many ways, NAFTA would address that deficiency and move toward an equalization of the economic colonization of both Canada and Mexico by the American empire. While Canadian workers had opposed the US-Canada FTA because of the fear that the higher labor productivity of the United States would give the United States a labor cost advantage, American workers opposed NAFTA because of the fear that the much lower wages paid to Mexican workers would give Mexico a labor cost advantage.

What many Americans did not know was that both the Maquiladoras Program and NAFTA were put into place by American leaders more as a substitute for the military conquest of Mexico than for economic benefits to American workers. As we have said above, the United States had abandoned its determination to conquer all of Mexico after its involvement in the First World War. But it still wanted to control Mexico through economic colonization as it had done with Canada. This economic colonization of Canada and Mexico, by the United States, is no different from the economic colonization of East Germany by West Germany. The unification of East and West Germany, after the fall of the Berlin Wall, was not motivated by any economic benefit to West Germany. It was clear that West Germany would subsidize the economic development of East Germany. The unification was motivated by political leaders wanting a larger unified Germany to increase its "imperial" power and clout in the world. It's the same reason that a unified Germany, today, subsidizes the EU. Candidate Trump was correct in claiming that NAFTA was detrimental to American workers in the U.S. manufacturing sector. Candidate Trump was also correct in claiming that the U.S. post–World War II economic colonizations of Japan, Germany, Saudi Arabia, and South Korea were costly to the United States because of the very expensive military defense of these economic colonies by the United States. This is a key reason for the rise of Trump, Brexit, and Far Right political parties in many countries of the EU. These groups see these economic colonizations as a new but costly form of Western imperialism where the military cost far outweighs what can be stolen. Prior military colonizations stole far more than the military costs. As candidate Trump proclaimed, if we invaded Iraq to steal the oil, why didn't we steal it?

The evidence is clear that NAFTA benefited the Mexican economy by adding to the economic gains from the Maquiladoras Program. There was a significant increase in per capita GDP in Mexico, as well as an increase in the percentage of Mexicans earning middle-class incomes, after NAFTA. Unlike political colonization, which is a zero-sum game, economic colonization provides economic benefits to the colony in return for the surrender of some of its political sovereignty to the colonizer, which in this case was the American empire. NAFTA replaced the U.S.-Canada FTA, beginning in January 1994. Like the FTA, it dealt with both trade liberalization and the relaxation of foreign investment restrictions. While free trade does integrate economies, it's foreign direct investment that enhances economic and political influence and control of the "economic colony" by the empire. U.S. foreign direct investment had long "colonized" most of Latin America after the Monroe Doctrine of 1823. That economic colonization was enhanced under NAFTA, not so much because of trade liberalization but more because of increased U.S. foreign investment. This is why the term "free trade area" is misleading. Under NAFTA, U.S. foreign direct investment, FDI, was no longer restricted to the narrow border region where the Maquiladoras Program was implemented. It could, and did, penetrate all of Mexico. As a result of NAFTA, the United States accounts for almost half of the total FDI in Mexico.

While the increased U.S. foreign direct investment in Mexico enhanced the U.S. economic colonization of Mexico, it contributed to what we call the Global Shift from the developed economies to the emerging economies. The United States lost high-paying manufacturing jobs to Mexico, estimated to be over seven hundred thousand. Most of the American FDI in Mexico is in manufacturing. Since the American workers who lost their jobs in the U.S. manufacturing sector were not highly educated, it was difficult for them to find alternative jobs that paid as much as the lost manufacturing jobs. Their wages fell. NAFTA made the United States the largest trading partner for Mexico. Cheaper Mexican imports into the United States benefitted consumers as a group, but that gain was distributed over a much larger number and could therefore not compensate fully for the lower wages received by the seven hundred thousand displaced manufacturing workers.

But the Mexican Maquiladoras Program and NAFTA were only the beginning of the massive job losses in manufacturing in the West, which the Global Shift has created, and will continue to worsen, which gave birth to the *Trump phenomenon* in the 2016 U.S. federal election. Our primary reason for digressing to both NAFTA and the many U.S.-Canada economic integration programs is to provide the difference between pre–Global Shift FDI and post–Global Shift FDI. In general, pre–Global Shift FDI had an important inherent limit. That limit was limited numbers of high-income consumers in the *host* country. The pre–Global Shift FDI targeted high-income consumers in the *host* countries such as Canada. The post–Global Shift FDI has no such constraint, since the goods manufactured by the branch plants of the Western corporations would be sold to Western consumers in the *home* countries. Donald Trump was correct in pointing out to the American voters that the U.S. corporations were not simply moving their plants to Mexico but shipping back the manufactured goods across the "open" border to be sold to American consumers. American consumers loved the lower prices, but American workers who lost their high-paying manufacturing jobs were mad as hell.

The Global Shift, which began with the Mexican Maquiladoras Program and enhanced by NAFTA's easing of restrictions on U.S. foreign direct investment in Mexico, did not stop in Mexico. It penetrated all of Latin America and the Caribbean, creating new emerging economies in Brazil, Argentina, and elsewhere. However, we will address those emerging economies in a later chapter. To pursue a minimal chronological order of the Global Shift, we need to move from Mexico, where it began, to China and India, where it changed from a minor New World phenomenon to what we consider the greatest economic revolution since the accidental rediscovery of the New World by Columbus. Just as the voyages of Columbus created the American empire, which enabled the West to continue to dominate the world, after the birth of the Western European empires, the Global Shift to China and India, after Mexico, will, by 2030, rearrange the global world order against the West and in favor of the emerging economies.

We will begin with China since China became the first of the emerging economies created by the Global Shift, after Mexico. As it turned out, China is also the largest of the emerging economies created by the Global Shift. By comparison, Mexico is the sixth largest of the emerging economies, behind China, India, Brazil, Russia, and Indonesia. In fact, not only is China the largest of the emerging economies, but also it has even overtaken in size the large non-emerging economies of Japan, Germany, France, Italy, and the United Kingdom. It is second only to the largest of the non-emerging economies, the USA.

CHAPTER 4

China: The Awakening of the Real Sleeping Giant: 1965–2018 (Part 1: Southern China Maquiladoras)

We begin in 1965 because that was when the U.S.-Mexican Maquiladoras Program began. In that year, China had the fifth-ranking economy, as measured by GDP. But that GDP was less than 10 percent of the GDP of the United States, as measured by U.S. dollars and existing exchange rates at the time. China had long dominated the world before the rise of the West. But like the Ottoman Empire, China failed to understand the shift from conquests based on superior armies to superior naval power. This enabled the maritime powers bordering the Atlantic, Portugal, Spain, France, and England to dominate both China and the Ottoman Empire. While the demise of the Ottoman Empire was aided by the rise of Russia, the demise of China was aided by the rise of Japan. But that Western invasion and control of China, which we have documented at length in our previous books, ended with China's embrace of Communism under Mao Zedong. While Mao ensured the political sovereignty of China, it was China's post-Mao leaders who ensured the economic sovereignty of China. They did that by embracing the Global Shift, which had originated in Mexico with the Maquiladoras Program. As in so many of the calamities inflicted on Western Europe, after their leaders prostituted themselves to American hegemony, the creation of the Maquiladoras Program in Mexico by the United States, followed by President Nixon's rapprochement with China to isolate the Soviet Union, is the single reason for the loss of high-paying manufacturing jobs in both the United States and Western Europe.

While superior naval power had enabled relatively tiny Western European states to colonize vast areas of the globe, it was the industrial revolution that had enabled those states to grow into massive empires. In like manner, it was the combination of superior air power with its own industrial revolution that had enabled the American empire to wrest hegemony from the Western European empires and to ally with them to continue the domination of the world by the West. It is for that reason that the largely accidental shift of the manufacturing base of the Western economies to the emerging economies will bring about the end of Western domination.

One important difference between this current shift from West to East, compared with the prior shift from East to West, is the absence of military conquests and colonizations. When Portugal, Spain, France, and England initially engaged with the East, it was an engagement forced on Asia and Africa by the superior military force of invaders and conquerors. Likewise, the United States, Canada, and Mexico used military force to steal the lands and resources of the First Nations. This current Global Shift is mutually agreed to by both sides. Both sides see the economic benefits to each and are willing to integrate their economies to chase the never-ending dream of economic growth. But so far, the rate of economic growth by the emerging economies has outpaced the rate of economic growth in the West. If this trend continues, it is inevitable that the emerging economies will become larger than the Western economies, despite their huge initial advantage. This was never envisaged by the West when it began to engage with China. The high growth rates achieved in China had never been achieved before by such a large economy. Previously, they had only been achieved by relatively small economies such as Singapore, Taiwan, and Hong Kong. As we said earlier, the United States began its rapprochement with China for political reasons. Never, in its wildest dreams, could it have ever imagined that dirt poor China would rapidly grow to challenge it for economic hegemony. Let's begin with some background to that historic visit to China by President Nixon in 1972.

U.S.-China Relations before 1972

The United States, like Britain and France, began its modern relation with China by using superior military force to bully China into economic and political engagement. Some of this we have documented in our previous books. We will review briefly here this stormy and often one-sided U.S.-China engagement prior to the historic Nixon visit. The United States began to engage with China in 1784 when its first ship, *Empress of China,* arrived in the single open Chinese port of Canton. That was only a year after the United States had successfully fought the

British Empire to secure its independence in 1783. As the French had complained, England had "bought peace" with its American colonies and began a lasting military and economic alliance with the newly independent USA. Since America's new ally, Britain, was on a quest to add China to its worldwide empire, the Americans wanted its piece of China, alongside the great powers of the world. The American empire began to flex its military muscle against China in 1835 when it stationed warships of its navy in Mirs Bay off the southern coast of China.

The British had found a new weapon to colonize China. Having already colonized India, England began to produce opium on some of the lands stolen from India. The British Empire smuggled the opium into China to enrich its empire by addicting the Chinese people. The new American empire was only too happy to join with its ally, the British Empire, to participate in the very "civilized" drug trade with China. Ever since the Portuguese had found a sea route to Asia, the Western European empires of Portugal, Spain, France, and Britain were colonizing every country in Asia. The American alliance with Britain gave the new American empire easy access to this growing list of empires colonizing China. After the British had forced the Chinese to sign the Unequal Treaty of Nanking in 1842, the American empire forced the Chinese to sign the Unequal Treaty of Wanghia in 1844. This provided Americans the same right of extraterritoriality in China, which the British had secured with its treaty of Nanking. The American empire became an equal player with Britain and France in leading the Western colonization of all of China.

The American empire joined the British and French to defeat China in the Second Opium War of 1856. This military defeat of China emboldened the American empire to force China to sign an even more unequal treaty in 1858, the Treaty of Tianjin. This treaty forced China to legalize imports of the deadly drug opium into China. This marked the beginning of the American empire becoming the *world's largest drug lord*. In addition to the wholesale theft of First Nations lands and enslavement of Africans, the American empire had added *drug lord* to its claims to be the most "civilizing" nation on the planet. It was an indication that American propaganda and hypocrisy has no historical parallel. The Treaty of Tianjin forced China to open twenty-three ports to American trade and to allow Christian missionaries into China. The Christian Church has been at the forefront of Western colonization since the leading Christian monarchs of the day, Queen Isabella and King

Ferdinand, financed the first voyage of Columbus in 1492. Converting Chinese citizens to Christianity was a sure fire way of getting Chinese to help the Americans colonize China.

China was fully aware that the West was far more committed to colonization than trade. But China had been blindsided by the shift of military superiority from armies to navies. The American empire had wisely recognized the growing importance of naval superiority much earlier than China. The size and power of the U.S. Navy expanded rapidly after Teddy Roosevelt became assistant secretary of the navy in 1897. The opening of China's ports was forced on China by what came to be known as "gun boat diplomacy." Once the West had forcibly opened China's ports, allowed foreign diplomats and their armies, as well as Christian missionaries, into China, China was literally doomed. It was simply a matter of time before China would become a colony of the West, similar to India, Indochina, Malaysia, and other parts of Asia.

After the forced opening of ports, the next military battle came in 1899 with the Boxer rebellion. By 1899, the American empire had built a navy strong enough to conquer Cuba and the Philippines from the Spanish empire. In addition, the American empire had colonized Hawaii in 1893 and acquired a strategic military base in Pearl Harbor. With naval bases in Hawaii and the Philippines, the American empire could quickly move its military forces to defeat armed Chinese resistance to Western colonization. Despite the millions of Chinese citizens who participated in the Boxer rebellion, the rebellion was crushed by the superior arms of the West. This military defeat emboldened the American and other Western empires to compete for the total colonization of China. The American empire called this colonization effort the "Open Door Policy." American propaganda is the best at finding misleading names for American military aggression.

American Japanese Competition for Asia and the Pacific

American determination to colonize China was disrupted by the rise of the Japanese empire. Japan, like China, was threatened by Western colonization. The American empire began its efforts to colonize Japan in 1791, just seven years after it had begun its efforts to colonize China. Like China, Japan was threatened by all the Western European empires in addition to the American empire. But Japan responded to the Western threat very differently than China, India, Malaysia, and other Asian countries. Japan decided to build a strong military not only to prevent Western colonization but also to compete with the West for colonies in Asia and the Pacific.

After the relative decline of the Portuguese, Spanish, and Dutch empires, the American empire was primarily in competition with the British and French empires for continued Western colonization of Asia and the Pacific. With the large number of colonies already acquired by the British and French empires, the American empire became the prime Western empire competing with the Japanese empire for Asia and the Pacific. When the Japanese empire invaded Manchuria in 1931, the American empire found the opportune excuse to further its colonization of China. It's important to understand that every American military invasion has been falsely portrayed by the American empire as intervention to save the country from continued colonization. In the case of Cuba and the Philippines, the American military had supposedly intervened to remove Spanish colonization. In the case of China, the American military intervention was portrayed as saving China from Japanese colonization.

Japanese attempts to colonize China ushered in a period of military cooperation between China and the United States. Once the Japanese threat had been destroyed by the Second World War, China was once again threatened by American colonization. The American empire had found a useful puppet Chinese leader in Chiang Kai-shek. But the Chinese people had also found a powerful Nationalist leader in Mao Zedong. Prior to the Second World War, the American empire had focused its imperial ambitions exclusively on the New World, Asia, and the Pacific. But the Second World War had unintentionally made the American empire the prime leader of the entire West. Western Europe was now the key concern of the American empire. This was fortunate for China as it meant fewer American resources to support Chiang Kai-shek. As a result, the nationalists won the Civil War in China, and America's puppet was forced to flee to Taiwan, then called Formosa, in 1949.

With its hands full trying to rebuild the war-torn economies of Western Europe as well as colonizing Japan, the American empire was forced to delay its colonization of China. But it continued to collude with

Chiang Kai-shek and promote the ridiculous notion that the government of Taiwan was the only legal government of China. Taiwan was referred to as the Republic of China and given China's seat at the UN Security Council by the American empire. Since the Nationalist government in China was a *Communist* government, the American empire found a new excuse for continuing its efforts to colonize China. That new excuse was "fighting Communism."

American Efforts to Colonize Korea and Vietnam Worsens Sino-U.S. Relations

As we saw above, the American empire pivoted from military colonization of Canada to economic colonization after two failed military invasions. In like manner, after invading and conquering half of Mexico, the American empire pivoted from further military invasion of Mexico to economic colonization following the end of the First World War. But the biggest catch from this pivot from military to economic colonizations was Japan. Prior to the Second World War, the American empire had made several attempts to colonize Japan by using military force. After Japan's defeat in the Second World War, the American empire pivoted to the economic colonization of Japan. As we have also explained earlier, those colonized prefer economic over military colonization, since the economic colonization brings significant economic benefits to the colony. It's an exchange of economic growth for the surrender of political sovereignty. Canada was the first country willing to surrender its political sovereignty to the American empire in exchange for economic growth.

Prior to the Second World War, the American empire used the Canadian model primarily in other parts of the New World, beginning with Mexico. After the Second World War, the Canadian model was pursued aggressively in Asia. While Japan was the biggest catch, other important Asian countries that succumbed to economic colonization by the American empire included the Philippines, Taiwan, South Korea, and South Vietnam. With the American empire taking on the leadership of the West from the older Western European empires of Britain, France, Italy, Germany, Holland, Spain, and Portugal, after the Second World War, economic colonizations in Asia became a much more practical alternative to military colonizations. The Soviet Union had become the prime competitor of the American empire for world domination. By using the propaganda that private property was morally superior to communal property, these economic colonizations provided the American empire with increasing numbers of allies forced to support the American empire against its rival, the Soviet Union.

However, not every Asian country was as willing as Canada or Japan to surrender political sovereignty for economic growth. Two countries that resisted, in addition to China, were North Korea and North Vietnam, both allies of China. Having failed to invade and colonize China, the American empire used the excuse of *fighting Communism* to invade and colonize China's allies. While holding its economic colonies of Taiwan, Japan, South Korea, South Vietnam, and the Philippines, it wanted to add North Korea and North Vietnam, in an effort to isolate China, and eventually add China, to its growing empire. But America's military invasions of both North Korea and North Vietnam failed, as it had failed twice in Canada. Failures in Canada were largely due to the defense of Canada by the British Empire. Failures in North Korea and North Vietnam were due to military support for both North Korea and North Vietnam, by China and the Soviet Union.

When the American empire invaded North Korea in 1950, Sino-U.S. relations were already at an all-time low. The American empire had refused to acknowledge the legitimate government of China, insisting instead that the tiny island of Taiwan was China. When China decided to provide military support to North Korea against the American invasion, Sino-U.S. relations worsened. But China's military aid to the North Koreans led to the military defeat of the American empire in North Korea. North Korea continued to be an independent country and a prime example of how vicious the American empire would be if a country would choose political independence over economic colonization by the American empire.

While the American empire had forced Japan into submission to its will by nuking Hiroshima and Nagasaki, it could not nuke either North Korea or China. The reason was that in 1950, the Soviet Union had acquired nuclear weapons, and both China and North Korea were allies of the Soviet Union. The evidence that the only reason that the American empire did not nuke China during the Korean War, because of Russia's nuclear arsenal, is so overwhelming, that every country that is not an economic colony of the American empire recognizes that the only guarantee against American military invasion is the nuclear deterrent. That is why North Korea will never surrender its nuclear program no matter how much the American empire impoverishes its people. The most recent example is Libya. Libya had been pursuing nuclear weapons and was being impoverished by the American empire. Libya foolishly believed that if it gave up its nuclear program, the American empire would ease economic sanctions, without requiring Libya to surrender its political sovereignty and become an economic colony of the American empire. Instead, the American empire invaded and destroyed Libya.

The failed American invasion of North Korea only served to reinforce the resolve of the American empire to tighten its leash on its many economic colonies in Asia and to prevent them from ever acquiring nuclear weapons. Candidate Donald J. Trump, unfortunately, does not understand the reason behind the huge military subsidies to America's many economic colonies in Asia and to Germany and Saudi Arabia. As a business person, those subsidies make no logical sense. But to those who have long understood the need to prevent the economic colonies of the American empire from ever acquiring nuclear weapons, they fully understand the naivety of the business person turned politician. The only sure way to prevent America's economic colonies from pursuing political independence is to control their military defense. By paying for some of the military defense of Germany, Saudi Arabia, Japan, South Korea, Taiwan, and the Philippines, the American empire keeps the colonies in line. While the economic colonies opted for economic growth over political sovereignty, many in the colonies still yearned for freedom from American colonization. Many would be willing to accept economic impoverishment by the United States in exchange for political sovereignty. One prime example of domestic rebellions against American economic colonization is Bin Laden's revolt against his own Saudi royal family to fight for the political independence of Saudi Arabia.

There are increasing domestic protests against American economic colonizations in many of the colonies. The most extreme example of this today is the Philippines, under Pres. Rodrigo Duterte. Duterte became the president of the Philippines in 2016. He has used the threat of an alliance with China to coerce more political independence from the American empire. There have been rumblings for greater political independence in Japan, South Korea, and Taiwan. The only sure guarantee that the American empire has to prevent economic colonies from demanding political sovereignty is controlling their defense budgets and preventing them from acquiring nuclear weapons. That means that U.S. taxpayers must subsidize the defense of the economic colonies. But as the Philippines has indicated, the American empire now faces a new threat from its *Asian* economic colonies. That new threat is an economic and military alliance with China, which has the geographical advantage over the American empire. Such an alliance undermines both the American threat of economic impoverishment and the American threat of military invasion. That is why the failure of the American empire to colonize China, either militarily or economically, will gradually roll back its empire in Asia.

The other American invasion that worsened Sino-U.S. relations was its invasion of Vietnam. Initially, the American empire provided military support for the post–World War II French recolonization of Vietnam. When the French empire failed to recolonize Vietnam and abandoned their efforts in 1954, the American empire decided to invade. As in the case of North Korea, China provided military support to its ally Vietnam. The American invasion of Vietnam proved no easier a task for the American empire than the French empire. The French had fought the Vietnamese people for almost a decade, 1946–54, and failed. The American attempt to colonize Vietnam lasted until 1972 and also failed. With China supporting Vietnam during the American invasion, there could be no hope of the American empire softening its economic punishment of China. But once the American empire had accepted its failure to colonize Vietnam and withdrew its forces from Vietnam, it could begin to reach out to China. That is why President Nixon could not visit China before 1972. President Nixon withdrew the last of the U.S. forces in Vietnam in August 1972.

The Sino-Soviet Split and the Sino-U.S. Reset

The military defeat of the American empire by Vietnam was a severe blow to the American empire in its Cold War against the Soviet Union. It created deep fears regarding the ultimate outcome of that war. During the 1950s and 1960s, Russia had achieved higher rates of economic growth than the United States. But the United States had turned that around during the Vietnam War. That had given the American empire the economic edge in the Cold War. But its military defeat in Vietnam worried its military as to whether it could win a hot war against the Soviet Union. President Nixon was under enormous pressure to change the public perception that the American empire had fallen militarily behind the Soviet Union.

President Nixon saw an opportunity to reverse the damage done to the American empire by its military defeat in Vietnam. That opportunity was to wean China away from the Soviet Union and into an alliance with the American empire. China had been Russia's largest ally against the United States. Getting China to switch sides would be the coup of the century. China was a prime target for a U.S. reset because Sino-Soviet relations were at an all-time low and China's economy was a disaster. What is of the greatest importance in explaining the Global Shift of both economic and political power from the West to the emerging economies was the willingness of the American empire to ally itself with a *Communist* country without requiring China to change its political system. The American empire was willing to form an alliance with China similar to the great power alliances before the Second World War. This was a revolutionary departure from the post–World War II alliances where previously powerful empires like the British, French, Japanese, German, Italian, Spanish, Dutch, and Portuguese had effectively become economic colonies of the American empire. They had been deprived of their political and military independence in exchange for U.S.-supported economic growth. American alliances with Asian countries such as Japan, South Korea, Taiwan, and the Philippines had all been conditional on them being strongly anti-Communist and willing to join the Western Cold War against the Soviet Union. In addition, the American empire had developed military agreements with these countries, as well as Germany and Saudi Arabia, that would guarantee American control over their future military spending and military independence. This was imposed on these economic colonies by the American empire to guarantee that their populations would never rise up to claim political independence from the American empire.

When candidate Donald Trump spoke of the cost to the United States of defending Germany, Japan, Saudi Arabia, South Korea, and Taiwan, he was implicitly referring to these post–World War II military agreements where the United States agreed to subsidize the military defense of these countries in return for American military control, to guarantee the subservience of their populations to economic colonization by the American empire. In like manner, the American empire agreed to fund the lion's share of the huge NATO military budget, to keep countries like Britain, France, Germany, Italy, Canada, Spain, Greece, Portugal, Australia, and New Zealand in line, and to transform them into economic colonies of the American empire. Again, it's this cost to the U.S. taxpayers that candidate Donald Trump indicated when he chastised the NATO members for not paying their fair share. It's also the reason that Trump's attackers claimed that Trump did not understand American foreign policy. In the immediate post–World War II period, America was rich and every other country was broke. American leaders agreed to create a world in which the U.S. taxpayer would subsidize the militaries of all of America's allies in exchange for their subservience to American imperialism. The Sino-American alliance would be different. At the time, this difference was insignificant because China was poor. Today, the difference is *monumental,* because China's economy is almost as large as that of the United States.

As we have explained earlier, the American empire had transformed its imperialism from invading and conquering, in the way that the Western European empires had done, to amassing economic colonies, beginning with Canada and Mexico. But all the economic colonies had to be strongly anti-Communist and dedicated to joining the fight against Communist states. They also had to be made dependent on the American military and American control of political, economic, and financial institutions such as the UN, the IMF, the WTO, the World Bank, and the reserve currency. The planned Sino-American alliance would not require China to become an economic colony of the American empire. China would be allowed its own *independent* political and military systems. In that sense, it was more similar to a *free trade agreement* than to economic or political colonization.

The American empire had imposed an economic embargo on China since the Korean War to impoverish China, as it had impoverished Cuba and North Korea. The American empire began to relax this economic embargo in 1969 to signal to China its desire for a reset to Sino-American relations. This timing coincided with the Sino-Soviet military border clashes and a growing desire by Americans to find an honorable way of ending the disastrous war in Vietnam, Cambodia, and Laos. President Nixon and his national security advisor, Henry Kissinger, were looking for a way to simultaneously end the Vietnam War and form an alliance with China against the Soviet Union. China was desperate to have the American economic embargo lifted because millions of its people were dying from starvation. China was also growing more suspicious about Soviet military incursions into its territory on the border with Soviet-controlled Tajikistan.

A stumbling block in beginning this reset was that the United States and China had severed diplomatic relations. Enter ping-pong diplomacy. In March 1971, the United States eased restrictions on Americans visiting China. China invited the U.S. ping-pong team to visit China after playing in the World Table Tennis Championships held in Japan in April 1971. The team accepted the invitation and visited China from April 10 to April 17, 1971. They were accompanied by journalists. In April 1971, the United States eased restrictions on Americans converting U.S. dollars to Chinese yuan, and the United States also made it easier for Chinese citizens to get visas to visit the United States. On June 10, 1971, the American empire lifted the economic embargo it had imposed on China since 1949. This was followed by a secret visit to China by Henry Kissinger in July 1971. Kissinger paved the way for an official visit by his boss, President Nixon, in February 1972. Most of America's allies supported the visit without understanding the special nature of the Sino-American alliance it would give birth to. China would not be an economic colony of the American empire, whereas all the other American allies were economic colonies.

Nixon Goes to China

President Nixon's visit to China in 1972 was so totally unexpected that the term "Nixon goes to China" has become a political metaphor for a politician, seen as a hawk, reversing course and acting as a dove to make peace with an enemy. In 2016, it would be the equivalent of candidate Hillary Clinton visiting Russia to make peace with Vladimir Putin. Since China's defeat of the American empire during its civil war, the American empire had insisted that the Republic of China, ROC, was China. The People's Republic of China, PRC, was not recognized by the American empire. President Nixon, by accepting an invitation to visit China, signaled that the American empire was willing to abandon its long-held ridiculous assertion that Taiwan was the legitimate China. The visit would pave the way for the American empire to recognize the PRC as the legitimate government of China. Since America's allies were

really economic colonies, they would all follow suit and recognize the
PRC. This would include the world's most powerful countries such as
Germany, Britain, France, Japan, South Korea, Italy, Spain, Portugal,
Greece, Canada, Australia, New Zealand, and the ROC. It would end
the economic isolation of China, which had been imposed on China by
the American empire, to impoverish China in the hopes of reigniting the
Civil War and replacing the PRC with the ROC.

President Nixon had concluded that the American policy to reignite
the Chinese Civil War had failed and that it was time to reengage
with China to help it win its Cold War against the Soviet Union. The
American empire had concluded that it was difficult, if not impossible,
to win the Cold War without the aid of China, despite its many powerful
allies. This was an astonishing conclusion, given that in 1972, China was
such a poor country. At least *five* of the American empire's allies, Japan,
Germany, France, Italy, and the UK, had GDPs larger than China in
1972. History would show that Nixon's strategy would help the American
empire defeat the Soviet Union. But it would simultaneously create a
new and equally formidable rival in China. The American empire would
become the only superpower after the fall of the Soviet Union. But the
American empire would abuse its superpower monopoly by waging
expensive wars and military invasions in Afghanistan, Iraq, Libya,
Syria, Yemen, and elsewhere. It would use debt to finance these wars,
causing its debt to grow much faster than its GDP. In the meantime, the
reengagement with China will energize the Global Shift, begun with the
Mexican Maquiladoras Program, and create a growing list of emerging
economies, which were *never* economic colonies of the American empire.

The majority of Americans welcomed the decision of their president
to accept the invitation to visit China. As expected, Nixon's decision
was denounced by the hawks and dedicated warmongers. The Chinese
response was similar. Most Chinese were eager to experience the
American dream of abundant consumer goods and services. But the
minority of hardline military men opposed the decision. President Nixon
and his wife arrived in China on February 21, 1972. Air Force One
landed at the airport in Beijing, and President Nixon had a one-hour
meeting that same day with Chairman Mao in Beijing. There were no
other meetings with Mao, possibly because of Mao's poor health. Further
meetings were with the Chinese premier Zhou Enlai. President Nixon
and his delegation, which included Kissinger and Secretary of State
William Rogers, spent a week in China, visiting the Great Wall, China's

largest city, Shanghai, as well as Beijing and Hangzhou. Pat Nixon visited hospitals, schools, and factories in addition to the Great Wall.

The result of the visit was the Shanghai Communique in February 28, 1972. The key point of the Communique was the expressed intent of both countries to normalize economic and political relations as equally *independent* and *sovereign* states. In addition, the American empire agreed to recognize that Taiwan was a part of China, as China had long claimed. In this regard, the American empire implicitly abandoned its puppet ruler of "China," who had escaped to Taiwan, and was protected in Taiwan by the American military after the Communists had won the Civil War in China. As Chairman Mao remarked when he met President Nixon, "I believe our old friend Chiang Kai-shek would not approve of this." The American empire also agreed to reduce its military forces in Taiwan and expressed its desire for a peaceful settlement of the Taiwan question by the Chinese themselves.

This decision by the American empire, not to add China to its long list of economic colonies but still have normal diplomatic and economic relations, was a *revolutionary departure* from its post–World War II diplomatic and economic relations with all other countries. It was a price the American empire was willing to pay to help win its Cold War against the Soviet Union. President Nixon called his visit "the week that changed the world." Little did he know at the time how truly *revolutionary* his visit would be. In particular, no one imagined poverty-stricken China would become the economic equal of the USA. That was what changed the world, not what Nixon imagined or intended. The willingness of the American empire to engage politically with a *Communist* state was of equal significance in unleashing the Global Shift as was China's subsequent enormous economic growth. China's political and military independence, combined with the new Mexican maquiladoras type foreign investment in China, are the two key elements in understanding how the Global Shift is very different from traditional *Globalization* and Western imperialism.

Under Mao Zedong, China had copied Stalin's economic model of a planned economy based on five-year plans. Stalin's planned economy model had outperformed the free enterprise model copied by the United States from Britain. This was an amazing achievement given that the free enterprise model had been touted for centuries by economists as the model that would use Adam Smith's invisible hand to maximize wealth. Most economists were skeptical as to whether any economy could be planned, much less be more efficient. Economists pointed to the enormous data required for central planning and the waste of resources used in creating and implementing a central plan. Under the free enterprise system, no resources are used to set up a plan or pay central planners. The invisible hand and markets are free and use none of the economy's scarce resources. Stalin proved that economists were wrong. Not only was a centrally planned economy functional, but also it could generate higher rates of economic growth than a free enterprise system. Under Stalin's Soviet model, the Russian economy grew twice as fast as that of the United States, around 5 percent annually compared to 2.5 percent in the United States.

Given the success of Stalin's economic model, it was understandable why Mao Zedong would copy that model and apply it to China. As a Communist country, it was also understandable that China would look to the USSR for economic and military assistance. China and the USSR were natural allies at a time when the American empire was forming alliances with Western European empires, Japan, Canada, Australia, and South Korea, to wage a cold war against all Communists. The Sino-Soviet alliance initially worked well both militarily and economically. But the military alliance fell apart over border disputes, and the economic alliance fell apart when the centrally planned system failed to deliver better growth rates than the free enterprise system.

The change from rapid to sluggish growth rates in the Soviet Union can be largely attributed to the ousting of Stalin's successor, Nikita Khrushchev, in 1964. While economic growth had begun to slow somewhat before 1964, under the leadership of Brezhnev and Kosygin, Soviet economic growth worsened. This enabled the American empire to dominate in the 1970s. In China, economic growth had also deteriorated under Mao's leadership. Mao's cultural revolution, beginning in 1966, was an economic disaster. Both Russia and China stagnated in the 1970s, while growth continued in the West. By the 1970s, confidence in the free enterprise economic system had been restored. It was once again touted by both economists and world leaders as the superior economic system.

In reality, the West had shifted to a *mixed economy* where there was a growing centrally planned *Communist* sector. It was, of course, called the public sector instead of the "Communist" sector. While the free enterprise sector was larger, it was shrinking in every Western country. In time, many Western countries would have a public sector almost as large as its free enterprise sector. This public sector is essentially a "Communist sector" as it is communally owned. It implicitly denied the sanctity of private property, touted by the American empire as an excuse to *steal* the lands and resources of the First Nations, by denying communal property rights. Western propaganda is so powerful that it could increase the "Communist sector" in all Western economies while simultaneously waging a Cold War against *Communism.*

While the economies of both Russia and China were stagnating, relative to the Western economies and the Asian free enterprise economies of Japan, South Korea, Taiwan, Hong Kong, and Singapore, Russia and China engaged in a very divisive border dispute. In addition, Mao attacked the Soviet leaders as revisionists, not true Communists. The border dispute between China and Russia began in 1964 when Mao publicly accused Russia of stealing Chinese territory. Soviet leader Khrushchev was outraged. Both countries began a massive build-up of troops and arms along the disputed border of the Soviet Republic of Tajikistan and the Chinese province of Xinjiang. Armed conflict broke out in March 1969. A full-blown war was avoided, but this open conflict between the two major Communist countries inspired the American empire to form an alliance with China against its major Cold War enemy, the Soviet Union. Mao's ideological split with Russia's leaders, China's military conflict with the Soviets over China's border, and China's dismal economic growth under Mao's leadership were the reasons why China was receptive to an alliance with the American empire against the Soviet Union.

When the USA began its rapprochement with China by sending Henry Kissinger to China in 1971, China was still a very poor country compared with the United States. Despite its much larger population, China's GDP in 1971 was barely 10 percent of that of the United States. The thought of China ever rivaling the United States for global hegemony never entered the minds of anyone. Russia was still the one country capable of challenging the United States. Just as no one predicted the future hegemony of the USA when Columbus discovered the New World in 1492, no one predicted the rise of China when Kissinger visited China in 1971. Even today, American and Western leaders do not understand the revolutionary nature of the Global Shift, which began with the Mexican maquiladoras in 1965. Western leaders and economists continue to treat this revolution as an evolution of centuries of *Globalization. They are mistaken.*

The Shanghai Communique was a statement of intentions. Chairman Mao returned President Nixon's state visit by visiting the United States in April 1972. It took another seven years to bring those intentions to fruition. In May 1973, liaison offices were set up in Washington and Beijing. Pres. Gerald Ford visited China in 1975 to reassure China that the United States was working toward restoring full diplomatic relations. In 1978, Pres. Jimmy Carter sent his secretary of state, Cyrus Vance, to China, to wrap up the negotiations. In late 1978, the United States and the PRC announced to the world that they would restore full diplomatic relations, beginning January 1, 1979. By that time, Chairman Mao had passed away. Vice Premier Deng Xiaoping had effectively succeeded Chairman Mao after Mao's death in 1976. He visited Washington in January 1979. This officially ended the U.S. recognition of the ROC as the legitimate government of China and began the official recognition by the United States, of the PRC, as the legitimate government of China. Embassies were established in Washington and Beijing in March 1979.

The Global Shift Moves from Mexico and Latin America to Southern China after 1980

China is the key to understanding why the Global Shift is truly revolutionary and not simply a continuation of *Globalization*, free trade, or Western imperialism. President Nixon's visit to China was intended to be mostly political for the United States and only marginally economic. The American empire had engaged in a Cold War with the Soviet Union since the end of the Second World War. Despite strong political alliances with Britain, France, Germany, Italy, Spain, Portugal, Greece, Japan, South Korea, Canada, Australia, New Zealand, Saudi Arabia, Mexico, the Gulf States, Taiwan, the Philippines, and many others, the American empire failed to win the Cold War. Reengaging with China was intended to add yet another *political* ally to destroy the Soviet Union. President Nixon was simply pursuing an agenda that would secure the continuation of six centuries of Western imperialism, military conquests, and world leadership. Neither President Nixon nor his political advisors nor any of his allies had a clue of the Pandora's box his visit would open.

The Global Shift to China was never envisaged by China either. While China's motive for reengaging with the West was somewhat more economic than political, China was no wiser than the Americans as to the revolutionary nature of the outcome. China simply hoped for a modest boost in economic growth and slight improvement in the standard of living of its destitute millions. Economists across the globe had long written off prosperity for China, India, and the billions of poor who had the misfortune of inhabiting the Third World. They were doomed to permanent poverty because their populations were far too large to ever grow their real GDP much more than their population. Low per capita land, resources, savings, and investment, caused by overpopulation, guaranteed low and insignificant growth in per capita GDP. Western politicians, economists, and China would be proved wrong.

America's reengagement with China differed from America's previous engagements with countries across the globe, including its reengagement with Germany and Japan, after the Second World War. Reengagement with China was different both at the political level and at the economic level. At the political level, China was allowed to keep its political system. It marked the departure of traditional U.S. policy of forcing the American economic colony to conform to a standard free enterprise political system. At the economic level, China would produce manufactured goods for Western consumers. Neither of these differences were significant in 1972 but turned out to be crucial in explaining why the Global Shift is very different from historical *Globalization* and Western imperialism. Since no one fully understands the significance of this difference, even today, we have our job cut out for us in trying to convince you to understand that difference. To do that, we will use both the historical evolution of the Global Shift in China, as well as comparisons with prior American reengagements with countries like Germany, Japan, and South Korea, to see how those American alliances were both politically and economically different and, therefore, were a continuation of traditional *Globalization* and Western imperialism.

Birth of the U.S.-Mexican Maquiladoras-Type Program in Southern China

We have identified the U.S.-Mexican Maquiladoras Program, implemented by the U.S. factories along the Mexican side of the U.S.-Mexico border, beginning in 1965, as the accidental reason for what we

call the Global Shift. We have compared this accident to the accidental
rediscovery of the New World by Columbus in that the latter gave rise
to the American empire, while the former will cause the demise of the
hegemony of the American empire. Initially, Columbus's rediscovery
created the Spanish empire in the Southern part of the New World before
creating the American empire in the northern part of the New World. In
like manner, the Maquiladoras Program began in Mexico, moving south
into Latin America before moving to China. Just as the creation of the
American empire led to the extreme dominance of the West, China holds
the key to the ultimate dominance of the emerging economies. While it
took centuries after Columbus's rediscovery for that rediscovery to give
birth to the American empire, it took only decades for the Maquiladoras
Program to reach China.

Mexico had a clear and decisive head start over China for several
reasons. First, Mexico was already one of the older economic colonies
of the American empire when the Maquiladoras Program began in
1965. Second, this so-called Border Industrialization Program, BIP,
was specifically designed from its inception to be different from the
traditional economic development programs pursued by all the Western
imperial powers in their colonies, including branch plant economies
like Canada. Though not meant to be a revolutionary program, it was
revolutionary in that it would produce manufactured goods *not* for the
consumers in the economic colonies but for consumers in the imperial
power, the USA. This is the key difference between centuries of political
and economic colonizations by the West and the Maquiladoras Program.
The question that we must now address is how did this type of program
end up in China, even though China was not an economic colony of any
imperial power, kept its *Communist* government, and kept its political and
military *independence,* after reengaging with the United States? In many
ways, the answer to this question lies with another accident. That other
accident was the decision by China not to embrace a *national* strategy of
capitalism or free enterprise, as many previously Communist "colonies" of
the Soviet Union have done, but to create special economic zones, SEZs.
As a nation, China would still be a *Communist* state. But within the
SEZs, capitalism and free enterprise would flourish. These SEZs turned
out to be similar to the Mexican Maquiladoras Program in its singularly
key difference from centuries of Western development in their colonies.
That key difference is that foreign factories located in the SEZs would
produce manufactured goods *not* for Chinese consumers but for Western

consumers. This is how the Global Shift emigrated from Latin America to China and Asia.

We should not be surprised that the SEZs created by China would be located by China along its southern border, with easy port access to Western markets, just as the Maquiladoras Program was located by Mexico, along its northern border, with easy land access to the U.S. market. China's choice of the city of *Shenzhen* in Guangdong Province to locate its first of many SEZs was no accident. It was ideally located for many reasons. The most important reason was that it was along the border with Hong Kong. As a colony of the British Empire, Hong Kong had become more capitalist and free enterprise than both Britain and the USA. Hong Kong was a port city with global access. It had one of the largest container ports in the world. It had developed financial markets and infrastructure. Hong Kong was to be returned to China by the British Empire in 1997. Guangdong was the new name for Canton, the Chinese province that was the first province in China that had opened a port to foreigners long before the creation of the Shenzhen SEZ.

When Chairman Mao passed away in 1976, the new Chinese leader, Deng Xiaoping, was far more receptive to a free enterprise economic system than Mao. This is not surprising. As we said above, Chairman Mao had adopted the planned economy system from Stalin's Russia at a time when Russia's planned economy system was outperforming free enterprise economies in the West. But by 1976, free enterprise economies were far outperforming planned economies. With the American empire willing to reengage with China without requiring China to change its political system, Deng was able to have the best of both worlds. He would keep the Communist Party's governance of China but allow free markets to determine outcomes in the SEZs. Since the SEZs would be located initially in Southern China, China would be the only country to move toward a mixed economy on a *geographical* basis. By the time the SEZs were introduced in China in 1980, all Western countries had moved from capitalist economies to mixed economies. But that mixture of private and public sectors was based on the type of product produced, not on geographical regions. Defense, policing, health care, education, parks, and recreation were examples of products produced by the "Communist" public sector. Cars and electronic gadgets were examples of products produced by the private sector. Unlike the mixed economies of the West, China would experiment with a system that introduced private sector capitalism in its southern provinces and moved geographically further and further north. This experiment, in our view, is the true meaning of *capitalism with Chinese characteristics.*

It was August 1980 when the National People's Congress created its first SEZ in Shenzhen. After President Nixon's visit to China in 1972, both the United States and China were working on how to take advantage of the Shanghai Communique, agreed to during that visit. American leaders were working on the American side to find an acceptable way to switch from its political recognition of the ROC and Taipei to political recognition of the PRC and Beijing. Chinese leaders were working on the China side to open up segments of the Chinese economy to free markets and inflows of foreign capital. By the time the United States and China restored full diplomatic relations in January 1979, China was well on its way to creating the SEZs. In July 1979, the PRC issued a directive to create SEZs in the *southern* provinces of Guangdong and Fujian. This directive was followed by the brainstorming of a group of officials and economists from the PRC, Guangdong, Hong Kong, and Macau, to come up with draft regulations for SEZs. While free trade zones had a long history in other Asian countries such as Taiwan, South Korea, and the Philippines, it was a novel departure in a *Communist* state. By involving Hong Kong and Macau, as well as the Taiwan border province of Fujian, the PRC was combining its new economic strategy with its political goal of reacquiring Hong Kong, Macau, and Taiwan. Kill two birds, as it were, reunification and economic growth, with one stone.

Since three of the planned initial SEZs were to be located in Guangdong Province, the Guangdong Provincial People's Congress was actively involved in drafting the regulations that would govern the SEZs. This draft was completed in December 1979 and submitted to Beijing. The draft was modified and approved by the National People's Congress in August 1980. Shenzhen had been identified to be the first of the SEZs on May 1, 1980. Two others, Zhuhai and Shantou, were also to be located in the same province of Guangdong. A fourth was to be located in the city of Xiamen in Fujian Province.

Shenzhen: The First Chinese Maquiladora Established in 1980

There are many similarities between the U.S.-Mexico Border Industrialization Program of 1965 and China's first SEZ established along the border with Hong Kong in 1980. What is often not known, the island of Hong Kong is only the financial center of Hong Kong, much like New York is the financial center of the United States. The geographical area of Hong Kong, known as the *New Territories,* with its land border with China, is far larger than the geographical area of Hong Kong Island. While no one confuses New York with the USA, many confuse Hong Kong Island with Hong Kong. Just as the BIP was not located in New York, the Shenzhen SEZ was not located on Hong Kong Island. It was located on the Chinese side of the China-Hong Kong land border, just as the BIP was located on the Mexican side of the Mexico-U.S. border. The reason for these choice of locations were identical. In the case of the BIP, the factories would be financed by U.S. entrepreneurs owning factories in the United States, located close to the Mexican border. They would locate the new BIP factories on the Mexican side to take advantage of the cheaper Mexican labor and transport the output to their customers located on the American side of the border. By being close to the border, transportation cost would be minimized, thereby keeping the selling price of the products lower than if they were produced by American workers.

In like manner, Hong Kong entrepreneurs would locate their new factories on the Chinese side of the Hong Kong-China border to take advantage of the cheaper Chinese labor. Since the factories are close to the border, the increased transportation cost would be minimal compared to the lower labor cost. While China was intending to open the SEZs to foreign investment from many countries, it began this program by focusing almost exclusively on Hong Kong, in the same way that the Mexican Maquiladora Program initially focused exclusively on the USA. Replace Mexico with China and replace USA with Hong Kong, and the two programs are identical. Furthermore, we explained in the previous chapter the importance of similar experiences and values and family ties on both sides of the U.S.-Mexico border because the U.S. border states had initially been part of Mexico. In the same way, the Chinese living on both sides of the China-Hong Kong border had long historical ties and common ethnicity and language. Unlike most of China, where the common language is Mandarin, in Hong Kong and Shenzhen, the common language is Cantonese. English colonization of Hong Kong was the equivalent of the U.S. invasion and conquest of the northern half of old Mexico. The fact that in 1997 the English would return Hong Kong to China was an added incentive for the Hong Kong entrepreneurs to take advantage of this opportunity to get a head start on future competitors.

A final similarity between the U.S.-Mexico program and the Hong Kong-Shenzhen program was the residence of the managers, trainers, and technical support workers. In the United States, those workers preferred to continue to reside in the United States but have quick mobility across the border to the factories located in Mexico. In like manner, the managers, trainers, and technical support workers continued to reside in Hong Kong but had quick mobility across the border into Shenzhen. Such quick border access also enabled parts not available in Shenzhen to be quickly shipped out from Hong Kong for speedy repairs to machinery and equipment.

The Shenzhen-Hong Kong maquiladora is an excellent example of the difference between trade and colonization. Unlike colonization, which uses military force to conquer and benefit the imperial power at the expense of the colony, the Shenzhen-Hong Kong maquiladora would be mutually beneficial to both parties, Shenzhen and Hong Kong. China was aware that when Hong Kong was returned by Britain in 1997, it had two options. One option was to impose its Communist form of government on Hong Kong. The alternative option was to keep capitalism in Hong Kong and implement Hong Kong's capitalism in its SEZs, beginning with Shenzhen. China chose the latter option, and Hong Kong entrepreneurs were delighted. They were delighted not simply because they were able to keep their wealth and businesses as private property but because they could now expand into neighboring Shenzhen, thereby *increasing* their wealth and private property value.

The British took advantage of a militarily weak China to colonize Hong Kong in 1842. Hong Kong's location provided a strategic port for the British to access China's Guangdong Province, then called Canton. The British colony attracted foreign businesses that specialized in trade, shipping and shipbuilding, banking and other financial services, and small-scale manufacturing. Hong Kong benefitted from the Western isolation of China during the Cold War. Its manufacturing sector experienced significant growth during this period. As the first of the four so-called Asian Tigers of the 1960s and 1970s, Hong Kong had experienced exceptionally high growth rates, unheard of historically, before the Asian Tigers. By 1980, Hong Kong was an export-led developed economy with a highly educated and trained labor force. Two decades earlier, it was considered a Third World country. By 1980, it was very open to international trade with exports accounting for 65 percent of its GDP. It attracted foreign capital with low corporate and income taxes. It had a sound banking system and one of the highest indices of economic freedom. By 1980, Hong Kong was also well on its way to becoming one of the world's leading financial centers, not too far behind Tokyo or New York and London. Hong Kong Stock Exchange provided a bridge to stock exchanges in Tokyo, Europe, and the United States.

Entrepreneurs are always looking for opportunities to expand. The creation of the Shenzhen SEZ in 1980 came at an especially opportune time for Hong Kong entrepreneurs. Hong Kong had achieved those high-growth rates by specializing in a narrow range of labor-intensive, low-tech, assembly-type, light manufactured goods using its low labor cost advantage relative to developed economies such as Japan. The products it specialized in were primarily textiles, clothing, plastics, and electronics. By 1980, Hong Kong's low labor cost competitive advantage was under threat from emerging Asian economies such as Thailand, Malaysia, Indonesia, and the Philippines. Enter Shenzhen's SEZ, cheaper land and labor, with an almost infinite supply of the same type of relatively unskilled labor that had driven the manufacturing sector of the Hong Kong economy. With a common language, ethnicity, custom, business ethics, family ties, and easy access of Hong Kong entrepreneurs to local officials in the SEZ, Hong Kong entrepreneurs were drooling at the mouth to expand from the New Territories into their new backyard. One of China's strategies in creating the SEZs was to provide new investment opportunities for the millions of overseas Chinese entrepreneurs, beginning with the Cantonese-speaking overseas Chinese with strong connections and homes in Hong Kong and Guangdong. Within the SEZ, taxes would be low as they had been in Hong Kong, to attract foreign capital. Prior to the SEZ, the inhabitants of Shenzhen struggled to migrate into Hong Kong, much like the Mexicans struggled to migrate to the United States before the creation of the maquiladoras. The SEZ was bringing the mountain to Mohamed, leading the Global Shift from the West to the emerging economies.

In choosing Shenzhen to locate its first SEZ, China was not simply connecting China to Hong Kong. China was tapping into Hong Kong's window to the West through its port. Hong Kong's port was strategically located in the Pearl River Delta. China would access the Hong Kong port by locating its manufacturing in neighboring Shenzhen. With two other SEZs located in the Pearl River Delta region, China was planning to use Shenzhen as a first step to the development of a giant manufacturing base in the much larger Pearl River Delta region in the province of Guangdong. The key evidence that China was not simply using Shenzhen as a gateway to Hong Kong but as a gateway to the world is the "containerization" of the port of Hong Kong and the establishment of another large container port in Shenzhen. Shenzhen's container port also acts as a feeder port to other container ports located in the Pearl River Delta region. The success of the Global Shift outside the Mexican maquiladoras is very dependent on low-cost water transportation from Asia to the West. Containerization has reduced transportation cost from Asia to the West to *one-twentieth* of precontainerization cost.

While the creation of the Shenzhen SEZ led to a rapid growth in Hong Kong's container port, Shenzhen's container port is currently busier than that of Hong Kong. Hong Kong's container port was the world's busiest port during the years 1987 to 1989. It's ranked the fourth-busiest container port in the world in 2018, while Shenzhen is ranked the world's third-busiest in 2018. This third- and fourth-place ranking implies that exports have grown sufficiently to keep both ports busy rather than Shenzhen's port growing at the expense of Hong Kong. Both ports are located in the Pearl River Delta region in Southern China. Shenzhen's container port is divided into an eastern and a western port, with the mainland area of Hong Kong separating the two halves. Shenzhen's eastern port is located in one of the best natural harbors in Southern China. To the north of Shenzhen's western port is China's third-largest city, Guangzhou, just over one hundred kilometers away. Both Shenzhen and Guangzhou are located in the province of Guangdong, previously called Canton. Since 1985, China has invested more in the expansion of its ports than the rest of the world combined. It's no coincidence that most of the world's largest container ports are located in China. The intent of China's SEZs was to transform all of Southern China into a free enterprise manufacturing giant supplying the world with cheap manufactured goods while providing jobs for millions of Chinese workers moving from the farms to cities in Southern China. While wages were low relative to wages paid to industrial workers in the West, the wages far exceeded those earned by farmworkers in rural China. This transformation of Sothern China into the world's central manufacturing hub began in the Pearl River Delta region.

In the first year of the creation of the Shenzhen SEZ, many Hong Kong entrepreneurs located new factories in Shenzhen instead of Hong Kong, and over 90 percent of the foreign investment in the Shenzhen SEZ originated from Hong Kong. This foreign investment naturally targeted labor-intensive manufacturing using relatively unskilled workers for assembly-type work. The common language and culture of the employees in the Shenzhen factories with employees in the Hong Kong factories made the transition easier and cost effective. The SEZ was able to attract large numbers of workers from rural areas because farm labor was willing to move from the farms to the SEZ in search of higher wages. This steady flow of farm labor into the SEZ prevented any significant increase in labor cost, thereby maintaining the competitive advantage of the ever-increasing number of factories locating in the SEZ, instead of Hong Kong. Land was also cheaper in Shenzhen than in Hong Kong since Shenzhen was largely rural in 1980. Rents were less than one-third the cost in Hong Kong. In many ways, Hong Kong investors saw rural Shenzhen as a great relief to urban crowded Hong Kong where physical space was at a premium.

Hong Kong's access to cheap land and labor in Shenzhen was quickly recognized by Hong Kong entrepreneurs as the best way of keeping Hong Kong's exports competitive in world markets. The creation of the Shenzhen SEZ also enabled Hong Kong to shift its more highly skilled labor force from lower-skill jobs to higher-skill jobs by moving the lower-skill jobs to Shenzhen. Low-skill labor in Shenzhen was less than half the cost of low-skill labor in Hong Kong. Hong Kong entrepreneurs also used the Shenzhen SEZ to grow its services sector relative to its manufacturing sector. As an economy matures, its manufacturing sector shrinks while its service sector expands. This natural maturing of economies was enhanced in Hong Kong by the creation of China's SEZs just north of Hong Kong, in Shenzhen, and in the larger Pearl River Delta region. By the end of the first two decades of the creation of the Shenzhen SEZ, employment in the manufacturing sector in Hong Kong fell to 10 percent of its labor force while employment in services reached 80 percent.

One of the best measures of the immense success of the Shenzhen SEZ is the creation of a metropolis more populous than famous historical cities like London and Paris within a few decades. Its high-rises rival New York, the birthplace of high-rises. The SEZ transformed a largely rural Shenzhen, with a population of sixty thousand in 1980, into a megacity of twelve million, and a population exceeding twenty million within the greater Shenzhen area. It became the fastest-growing city in the world during the last two decades of the twentieth century. Its growth had been fueled largely by its economically advanced neighbor, Hong Kong, but it overtook the population of Hong Kong. While the population of Hong Kong grew from 4.6 million in 1980 to 7.3 million in 2015, the population of Shenzhen grew from sixty thousand in 1980 to eleven million in 2015. Shenzhen's GDP grew at the staggering annual rate of 40 percent between 1980 and 1995. Since 1995, its economy has continued to grow in excess of 10 percent annually. By 2018, its GDP was over $300 billion, larger than Portugal, the country that launched Western colonizations before 1450. Its per capita GDP exceeded US$30,000. Shenzhen remains one of China's leading manufacturing hubs and is increasingly switching from low-tech to high-tech manufacturing. Despite the rapid growth of China's largest cities, Shanghai, Beijing, and Guangzhou, Shenzhen retains its fourth-place rank as measured by GDP. Shenzhen is the largest of the many SEZs created by China after 1979.

Another measure of the Shenzhen SEZ's success is the development of a stock exchange rivaling that of its more advanced neighbor Hong Kong. Initially, the Shenzhen SEZ gave a big boost to the growth in Hong Kong's financial and banking services. The Hong Kong Stock Exchange also linked Chinese businesses to stock exchanges in Japan and London. By 1990, Hong Kong had become an important financial center in Asia. This prompted the creation of a separate Shenzhen stock exchange in 1990. As with all other economic indicators in Shenzhen, its stock exchange grew rapidly to be ranked nineteenth in the global ranking of the world's financial centers. By 2018, it had a market capitalization exceeding US$200 billion. By 2018, both the Shenzhen and Shanghai Stock Exchanges had been merged with the Hong Kong Stock Exchange.

Shenzhen's integration with Hong Kong has continued through increasing the number of border crossings by land, sea, and air. A new high-speed rail link was completed in 2018. There is a continuous flow of goods and services, as well as people, by rail, roads, ships, and planes. In many ways, it is a replica of the border crossings between the United States and Mexico. The border states of the United States were once a part of Mexico. Hong Kong was once a part of China, colonized by the

British, and returned to China in 1997. While the U.S.-Mexico economic integration, begun with the maquiladoras and strengthened by NAFTA, would be limited by the political sovereignty of two independent states, there would be no such limit on the Hong Kong-Shenzhen economic integration, since both Hong Kong and Shenzhen would be politically integrated into the larger Chinese state. In fact, we can foresee Shenzhen moving from junior partner in the early decades of the Hong Kong-Shenzhen economic integration to *senior* partner as its population, GDP, management expertise, technical labor expertise, component parts production, container port, and stock exchange surpassed that of Hong Kong in 2018.

Think of the Shenzhen SEZ as the Hong Kong gateway into China's Guangdong Province and the Pearl River Delta, just as the BIP was America's gateway into Mexico. As America's gateway into Mexico would eventually penetrate all of Latin America, Hong Kong's gateway into Guangdong and the Pearl River Delta would eventually penetrate all of China. On the other side of the coin, China's access to Hong Kong via Shenzhen gave China access to the West via Hong Kong's port, financial markets, and foreign investors outside Hong Kong. In 1980, China's ports were not equipped to handle any rapid increase in exports of manufactured goods, and its financial markets were not yet developed. The timing was crucial to both China and Hong Kong. China's post-Mao goal was rapid economic growth based on free enterprise principles. Hong Kong's impending end of British colonization and return to China led to Hong Kong's business elite recognizing that their best weapon in maintaining their capitalist preferences in *Communist* China was to create a lasting economic bond with China via economic and financial dominance of the Shenzhen SEZ. By creating this lasting economic bond, rather than China attempting to reduce capitalism in Hong Kong, China would harness Hong Kong's capitalism to grow all of China. Shenzhen's SEZ was seen as a win-win by both sides. As Hong Kong entrepreneurs developed lasting relationships with local politicians in Shenzhen, they would later use those relationships to assist Western entrepreneurs outside Hong Kong to negotiate business deals with local politicians in Shenzhen and then further into Guangdong Province. This growing "middle man" role for Hong Kong entrepreneurs was one strategic factor that China had counted on in choosing Hong Kong's Cantonese-speaking neighbor Shenzhen to locate its first SEZ.

Just as the USA had a decisive location advantage to move its factories from the United States to Mexico and further southward into Latin America, the developed economies in Asia, Hong Kong, Taiwan, Japan, and South Korea had a decisive location advantage to move their factories into China's SEZs. It was therefore a strategic move for China to initially target Hong Kong and Taiwan, followed by Japan and South Korea, before targeting the United States. But without the restoration of diplomatic relations with the United States, the English colony of Hong Kong and the American economic colonies of Taiwan, Japan, and South Korea would not have dared to antagonize their Western masters. During the first two decades of the creation of China's SEZs, trade between Hong Kong and China grew at a staggering annual rate of 30 percent.

The Zhuhai SEZ and Macau

While the Shenzhen SEZ targeted the economic and financial advancement of Hong Kong, the intent of the Zhuhai SEZ was to harness the dynamic forces of Macau. In 1980, when the first SEZs were created by China, Hong Kong was a much more advanced economic, financial, and trading center than Macau. Its population of 4.6 million dwarfed that of Macau's population of 243,000. This explains China's initial focus on Hong Kong, by creating its first SEZ in Shenzhen. But Macau had been opened up by Western colonization long before the British colonized Hong Kong. The Portuguese empire, which predated the British Empire by centuries, colonized Macau in 1557. But Macau's port had been doing trade with foreign countries since the fifth century. Macau's population increased during the Song dynasty as a result of the Mongol invasions. In the later Ming dynasty, Chinese continued to migrate from Guangdong and Fujian Provinces into Macau to trade and fish. But the biggest boost to the development of Macau occurred as a result of the Portuguese colonization.

The Portuguese were first allowed to anchor their ships in Macau as a result of a shipwreck in 1535. The Portuguese empire decided to cooperate with the Ming dynasty to reduce piracy along China's southern coastline. This influenced the Ming dynasty to allow the Portuguese to establish a permanent trading post in Macau in 1557 and administer the island. The Portuguese administered the island as a Portuguese colony, with a Portuguese governor, while paying an annual tribute to the Ming emperor. Chinese inhabitants were subject to Chinese law. Portuguese colonization of Macau attracted merchants from both Portugal and China to the island. By the time of the Portuguese colonization, Macau had become an important trading center for Southern China. Portuguese colonization enhanced Portuguese and Western trade with China via Macau. The Portuguese used Macau to expand their international trade via both Goa in India, and via the Philippines and Mexico. The union between the Portuguese and Spanish empires in 1580 boosted this trade. The Portuguese also acted as middle men in expanding trade between China and Japan. China's concern over Japanese and Chinese pirates led China to ban direct trade between China and Japan in 1547.

The Portuguese linked China and Japan by connecting Macau with Guangzhou and Nagasaki. The Portuguese exchanged Chinese silk for Japanese silver. But the Portuguese used its colony of Macau to convert many Chinese to Catholic Christianity. The Christian religion was an important tool of Western imperialism. Under Portuguese colonization, Macau became a magnet for Christian missionaries. With the trade linkage the Portuguese empire provided between China and Japan, missionaries saw Macau as the gateway to Christianizing both the Chinese and the Japanese. What a bonanza this would be! It was this fear of Catholic influence on the Japanese people that led Japan to restrict the Portuguese middle-man trade between China and Japan beginning in 1637.

In 1685, China opened its ports to all foreign traders. This added traders from Holland, England, France, the United States, Russia, Sweden, and Denmark to the Portuguese and Spanish traders in Macau. Macau was also used as a transit port for the "trade" in Chinese slaves. Africans were not the only people enslaved by the West. Many Chinese were kidnapped from China and sold into slavery in the New World. Macau's close proximity to Guangdong Province enabled it to act as a transit hub for Chinese slaves kidnapped from Guangdong Province and other parts of Southern China. Many refugees entered Macau during World War II as the Japanese recognized Portugal's neutrality. Japanese occupation of Hong Kong and Guangzhou boosted Macau's position as a free port. Gambling was introduced to Macau in 1962. Most of the gamblers came from the British colony of Hong Kong. The first bridge linking the two islands in Macau, Coloane and Taipa, was built in 1966. A second bridge was built in 1994. Land reclamation has physically connected the two islands. Many new casinos have been built and are being built on this reclaimed land. Portugal agreed to return Macau to China in 1999.

The Shenzhen SEZ was created in 1980 in anticipation of the British returning Hong Kong to China in 1997. In like manner, the Zhuhai SEZ was also created in 1980 in anticipation of the Portuguese returning Macau to China in 1999. Macau is Zhuhai's southern border. Just as Shenzhen enabled China to use Hong Kong to attract foreign investment, Zhuhai enabled China to use Macau to attract foreign investment. While many Chinese and foreign residents of Hong Kong and Macau had feared China turning these Western colonies into Communist cities, China did exactly the opposite. It used these two capitalist colonies to bring capitalism and free enterprise into Southern China. Zhuhai would join Shenzhen, Hong Kong, and Macau as major deepwater port cities of China. Zhuhai includes several islands in the South China Sea, close to Hong Kong. Zhuhai has therefore attracted foreign investment from both Macau and Hong Kong. Foreign investment in Zhuhai targeted five major manufacturing industries. These were machinery and equipment, electronics, computer software, pharmacy, and biotechnology.

Unlike Shenzhen, which was of little significance except for its land border with Hong Kong, Zhuhai was China's equivalent of the French Riviera. It has a long coastline and was therefore a popular tourist destination in China. Since becoming an SEZ, it has attracted millions of both domestic and foreign tourists each year. Zhuhai recognizes that it can use its enhanced growth as a manufacturing center to leverage its pre-SEZ tourism attraction. Currently, it hosts China's largest air show and is developing many other tourist attractions such as the New Yuan Ming Palace.

In the meantime, Macau has become the Asian Las Vegas. Macau's population of six hundred thousand is about the same as Las Vegas. China leveraged the casino gambling introduced by the Portuguese to tap into gamblers from Hong Kong, China, and Asia. Many Las Vegas casino owners built casinos in Macau after Macau was returned to China. In 2004, a third bridge was built to connect the two islands and facilitate the ever-increasing numbers of gambling tourists. As the gambling boom expanded opportunities in Macau, economic growth spilled over into Zhuhai. One example of this is the development of Hengqin Island, one of the many small islands making up Zhuhai, and connected to the mainland area of Zhuhai by bridges. In addition to commercial and residential developments on the island of Hengqin, the University of Macau built a new campus there. Bridges, land reclamation, gambling, tourism, and the SEZ are creating an integrated geographical, financial, and manufacturing area encompassing the old Portuguese colony of Macau with the new emerging China. Hong Kong straddles both the economic miracle produced by the Shenzhen SEZ with the economic miracle produced by the Zhuhai SEZ. Shenzhen is the much larger of the two SEZs. Shenzhen's population of twelve million is about ten times as large as Zhuhai's population, just as Hong Kong's population of eight million is about ten times as large as Macau's population. In 2018, the geographical area combining Shenzhen, Hong Kong, Macau, and Zhuhai has become a single integrated manufacturing and financial powerhouse for China's economic growth and China's attempt to influence the global economy. A thirty-four-mile-long bridge tunnel linking Zhuhai to Hong Kong and Macau, costing US$16 billion, completed construction in 2017 and was open for traffic in 2018. The US$20 billion bridge was constructed over a ten-year period and is the world's longest bridge. It provides a fast alternative to the existing road and rail links. It is also a symbol of China's engineering prowess.

The Shantou SEZ, Guangdong Province, and the Pearl River Delta Region

As we have mentioned before, the SEZs of Shenzhen and Zhuhai are located in China's southern province of Guangdong. A third SEZ, Shantou, was also added in the same province at the same time. If you look at a map of Southern China, you will observe the three SEZs lined up along the southern coast line of Guangdong, with Zhuhai to the left, Shenzhen in the middle, and Shantou to the right. Zhuhai is just north of Macau, and Shenzhen is just north of Hong Kong. Shantou is further east of Shenzhen and close to the border of Guangdong Province with Fujian Province. In terms of relative size, it is larger than Zhuhai but smaller than Shenzhen. The population of Zhuhai today is about two million, while that of Shantou is about six million. Shenzhen has a population of twelve million. The Shantou SEZ expands significantly the length of the Guangdong coastline, which can be used to ship out manufactured goods produced by Guangdong's SEZs. It makes effective use of the eastern coastline of Guangdong. Guangdong is China's most populous province with a total population exceeding 110 million in 2018. It has the highest provincial GDP as well, contributing about 12 percent of China's total GDP. Its GDP was a modest 24 million yuan when the SEZs were created in 1980. By 2010, it had reached almost 5,000 million yuan.

Shantou was one of the ports used in the nineteenth century after China was forced by the Opium Wars to open its ports to the British, Americans, and other Western empires. Under the Canton system, 1757–1842, China ensured that all foreign trade was channeled through the province of Guangdong, then called Canton. This was done to make it administratively easier for the emperor to limit and control how much foreign trade was in China's best interests. All countries, even today, limit their levels of foreign trade. Limiting foreign trade is an age-old custom practiced by every nation state throughout history. What was unique about the Canton system was to use a single province to exercise that limit. The historical significance of the Canton system to China's SEZs is that it was used by the *Communist* government of China to introduce into China, after 1980, its own brand of our special interpretation of capitalism with Chinese characteristics. We interpret this to mean that China introduced capitalism by geography, beginning with the same province used for the Canton system.

Under the Han dynasty (206 BCE–220 CE), Guangdong and neighboring Guangxi Province linked China to the West through trade, long before the birth of Western imperialism in the fifteenth century. China became the wealthiest country in the world. The Mongol invasion from the north during the thirteenth century pushed the Song dynasty south into this area of China. Much of Southern China was free from Mongol rule. China closed its ports and economy to foreign trade during the Ming dynasty (1368–1644). That began the era of China's closed-door policy. The Portuguese empire was determined to find ways around China's closed-door policy. Portuguese sailors first arrived in the Pearl River region in 1513. The Portuguese began to trade with Chinese merchants in Guangzhou in 1516. But the Portuguese also engaged in piracy and enslaving Chinese women. Such bad behavior by the Portuguese led to conflicts with the Chinese. Trade was limited by the Ming emperor because of the bad behavior of the Portuguese. But the Portuguese were very determined to trade or steal by any means. Their ships continued to arrive in the Pearl River region.

Portugal's colonization of Macau in 1557 diverted Chinese foreign trade from Canton to Macau. This linked Macau to Guangdong during the Song and Ming dynasties. Many Chinese inhabitants migrated from

Guangdong Province to Macau during the Ming dynasty. After the reopening up of China to foreign trade in 1685, Macau's special position as the primary trading hub between China and the West declined. This initial closed-door policy ended under the Qing dynasty in 1685, when foreign traders received permission to enter Chinese ports. The Qing emperor regulated trade by channeling it through Canton. Spanish, Dutch, British, French, and Scandinavian traders joined the Portuguese in trading with China. China's primary exports were tea and porcelain. Western imperialism took advantage of China's open-door policy to convert Chinese to Christianity. Christian converts have served Western imperial powers as one of its key instruments of colonization. In an effort to control and limit foreign trade and minimize the colonization efforts of Christian missionaries, all China's ports were closed to foreign trade in 1757, with the exception of a single open port in Canton. This came to be called the Canton system (1757–1842).

The Canton system made Guangdong's capital city, Guangzhou, a major international port city. The creation of the SEZs in 1980 has led to significant growth of Guangzhou and made it a primary manufacturing hub for the Pearl River Delta region. Its population grew from 2 million in 1980 to 12.5 million in 2015. It is China's third-largest city after Shanghai and Beijing. It has a population close to fourteen million in 2018. It attracts immigrants from Africa, the Middle East, Eastern Europe, and Southeast Asia. With a per capita GDP exceeding US$25,000, it is one of China's most prosperous cities.

Foreign trade was controlled through thirteen factories in Canton. The choice of Canton gave a great economic boost to the growth and development of Guangzhou and the Pearl River Delta region of Guangdong, Guangxi, Hong Kong, and Macau. Under the Canton system, trade between China and the West grew rapidly, leading to rapid economic growth in the province of Guangdong and in its capital city, Guangzhou. It was the port of Canton that the British used to forcibly import their opium into China and establish themselves as the world's primary *drug lord*. On the Chinese side, the government attempted to control the foreign trade by creating a privileged bonded merchant class, called *Hongs,* to deal with the foreigners. In return for this special privilege, the Chinese merchants were held responsible for the good behavior of the foreigners and their payment of taxes to the Chinese government. These merchants were given a monopoly by the Chinese emperor to create thirteen factories on the banks of the Pearl River to conduct all trade with the foreigners.

Western empires have never been content with trade. Their ultimate goal has always been colonies. Trade requires free and equal exchange of goods for goods. Both trading partners benefit. Colonization enables the Western powers to steal by using superior military force. With colonization, the imperial power gets all the benefits at the expense of the colonies. In the case of China, it was the British who first determined to colonize China rather than trade with China. The British had already colonized India and most of Asia and had the world's most powerful navy. Its switch from trade to colonization began in 1839 with what has been called the First Opium War. The British invaded and conquered Guangzhou on March 18, 1841.

After defeating the Chinese empire in the First Opium War in 1842, the British forced China to open four other ports, Shanghai, Xiamen, Fuzhou, and Ningbo. This abolished the Canton system and removed Guangzhou's privileged position. This military defeat also marked the steady military decline of the Qing dynasty and its ability to prevent Western colonization of China.

The American empire joined the British in the illegal drug trade in opium in China. While the British produced their opium in their colony of India, the Americans found their opium in Turkey. American merchant Samuel Shaw first arrived in Guangzhou in 1784 on the infamous *Empress of China.* Shaw joined other foreign merchants in Canton to trade his cargo of ginseng with the Chinese for a handsome profit. Shaw had opened up China for the subsequent lucrative sale of Turkish opium by the American company Russell & Co. to Chinese drug addicts. Russell & Co. began their operations in Guangzhou in 1808. Initially, it sold ginseng, furs, grain, rum, cheese, and opium purchased from the British. But by the 1820s, it was competing fiercely with the British for the more lucrative opium trade by switching from Indian opium to Turkish opium. In 1844, the American empire was able to force China to sign the Unequal Treaty of Wangxia, which granted similar privileges to Americans as the British had forced out of China with its earlier Unequal Treaty of Nanking in 1842.

The Qing dynasty was caught between a rock and a hard place. It was forced by the superior Western militaries to make colonial concessions to the Western powers. But such concessions angered the Chinese people who increasingly rebelled against their emperors. This forced the emperors to ask the foreigners for military aid to quell the rebellions. This further angered their subjects and increased the rebellions. The foreign invaders were only too happy to exploit the civil unrest. The British colonized Hong Kong in 1842, turning the island into a foreign trade hub and financial center, rivaling Macau and Guangzhou. Hong Kong's deepwater port in Victoria Harbour gave Hong Kong a strategic advantage over Macau. It provided a natural port for Guangdong Province. Many Chinese moved from Guangdong Province to Hong Kong to take advantage of the economic opportunities. In many ways, what occurred in Hong Kong after 1842 was replicated in Shenzhen after 1980. Both became magnets for population and economic growth. Both relied heavily on international trade and global finance.

While the easily accessible land border between Mainland Hong Kong and Shenzhen was the driving force behind the location of China's first SEZ in Shenzhen, China had simultaneously planned the economic development of a much larger area of Southern China located in the Pearl River Delta and the province of Guangdong. These were the areas of Southern China that had a long historical trade connection with the West. Hong Kong's natural deepwater port is ideally located in the South China Sea to serve Southern China. The Pearl River Delta refers to the low-lying area where the Pearl River flows into the South China Sea. It includes the Chinese province of Guangdong as well as Hong Kong and Macau. Guangdong's southern border has a long coastline along the South China Sea.

While Hong Kong expanded relative to Macau and Guangzhou, since all three trading hubs were in the Pearl River Delta region, this region experienced enormous economic growth. In the nineteenth century, many Chinese used the port of Canton, now Guangzhou, to migrate to the New World and to other parts of Asia. This established a permanent link between overseas Chinese and Guangdong Province. During the nineteenth century, the Portuguese also captured many Chinese from Guangdong Province and sold them as slaves in the New World. Civil War erupted in Southern China in the 1850s with the *Taiping Rebellion*. It began in Guangdong's neighboring province Guangxi and was led by Hong Xiuquan, who was born in Guangdong. It was the largest uprising against the Qing dynasty. The Chinese empire suffered a second military defeat by the Western imperial powers during the Second Opium War of 1856. In 1894–95, the Japanese empire defeated the Chinese empire in the first Sino-Japanese war.

These military defeats greatly weakened the Qing dynasty and led to its overthrow by the Chinese people in 1911.

As in the Taiping Rebellion, the movement that would successfully overthrow the Qing dynasty began in Southern China. It was led by Dr. Sun Yat-sen, who, like Hong Xiuquan, was born in Guangdong Province. The Xinhai Revolution of 1911 overthrew the Chinese emperor and created the Republic of China, ROC. Dr. Sun Yat-sen was elected as its provisional president on December 29, 1911. Emperor Puyi abdicated on February 12, 1912. China began a period of increased civil unrest and foreign interventions. The same forces that had led to the overthrow of the emperor haunted the new republic. Military invasions and threats from foreign empires combined with civil wars and unrest to keep China in chaos. On the foreign front, the threat from the Japanese empire was seen as more disastrous than the continued threats from the British and American empires. This led the leaders of the ROC to form alliances with the British and Americans against the Japanese. On the domestic front, the leaders of the ROC faced a civil war with the Chinese Communist Party, CCP. Chiang Kai-shek emerged as the leader of the ROC, and Mao Zedong emerged as the leader of the CCP.

After the Second World War, the American empire emerged as the dominant world power, replacing the British Empire. Both Japan and Britain became economic colonies of the American empire. The American empire was on a mission to dominate the world by political and economic colonizations. It did not allow any country their political independence. If a country insisted on political independence, the American empire would invade and colonize it or impose economic and financial embargoes to impoverish it. In an effort to mitigate the economic consequences of defying the American bully, many countries turned to the Soviet Union for help. This is what China did after the CPP had defeated the American ally Chiang Kai-shek. Led by Mao Zedong, China refused to become an economic colony of the American empire as Japan had done. As a result, the American empire isolated China by preventing all of its worldwide economic colonies to do business with China. The irony of this policy is that prior to World War II, the Americans, led then by the British, forced China to be nonisolationist. After the Second World War, the American empire and her many global economic colonies forced China into isolation.

Our analyses focus on the period after the end of the isolation forced on China by the American empire and her economic colonies. As we have explained earlier, the American empire ended its policy of isolating China because it needed China's help to defeat the Soviet Union. Had the American empire not been so impatient, it would have witnessed the collapse of the Soviet Union without the aid of China. China may have been impoverished to the point where it may have agreed to become an economic colony of the American empire like Japan, South Korea, Taiwan, Canada, Australia, New Zealand, Britain, France, Germany, Italy, Spain, Portugal, Ireland, Greece, Brazil, Argentina, Chile, and many more. Instead, American impatience led to China becoming a new rival to the American empire, which could surpass the earlier rival of the Soviet Union. That is the premise of this book.

We have seen that the Pearl River Delta region had forged economic, financial, and people links with foreign countries for centuries before the Global Shift and the creation of the SEZs. It was this long historical connection of this region with Asia, Europe, and the United States that had led China to establish the first three SEZs, Shenzhen, Shantou, and Zhuhai, in this region. The intention was to unleash the maquiladora forces to enhance the existing dynamism of Hong Kong, Macau, and Guangzhou. The combined effects of the SEZs and the long historical connections with foreign trade led to the region recording double-digit growths in real GDP for several decades after 1980. Together, the entire Pearl River Delta region would drive China's economic growth and unleash Chinese entrepreneurship to challenge American entrepreneurship. At the same time, the area would draw workers from China's vast rural areas to the north. As its economic opportunities grew, so would its population. The largest province within the region is Guangdong. The GDP of Guangdong Province exceeds 10 percent of China's total GDP.

Today, the Pearl River Delta region is the world's largest single urban area both in geographic size and in population. Its population of seventy million far exceeds that of the whole of Canada. Exports from this region account for over 40 percent of China's total exports. Most of the businesses in Hong Kong have branches in this region today. In addition to the cities of Guangzhou, Shenzhen, Hong Kong, and Macau, there are two other major cities, *Foshan* and *Dongguan,* with populations close to eight million. Foshan is an important manufacturing center about sixteen miles southwest of Guangzhou. The Foshan Hi-Tech Development Zone was established in 1992. It has attracted massive amounts of foreign investment, much of it from Taiwan. Dongguan is on the southern border of Guangzhou and the northern border of Shenzhen. It is strategically located within short distances from Hong Kong, Macau, Shenzhen, and Guangzhou. Other cities within the region include Zhuhai, Zhongshan, and Jiangmen to the south of Guangzhou, Huizhou to the east of Guangzhou, and Zhaoqing to the west of Guangzhou. Their populations range from a high of five million for Huizhou and Jiangmen to four million for Zhongshan and Zhaoqing with Zhuhai being the least populous at two million.

The Xiamen SEZ, Fujian Province, and Taiwan

In establishing the first four SEZs, China targeted not only Hong Kong, Macau, and Canton but also Taiwan and Canton's neighboring province of Fujian. The Portuguese empire had opened its colony of Macau to the world, and the British Empire had done likewise with its colony of Hong Kong. The American empire had followed suit with its *uncolony* of Taiwan. All three of these colonies of Western empires were to be returned to China. China decided to use these three Western colonies to introduce its unique brand of capitalism with Chinese characteristics.

The SEZ of Xiamen in Fujian Province looks across to the island of Kinmen, which is part of the state of Taiwan. The island is just a few miles from China and claimed by China as part of Fujian Province. It is still claimed by both China and Taiwan. The island of Taiwan is separated from Fujian Province in China by the Taiwan Strait, which is about one hundred miles wide and is part of the South China Sea. China has laid claim to the entire South China Sea, despite objections by the American empire. Looking at a map of Southern China, you can see all four of China's initial SEZs stretching along the coastline of Southern China from Zhuhai on the left to Xiamen on the right. They form an arc with easy access to the South China and East China Seas, and to the Pacific Ocean. The area is ideally located to transport goods manufactured on the Chinese mainland, to Macau, Hong Kong, Taiwan, South Korea, Japan, and the United States. These would be the countries that would build the factories in China and buy the goods produced in those factories. The goods are shipped by sea using containers to reduce transportation cost.

The Xiamen SEZ was established in Xiamen City, Fujian Province, in October 1980. Its deepwater port is ice-free all year. Portuguese and other European imperial powers first visited Xiamen in 1541. During the First Opium War, the British captured the city on August 26, 1841. Its port was one of the four treaty ports forcibly opened by the British after China was defeated in the First Opium War in 1842. It therefore has a long history of foreign trade and European influence. It also has a long history as a tourist destination. The city and its surrounding area also have a long historical connection with Chinese who migrated to Taiwan and many countries in Southeast Asia, including Singapore, Malaysia, and Indonesia. These overseas Chinese never severed their historical connections and financial support for their homeland. One of the reasons for choosing Xiamen as one of the four original SEZs was to attract investments from these overseas Chinese with strong historical ties to Xiamen. The area of the SEZ was expanded in 1984 from Xiamen city to include all of Xiamen Island.

After the Dutch colonized Taiwan in the seventeenth century, many Chinese migrated from Guangdong and Fujian Provinces across the Taiwan Strait to Taiwan. China defeated the Dutch in 1662 and colonized Taiwan. The Japanese empire defeated the Chinese in 1895 and colonized Taiwan. When Japan was defeated in the Second World War, Taiwan was returned to China. When Mao Zedong defeated Chiang Kai-shek in the Chinese Civil War, Chiang fled to Taiwan and renamed it the Republic of China, ROC. During the Cold War, Taiwan became an economic colony of the American empire. As one of the four Asian Tigers, along with Hong Kong, Singapore, and South Korea, it experienced high rates of economic growth.

In many ways, the creation of the SEZs by China in 1980 came at an opportune time for Taiwan as it did for Hong Kong. Hong Kong's colonization by Britain had helped to produce its high rates of economic growth as an Asian Tiger. In much the same way, Taiwan's high rate of economic growth as another Asian Tiger was largely due to its special relationship with the American empire. But both of these relatively small Asian economies were facing greater competition during the 1980s. Taiwan's specialization on relatively small- and medium-size businesses placed it at a competitive disadvantage with countries such as Japan and South Korea. Just as Hong Kong entrepreneurs rushed to offset that increased competition by expanding into the Chinese SEZ in Shenzhen, the Taiwan entrepreneurs rushed to offset their increased competition by expanding into the Xiamen SEZ.

There was one important difference between Hong Kong and
Taiwan. Unlike Hong Kong, which was to be returned to China for
sure, it was unclear if Taiwan would be returned to China. As a result,
Taiwan's government was not willing initially to permit Taiwan's
entrepreneurs to legally invest in the Xiamen SEZ. The initial foreign
investors were primarily from Hong Kong and Macau. Nevertheless,
many Taiwan entrepreneurs invested indirectly via Hong Kong or other
third parties because of the expectation of high profits. In addition,
Taiwan had a population about three times as large as Hong Kong.
Government restrictions on Taiwan's investments in Xiamen were
gradually eroded. In 1989, the Taiwan Investment Zone and the Taiwan
Merchants Development Zone were established in Xiamen. Taiwan's
investments in Xiamen skyrocketed, targeting industries such as textiles,
chemicals, fisheries, real estate, and tourism. Most of the output was for
exports using Taiwan's long-established marketing networks.

In 2001, China established commercial, mail, and ferry links
between the Xiamen SEZ and Taiwan. Flights and travel followed. An
international airport was built in 1983. Xiamen attracts tourists from
Hong Kong and Macau as well as Taiwan. China is Taiwan's largest
trading partner and increasing as the two economies become more and
more integrated. In June 2010, China and Taiwan signed an Economic
Cooperation Framework Agreement, ECFA. As with Hong Kong,
Taiwan's increasing integration with China has enabled its economy to
shift from producing goods to producing services. As China's domestic
market grows, Taiwan's entrepreneurs have an additional incentive to
expand investments in Xiamen. Xiamen's population is twice as large
as that of Zhuhai. If we ranked the size of the four SEZs by population,
it would be twelve million for Shenzhen, six million for Shantou, four
million for Xiamen, and two million for Zhuhai.

Hainan, Guangxi, and all of Southern China

This first of two chapters on China deals exclusively with *Southern
China*. Since it's difficult to identify exactly what area constitutes
Southern China, we take it to mean the provinces/autonomous regions of
Guangdong, Fujian, Guangxi, and Hainan Island, as well as the special
administrative regions, SARs, of Hong Kong and Macau. The population

of this area was over two hundred million in 2018. More than half of that population was in Guangdong Province. Fujian and Guangxi had populations of about forty million and fifty million, respectively. Hong Kong and Hainan Island had populations of about ten million each. Macau's population was under one million. Historically, Northern China was more developed than Southern China. The Mongol invasions led to Chinese migration from Northern China to Southern China. This begun a gradual shift of economic and political power from north to south. But it was the Global Shift, beginning with the creation of the SEZs in 1980, that has made Southern China more economically developed than Northern China. We have documented the effect of the four initial SEZs on Guangdong, Fujian, Macau, and Hong Kong, where most of the economic development of Southern China took place. We will now address China's fifth SEZ, Hainan Island, and the Guangxi Zhuang Autonomous Region. We begin with Hainan Island.

Hainan Island is the most southern province in China. It became a province only in 1988, the year it also became China's fifth SEZ. Prior to 1988, it was part of the province of Guangdong. Creating the fifth SEZ in Hainan Island is consistent with our explanation that capitalism with Chinese characteristics is best interpreted to mean that China implemented a free enterprise system first in Southern China before moving other *geographic* parts of the country from centrally planned areas to free enterprise areas.

The province of Hainan Island is made up of several islands in the South China Sea. Like the islands that make up a large part of the Hong Kong SAR, Hainan Province is not on the mainland. Unlike the Hong Kong SAR, which has a large part on the mainland, no part of Hainan Province is on the mainland. It further differs from Hong Kong SAR in that whereas Hong Kong Island is only a small portion of the total area of Hong Kong SAR, the island of Hainan Island is a much larger portion, 97 percent, of the Province of Hainan Island. In terms of area, it is the largest of the first five SEZs created by China. As an island with 1,500 kilometers of coastline, it has many ports providing easy access to water transportation for exports to Hong Kong, Taiwan, South Korea, Japan, and further away. Its total population is similar to that of Hong Kong SAR. In addition to completing China's goal of creating a mixed economy by making Southern China capitalist before "capitalizing" other parts of China, developing Hainan Island is consistent with another goal of China, which is its claim to all of the South China Sea.

Prior to its creation as an SEZ, Hainan specialized on agriculture, minerals, and tourism. While the intent of making it an SEZ was to attract investment in manufacturing, China did not lose sight of its tourism potential. Its tropical climate and many white sand beaches are used to portray the province as China's *Hawaii.* In addition, the province is expanding its mineral, agricultural, pearl breeding, and fisheries output.

The Guangxi Zhuang Autonomous Region borders the South China Sea as well as the province of Guangdong. While Fujian Province is to the east of Guangdong, Guangxi is to the west of Guangdong. While not as developed as its northeastern neighbor, the history of Guangxi has long been tied to the history of Guangdong. China's decision to open all of Southern China to the Global Shift has once again tied the development of Guangxi with that of Guangdong. Just as Fujian provides a southern link to Taiwan, Guangxi provides a western link to Vietnam, which is on its southwestern border.

Guangxi became a part of China during the Qin dynasty, 221–206 BCE. During the Tang dynasty, it was integrated with Guangdong in 627, with Guangxi being the western half of the Lingnan Circuit and Guangdong being the eastern half of the Lingnan Circuit. The name Guangxi is traced to the Song dynasty, 960–1279. After the defeat of the Song dynasty by the Mongols in 1279, Guangxi became a province. Under the PRC, Guangxi Province became an autonomous region for its indigenous Zhuang ethnic population in 1958. Over 90 percent of China's eighteen million Zhuang people live in Guangxi.

China's Global Shift came to Guangxi later than Guangdong. As we explained, China's initial SEZs were located in Guangdong and Fujian Provinces in 1980. But this Global Shift expanded to Hainan Island and Guangxi only a few years later. In 1985, Guangxi was declared an open economic zone. As we saw above, Hainan Island became an SEZ in 1988. Like Hainan Island, the city of Beihai in Guangxi was also a major tourist destination for Chinese and foreign tourists before China's Global Shift. Beihai is a seaside resort adjacent to the South China Sea. After China's Global Shift, it became the fastest-growing city in the world. Beihai was one of fourteen coastal cities identified as SEZs in 1984. This is only four years after China's first four SEZs were created. In 1992, Beihai's famous white-sand Silver Beach, six miles from the city, was designated a free economic zone as "Beihai Silver Beach National Tourist Holiday Resort." Like Hainan Island, Beihai also has a thriving natural pearl-breeding industry. The Beihai Export Processing Zone was created in 2003. The city of Guilin is also a huge tourist attraction. Its beautiful scenery and famous Li Jiang River draw painters from all over the world. It was also the capital of Guangxi before Nanning. The Guilin National Hi-Tech Industrial Development Zone was created in 1988. It specializes in electronics.

Guangxi has become a manufacturing hub producing cars, steel, and nonferrous metals such as tin and manganese. In addition, Guangxi has a large and growing primary products sector specializing in star anise, rice, sugar cane, tobacco, and peanuts. It produces 85 percent of the world's output of star anise. During the years 1999–2001, Guangxi's GDP grew at an annual rate of 30 percent. In 1999, China began to increase its focus on China's Western region. This region includes Guangxi, in addition to five other autonomous regions, six provinces, and the city of Chongqing. The region as a whole accounts for over 70 percent of China's area. As part of this "Western development" strategy, the Beibu Gulf Economic Zone was created in 2006. The Beibu Gulf Economic Rim is on the southern border of Guangxi with Vietnam and the Gulf of Tonkin. The region includes Guangxi, Vietnam, Guangdong, and Hainan Island. It connects China to the Association of Southeast Asian Nations, ASEAN, economies, via its close border with Vietnam. It's part of China's strategy to engage more with the ASEAN nations. In 1997, China, along with Japan and South Korea, became a member of what has been called "ASEAN plus three."

CHAPTER 5

China: The Awakening of the Real Sleeping Giant, 1965–2018 (Part 2: Northern and Western China Maquiladoras)

We have allocated two chapters of this book to China because China is to the Global Shift what the American empire was to the domination of the world by the West. While the Global Shift began in Mexico, and many other countries like India and Russia are important contributors, those other countries are the equivalent of the British and French empires in explaining the dominance of the West after Columbus. Our division of China into southern and northern is based solely on what we have identified as capitalism with Chinese characteristics. As such, our definition of Southern China is a direct result of the geographic beginning of China's move towards a mixed economy. This is the Pearl River Delta region of China. It represents an area much smaller than what is more commonly thought of as Southern China. It also represents a much smaller area than the area of China ruled by the Southern Song dynasty, 1127–1279, when the capital city was Hangzhou. As a result of our definition of Southern China, what we will call Northern China is the much larger area outside our definition of Southern China. This can be misleading, since this much larger area includes areas often designated as Northern China, Central China, Eastern China, and Western China. In the previous chapter, we alluded to this more common definition of Western China by addressing the autonomous region of Guangxi, which we included in our definition of Southern China.

Another clarification we need to address before discussing China's Global Shift in Northern China is the many terms used to define different ways in which China opened up areas of the country to foreign investments. So far, we have used two terms primarily. These terms are SEZ and maquiladora. The term "maquiladora" comes from the original Border Industrialization Program, begun in Mexico in 1965. The term SEZ comes from China's use of that term in 1980 as applied to Shenzhen, Zhuhai, Shantou, and Xiamen. As many authors have pointed out, China's SEZs were similar to export processing zones, EPZs, previously established by Asian countries such as India, Taiwan, South Korea, Singapore, and Malaysia. Since the use of the term "SEZ" in 1980, China has used numerous other terms to identify how it opened other areas of China to foreign investment. These other terms include "EPZ, special investment zone, high-tech development zone, high-tech industrial development zone, free trade zone, economic and technical development zone, high-tech industrial park, tourist holiday resort, coastal development areas," and many more. We will not make much of an effort to explain the ways in which these terms differ. Our goal is to explain the role of China in what we call the Global Shift. As such, we will generalize these terms as Maquiladora programs. As explained before, the key difference of all these Maquiladora-type programs and old-fashioned *Globalization* and Western colonization is that the foreign investments are attracted by cheap labor to build factories in the Third World to produce consumer goods for people in the First World.

The Yangtze River Delta Economic Zone

Once President Nixon's visit to China had given Western countries from South Korea to Canada, the green light to do business with China, China embraced this opportunity with an impatience never witnessed before. Other countries would have waited to see if the Chinese experiment with the four SEZs created in Southern China would work, given that it had never been tried by a Communist regime, but not China. China was burning with impatience and dashed headlong into the unknown. Just two years after creating the four SEZs in Southern China, China opened up a second even larger area to the Global Shift, beginning in 1982. China had no time or desire to take a wait-and-see attitude to the economic and financial opportunities presented to it by the Nixon visit. This impatience to plunge headlong into this abyss was even more amazing given that China was plunging into the unknown on its own terms. It refused to be like Canada, Britain, France, Germany, Japan, or South Korea and many others, all of whom had embraced the American offer to develop their economies, by surrendering their political and military sovereignties. Not China. China agreed to the American offer on condition that it remained a sovereign nation, not an economic colony like Britain, Germany, Japan, Canada, and others. China's impatient plunge into the unknown turned out to be an unimaginable economic, financial, and political success. Far from China trading off its political sovereignty for economic gain as all others had done, China's massive economic success boosted its political independence. As an independent nation state before Nixon's visit, it could be ignored by the powerful American empire as it was puny. But as an economic power house after Nixon's visit it can, and has, challenged the once unchallengeable American empire for world leadership. It was China's impatience in risking everything to plunge into the unknown that enabled it to do in fifty years what others took, and would have taken, at least two hundred years.

China's selection of the Yangtze River Delta Economic Zone, as its second area to plant SEZs, was based on some of the same reasons for beginning with the Pearl River Delta Economic Zone. As we saw in the previous chapter, the Pearl River Delta had a long history of engaging with the world outside China. This was also true of the Yangtze River Delta. What Canton was to the Pearl River Delta, Shanghai was to Yangtze River Delta. The difference, of course, was that the Pearl River Delta was also selected because of its connections to Hong Kong, Macau, and Taiwan. That explains why it was selected before the Yangtze River Delta. But China was impatient, and two large economic zones would grow China much faster than one. There was no time or desire to wait for the outcome of the first zone before proceeding to the second. Instead, a second zone would both imitate and reinforce the success or failure of the first. It was a chance China was willing to take in its burning desire to hasten economic development after decades of stagnation under American-imposed isolation. While the Pearl River Delta concentrated on light industries, the Yangtze River Delta concentrated on heavy industries. In this way, the two zones complemented each other.

While we begin this chapter with the Yangtze River Delta because it was the first to get the SEZs outside what we defined as Southern China, this chapter will look at all of China outside the area we addressed in the previous chapter. The Yangtze River Delta has a larger population, some 125 million in 2018, than the Pearl River Delta. It accounts for over 25 percent of China's total GDP per year. It includes a total of twenty-eight cities, including China's largest city, Shanghai. Shanghai was central to the choice of this area as China's second economic zone just as Guangzhou was central to the choice of the Pearl River Delta.

But the Pearl River Delta had the added advantage of Hong Kong, Macau, and Taiwan. The Yangtze River Delta did not have this extra advantage but pulled in the eastern *coastal* provinces of Zhejiang and Jiangsu, as well as the province of Anhui to the west of Shanghai, to make an economic zone of formidable size. Easy access to the *South China Sea* was a huge consideration in choosing the Pearl River Delta as China's first economic zone. In like manner, easy access to the *East China Sea* was a huge consideration in choosing the Yangtze River Delta as China's second economic zone. While the Pearl River Delta has its southern border as the South China Sea, the Yangtze River Delta has its eastern border as the East China Sea. Easy access to these seas are crucial since the manufactured goods have to be shipped cheaply to the West. It's not surprising that the port of Shanghai became the busiest container port in the world. A second container port, the port of Ningbo, in the Yangtze River Delta, became the fifth-busiest container port in the world. We have already mentioned that the Pearl River Delta has the third- and fourth-busiest container ports in the world. These two massive economic zones are adjacent to each other stretching overland along China's southeastern coastline to form one giant economic zone linked by land and the South and East China Seas. Together they contain four of the five busiest container ports in the world.

The Yangtze River Delta had become China's most populous and economically prosperous area during the latter part of the Tang dynasty, 618–907. Initially, Ningbo was the dominant port of the region, but it was gradually overshadowed by Shanghai during the nineteenth century. During the nineteenth century, the region industrialized, and Shanghai became the leading commercial center throughout the Far East. In 2018, Shanghai is the most populous city in the world, far outpacing Western cities like London, Paris, New York, and Tokyo. It is located in East China in the Yangtze River Delta. The Yangtze River is China's largest and most important river. The Yangtze is the longest river in Asia and the longest river in a single country in the entire world. One-third of China's population live in the river basin. It flows into the East China Sea, thereby providing relatively cheap water transportation for the manufactured goods produced in the current economic zone for the West. It is home to the famous Three Gorges Dam, the largest hydroelectric dam in the world. The dam supplies clean electric power, which reduces pollution caused by burning coal. It increases shipping on the Yangtze River. Most importantly, the dam will reduce floods, which have killed millions over the centuries and destroyed the crops of those who survived. The dam will now protect the industries being developed in the Yangtze River Delta.

Shanghai was one of the five ports forcibly opened by the British after China's defeat in the First Opium War. China remembers this military humiliation by the British as well as the subsequent military humiliation by the American empire. It was an important reason not to become an economic colony of the American empire as Britain has done. Today, China is militarily stronger than the British and is the dominant military power in Asia. In many ways, Shanghai had been forced to become an economic colony of the West after concessions were granted to other Western imperial powers such as the French empire. As an important economic colony of the West, Shanghai naturally flourished much as Taiwan, Hong Kong, Singapore, South Korea, and Japan, later flourished as economic colonies of the West. In fact, when China decided to reassert its independence from the West, Shanghai declined, while the new Western economic colonies in Asia prospered. China was wise to not trade its political independence for economic gain as it now has both. Shanghai, along with the entire Yangtze River Delta, has experienced rates of economic growth far exceeding those of the Western economic colonies in Asia. Of course, Hong Kong is now a part of China, while the other Western economic colonies are at a crossroad in shifting their economic, political and financial alliance increasingly from the West to China.

The Yangtze River Delta Economic Zone became the fastest-growing region of China, even surpassing the Pearl River Delta Economic Zone. Together they became the driving force for transforming China from a centrally planned economy to a capitalist/free enterprise economy with Chinese characteristics. Like the Pearl River Delta, the Yangtze River Delta has attracted foreign investment from Hong Kong, Taiwan, Japan, South Korea, Singapore, and the United States. In the previous chapter, we provided details for the Pearl River Delta Economic Zone. These details included the role of the initial four SEZs created in Guangdong and Fujian, the special role of Hong Kong, Macau, and Taiwan, the role of the SEZ created in Hainan Island, and the role of the autonomous region of Guangxi. In like manner, we now provide similar details for the Yangtze River Delta Economic Zone. The Yangtze River Delta Economic Zone is made up of the Shanghai Municipality and the provinces of Anhui, Jiangsu, and Zhejiang. We begin with the Shanghai Municipality since the ancient city of Shanghai was the key to China's choice of this area to locate its second free enterprise hub to embrace the Global Shift.

The Shanghai Municipality

The Shanghai Municipality is administratively equal to that of a Chinese province. It is surrounded by the East China Sea and the provinces of Jiangsu and Zhejiang. It is conveniently located halfway between the city of Guangzhou in the south, and China's capital city, Beijing, in the north. The city of Shanghai, located within the municipality, is not only China's largest city but also the financial center of China, the equivalent of New York for the United States. It has been the world's fastest-growing city in the last three decades. The Shanghai Stock Exchange is ranked third after London and New York. The Global Shift has turned the Shanghai Municipality into one of the main industrial centers of China and in the world. Like Shenzhen, it symbolizes the twenty-first-century revolution, which will reverse the revolution that began with the discoveries of Columbus and da Gama. The city of Shanghai is the largest of the twenty-eight cities within the Yangtze River Delta Economic Zone. It produces 20 percent of China's output of cars and 15 percent of China's output of electronics.

The Coastal Province of Zhejiang

It was natural for China to add the coastal province of Zhejiang to bolster the opening up of Shanghai to the Global Shift. The manufactured goods had to be transported by sea. Easy access to the sea was crucial in determining where to locate the SEZs. In creating the Pearl River Delta Economic Zone, many coastal areas in Southern China were included. In the case of the Yangtze River Delta Economic Zone, China was extending the coastal areas in Southern China eastward along the coast from the South China Sea to the East China Sea. This entire area stretching from Hainan Island to Shanghai hugs the south and southeastern extremities of China. Check any map of China. Fujian

Province, part of Pearl River Delta Economic Zone, borders the province of Zhejiang. It is the province that links Shanghai seamlessly to the Pearl River Delta. Moving north along the southeast coast of China, you get from Fujian to Zhejiang to Shanghai with a continuous stretch of coastal territory. Including Zhejiang in the Yangtze River Delta Economic Zone not only bridges the Yangtze River Delta Economic Zone with the Pearl River Delta but also adds to the size and economic viability of the economic zone in much the same way that Hainan Island and the autonomous region of Guangxi added to the size of the Pearl River Delta Economic Zone.

As a coastal province, Zhejiang has several ports, the largest of which is Ningbo, the fifth-busiest container port in the world. This means that the Yangtze River Delta Economic Zone contains the world's first- and fifth-busiest container ports in the world, making it competitive with the Pearl River Delta Economic Zone, which contains the second- and third-busiest container ports in the world. The province contains eleven large cities. The important Chinese city of Hangzhou is also located in Zhejiang. Hangzhou became the capital city of China in 1132 during the Southern Song dynasty, 1127–1279. As a result, Hangzhou became an important cultural and commercial city in China, and its international reputation increased significantly. As many Chinese fled from the Mongol invasions of Northern China, the population of Hangzhou grew to two million, making Hangzhou the most populous city in the world at the time. The Mongols conquered the city in 1276. Marco Polo wrote that Hangzhou was greater than any city in the world. The Hangzhou Tourism Commission capitalized on this historical gem to launch the Modern Marco Polo campaign to attract more tourists, in 2013. Many Chinese regard Hangzhou as one of the most beautiful and scenic cities in China. The famous West Lake, located in Hangzhou, is one of the most popular tourist attractions in China. West Lake was designated a UNESCO World Heritage Site.

Hangzhou took advantage of the Global Shift to boost its historical attraction as a tourist destination as well as its strategic location in the Yangtze River Delta, between the port city of Ningbo and Shanghai. Located in the city of Hangzhou today is the Hangzhou Zhejiang National Tourist Holiday Resort. Tourism remains an important engine of economic growth. But the Global Shift is more about manufacturing than tourism. The Hangzhou New and Hi-Tech Industrial Development Zone was established in 1991. This was followed by the Hangzhou

Economic and Technological Development Zone in 1993 and the Hangzhou Export Processing Zone in 2000. Hangzhou has become a major manufacturing hub for China. It is to Zhejiang Province in the Yangtze River Delta what Guangzhou is to Guangdong Province in the Pearl River Delta. Hangzhou is the largest city in Zhejiang Province and the capital city of the province. It is located in the northwestern part of the province at the southern end of the Grand Canal of China. It has experienced rapid economic growth since the creation of the Yangtze River Delta Economic Zone in 1982. It is connected by high-speed trains to Shanghai and provides rail link to fifty other cities in China. It has a population of about eleven million with a total population exceeding twenty-three million in its greater metropolitan area. It is the fourth-largest metropolitan area in China. Its metro system was built in 2012. Hangzhou hosted the eleventh G20 summit in 2016 and will host the Asian games in 2022. Hangzhou is geographically located close to Japan, South Korea, and Taiwan. These are the Asian countries that are building the factories in the Yangtze River Delta Economic Zone.

The Coastal Province of Jiangsu

While the coastal province of Zhejiang both expanded the size of the Yangtze River Delta Economic Zone, outside the Shanghai Municipality, and provided a seamless continuity between the Pearl River Delta Economic Zone and the Yangtze River Delta Economic Zone, the government of China wanted to create an even larger economic zone that would extend northward along the coast from Shanghai. Looking at a map of Southeastern China; you can see how the coastline of the East China Sea moves seamlessly in an arc from Zhejiang Province to Shanghai and north to Jiangsu Province. The southern border of Jiangsu touches both Zhejiang and Shanghai. Initially, Shanghai was part of Jiangsu Province. In 1732, the emperor gave Shanghai exclusive control over collecting customs revenue for the international trade done by the entire province of Jiangsu. This marked the beginning of Shanghai and Jiangsu Province becoming important trading centers for China. In 1854, the Shanghai Municipal Council was created and tasked with managing the many foreign concessions forced on China by the unequal treaties of Nanking and Wanghia. But it was not until 1927 that Shanghai was separated politically from Jiangsu Province by becoming a separate municipality with its own mayor. In China, only four cities, Shanghai, Beijing, Chongqing, and Tianjin, have their own municipal government separate from the provincial government.

The Grand Canal of China cuts through Jiangsu Province from north to south. This made Jiangsu Province a commercial hub for China since the Sui dynasty, 581–618. The Yangtze River also cuts the province to connect with the East China Sea. Jiangsu Province has over six hundred miles of coastline along the Yellow Sea. The Grand Canal links the Yangtze River to the Yellow River. This makes it an enormous coastal area to be included in launching China's second economic zone, to attract foreign factories that would have easy access to sea transportation to Western markets for their output of manufactured goods. Since 2006, Jiangsu has received more foreign direct investment than any other Chinese province. Its GDP is second only to Guangdong Province. It plays host to many of the world's largest exporters of electronics, chemicals, and textiles.

Jiangsu is the fifth most populous province of China. It contains fourteen cities, including major cities such as Nanjing, Yangzhou, Suzhou, and Wuxi. Nanjing, formerly Nanking, served as the capital city of China several times, beginning in 222. This made it the commercial and cultural center of China. Many of these historic cultural sites are preserved and celebrated to this day. Nanjing first became the capital for the Eastern Wu, during the Three Kingdoms period, 211–280. It served as the capital of China again during the Eastern Jin and the Southern dynasties, 317–976. After the defeat of the Mongols, Nanjing became the capital of China again during the Ming dynasty, 1368–1421. Beijing became the capital in 1421, but Nanjing became the capital again under the Republic of China, 1927–1937 and 1945–1949, before moving the capital to Beijing again in 1949. Nanjing is now the capital of Jiangsu Province.

The Inland Province of Anhui

With such a large coastal area, one can reasonably ask why the inland province of Anhui was part of the initial Yangtze River Delta Economic Zone. The province of Anhui is located east of Shanghai, between the coastal provinces of Zhejiang and Jiangsu. Its inclusion in the Yangtze River Delta Economic Zone could be simplistically justified by "adding space for Shanghai to grow." But the Chinese government had more foresight than that. As I said earlier, the Chinese government was impatient. Just as it was willing to take the risk to create two large free enterprise economic zones instead of one, it was signaling from the very beginning that its embrace of the Global Shift would move inland from its origins in the coastal regions.

In our *American Invasions* we explained how the Western European empires of Spain, France, and Britain had begun the conquest of the New World from the coasts reached by their ships. But they had signaled their intent to penetrate and conquer the entire mainland. In like manner, China began its embrace of the Global Shift in the southern coastal areas but signaled its intent to gradually penetrate all of China, moving northward. The province of Anhui was just the beginning. In many ways, this Chinese experiment is similar to the original Global Shift, which began on the Mexican side of the U.S.-Mexico border. While the original BIP program was never intended to move inland, it did. If it had not, its impact on Mexico would have been minimal. In like manner, for China to lead the Global Shift and challenge the American leadership of the world, China's free enterprise economic zones must move further and further inland. Just as Mexico's experiment with the Global Shift was imitated by Brazil and other countries in Latin America, China's experiment with the Global Shift was imitated by India and other countries in Asia.

The inland province of Anhui was selected to indicate China's intent to move inland from the coast because it bordered the coastal provinces of both Zhejiang in the south and Jiangsu in the north, as well as being on the western border of the Shanghai Municipality. It was the inland province ideally located to push the coastal Yangtze River Delta Economic Zone deeper into the heart of China. It added an area of fifty-four thousand square miles and a population of sixty-two million to the economic zone. While the province of Anhui is still much less developed than Shanghai, Zhejiang, and Jiangsu, its inland location is vital to the Yangtze River Delta Economic Zone becoming the key driver of China's plan to move its embrace of free enterprise from its southern and eastern coasts to inland areas of China. Just as the American empire took the eastern coastal English colonies and moved inland across the continent, China will take the Global Shift from its two coastal economic zones across all of China.

Western China and the Megacity of Chongqing

We turn now to China's equivalent of America's development of its Midwest during the nineteenth century. Just as the Yangtze River Delta Economic Zone has its megacity of Shanghai, and the Pearl River Delta Economic Zone has its megacity of Guangzhou, the Western China Economic Zone has led to the creation of China's fourth-largest megacity of *Chongqing*. China's Western region includes the mega cities of Chongqing, Chengdu, and Xian, six provinces, and three autonomous regions. Chongqing has a population of nineteen million. Chengdu has a population of eighteen million, and Xian has a population of nine million. The total population of China's Western region exceeds three hundred million, which is equal to the entire population of the United States.

Western China covers a very large area of China, over 70 percent, but the two Western autonomous regions, making up more than half the total geographical area, are very sparsely populated, accounting for less than 10 percent of the total population of Western China. The two western autonomous regions, Tibet and Xinjiang, are on the western border of China with India, Pakistan, Afghanistan, Kazakhstan, Russia, and Mongolia. To the east of these two autonomous regions, China's western region stretches from the province of Yunnan in the south to the cities of Yumen and Golmud in the north. Yumen is located in the province of Gansu, one of the six provinces included in Western China. Gansu has a population of twenty-seven million. The city of Yumen provides overland transportation by road and rail to China's autonomous region of Xinjiang and further to Kazakhstan. The city also refines the oil produced in the nearby Jiuquan basin, which is piped to the capital city of the province, Lanzhou.

To the southwest of Yumen is the city of Golmud. It's the closest city to the Tibet border. Golmud is in the province of Qinghai, the least populated of the six provinces in Western China. The other three provinces in Western China are Qinghai, Sichuan, and Shaanxi. In the extreme east of China's western region is the city of Chongqing. Chongqing is one of only four autonomous municipalities in all of China. Chongqing is the gateway to Western China. Just as China chose its first SEZ in Shenzhen to develop the Pearl River Delta Economic Zone, it chose the city of Chongqing to begin the development of its equivalent of the American "Wild West," all the way into Tibet and Xinjiang. Most of the economic development in Western China has taken place in the three cities of Chongqing, Chengdu, and Xian. In 2009, these three cities were designated as the West Triangle Economic Zone. We begin by looking at the role played by this more recent major economic zone in pushing China's Global Shift from the coastal areas into the heart of inland China.

The West Triangle Economic Zone

As we saw above, China embraced the Global Shift by creating two massive economic zones, the Pearl River Delta Economic Zone bordering the South China Sea and Yangtze River Delta Economic Zone bordering the East China Sea. But China was not content to sit on its laurels and hope for some kind of trickle-down effect into its hinterland. China would follow the U.S. example and actively open up its inland regions to economic development. The United States had taken control of the English colonies founded on stolen First Nations lands bordering its Atlantic coast. Next, the United States had seized the Spanish colonies founded on stolen First Nations lands bordering its Pacific coast. China's two earliest economic zones bordering its southern and eastern coasts would be the equivalent of the American Atlantic and Pacific growth regions. Just as the United States pushed its economic development into the heart of First Nations territory with canals and railways and white immigrants from Europe, China is pushing the Global Shift into its relatively undeveloped west all the way to the Tibetan highlands. Just as the United States needed the canals and railroads to enable its push westward from the Atlantic Coast, China used the mighty Yangtze River and its mega hydroelectric project, the Three Gorges Dam, to enable its push westward.

The city of Chongqing in Southwest China was chosen by China to begin its push westward from its eastern coast all the way into Tibet. Chongqing has a long history dating back before the fourth century, BCE, when the State of Ba was forced to move its original capital westward from Yicheng in Hubei Province to Chongqing in Sichuan Province. In 1891, Chongqing became the first inland port open to foreign trade. As a result, foreign embassies were established in Chongqing by the British, French, Japanese, Americans, and Germans.

During the Sino-Japanese war of 1937–1945, the Republic of China, led by Chiang Kai-shek, established its capital in Chongqing. In 1997, China merged surrounding areas of the city to create a municipality independent of Sichuan Province. It's one of only four independent municipalities in China, on a par with Beijing, Shanghai, and Tianjin. In conferring this special status on Chongqing, China was signaling its intention to create an inland mega economic zone that could rival the coastal zones of the Pearl River Delta and the Yangtze River Delta. The independent municipality boasted a population of thirty-two million, making it the most populous municipality in China.

In creating economic zones, China has attempted to combine economic growth with other goals. As we saw earlier, one of the additional goals in creating the Pearl River Delta Zone was to integrate Hong Kong, Macau, and Taiwan into China. Likewise, one of the additional goals of the West Triangle Economic Zone was to resettle those who had to be moved to construct the Three Gorges Dam and harness the hydroelectric power created by the dam. The mighty Yangtze River has played a dominant role in China's economy for thousands of years. As with most countries, the people tend to settle along the banks of a mighty river and farm, fish, and develop crafts, art, culture, and industry close to their settlements. The Yangtze was also the key transportation system for inland China. It connected China's major port city, Shanghai, to the interior of China. This is one reason why the Western countries, with concessions in Shanghai, demanded access to an inland port in Chongqing. After the British had defeated China and colonized Canton in 1840, they sailed up the Yangtze River to flaunt their naval prowess. The Americans followed suit in the 1860s. The French joined during the 1880s. Initially, the foreign ships could only navigate as far as Yichang but eventually reached Chongqing by 1890.

The area inhabited by the Chinese on the banks of the Yangtze for thousands of years were subject to devastating floods, which killed thousands and destroyed crops. Modern China was determined to find a way to reduce the devastation from these floods and simultaneously harness the hydroelectric power of the Yangtze. Plans for a dam across the Yangtze began in 1919 with the Republic of China. Devastating floods in 1931, 1934, and 1954 heightened China's determination to build a dam. Construction on the Three Gorges Dam began in 1994. With the completion of the dam in 2012, China had built one of the largest power stations in the world. This would provide the power needed to develop

Chongqing and all of Western China. China had to relocate close to two million residents displaced by the construction of the dam. Most of them were settled in Chongqing. Another five million are expected to relocate voluntarily to Chongqing because of better economic opportunities.

The Three Gorges are known for their spectacular scenery and have long attracted both Chinese and foreign tourists. The dam has given a boost to tourism as it has widened and deepened the river, enabling more and larger cruise boats. The boost in tourism adds to the use of the river for transporting commodities resulting from the creation of the West Triangle Economic Zone. Without the dam, it would have been very difficult to achieve the recent high rates of economic growth in Chongqing and Western China.

The West Triangle Economic Zone was created in 2009 by adding the cities of Chengdu and Xian to Chongqing. This zone is responsible for 40 percent of the total GDP of Western China and is the key to China's push westward. The zone has a population of about 125 million. Chengdu is the capital city of Sichuan Province, one of the six provinces included in China's Western Development Plan. Sichuan Province is located in Southwest China with Chengdu directly east of Chongqing. Adding the city of Chengdu to the municipality of Chongqing to create the West Triangle Economic Zone made sense because of the geography. The Yangtze River connected many of China's major cities beginning with Shanghai at its mouth and flowing westward through Nanjing, Wuhan, Chongqing, and all the way to Qinghai and Tibet. Shanghai is China's largest city with a population of twenty-six million. Wuhan has a population of twelve million, and Nanjing has a population of ten million. The first bridge across the Yangtze was built in Wuhan in 1957. The second bridge was built in Chongqing two years later. Today, there are hundreds of rail and road bridges across the river. Wuhan alone has six bridges as well as a tunnel.

Chengdu is located in the more fertile eastern part of Sichuan Province, thereby linking Eastern Sichuan to the West Triangle Economic Zone. Linking Chongqing with Chengdu helped develop the upper reaches of the Yangtze River. There are easy road and rail linkages. High-speed rail service between Chongqing and Chengdu was added in 2015. Chengdu is the primary rail hub for all of Southwestern China. Its international airport is the busiest in Western China. In 2013, a direct rail link between China and Europe was created when Chengdu was linked to Poland. In 1988, China created a high-tech industrial development zone in Chengdu. This was followed by a Taiwan investment zone in 1992, an economic and technological development zone in February 2000, and an export processing zone in April 2000. The creation of the Chengdu-Chongqing Economic Zone was announced at the first Sichuan-Chongqing High-Level Forum held in 2007. An agreement was signed between the two local governments. The two governments also agreed to cooperate in eco-friendly development of the upper reaches of the Yangtze River.

While Chengdu is world famous as the home of the giant panda, Sichuan is world famous for its uniquely spicy brand of Chinese cuisine. Sichuan Province was the most populous of the twenty-three provinces of China prior to the creation of Chongqing as a separate municipality in 1997. When Deng Xiaoping took over the leadership of China in 1978, he began China's experimentation with a market economy in Sichuan. The province is divided into an economically prosperous half in the east and a much less developed western half, which borders the sparsely populated autonomous region of Tibet and the province of Qinghai. The Yangtze River runs through the province, thereby connecting it to the major cities of Shanghai, Chongqing, Wuhan, and Nanjing. Sichuan has historically been an important agricultural province in China, specializing in rice and wheat. It is also rich in minerals such as iron, natural gas, titanium, cobalt, vanadium, and lithium. The Global Shift has added significant industrial development in both heavy and light industrial products, steel, coal, electronics, cars, and aerospace.

Two years after the creation of the Chengdu-Chongqing Economic Zone, the city of Xian was added to create the West Triangle Economic Zone. While Chengdu is located west of Chongqing, Xian is located north of Chongqing. The West Triangle Economic Zone was therefore pushing China's Global Shift inland, both to the west and to the north. Xian is the third most populous city in Western China, with a population close to ten million. Xian is world famous as the home of the terracotta soldiers. Xian is one of the four ancient capital cities of China. The beginning of the famous Silk Road is also located in Xian. These historical facts have made Xian a world-famous tourist destination and is one of the most popular tourist destinations in China. With the Global Shift, Xian specialized in software production and outsourcing services, an important part of the Global Shift, for which India is far more famous than China. Like Chengdu and Chongqing, Xian established a high-tech industrial development zone in 1991, an economic and technological development zone in 1993, the Xian Software Park in 1998, and the Xian Aerospace Science and technology Zone in 2006.

Xian is the capital city of Shaanxi Province, one of the six provinces of Western China. Shaanxi Province has a population of almost forty million. The province is separated from the autonomous region of Inner Mongolia by the Great Wall of China, another famous tourist destination. Xian is located in the south-central part of the province. The province is China's third-largest producer of coal, oil, and natural gas. The Global Shift led to the creation of the Baoji Hi-Tech Industrial Development Zone, the Shaanxi Export Processing Zone, and the Yangling Agricultural Hi-Tech Industrial Zone within the province.

Tibet, Xinjiang, Inner Mongolia, Yunnan, Gansu, Guizhou, Qinghai, and Ningxia

The provinces of Sichuan and Shaanxi, as well as the municipality of Chongqing, are located in the more developed eastern portion of Western China. They spearhead China's drive to push the Global Shift into its "Wild West." Together, they have a population of 150 million, half the population of Western China. By contrast, the autonomous region of Ningxia has a population of only seven million. The autonomous region of Tibet has an even smaller population of 3.5 million. Apart from the autonomous region of Guangxi, which we covered in our previous chapter on China, the provinces and autonomous regions listed in the title above make up the rest of Western China. If China can succeed in taking the Global Shift to this relatively remote area it would have succeeded in penetrating all of China.

We explained before that China incorporates political and other goals while embracing the Global Shift for economic development. In the case of pushing the Global Shift into this remote region, it was simultaneously protecting its Western borders while dealing with its Western-backed Tibetan leader in exile, the Dalai Lama. During the Cold War, the United States had used the Dalai Lama to help isolate China. The CIA had not only funded the separatist activities of Tibetans, led by the Dalai Lama, against China, but also provided personal funds to maintain the high lifestyle of the exiled Dalai Lama. While maintaining an affluent lifestyle and never criticizing Western warmongering, the West was able to use its powerful propaganda machine to portray the Dalai Lama as a spiritual leader. The Dalai Lama fully embraced this example of Western hypocrisy, taking advantage of every invitation by Western countries to flaunt his fake spirituality. Canada was especially proud of its public support of the Dalai Lama since it had no economic cost at the time China was still a poor country.

Once the United States had decided to cozy up to China to help it fight the Soviet Union, CIA funding to support the sumptuous lifestyle of the Dalai Lama and his separatist activities dried up. As usual, Canada did not put its money where its mouth was but continued to host visits by the Dalai Lama, prior to its prime minister Steven Harper doing a U-turn on chastising China for Western-invented human rights abuses, to embracing China for economic gains from trade and investment. That a country like Canada, originating entirely from stolen First Nations lands, can still have Western support for protecting human rights is a testimony to Western hypocrisy. The final stand against China by the Dalai Lama took place in the year prior to China's hosting of the 2008 Olympic games in Beijing. Many Canadians, Americans, and other Westerners joined with the Dalai Lama in protesting against the games, but in the end, Western governments recognized the economic cost of backing the Dalai Lama. China's efforts in pushing the Global Shift into Tibet will put the final nail in the coffin of the Dalai Lama's pretend spiritual resistance to China and benefit the Tibetan people.

China's claims to Tibet dates back to the Yuan dynasty, 1271–1368. When imperial rule of China ended in 1912, the Republic of China claimed Tibet as an integral part of China. However, the thirteenth Dalai Lama returned from exile in India in 1913 and attempted to rule Tibet as an independent country. That was the beginning of a dispute between China and Tibet that continues to this day. It's similar to the ongoing dispute between China and Taiwan except for a very important difference. Both the ROC and the PRC claimed jurisdiction over Tibet. In the case of Taiwan, however, the government of the ROC, led by Chiang Kai-shek and supported by the United States, fled to Taiwan and governed it as the ROC. While the ROC, the United States, and the Dalai Lama attempted to secure independence for Tibet, they never succeeded. The PRC has increased its control over Tibet as it has over Hong Kong and Macau.

Under the Dalai Lamas, Tibet was ruled as a feudal state like England had been during the Middle Ages. The church and the Monks owned the land, and the people were serfs. While England had removed serfdom, and serfdom had never been practiced in the United States or Canada, these Western countries turned a blind eye to this barbaric type of governance to support the claims of the Dalai Lama because of their intense dislike of Communism and the rule of China by the PRC. But many Han Chinese immigrated into Tibet as the PRC developed the economy of Tibet. What China has done with all its regions where there is a significant non-Han ethnic minority is to give the region a greater degree of autonomy than a province. Tibet is one of five autonomous regions in China. In an autonomous region, the governor of the region is appointed from the ethnic minority population, in this case a Tibetan. In 1959, the fourteenth Dalai Lama fled to India to establish a Tibet government in exile, the Central Tibet Administration. India allowed the Dalai Lama to set up the Central Tibet Administration in Dharamshala, close to the Tibet border. The British had stolen nine thousand square kilometers of Tibetan territory in South Tibet and incorporated it into India when India was a British colony. China and India fought a war in 1962 over this border dispute, but the dispute is still not resolved. Many Tibetans followed the Dalai Lama into Dharamshala, which had a long historical connection with Buddhism. As I said above, the United States and its allies, including Canada, also supported the government in exile because they opposed the PRC government of China and supported the ROC government in Taiwan.

The PRC has built highways that run through Tibet all the way to the borders with India, Pakistan, and Nepal. As part of its strategy to develop Western China, including Tibet, the PRC embarked on several large-scale infrastructure projects including the Qinghai-Tibet Railway. While the primary reason for building this railway was to take the Global Shift all the way to Lhasa, the capital of Tibet, China was using this project to flex its technological muscle to the Western world. It was the British who had inspired the railways built in India. Now, the Chinese were showcasing their railway building prowess with this railway over the most challenging terrain. A railway to Tibet would connect every province and autonomous region of China by rail. Qinghai Province is further west of the West Triangle Economic Zone. The railway would connect Tibet to the West Triangle Economic Zone via Qinghai Province. The first section of the railway from the cities of Xining to Golmud, in Qinghai Province, was completed in 1984. The section from Golmud to Lhasa was far more challenging because of the steep altitude. Technical difficulties associated with building a line through permafrost had to be solved before construction could begin. But these difficulties were resolved for construction to begin in 2001. The line was completed in 2005. It is regarded as one of China's major technological achievement. Tanggula Pass is the world's highest point for any rail line, and Tanggula station is the world's highest railway station. The railway also sets the record for the highest railway tunnel. The trains provide oxygen supplies for every passenger. The Qinghai-Tibet Railway has linked Lhasa to China's major cities, including Shanghai, Beijing, Guangzhou, Chongqing, and Chengdu. But it is intended to link China internationally to countries such as Nepal, India, Pakistan, and Bangladesh. China reached an agreement with Nepal in 2008 to extend the line into Nepal.

Xinjiang Uyghur Autonomous Region

While Tibet has a massive area of 1.228 million square kilometers, Xinjiang has an even larger area of 1.665 million square kilometers. Together, they make up 30 percent of the total area of China. However, they are both sparsely populated. Nevertheless, these relatively remote border regions of China are strategically important to China's national integrity. Xinjiang borders the countries of India, Russia, Pakistan, Afghanistan, Kazakhstan, Kyrgyzstan, Tajikistan, and Mongolia. We saw above that China and India have an ongoing border dispute over a portion of Tibet. In like manner, China and the Soviet Union had a border dispute over a portion of Xinjiang, which led to military conflict in 1969. The Soviet Union had previously invaded Xinjiang in 1934. The Soviet Union had also supported the Uyghur movement for an independent state in Southern Xinjiang. In addition to these border concerns, both Tibet and Xinjiang have ethnic minorities willing to use protests and violent means to secure independence from China. In Tibet, it's the ethnic Tibetans. In Xinjiang, it's the ethnic Muslim Uyghurs. These are some of the noneconomic reasons for China wanting to push the Global Shift into this underdeveloped, sparsely populated western region.

China has a long history with Xinjiang, dating back to the documentation of the trade in jade in 645 BCE. The nomads of Xinjiang sold jade to China. This area was accessible by the Silk Road. The Han dynasty, 206 BCE–220 CE, sent military expeditions into Xinjiang. During the eighth century, the Uyghur Khanate invaded Northern Xinjiang and captured it. The Uyghurs had previously revolted against the Turkic khanate and allied with China. China used this alliance against an invasion by the Tibetan empire in the eighth century. The Uyghur khan, Bayanchur, married the daughter of the Chinese emperor. The Uyghur khanate prospered under the rule of Bayanchur's son, who continued the alliance with the Tang dynasty. Uyghurs living in Tang China were given special privileges. The Turks brought Islam to Xinjiang during the ninth century. The Qing dynasty created the province of Xinjiang in 1884. The province was made an autonomous region in 1955 to recognize its Uyghur ethnic minority, formally the Xinjiang Uyghur Autonomous Region. The Uyghurs make up over 40 percent of the total population.

Xinjiang is well endowed with oil, natural gas, coal, and minerals. It produces many farm products such as wheat, rice, maize, cotton, fruits, and raisins. There is significant fishing in its lakes and rivers. Its primary livestock is sheep. The Global Shift has established free trade and technology zones. Most of its trade is with neighboring Kazakhstan. There are several economic and technological economic zones. The Urumqi New and Hi-Tech Industrial Development Zone was established in the capital city in 1992. Han Chinese entrepreneurs have moved into Xinjiang to take advantage of the business opportunities provided by the Global Shift.

Xinjiang is geographically split into two parts by the Tian Mountains. The Tarim Basin in the south is where the majority Muslim Uyghur people would like to create a separate state, East Turkestan. This is the lesser developed part of Xinjiang. After the Global Shift, many Uyghurs migrated to the cities, especially the capital city, in search of better jobs. In general, Han Chinese have higher-paying jobs than Uyghurs. Since the West created Islamic "terrorism" by their incessant bombing of Muslim countries in the Middle East, China has come under attack by Uyghur Muslims who want a separate "Islamic" state in southern Xinjiang. There was an attempted suicide bombing of a China Southern Airlines flight in 2008. Another attack killed sixteen police officers in Xinjiang just four days before the Beijing Olympics. There have been many more attacks, bombings, riots, and protests since 2008. The rebels have recently been supported by the Western-created Al-Qaeda and ISIL jihadi movements fighting Western bombings of Middle East and African Muslim countries.

The Provinces of Yunnan, Guizhou, and Gansu

Within the geographical vicinity of the West Triangle Economic Zone lies three large Western provinces that are an important part of China's Western Development Strategy. Yunnan is the most populous of these three Western provinces with a population of fifty million. It lies south of Sichuan Province. Guizhou has a population of forty million and lies south of Chongqing. Gansu has a population of thirty million and lies north of Chengdu. These are the more immediate areas that the Global Shift will reach from the West Triangle Economic Zone. We now look at their potential, beginning with the most populous province and the southern limit of Western China.

The province of Yunnan is strategically located to be reached by the West Triangle Economic Zone, as it moves southward, and also by the Pearl River Delta Economic Zone, as it moves westward across Guangxi Autonomous Region. We included the Guangxi Autonomous Region in Pearl River Delta Economic Zone, but the Guangxi Autonomous Region is included in China's Western Development Strategy. In this way, the Guangxi Autonomous Region and neighboring Yunnan Province links China's first economic zone with its later West Triangle Economic Zone. We explained above how the Pearl River Delta Economic Zone was linked to the Yangtze River Delta Economic Zone through the provinces of Fujian and Zhejiang. Now we see that all three of these massive economic zones are linked to take the Global Shift into all of China.

The province of Yunnan is also important in protecting China's borders with Vietnam, Laos, and Myanmar. Yunnan also borders the important Tibet Autonomous Region. It can therefore help China's goal of developing Tibet. More importantly, it's the gateway for China to increase trade and investment links with Southeast Asia and ASEAN. Initially, China embraced the Global Shift mostly for economic advantage. But the Global Shift has been far more successful economically than any could have imagined. We have compared the magnitude of its global effect with the rediscovery of the New World by Columbus. The United States, belatedly and reluctantly, was awoken to this global revolution by candidate Donald Trump. But President Trump has great difficulty convincing the American media and American politicians of this new reality. Just as the British initially referred to the American empire derogatively as a "puny empire," so too establishment leaders in the West misunderstand what they derogatively refer to as "populist" politicians. Many in the West are rightly concerned about the economic and political effects of the Global Shift, but traditional leaders and the mainstream media are totally oblivious of the new reality.

This brings us to the importance of Yunnan being a strategic province for China to flex its economic, political, and military muscle within ASEAN. China is no longer content with using the Global Shift to reduce poverty in China. Since the Global Shift has made it the largest economy in Asia, China is determined to lead Asia in the twenty-first century. Just as the United States decided to lead the New World after the Monroe Doctrine, China decided to lead Asia after overtaking Japan as Asia's largest economy. As part of this strategy to lead Asia, China wants influence in ASEAN, and Yunnan Province is its geographical gateway. The Burma Road was built by China during its war with Japan in 1937. It connects China with Myanmar through Chongqing and the capital city of Yunnan, Kunming. Today, there is an expressway between Kunming and Bangkok. The French had connected Yunnan to Vietnam since 1905. Today, many of the neighboring countries in Southeast Asia, all members of ASEAN, are linked by rail to Yunnan.

ASEAN began modestly in 1967 with five members, Indonesia, Singapore, Malaysia, Thailand, and the Philippines. Apart from the tiny island state of Singapore, they were all relatively poor developing countries. The French Indo-China colonies of Vietnam, Laos and Cambodia, joined ASEAN after the Vietnam War. By 1999, ASEAN had ten members, including Myanmar and Brunei. During the first two decades of the twenty-first century, ASEAN has seen rapid economic growth with a combined GDP today almost as large as that of Japan. In 2000, China initiated talks with ASEAN to create a free trade area, ACFTA. After a decade, ACFTA became a reality in 2010. This free trade area has the largest population of all FTAs in the world. It is the third largest, after the European Union and NAFTA, in terms of volume of trade. Before and after the creation of ACFTA, China's investments in ASEAN were an important contributor to the economic growth of ASEAN. These Chinese investments took place through what has been called the *Bamboo Network*. These are Chinese entrepreneurs who have family ties in the ASEAN

countries. Many Chinese had immigrated into the ASEAN countries
during British and French colonizations. These "overseas Chinese" had
established businesses throughout the region and have played an important
role in connecting with China after the Global Shift.

The Global Shift brought economic development to Yunnan,
which had previously been a relatively poor province of China. It was
rich in minerals such as lead, aluminum, zinc, tin, copper, cadmium,
coal, gold, silver, iron, and nickel. But it was a mountainous region with
little economic development. Agricultural products include rice, tobacco,
cotton, sugarcane, wheat, corn, mushrooms, and tea. Tobacco is its main
agricultural export crop. Manufacturing came with the Global Shift as
well as dairy products and a thriving flower production industry. Several
economic zones have been established in Kunming. In 1992, the Kunming
Economic and Technological Development Zone and the Kunming High-
Tech Industrial Development Zone were created. Other economic zones
in Kunming include the Kunming Airport Economic Zone and the
Kunming Tourism Zone. Economic zones were established in other cities
such as Qujing, Yuxi, Dali, and Chuxiong. The Ruili Border Trade Zone
and the Wanding Border Zone were set up to boost trade with Myanmar.
Myanmar is Yunnan's largest trading partner. Likewise, the Hekou Border
Zone was set up to boost trade with Vietnam.

While Yunnan links Southern China with the West Triangle
Economic Zone, the province of Guizhou, northeast of Yunnan, pushes
the economic boom of Southern China, begun by the Pearl River Delta
Economic Zone, north toward Sichuan Province and the two large
Chinese cities of Chongqing and Chengdu. Like Yunnan, Guizhou was
a relatively poor mountainous province of China before the Global Shift.
Like Yunnan, it was dependent on minerals, agriculture, and forestry.
Minerals include coal, gold, iron, and lead. Its primary agricultural
product is tobacco. The Global Shift led to the establishment of the
Guiyang Economic and Technological Development Zone in its capital
city in 2000. It has rail connection to all of China's major cities including
high-speed rail to Chongqing and Guangzhou.

Gansu is another of China's poor provinces that is now being
developed by the Global Shift. Located north of the West Triangle
Economic Zone, it is pushing the Global Shift north of the West Triangle
Economic Zone into the autonomous regions of Ningxia and Inner
Mongolia. Prior to the Global Shift, Gansu was also heavily dependent
on minerals and agriculture. Agricultural crops include wheat, cotton,

melons, maize, and linseed oil. Minerals include rare earth, cadmium, chromium, coal, oil, copper, iron, nickel, cobalt, and lead. The province is home to one of the most popular Great Wall tourist attractions, the Jiayuguan Pass, built by the Ming dynasty in the fourteenth century. The Global Shift established the Technological Development Zone in its capital city, Lanzhou, in 1993. In 1998, the High-Tech Industrial Development Zone was added.

Qinghai, Inner Mongolia, and Ningxia

Qinghai is the Western province that links the West Triangle Economic Zone to Tibet and Xinjiang. Like Tibet, it is sparsely populated, a mere seven million inhabitants. But it covers a very large geographical area, 720,000 square kilometers. As we explained earlier, its capital city, Xining, was an important link for the railway to Tibet. As with all other provinces and autonomous regions, the Global Shift to Qinghai meant locating economic zones in the capital. The Xining Economic and Technological Development Zone was established in 2000. Its primary industries are steel, oil, natural gas, iron, salt, and tourism.

Inner Mongolia also has autonomous region status because of its ethnic minority Mongol population. Taking the Global Shift to Inner Mongolia serves to develop and protect China's border with Mongolia and Russia in China's far north. It covers an even larger area than Qinghai, 1.18 million square kilometers. Xinjiang, Tibet, Inner Mongolia, and Qinghai are ranked first, second, third, and fourth in China in terms of geographical area. They are all located in Western China. Prior to the Global Shift, Inner Mongolia depended on herding goats, reindeer, and sheep as well as forestry, minerals such as coal, rare earth, and natural gas. Agricultural crops included wheat and grapes. With the Global Shift, Inner Mongolia has established several economic zones in its capital city, Hohhot, and in other areas. It has added a thriving manufacturing sector based on its natural resources as well as construction, chemicals, and equipment production. The tourism sector has also grown. Since the Global Shift, Inner Mongolia has experienced annual economic growth exceeding 10 percent.

The last of the twelve provinces, autonomous regions, and independent municipalities making up Western China is the autonomous region of

Ningxia. Like Tibet and Xinjiang, it has autonomous region status because of its ethnic minority Hui population. This status was granted in 1958. It borders Inner Mongolia in the north, Gansu in the south, and Shaanxi in the east. Prior to the Global Shift, Ningxia was famous for its production of wolfberries. The Yinchuan Economic and Technological Zone was established in its capital city in 1992. The major manufacturing industries created by the Global Shift include machinery and equipment, steel, and chemicals. Wine production has also been expanded.

Northern China, Beijing, and the Bohai Economic Rim

This section completes our analysis of the Global Shift in China. China is the largest economy leading the Global Shift. It's the equivalent of the American empire leading the West. In the next chapter, we will analyze the Global Shift in India. India is the second-largest economy transformed by the Global Shift. As we saw in the previous chapter, China's Global Shift began in the South. It was centered on the South China Sea, Guangdong Province, Hong Kong, Taiwan, and Macau. It created a new city in Shenzhen and incorporated China's third-largest city, Guangzhou. In this chapter, we began with the Global Shift moving to Central China. This second region was centered on the East China Sea and China's largest city, Shanghai. Next, we analyzed the Global Shift in Western China. This region moved the Global Shift inland, creating China's fourth-largest city, Chongqing, harnessing the powers of the mighty Yangtze River and pushing the Global Shift into Tibet and to the remotest borders of Western China. Here we complete the circle by analyzing the Global Shift in China's capital city, Beijing, and areas north of the Yellow River. The Yellow River flows into the Bohai Sea. While the Global Shift in China is very confusing, involving hundreds of different kinds of economic zones, free trade zones, high-tech zones, tourist zones, border zones, and special zones, it can be simplified by thinking in terms of four large connected regions. The Pearl River Delta region is in the *south*. The Yangtze River Delta is in the *center*. The West Triangle Zone is in the *west*, and the Bohai Economic Rim, including Jingjinji, is in the *north.* The Yangtze River Delta borders both the West Triangle Zone and the Bohai Rim Zone.

Beijing-Tianjin-Hebei: Jing-Jin-Ji

China's Global Shift into Beijing and north of the capital city is centered on the creation of a megacity that combines the two large cities Beijing and Tianjin as well as the surrounding province of Hebei. The word *Jingjinji* combines the "jing" in Beijing, the "jin" in Tianjin, and the "ji" from the old name for Hebei, Ji. As we saw above, China has always attempted to combine other goals with the economics of the Global Shift. In this northern region, China is attempting to combine the economic advantages of the Global Shift with an innovative way of addressing the worldwide problem of congestion in capital cities such as London, Paris, Tokyo, Mexico City, Beijing, and elsewhere. The United States and Canada, for example, resolved this problem by establishing their capitals outside a major city. Brazil and the Philippines, for example, attempted to resolve their capital city congestion by creating new capitals. London, for example, attempts a solution by banning cars from the inner city. All of these solutions have downsides. What China is attempting is expanding the area of the capital outward to increase significantly its total geographical area. Beijing Municipality has a total area of 16,411 square kilometers. Tianjin Municipality has a total area of 11,760 square kilometers. Hebei Province has a total area of 187,700 square kilometers. The municipalities of Beijing and Tianjin were carved out of the province of Hebei.

This novel experiment by China is still in its infancy. It will connect the port city of Tianjin, which is basic to the Global Shift, to the inland city of Beijing and by high-speed rail to several other cities in the surrounding areas, mostly in the province of Hebei. Beijing is China's second-largest city with a population of nineteen million. Tianjin has a population of thirteen million. Large cities in Hebei with populations of eight million or more include Baoding, Shijiazhuang, Handan, Tangshan, Cangzhou, and Xingtai. Other large cities include Dalian, Qingdao, Qinhuangdao, Dandong, and Shenyang. This planned megacity is expected to have a population of 130 million. While the key focus of this megacity is to complete the Global Shift throughout China, the hope is that it will relieve the pressure on the capital that the Global Shift inevitably brought. Beijing was a densely populated city before the Global Shift. One can argue that an economy five times its pre–Global Shift size requires a capital city five times as large.

Hebei Province

The name Hebei means "north of the Yellow River," the traditional separation of north and south China. To the south of Heibei are the provinces of Henan and Shandong, which link the Bohai Rim Zone with the Yangtze River Delta. To the west of Hebei is Shanxi Province, which links the Bohai Rim Zone with the West Triangle Zone. To the east of Hebei is the Bohai Sea. Easy and cheap access to the sea is key to locating all the economic zones. The economic zones established in Hebei as a result of the Global Shift include the Baoding Hi-Tech Industrial Development Zone in the largest city, the Shijiazhuang Hi-Tech Industrial Development Zone in the capital city, the export processing zones in Langfang and Qinhuangdao, and the economic and technological zone in Qinhuangdao. Hebei is connected by rail to all the major cities in China and by high-speed rail to China's three largest cities, Shanghai, Beijing, and Guangzhou.

Tianjin, Dalian, and Northeast China

Tianjin is the fifth-largest city in China. As a port city, it is ideally located on the west coast of the Bohai Gulf to benefit from the Global Shift. The Global Shift led to the creation of China's seventh-largest container port in Tianjin. This has made Tianjin the gateway to Beijing on its northern border. Since it is surrounded by Hebei Province, it is also the gateway to the megacity of Jingjinji. Historically, its location at the northern end of the Grand Canal was significant in linking the Yellow and Yangtze Rivers with the Grand Canal. It became one of China's treaty ports in 1860 when China was forced to open ports to the West after China lost the Opium Wars.

The Global Shift established numerous economic zones in Tianjin, including the Tianjin Port Free Trade Zone, the Tianjin Export Processing Zone, the Tianjin Economic and Technological Development Zone, the Tianjin Airport International Zone, and the Tianjin Marine Zone. Tianjin experienced rates of economic growth exceeding 10 percent annually after the Global Shift. Its manufacturing sector has become the driving force of this rapid growth and now accounts for over half its total GDP. The more recently created Tianjin-Binhai Economic Zone, where the Port of Tianjin is located, is intended to make Tianjin the gateway to all of northern China. Tianjin is the largest port in Northern China. Since 2007, Tianjin has alternated with Dalian to host the Summer Davos, referred to as the Annual Meeting of New Champions of the Word Economic Forum. As host of this world event, Tianjin has attracted even more foreign investments.

Dalian is a port city on the southern tip of the Liaodong Peninsula, ideally located for access to both the Bohai Sea and the Yellow Sea. It lies directly east across the Bohai Sea from Tianjin. It serves as an ideal complement to Tianjin in providing access to sea transportation for the increased output of Northern China resulting from the Global Shift. It is also the second-largest city in the province of Liaoning, with a population of seven million. Liaoning Province is northeast of Beijing, hugging the eastern coast of China. It was occupied by the British between 1858 and 1885. The entire Liaodong Peninsula was ceded to Japan in 1895 after China's defeat in the first Sino-Japanese War. Russia intervened in 1898, built a modern port in Dalian, and linked Dalian to China's northern city of Harbin by rail. This linked China to Russia's Trans-Siberian railway. Russia lost the port city to Japan in 1905 after the Russo-Japanese War. Japan modernized the port. The city was returned to China in 1950.

Dalian was designated a special economic zone in 1984. Economic zones include the Dalian Free Trade Zone, the Dalian Export Processing Zone, the Dalian Economic and Technological Development Zone, and the Dalian Hi-Tech Industrial Zone. Foreign investments poured in from Japan, South Korea, Europe, and the United States. GDP increased annually by 10 percent or more after 1992 as a result of the Global Shift. Like Tianjin, cohosting the Summer Davos since 2007 has led to even more foreign investments. China has taken advantage of the rail link to its north and Russia, first initiated during the coerced lease of the port to Russia in 1898. The Russians built the Chinese Eastern Railway linking Dalian north to Beijing, Shenyang, Changchun, and Harbin, and then west across the Russian border to Siberia and east across the Russian border to the Russian port of Vladivostok. Since the Global Shift, China has linked Dalian by rail and expressways to the city of Shenyang, which is the capital of Liaoning Province. This is part of China's plan to push the Global Shift into Northeast China with its Northeast Area Revitalization Plan. This plan was first announced in 2003 but did not gain traction until a lead group was established in 2009.

Shenyang will act as the central hub of this push of the Global Shift into China's northeast provinces of Liaoning, Jilin, and Heilongjiang. Shenyang is the largest city in Northeast China with a population of eight million. Shenyang had served as the capital of China during the Manchu dynasty. It became an important rail hub city after the Russians built the Chinese Eastern Railway. Shenyang is also well linked by air and expressways. Shenyang began to develop heavy industry in the 1920s and became an important industrial center in Northeast China. By the 1970s, it ranked among the top-three industrial centers in all of China, along with Shanghai and Tianjin. As the center of China's post-2009 plan to revitalize Northeast China, Shenyang has attracted new foreign investments from South Korea, Hong Kong, Singapore, and Japan. Economic zones include the Shenyang Economic and Technological Development Zone, the Shenyang Hi-Tech Industrial Development Zone, and the Shenyang Finance and Trade Development Zone.

North of Shenyang is the capital city of Jilin Province, Changchun. Changchun lies in the middle of the Northeast China Plain. The Chinese Eastern Railway built a station in Changchun in 1898. This provided an early link to Beijing and Russia. In 1931, Japan invaded and captured Manchuria, the area of Northeast China and Inner Mongolia. Japan established the state of Manchukuo, and Changchun served as the capital of Manchukuo between 1932 and 1945. During those years, the population more than quadrupled, making Changchun one of the most populous cities in Manchukuo. Today, it has a population of five million. It became the capital of Jilin Province in 1954. Jilin Province lies between Liaoning Province in the south and Heilongjiang Province in the north, in China's northeast region. It borders both Russia and North Korea. Jilin Province has large reserves of oil, gas, coal, gold, silver, and many other minerals. Agricultural produce includes rice and wheat. It has plentiful supplies of lumber. Sheep herding is common in its mountains. It has a growing tourism industry. Its population exceeds twenty-eight million. The Global Shift led to the creation of the Jilin New and Hi-Tech

Industry Development Zone in 1992. Other economic zones outside the capital city include the Hunchun Border Economic Cooperation Zone and the Hunchun Export Processing Zone. Jilin has experienced double-digit growth rates since 2003.

Changchun began to industrialize before the Global Shift came to China. In 1953, Changchun began to produce cars and trucks with technical assistance from Russia. This early association with the auto industry earned Changchun its nickname of "Detroit of China." Today, it produces 10 percent of China's total output of cars. First Automotive Works, built in 1953, is still China's largest auto maker. Changchun also produces passenger trains, including carriages for high-speed trains, and tractors for farmers. It produces metro cars for many of China's city metros, such as the Metros of Shanghai and Guangzhou, via a joint venture with Canada's Bombardier Corporation. Changchun is the host city for the annual Changchun International Auto Fair. As a result of the Global Shift, the Changchun Automotive Economic Trade and Development Zone was created in 1993. Other economic zones include the Changchun Hi-Tech Development Zone, the Changchun Economic and Technological Development Zone, and the Changchun Film Theme City. Changchun is connected by rail to China's major cities, including Shanghai, Beijing, Guangzhou, Dalian, and Harbin. It is connected by high-speed rail to Harbin and Dalian. Changchun hosted the Winter Asian Games in 2007.

The most northernmost province of Northeast China is the province of Heilongjiang. As the Global Shift pushes into Heilongjiang Province, it will have penetrated all of Northern China from the border of North Korea in the east, to Russia and Mongolia in the east and north, and Tibet, Kazakhstan, Tajikistan, Pakistan, and India in the west. Just as the West Triangle Economic Zone pushes the Global Shift into China's remote northwest regions, Jing-Jin-Ji pushes the Global Shift into China's remote northeast regions. As Tibet represents the furthest reach of the West Triangle Economic Zone, Heilongjiang and its capital city of Harbin represent the furthest reach of Jing-Jin-Ji. This province was created from the northern part of Jilin Province in 1683. The province was captured by the Japanese in 1932 and became part of Manchukuo. Japan was driven out of Manchuria by Russian forces, and Russia subsequently aided Mao Zedong in capturing Heilongjiang from the U.S.-backed forces of Gen. Chiang Kai-shek. Heilongjiang became the first province in China to be controlled by the People's Republic of

China. It's the sixth-largest province of China by geographical area, more than twice the area of neighboring Jilin Province. Like other parts of Northern China, it is relatively sparsely populated with a total population under forty million. As expected, it contains much of what is still left of China's forestry industry.

Agricultural crops in Heilongjiang include wheat, soybeans, potatoes, and sunflowers. It produces more milk than any province in China. Horses are also bred. Minerals include oil, coal, gold, and graphite. It is the natural gateway for trade expansion with Russia. Russia played a key role in China's Civil War and post–Civil War economic development. Heilongjiang provides the most important geographical link between these two ex-Communist allies. In a rather ironic twist, the Global Shift reconnected their economic and political ties as two of the four members of BRIC. Decades after the Global Shift began to change dramatically the economic fortunes of poor Third World economies, in 2001, Jim O'Neill, chief economist of Goldman Sachs, coined the acronym BRIC to link the emerging economies of Brazil, Russia, China, and India. It was not until 2009 that the leaders of these four countries decided to formally meet as a single group. China has the largest economy among the emerging economies, and Russia is the largest country by geographical area. Goldman Sachs has predicted that by 2050, China's economy will surpass the U.S. economy to become the world's largest economy, while Russia will become the world's sixth-largest economy, larger than every European economy, including Germany, and even larger than the Japanese economy.

As a result of the Global Shift, economic zones have been established in Heilongjiang Province. The Suifenhe Border Economic Cooperation Area was established north of Suifenhe city, close to the Russian border. It is linked by the Binzhou-Suifenhe Railway to the old Chinese Eastern Railway, which crosses the Sino-Russian border at the Chinese city of Suifenhe, and the Russian city of Pogranichny, fifteen kilometers from the border. Pogranichny is the first rail station in Russia after crossing into Russia from China using the old Chinese Eastern Railway from Beijing to Harbin. In 2014, Suifenhe became the first Chinese city to trade with Russia using the Russian ruble. Other economic zones created in Heilongjiang, outside the capital city of Harbin, include the Sino-Russia Dongning-Piurtaphca Trade Zone, the Daqing New and Hi-Tech Industrial Development Zone, and the Heihe Border Economic Cooperation Area. As usual, many more economic zones were created in the capital city.

Economic zones created in Harbin after the Global Shift include the Harbin Economic and Technology Development Zone, the Harbin New and Hi-Tech Industry Development Zone, the Harbin Songbei Economic Development Zone, the Harbin Limin Economic Development Zone, and the Harbin Pingfang Auto Industrial Zone. It was the building of the Chinese Eastern Railway that changed Harbin from a small village to the most populous city in Northeast China, with a population of eleven million. Harbin became the capital of Heilongjiang Province in 1954. Harbin has a long historical connection to Russia and is still China's primary trade link with Russia. It is China's largest city closest to the Russian border, and there is a large Russian population living in Harbin. Many Russians immigrated to Harbin after the 1917 Russian Revolution. It was the Soviet army that captured the city from the Japanese in 1945. Russia handed over the city to the People's Liberation army in 1946. Harbin was the first major city in China to be governed by the People's Republic of China. It was natural that Harbin's close geographical location to Russia would make it a prime target for economic development during China's first five-year plan, 1951–56, because of Soviet aid to China.

After China's economic decline in the 1960s, Harbin waited for the Global Shift to revitalize its economy. Harbin's Economic and Technological Development Zone was created in 1993. The Harbin International Trade and Economic Fair has been held annually since 1990. In 2013, it was agreed by China and Russia to rename this fair the China-Russia EXPO. Harbin is the major destination for foreign investment in Northeast China today. Harbin is world famous for its annual Ice Sculpture Festival, which draws tourists from across the globe. In 2004, Harbin was voted the top tourist city of China. Harbin was named "City of Music" by the UN in 2010.

Beijing, Shandong Province, and the Bohai Economic Rim

China's capital city of Beijing plays a crucial role in pushing the Global Shift into Northeastern China. Beijing has served on and off as China's capital since the first emperor of China, Qin Shi Huang, unified China in 221 BCE. Like Tianjin, it is one of only four cities in China with municipality status. Like Tianjin, Beijing was forcibly opened to the West by China's defeat in the Opium Wars. In 2008, Beijing hosted the Summer Olympics, and in 2015, it hosted the World Championships in Athletics. It will be the first city ever to host both the Summer and Winter Olympics when it hosts the Winter Olympics in 2022. As a result of the Global Shift, many economic zones were created in Beijing. These economic zones enabled the economy of Beijing to triple its GDP in just eight years between 2004 and 2012. The city is a primary tourist destination for foreign visitors. Tourist attractions include the Forbidden City, Tiananmen Square, the Summer Palace, the Old Summer Palace, the Great Wall, Beihai Park, the Temple of Heaven, the Temple of Earth, the Temple of the Moon, the Temple of the Sun, and the Beijing Zoo. Tourists from many countries can visit Beijing for three full days without a visa. Beijing is connected to the cities of Shanghai, Guangzhou, and Tianjin by high-speed rail. Beijing's Capital International Airport is the world's second-busiest airport.

To the southeast of Beijing is the coastal province of Shandong, on the eastern edge of the North China Plain. It provides another link between the Yangtze River Delta Economic Zone and China's Northern Economic Zone. Qingdao is one of the largest cities and a major seaport in Shandong Province. It has a long history with the West because it was colonized by Germany in 1898. The Germans developed the fishing village into a town and established a brewery in 1903. At the outbreak of the First World War, the Anglo-Japanese alliance captured the city from the Germans. Japan did not relinquish final control until the end of the Second World War. The most important legacy of the German colonization is the world-famous Tsingtao Brewery and Tsingtao beer. Tsingtao beer is China's most well-known international beer. As a result of its easy access to the sea, Shandong Province benefitted immensely from the Global Shift. It attracted large amounts of foreign investment from South Korea and Japan. In 1984, a special economic and technical development zone was created in Qingdao. Other economic zones in Qingdao include a free trade zone, a high-tech zone, and a university industrial zone. In June 2018, Qingdao hosted the eighteenth summit of the Shanghai Cooperation Organization, SCO. Prior to Qingdao, only Shanghai and Beijing hosted the SCO when China was the host nation. Economic zones were also established in the capital city, Jinan, and in the cities of Weihai, Yantai, Zibo, and Weifang.

The Bohai Economic Rim surrounds Beijing and Tianjin. The rim includes Jing-Jin-Ji as well as parts of Liaoning and Shandong Provinces. Major cities along the Bohai Coast, which we have not mentioned so far, include Qinhuangdao in Hebei Province and Longkou, Laizhou, and Penglai in Shandong Province. The Bohai Sea lies between the peninsulas of Liaodong in the northeast and Shandong in the southeast. The Global Shift requires access to cheap and efficient water transportation. This is why China's plan to add a fourth growth region in Northern China depends heavily on the Bohai Sea. Jing-Jin-Ji has easy access to the Bohai Sea from ports in Tianjin, Qinhuangdao, Tangshan, Yingkou, and Huanghua. As a gateway to China's north, the Bohai Sea has become one of the busiest waterways in the world.

CHAPTER 6

How the Global Shift Made India the Second-Largest Economy in Asia after China

It's natural to analyze the Global Shift in India after two chapters on China. First, in terms of the size of its economy, India is second only to China as the largest emerging economy that will challenge Western dominance. Second, in terms of population, India is as populous as China and is even expected to overtake China as the world's most populous country. Regardless, they are by far the world's two most populous countries. Third, in terms of geography, they are neighbors and both giants on the same continent, Asia. Asia will be the continent that will succeed Europe as the world's richest continent, and that will occur in this century. India is expected to overtake Japan as the second-largest economy in Asia. Prior to the Global Shift, Japan's economy was much larger than both India's and China's. In 1965, the year in which we identify the birth of the Global Shift, in the Mexican maquiladoras, the GDP of Japan was US$91 billion. China's GDP that same year was US$70 billion, while India's GDP that year was US$59 billion. The GDP gap among these three Asian economies had severely worsened by the time China embraced the Global Shift in 1980. In 1979, the GDP of Japan had increased to US$1,007 billion. China's GDP had increased to US$175 billion, and India's GDP had increased to US$151 billion. Japan's significantly higher growth was due to its decision to become an economic colony of the United States.

A fourth reason to analyze the Global Shift in India just after China is that India embraced the Global Shift only a decade after it reached China. India would have a lot of catching up to do, but had it waited several decades, it may have totally missed the boat. The final reason for analyzing the Global Shift in India just after China is that both China and India suffered from centuries of Western colonization, exploitation, and theft of their lands and resources. Both countries were determined to be *independent* after the Second World War. To secure their independence, they had to sever relations with the West even if that meant enduring poverty for many of their citizens.

In analyzing the Global Shift in India, it is natural to make comparisons with China. While we will explain differences, our focus will be more on commonalities than on differences. In particular, we see the difference between a "Communist" government in China and a "democratic" government in India as just Western hype rather than substance. The Western portrayal of "democracy" as the only good and moral form of government is pure propaganda. Western governments are neither democratic nor moral. Western governments are portrayed as moral simply because they are Western. It has nothing to do with morality or justice. It's just a name. Had the name been Timbuktu instead of democracy, it would have been equally propagandized as the best form of government.

In chapter 4, we identified the Global Shift as beginning in China in August 1980 when the National People's Congress created its first SEZ in Shenzhen. Prior to the Global Shift, *both* China and India had embraced *planned economic systems.* China's embrace of a planned economic system is much more well-known than that of India. China had fought a long and bitter civil war between those who favored the Soviet planned economic system and those who favored the U.S. free enterprise system. The planned economic system was implemented in China because that side won the Civil War. Although much less well-known, Indian postindependence leaders also embraced the planned economic system. In this regard, India was following many of the former British and French colonies in experimenting with planned economic systems. One reason for this was the great difficulty, if not impossibility, of engaging economically with past colonial masters. The second reason was that the Soviet Union, led by Josef Stalin, had shown that a planned economic system not only was functional but also could achieve higher rates of economic growth than Western free enterprise economies. We need to explain these two reasons more fully to convince our readers how similar India's postindependence economic system was to that of China, because Western propaganda implied that it was impossible for *Communist* China to have a similar economic system as the world's largest *democracy,* India. After all, the West fought a long and bitter Cold War with the Soviet Union during this time because of the Western propaganda that Communism was *evil* and democracy was *morally superior* in every respect.

The most important dilemma facing India and all the ex-colonies of the Western European empires was how to have any type of economic relations with the West without continued economic and political colonization by former colonial masters. Since all the Western countries had engaged in and/or supported Western colonizations, they were all equally threatening. These Western imperial powers had often hidden their military colonizations and thefts as trade and/or foreign investment. Trade is the exact opposite of colonization. Trade is a mutually beneficial exchange of goods and services for goods and services. Colonization is a zero-sum game in which the imperial powers use military force to steal the lands and resources of the colonies. However, Western writers deliberately speak of trade when it's not trade but theft. Adding to this deliberate lie is the fact that the Western colonial powers did not grant independence to their colonies voluntarily. The colonies had seized that independence after the Second World War had severely reduced the military powers of the colonial masters. Those ex-colonial masters were looking for every opportunity to recolonize lost colonies or ex-colonies of competing Western colonial masters. Postindependence Indian leaders were correct in assuming that Britain, the United States, and other Western European countries were plotting to use any opportunity presented to recolonize India economically and politically. This was India's key reason for turning to central planning and public control of the economy. By minimizing the opening up of the private sector to trade and investments by the West, India made it far more difficult for the West to recolonize India by conflating colonization with trade.

The second reason India chose the planned economy route was the increasing popularity among intellectuals of planning, socialism, and Communism as ways of reducing the injustices, and income and wealth inequalities, which were by-products of free markets and capitalist economic systems. Somewhat ironically, these criticisms of Western capitalist economies came from Western intellectuals and professors at Western universities. But the postindependence leaders of India and the other ex-Western colonies were educated at these Western universities by these Western intellectuals. While many of these Western intellectuals went into hiding after the United States branded them Communists and imprisoned or blacklisted them, the "colonials" returned home to become political, economic, and academic leaders in the ex-colonies. They could take comfort in the fact that the Soviet Union had proved that a planned socialist economy did not mean sacrificing economic growth. These are the two important reasons why India experimented with a planned economic system like China. China became a Communist state with a planned economic system in 1949. Postindependence India became a democracy with a planned economic system in 1947. They both copied the Soviet-style five-year economic plans. China implemented its first of many five-year plans in 1952–57. India implemented its first of many five-year plans in 1951–56, a year before China. Both countries were roughly at the same level of economic development with similar per capita GDP in 1950. Both countries were well aware of the Soviet model of a planned economic system. Both countries also copied Stalin's strategy of generating high rates of growth by switching economic resources from producing consumer goods to producing capital goods and by industrializing a predominantly rural economy. Like the Soviet Union, both countries embarked on a program to industrialize their economies using state control, central planning, and strict controls on foreign investment and international trade, including foreign exchange controls. State-owned enterprises, SOEs, were as common in India as they were in China.

As with the Soviet Union, this planned economy model was initially successful but encountered serious problems by the 1970s. In China, the economy went sideways during the Cultural Revolution and embraced the Global Shift to boost the anemic economic growth of the 1970s. It was a voluntary change implemented by the new leadership of Deng Xiaoping after Mao's death in 1976. In the case of India, it was initially forced into embracing the Global Shift by the IMF. The Indian government had mismanaged the economy. The success of a centrally planned economy depends crucially on efficient planning and minimal corruption. Unfortunately, central planning breeds bureaucracy, incompetence, graft, and corruption. Postindependence states like India began with good intentions. They had suffered from centuries of Western exploitation, which had impoverished their people. In the case of India, British colonization had sucked the wealth out of the country. In 1700, before the British had colonized India, India's GDP was a whopping 27 percent of the world's total GDP. By the end of the British Raj in 1947, India's share of the world's GDP had fallen to a miserable 3 percent. The postindependence leaders were determined to reverse this decline. By using the state to control and plan economic development and growth, the leaders hoped to use the lands, resources, and wealth, previously stolen by the imperial powers, to grow the economy for the benefit of the local inhabitants. They hoped to do this with minimal international engagement. They feared that international engagement would only replace political colonization with "economic" colonization.

Initial successes under a centrally planned, state-control-led, isolationist economic model became bogged down by increasing bureaucracy, inefficiencies, cost of an ever-expanding civil service, graft and corruption, and the lack of the benefits of international trade and foreign investment. One of the lessons still not learned by politicians and political economists is that while imperialism exploits the colonies for the exclusive benefit of the imperial power, international trade and foreign investment are essential for economic growth. Even under the most efficient centrally planned state control, without the benefits of international trade and foreign capital inflows, growth will be severely limited. Add to the deficiencies of isolationism, inefficient and costly bureaucratic SOEs, small tax base, large government expenditures or subsidies to help the poor, graft and corruption, and you have a recipe for continued postindependence economic decline. Both India and China had reached this dismal state by the 1970s. They were both rescued by the Global Shift. As we have explained, the Global Shift was a postimperial way of the Third World engaging with the West without fear of "economic" colonization.

While no engagement with the West is totally devoid of economic or political colonization, the Global Shift is historically the purest model of international engagement focused primarily on mutual economic benefits for both parties, with minimal political and economic control by the West. China is the best example of this since the United States was willing to let China keep its Communist form of government. As we explained in chapter 4, this was the single most important political concession made by the United States that guaranteed China's sovereignty after economic engagement with the West. Prior to China, the United States had not engaged with any country without that country surrendering some of its political sovereignty to the United States. This was true of Britain, Germany, Japan, France, Italy, South Korea, Spain, Greece, Portugal, Canada, Australia, Mexico, Ireland, New Zealand, Taiwan, Hong Kong, Singapore, the Philippines, other Latin American and Caribbean states, South Africa and other African states, Saudi Arabia, Egypt, Israel, and other Middle East states.

It was done with China only to get China on side to fight the Soviet Union, but it had a lasting effect and influence on how the West would in future engage with India and other ex-colonies of the West. All previous engagement of the Third World by the West was unable to separate trade from colonization. The West had decided since the 1450s that trade would be with colonies only, not independent states. Trade was never separate from imperialism. The reason was simple. Trade is mutually beneficial to both parties. Gains must be shared. Colonization is theft of lands and resources using superior military force. If you can use a gun to force someone to surrender his car to you, why would you pay for it? As long as the military cost of theft is less than what is given up in free trade, the West chose colonization over trade.

China and India were both fortunate that the Global Shift where the West, for the first time ever, came to the conclusion that trade produced more economic benefits than continued colonization, came along just when both countries needed international trade and foreign investment more than ever. The West had concluded that the military cost of theft outweighed what could be gained by free trade at the same time that emerging economies like China and India were desperate for international trade and foreign investment to reduce the dire poverty of their teeming millions. Under the Global Shift, India, like China before, would not have to surrender political sovereignty for economic growth. Having the IMF force reforms on India's leaders was just the icing on the cake in breaking down the postindependence barriers to international trade, free capital flows, free exchange rates, increased foreign and domestic competition to SOEs, and growth in the private sector relative to a large and inefficient bureaucratic public sector.

Why Did India Embrace the Global Shift?

There are several reasons why India followed China in embracing the Global Shift. By the time China embraced the Global Shift in 1980 by creating its first SEZ in Shenzhen, India was surrounded by Asian economies that were experiencing much higher economic growth rates than India. These included the economies of Japan, Taiwan, South Korea, Indonesia, Pakistan, Hong Kong, Singapore, and Thailand. What all these higher-growth economies had in common was more free markets and international engagement than India. It was becoming increasingly clear to India that its emphasis on a state-dominated economic model was not delivering the high growth rates it had anticipated. At the same time, the Soviet Union, which had invented the planned economy model, and China, which had copied it, were both performing as poorly as India.

By 1990, China had done two things that convinced India to change its economic model. The first was that China had successfully negotiated with the United States to open its economy to the West without surrendering its political sovereignty. No other country had succeeded in doing that. It set a precedent that India could follow. India, like China, was determined to never surrender its political sovereignty to imperial powers after centuries of Western colonization. The China precedent convinced India that it no longer had to close its economy to international trade and investment to keep its political sovereignty. The second thing that China had shown India was that an open economy will grow faster than a closed economy. Post–Global Shift, China experienced much higher growth rates than India and higher growth rates than it had achieved before embracing the Global Shift. These two factors were sufficient to convince India.

India and China had been Asian rivals to some extent and had fought a border war in 1962. If China grew at a much faster rate than India, China's economy would become much larger than India's. China would become a military threat to India. India's political sovereignty from the West would be of little significance. The only way to prevent this military threat was to match China's economic growth. The only way to do that was to embrace the Global Shift. In addition, India's population was growing faster than China's. With a lower growth rate than China, per capita GDP would stagnate relative to China's. Increasing poverty in India next to a rising China would further threaten India's independence and Asian influence.

Another important influence on India was the type of output India could specialize in after embracing the Global Shift. The Global Shift in China specialized in the output of manufactured goods. The Global Shift in India would specialize in services. This initial difference in output specialization would be more beneficial to India as the two dominant emerging Asian economies would be complementary rather than competitive after embracing the Global Shift.

The final reason for India embracing the Global Shift was a combination of growing trade deficits *and* budget deficits. Postindependence India was desperate to reduce the poverty of its teeming millions created by the British Raj. It needed high growth rates to do that. When its planned economy model failed to deliver the high economic growth rates, the government turned to budget deficits. Budget deficits are a temporary stopgap solution. If it is long term, it collapses under its own weight of rising debt and interest payments. By 1991, India had reached a limit in its ability to finance its public programs. No type of government, democratic or Communist, can long survive an uprising by the mass of poor people.

At the same time that India was incurring large and growing budget deficits, it was experiencing large and growing trade deficits. India's balance of payments deficits began in 1985. The government's large and growing budget deficits had begun before 1985. While it had largely insulated its economy from international trade, its Soviet style economic model required imports of capital goods to industrialize and transform its economy from rural to developed. India had no domestic capital goods industries when it initiated its industrialization strategy. As a result, all capital goods had to be imported. The Soviet-style emphasis on heavy industry meant costly imports. India was unable to export enough to earn the foreign exchange to pay for the capital imports. Like its public expenditure program, India decided to borrow. Budget deficits can be funded by borrowing from Indians. Trade deficits can only be funded by borrowing from foreigners. While a growing budget deficit can be managed by printing money, if the Central Bank cooperates with the government, trade deficits cannot be prolonged in that manner. If foreigners refuse further loans, no country can print money to resolve that, except the United States to a limited extent, because it produces the world's primary reserve currency. If the foreign lenders refuse further loans, you have to pay the piper. That was what India found out in 1991. Foreign investors had lost confidence in India's ability to service and repay its debts. By 1991, India had used up its foreign exchange reserves and faced bankruptcy.

India was forced to ask for a bailout by the IMF. The IMF would only bail out any country if they accept stringent conditions to reduce their debts. While there were many reasons for India to embrace the Global Shift, as explained above, it was forced to do so by accepting the bailout by the IMF. Had it not been in this crisis situation in 1991, the economic liberalization of both its internal markets and its external market would have been slower. This enforced liberalization was a blessing in disguise as India would have been left further and further behind, not only by its primary Asian rival, China, but also by other emerging Asian rivals such as Indonesia, Malaysia, Thailand, and Vietnam. We can use this forced liberalization of the Indian economy by the IMF in 1991 to date the beginning of the Global Shift. China had a head start of eleven years on India. Nevertheless, India had some advantages in its educated English-speaking IT workers, its younger labor force, its more advanced railway network, and its longer working relationship with both Britain and the United States. India was a member of the WTO before it reformed. China became a member after it reformed.

How Has India Benefitted from Embracing the Global Shift?

Every economy outside the West benefitted from the Global Shift. India is the largest beneficiary after China. Western imperialism, beginning in the 1450s, had benefitted the imperial powers at the expense of those colonized. These imperial powers were the United States, Britain, France, Germany, Russia, Japan, Italy, the Netherlands, Spain, and Portugal. After the Second World War, most of the colonies gained their independence. Some of these ex-colonies chose to align themselves with their ex-colonial masters to fight a Cold War with the Soviet Union. These ex-colonies included Canada, Australia, New Zealand, Taiwan, Hong Kong, Singapore, and the Philippines. The United States led a powerful coalition of countries that engaged in international trade and liberal capital flows, which produced high rates of economic growths, increasing per capita GDP, rising standards of living of their large, and growing middle classes and powerful WMDs. Outside the Soviet Union, the West controlled every "international" institution including the UN, the IMF, the World Bank, the WTO, the reserve currency, global capital and financial markets, the international media, and international propaganda.

Countries such as China and India who were unwilling to surrender political sovereignty and support Western military aggression across the globe isolated themselves from this single-minded club. They were rescued by the Global Shift when the United States unwittingly allowed China to engage with this club without surrendering its political sovereignty. I say unwittingly because the United States did not understand the forces it was unleashing when it allowed China to keep its political sovereignty in exchange for China's help in defeating the Soviet

Union. As we previously explained in our *How the West Was Won and Lost,* the American dominance will fall not because of the Soviet Union but because of the U.S.-enabled Global Shift to emerging economies such as China and India.

While the common term used to describe the Global Shift in China is "creation of SEZs," the common term used to describe the Global Shift in India is "economic reforms." Another common term is "economic liberalization." We will use the term "Global Shift" to refer to Mexico, China, India, and every other economy that experienced the inflows of foreign investments to take advantage of cheap labor, which began in 1965 with the Mexican maquiladoras. What has been called economic reforms refer to India's decision to abide by the conditions imposed by the IMF in 1991 to secure a bailout. These conditions included moving the economic model used by India, since its independence in 1947, from a centrally planned, state-controlled, and restricted international engagement model to an economic model based on capitalism, free enterprise, markets, international trade, capital inflows, larger private sector, and a smaller public sector. India was also required to reduce its highly bureaucratic red tape and abolish what was called the *license Raj,* an elaborate and cumbersome state system of regulations and licenses that made the creation of new businesses and operation of existing businesses costly, difficult, and subject to graft and corruption by officials of the government.

Unlike China, which had been black listed by the United States because of its Communist government, and therefore prevented Western countries from doing business with it, India was a democracy but had voluntarily isolated itself from international trade and foreign investment. As we said above, it had done so because it believed that the isolationist model would generate economic growth and because of fear of economic and political recolonization by the West. By the time of the financial crisis that required the IMF bailout in 1991, Indian leaders, like China's leaders after 1976, were rethinking their choice of economic model because of the overwhelming evidence of low growth rates. Just as post-Mao leaders of China were ready and willing to reduce China's isolationism and state control, post-1991 IMF bailout Indian leaders were ready and willing to reduce India's isolationism and state control. It matters not that China's desire for change coincided with the desire of the United States to engage with China to fight the Soviet Union. Likewise, it matters not that India's desire for change coincided with the conditions imposed by the IMF bailout. What matters, and this is our unique insight, is that international engagement between Western countries and Third World countries had been revolutionized by the creation of the maquiladoras in Mexico. This provided a much bigger boost to growth rates in the East than the previous six centuries of East-West engagement had done. It was a growth bonanza for the Third World economies never imagined by either side and which is still falsely analyzed by economists as if it were old-fashioned *Globalization* and outsourcing.

Some Indian leaders had attempted to reduce the built-in bureaucratic inefficiencies of the state-stifled Indian economic model before 1991, and there was limited success. But there was no consistent strategy to change. The balance of payments crisis of 1991 was the defining phenomenon that provided the consistent long-term move toward a free enterprise model that would follow the Chinese example of embracing the Global Shift but with Indian characteristics. Pre-1991 economic growth had averaged 3 percent annually. Per capita GDP grew much less because India was less successful than China in reducing population growth. Economists had given up on both India and China in finding any way out of the poverty of their teeming millions. In 1991, India could, for the first time since independence, look to a solution by observing the miracle occurring in its equally populous neighbor China. While there was opposition to the stringent bailout conditions imposed by the IMF, the prime minister could now argue that he had no choice. In addition, the collapse of the Soviet Union had served to convince even the diehards of proponents of Soviet-style economic planning that it was inefficient. The IMF gets a bad rap for imposing economic reforms, but in India's case, these imposed reforms were exactly what the patient needed and which the government of incoming prime minister Narasimha Rao supported.

The Global Shift, unwittingly brought to India by a financial crisis forcing IMF reforms, catapulted India to a place in the world where India would no longer be the world's largest but poorest democracy. The West had given up on India, and India had given up on itself. The only hope Indians had was to get an education in India to enable them to get a visa to a Western country. After the Global Shift, India, like China, are seen as potential rivals to old imperial powers like Britain and France, which had enriched their countries by preying on Third World countries like India and China. The world was witnessing a revolution the likes of which had not been seen since da Gama reached India and Columbus reached the New World.

India's embrace of the Global Shift began under the leadership of Prime Minister Narasimha Rao and his able finance minister and economist, Dr. Manmohan Singh. The so-called reforms or economic liberalization continued under future Indian administrations and continues today under the leadership of Prime Minister Narendra Modi. While there are many facets to what economists call "reforms," the key measure for us is foreign investment. Our definition of the Global Shift is the move of Western enterprises from their location in the West to location in a Third World country such as Mexico or India, to take advantage of cheap labor to produce goods or services for *Western* consumers. While the maquiladoras and China specialized in Western factories producing cheap manufactured goods for hungry Western consumers of junk, the Global Shift to India added services to goods. India's embrace of the Global Shift was significant in this regard. China would copy India in adding services to its exports as India would copy China in enticing the location of foreign firms in India to produce goods as well. Foreign investment in India grew from a low amount of US$130 million in 1991 to US$6 billion by 1997. In 1998, India's new prime minister Atal Bihari Vajpayee committed to enhancing this inflow of foreign investment. Prime Minister Rao's finance minister, Dr. Manmohan Singh, became India's prime minister in 2004 and continued opening up India to foreign direct investments. By 2005, India had become second only to China as the most favorable country for foreign direct investment, FDI. India attracted FDI into both goods and services sectors, especially the booming IT and business process outsourcing services sectors. The United States had fallen to third place for attracting FDI.

India's Post–Global Shift Economic Growth

In the twenty-first century, both India and China have emerged as the fastest-growing economies in the world. They are the new Asian Tigers, replacing Japan, South Korea, Taiwan, Hong Kong, and Singapore. The old Asian Tigers had never experimented with central planning. They had embraced what may be called the "economic colonies of the United States" model, which the United States had imposed on its Western European allies and on Canada and Australia. The driving force of this model was a free flow of goods and capital among a large number of highly developed rich economies. In the post–World War II period, trade and capital flows between the West and the Third World had shrunk, while trade and capital flows among the non-Communist developed economies under U.S. hegemony had grown.

With the Global Shift, the old Asian Tigers saw their growth rates fall, while the growth rates of the new Asian Tigers increased. China achieved average annual rates of growth of 10 percent, while India achieved annual rates of growth of 7 percent. At the same time, economic growth in Japan stagnated below 2 percent, while the other old Asian Tigers experienced growth rates much less than India and China. In addition to this switch in economic fortunes, the old Asian Tigers began to integrate their economies more with the new Asian Tigers and reduce their integration with the United States and Western Europe. While the *Asian Century* was being created by the new Asian Tigers, the old Asian Tigers wanted to be a part of it. The old Asian Tigers were willing to supply capital, expertise, and financial markets to the new Asian Tigers in return for profitable investment opportunities and new markets. Without this integration, growth rates in the old Asian Tigers would have plummeted even more, and the Global Shift would have been less successful in China, India, and other parts of Asia.

The IT revolution, India, and the Global Shift

India's important role in moving the Global Shift from Mexico and China to other emerging economies cannot be fully understood without explaining the complementary role played by the personal computer revolution in the Global Shift. So far, we have explained the Global Shift in terms of the location of manufacturing plants owned by Western corporations in emerging economies such as Mexico and China. Since these plants produced manufactured goods for Western consumers, they had to be located initially in Mexico alongside the U.S.-Mexico border and along the coast of China to minimize transportation cost. The development of container shipping and container ports have also been addressed. What we have not addressed so far is the fact that a personal computer revolution was taking place coincidentally at the same time as the Global Shift. The accidental Global Shift created by the maquiladoras and the decision of the United States to ally with China against the Soviet Union was enhanced by the personal computer revolution, which just happened to occur at the same time. We must now address how this *simultaneous* occurrence of the personal computer revolution with the Global Shift fed the Global Shift and how India, not China or Mexico, was at the forefront of this important fuel that enhanced the phenomenal economic growth rates produced by the Global Shift.

Personal Computers, Call Centers, Silicon Valley, and the Role of the Internet in Complementing the Global Shift

Who can think of the recent history of India without imagining call centers and the movie *Slumdog Millionaire*? The outsourcing of call centers by Western corporations to emerging economies such as India complemented the outsourcing of the manufacture of goods by these same Western corporations to the same emerging economies. While their simultaneous occurrence was coincidental, the underlying reason was the same, cheaper labor. While the call centers could be moved from the West to the emerging economies, without the advent of personal computers or the Internet or the IT revolution led by Silicon Valley, these simultaneous complementary occurrences made the shift of call centers from the West to the emerging economies more viable, efficient, and cost effective. In the beginning, the shift required only the decline in long-distance phone rates just as the shift in factories required the decline in shipping costs. But the advent of the digital revolution made it even cheaper to harness the personal computer and the Internet for Voice over IP calls and Internet chats. The development of computer software by Silicon Valley enabled call centers in the emerging economies to do much more for corporations and their customers than traditional call centers located in the West.

The Rise of Call Centers in the West

Call centers were initially set up by large corporations to deal with the large volume of calls expected from a large customer base. Calls were typically incoming from customers with complaints and queries. They began as in-house operations. In the days before the advent of personal computers, PCs, workers were equipped with a headset phone. Airlines and the banks were the first corporations to install call centers. It then spread to all large corporations to centralize the handling of incoming customer calls. It was from its inception a very labor-intensive operation, and that was the prime motivation to outsource it to cheap labor, emerging economies, after the Global Shift. The functions of call centers expanded to deal with credit checks and chasing customers for bad debts, airline and hotel reservations, telemarketing, catalogue shopping, technical help desks, soliciting charitable and political donations, market research phone surveys, and dealing with government service inquiries. With the advent of customer free 800 numbers, incoming calls grew rapidly. This required expanded call centers with larger numbers of workers. Call centers have progressed from "back office" addendums to businesses, to front-line drivers of sales, revenues, cost minimization, and profits. Unions capitalized on this expanding labor-intensive industry to grow their membership. Unionization increased the difference between wages in Western call centers and wages in emerging economies call centers, furthering the pace at which call centers were moved from the West to India and other emerging economies, after the Global Shift.

Many businesses outsourced their call center operations long before the Global Shift. It was a natural part of the outsourcing business where corporations use other corporate specialists to move some in-house operation to lower cost, to improve quality, or to better focus on their core business. As we have explained before, it is important not to confuse this traditional form of outsourcing with the post–Global Shift outsourcing to emerging economies to take advantage of cheaper labor. Just to remind you of the two key differences between pre–Global Shift and post–Global Shift outsourcing, the latter is a move from the West to an emerging economy to use cheaper labor, and the operation is often owned and managed by the same Western corporation, as opposed to outsourcing to a specialized corporation in the West. The *pre*–Global Shift outsourcing enabled corporations to remove the capital cost of in-house call centers and pay a specialized call center corporation that can provide the service cheaper by spreading the overhead cost by serving several corporations simultaneously.

The Shift of Call Centers to India:
Electronic City and Bangalore

In the 1990s, Western corporations began to look for cheaper labor to reduce the cost of their call center operations. By the 1990s, the call center functions of large corporations had grown from relatively small back-office addendums to its core business, to an essential and integral part of its core business. Whether it was done in-house or outsourced to a specialized provider, it had become a significant portion of the total cost of operating the business successfully. Since the functions provided by the call centers were labor intensive, finding a cheap source of labor would reduce cost significantly. Western corporations began to locate their call centers in India to take advantage of the much cheaper wage rates they could pay Indian workers compared to American, Canadian, or Western European workers. Indian workers were eager to work for the Western corporations as the job paid more and was more prestigious than the jobs they were currently doing. These workers were relatively well educated, spoke relatively good English, were highly motivated to succeed and move up the income class, and had relatively few good alternative employment prospects.

General Electric, Texas Instruments, American Express, British Airways, and Swiss Air were among the first Western corporations to establish call centers in India. Most of the large Fortune 500 corporations followed. GE's initial Indian call center was located in the city of Gurgaon, just outside India's capital city, New Delhi. Gurgaon is located in the Indian state of Haryana, twenty miles from New Delhi. It has a population just under one million. Indian entrepreneur Pramod Bhasin played a key role in convincing GE to set up its first call center in India in 1998. It began with eighteen employees. Bhasin was a British Chartered accountant employed by GE. He was still employed by GE when he convinced GE to set up the call center in Gurgaon. Just like the American corporations that had seen the obvious cost reduction from moving the location of a new factory from the American side of the U.S.-Mexico border to the Mexican side, in the 1960s, Bhasin was convinced that Indian workers could answer the phone almost as well as American workers at a fraction of the cost. The maquiladoras began the Global Shift for low-cost goods production, and the Indian call centers began the Global Shift for low-cost provision of services. India was on its way to becoming the world's third-largest economy after the United States and China.

Without the advent of container shipping, the Global Shift to China would not have been as successful as it is. In like manner, without the personal computer, the Internet, and VoIP (Voice over Internet protocol), the Global Shift to India would not have been as successful. In the beginning, call center workers were equipped only with a headset phone. Now they had both a headset and a personal computer. The computer served two important functions in the Global Shift. It enabled the use of VoIP and the Internet to lower the cost of international phone calls. In addition, call center workers would record a summary of the call for future reference by all workers and by supervisors. This led to superior service to customers. The data was also used for marketing. Telemarketing became an important additional function of call centers. Over time, the call centers attracted more and more skilled IT services technicians, enabling Western corporations to outsource more and more technical services that they provide to their customers. With the dawn of the computer age and digital technology, customers needed more and more technical assistance. Such technical assistance has been shifted from brick-and-mortar storefronts, where customers came for help, often bringing their computers or cell phones with them, to service over the phone. Business processing outsourcing is also a growing function provided by call centers. The ever-increasing call center business has led to a rapid growth of cities like Gurgaon. Today, over 250 Fortune 500 corporations have established call centers or local offices in Gurgaon. It has earned the nickname *Millennium City* and has become both a financial and industrial hub. Location of an auto plant by Maruti Suzuki India Limited predated its Millennium City fame. Today, Gurgaon is a world-famous offshore center for call center services as well as increasingly advanced IT services. It now develops new software for global corporations, and many of these corporations, such as BMW, All Nippon Airways, and Coca-Cola, have located their Indian head office in Gurgaon.

Offshoring

In China, the Global Shift began with the SEZ in Shenzhen. Over time, a large variety of special economic zones were created ranging from the original SEZ to high-tech zones, to economic zones, to industrial parks, to travel zones, and so on. The types and number of zones multiplied and became confusing. But they all had one thing in common, and that was to move manufacturing from the West to China. In like manner, the Global Shift of services to India began with the humble call centers but soon morphed into the provision of more and more services, both mundane and technical, to Western corporations. While equally confusing as the many types of economic zones in China, they had one thing in common, and that was to grow the Global Shift of services from the West to India. We now turn to another group of these services commonly referred to as *offshoring.*

Offshoring will be used here to explain the Global Shift of advanced IT and related services to emerging economies, beginning with India. Initially, call centers were located in India to employ relatively educated Indians without any specialized knowledge of computers, software, or IT. This was primarily "back office" services provided to Western consumers. At that time, Indians who had these technical skills had to immigrate to the West to get jobs in Silicon Valley or with Western corporations using those specialized IT skills. But this brain drain from East to West has been slowed, and in some cases reversed, because of the Global Shift. Even Silicon Valley is now losing more Indian IT workers, returning to India, than the new Indian IT workers emigrating from India to Silicon Valley. Western corporations have been forced by competition to offshore more and more of their core services. Competition comes not only from other Western corporations but also from Western consumers demanding ever lower prices and better services in a rapidly changing information age. With Western corporations willing to locate offices in the emerging economies, Indians no longer needed to immigrate to the West to find these highly skilled IT jobs. As a result, India became a key destination for offshoring. Western corporations could now develop new software in electronic parks in India using highly skilled but cheaper Indian workers instead of expensive IT workers living in the West.

While the offshoring of software development and related R & D is a key component of offshoring, offshoring is not restricted to IT services. Many other services previously done in the West for Western corporations or Western consumers are increasingly offshored. These services include accounting, finance, healthcare, legal, HR, marketing, sales, engineering, general R & D, analytics, AI, robotics, taxation, and ever more high-tech services. Initially, the Global Shift moved manufacturing to China, causing massive unemployment in Western factories. However, Western workers could be educated for higher-paying jobs in IT and professional services. Now, the Global Shift was moving more and more of these IT and professional services to emerging economies, beginning with India.

Western corporations offshoring to India include IBM, Microsoft, HP, Cisco, Oracle Corporation, and many more, including those located in Silicon Valley. Western corporations have also established business relationships with universities specializing in educating these highly skilled Indian graduates. This enables the Western corporations to influence the training to better fit their needs. As a result of this offshoring to India, India's IT and professional services sectors have experienced rates of growth as high as 15 percent annually. While wage rates have increased as a result of this offshoring boom, wages are still much lower than in the West for similar work. The Internet and personal computer age has transformed the world, not just the West. Like most new technologies, the Internet, personal computers, and computer software were invented in the West and first used by Western corporations to increase productivity and wages for Western workers. As with the industrial revolutions, Third World workers had to immigrate to the West to share the high-wage bonanza. But it's the same Internet, personal computers, and computer software that are now fueling the Global Shift of services to India and other emerging economies. Where once only a few workers from the Third World competed with Western workers because of strict immigration limits, offshoring creates the potential for masses of Third World workers to compete with Western workers. Wage differentials across the globe will be eroded as wages rise faster in emerging economies than they do in the West. In India, wage rates for workers providing the offshoring services to Western corporations are rising by 12 percent or more annually. As with the Global Shift in manufacturing to Mexico and China, Western workers will lose the five centuries of historical advantage they monopolized by severely restricting the free movement of labor from the Third World to the West. The advantage given to the West by the discoveries of da Gama and Columbus for five centuries will be taken away by the birth of the maquiladoras in 1965. Lower transportation cost created by the advent of containerization is combined with lower communication cost brought by the Internet, personal computers, and computer software to enhance the cost reductions created by Western corporations making the switch from using high-wage Western workers to using low-wage Third World workers. The mountain has indeed moved to Mohamed.

The major cities in India specializing in attracting the offshoring business include Gurgaon, Bangalore, Mumbai, Chennai, New Delhi, Noida, and Pune. Western corporations are now caught between a rock and a hard place. Offshoring ever higher-end technologically advanced services to India and other emerging economies means reducing their technological edge vis-à-vis emerging economies as they share research and knowhow. Western corporations face challenges with operating in new legal jurisdictions. Western corporations face increasing competition from knockoffs and copycats, which are closer and closer to the real thing. The monopoly advantage of patents and intellectual property rights are eroded by offshoring. India's increasing production of cheap medicines is one example of this erosion. But refusing to offshore these high-end services puts Western corporations at a competitive price disadvantage relative to other Western corporations that offshore. It's the same dilemma faced by Western politicians, such as President Trump, trying to bring back lost high-paying manufacturing jobs to the West. Just as the East could not undo the advantage the West got from the voyages of da Gama and Columbus and the military advantage of navies over armies, the West cannot undo the advantage that the Global Shift is now providing to the East. By 2006, India alone was the recipient of one-quarter of the total global investment in R & D. All of the major Western corporations had set up R & D centers in India. India's software exports are growing by 30 percent annually. As India's infrastructure improves and as its government moves toward a more open economy and away from its postindependence emphasis on central planning, India will attract even more of this offshoring business. India's rapidly growing labor force will dampen the pressure on wages to rise.

Silicon Valley of India

Bangalore is one of the many cities we identified above as attracting the offshoring businesses, specifically the outsourcing of IT-enabled services, ITES. But Bangalore is also regarded as India's copycat Silicon Valley or India's IT capital city. The city is India's leading exporter of IT services, accounting for a third of total exports. As in the case of Gurgaon, Bangalore postindependence India development began with manufacturing cars. The city also attracted other heavy manufacturing industries. But in 1985, Texas Instruments located its Indian head office in Bangalore. Other leading IT corporations followed the example set by Texas Instruments. In time, Western corporations such as Microsoft and Google established large research centers in Bangalore. This influx of Western corporations was complemented by Indian IT businesses fueled by the dotcom boom of the 1990s. As a result, by the 1990s, Bangalore had earned the nickname Silicon Valley of India. Bangalore employs over 35 percent of all IT workers in India.

As with cities in China that experienced rapid population growth after they became SEZs, attracting offshoring business led to rapid population growth in Bangalore. This provided the labor force needed to enable the rapid economic growth. Bangalore's economic growth was later fueled by the growth in its biotechnology industries. Today, Bangalore is both India's leading IT city as well as its leading biotechnology city. Bangalore is also a prime location for India's aerospace and aviation industries. In addition to domestic firms, the world's leading aviation industries, including the giants Boeing and Airbus, have R & D centers in Bangalore. Firms produce both commercial aircrafts as well as fighter jets for the Indian air force. India's National Aerospace Labs is also located in Bangalore, and well over half of India's Aerospace business is located in Bangalore. India's growing space program is also headquartered in Bangalore.

Electronic City is the primary location of India's Silicon Valley just outside Bangalore's city core. It is one of India's largest industrial parks, over 330 acres. It was created in 1978 and has since attracted over two hundred IT companies. The idea for the creation of the IT park came from the chair of the Karnataka State Electronics Development Corporation, R. K. Baliga, who, like Pramod Bhasin, had the vision of attracting Western outsourced services to India. His vision came at the right time as India began to move away from a centrally planned economy to a market-based open economy. The park is also the primary location for the biotech industries. Software Technology Parks of India, STPI, was created in 1991 by the Indian government to encourage the establishment of IT parks such as Electronic City to provide an attractive location for offshoring business. STPI was located in Electronic City by India's Ministry of Information Technology.

In 1994, another IT park, the International Tech Park Bangalore, was created in Bangalore. This was a joint venture between India and Singapore. As Bangalore attracted more and more domestic and international IT, R & D, manufacturing, aerospace, biotech, and related businesses, other parks were created in the suburbs surrounding the city. STPI Bangalore became India's first Internet services provider. STPI has influenced the creation of many more IT parks in other Indian cities such as Mumbai, Kolkata, Chennai, Pune, and Lucknow.

Growth in Bilateral Trade and FDI between India and China

While it's easy to date the beginning of the Global Shift in China with the creation of its first SEZ in Shenzhen in 1980, it's not as easy for India. However, we will date it at least a decade later as beginning after 1990. India's decision to phase out its dependence on central planning within a largely closed economy began in 1991 under Prime Minister Narasimha Rao and his finance minister, Dr. Manmohan Singh. But it was not until 1998 that Pramod Bhasin, an employee of General Electric, established India's first call center in Gurgaon, India. GE was convinced to outsource some of its services to this call center in India. In the two decades between 1979 and 2000, China's GDP had grown from US$175.6 billion to US$1,198.5 billion. India's GDP, by comparison, had only grown from to US$150.9 billion to US$460.2 billion. China's global ranking by GDP had increased from tenth place in 1979 to sixth place by 2000. India's global ranking by GDP, on the other hand, had slipped from twelfth place in 1979 to thirteenth place by 2000. India's decision to abandon central planning in favor of free markets was partly influenced by China's successful transition from central planning to free markets. But India had a lot of catching up to do and did not have the advantage of a developed financial market like that which China inherited from Hong Kong. Goldman Sachs forecasted a GDP of US$2,848 billion for India in 2020. This compares with a forecast of US$12,630 billion for China.

While the advent of cheap container shipping was essential to the Global Shift of manufacturing to China, the Internet was essential to the Global Shift of services to India. We have documented that above. Here we will look at how these two leading emerging economies, both created by the Global Shift, have since begun to combine forces to grow both of their respective economies while simultaneously fueling the Global Shift from West to East. As we saw above, China's advantage lay in goods production, while India's advantage lay in the production of services. It was natural that China would copy India's efforts to attract some of the global offshoring business, while India would copy China's creation of SEZs to attract manufacturing.

Initially, China and India became competitors for the Western outsourcing of both goods and services production, China vying for India's service production and India vying for China's goods production. But as both economies developed and grew from Third World status to emerging economy status, they recognized the gains that both could make by doing business with each other. In addition to competing for the Western outsourcing business, the two countries recognized that they could use the different strength of the other to boost their intercountry specialization and trade. China would outsource some of its goods production to India, and India would outsource some of its service production to China. Just as they both learned how to copy Western technologies by being recipients of Western outsourcing, they will copy each other's respective strengths by being recipients of outsourcing by each to the other.

In 2005, China's premier Wen Jiabao made the first visit of a Chinese leader to India. It marked the beginning of a deliberate effort by the governments of the two most populous Asian states to enhance bilateral trade and FDI. Within five years of Wen's visit, bilateral trade increased from US$14 billion to US$60 billion. Ten years after Wen's visit, China replaced the United States as India's largest trading partner. In addition to trade, partnerships are developing in the exchange of expertise with China exporting its expertise in manufacturing to India and India exporting its expertise in IT to China. FDI between the two countries has also increased as Chinese companies build plants in India. Somewhat ironically, India is attractive to Chinese FDI as a source of cheaper labor just as Shenzhen was initially attractive to Hong Kong entrepreneurs as a source of cheaper labor. Wages in China are now rising much faster than wages in India. This is partly explained not only by China's earlier embrace of the Global Shift but also by India's higher population growth, which led to India having a younger population than China. Today, China faces a rapidly aging population just like Japan and Western Europe. While FDI is flowing in both directions, the outflow from China to India is much larger and has grown by much more than India's since Wen's visit in 2005.

Historical Overview of India's Economic Growth since the Global Shift

We have identified the Global Shift as beginning in 1965 with the creation of the Maquiladoras Program. At the time, the GDP of India was US$58.8 billion. By comparison, the GDP of the United States was US$712.1billion, twelve times as large. In 1965, India was the seventh-largest economy in the world. Even though India embraced the Global Shift in the 1990s, by 2000, India's global ranking by GDP had slipped to thirteenth place. In 2000, India's GDP was US$460.2 billion. By comparison, the GDP of the United States was US$9,764.8 billion, 21.2 times as large. India had fallen behind both the United States and China despite having higher rates of growth after 1991. But as the Global Shift took hold in India during the twenty-first century, India's GDP would grow much faster than the United States, and the gap between India and Western economies would shrink as it had shrunk between China and Western economies.

During the first two decades of the twenty-first century, India's rate of economic growth has averaged 7 percent. This is more than twice the rate of growth of Western economies such as the United States. In 2014, India overtook China to become the world's fastest-growing large economy. With India's larger percentage of younger working age population compared to China, it is expected that India will continue to experience higher rates of growth than China into the next decade at least. India is projected to improve its global ranking from thirteenth place in 2000 to third place by 2025, just behind China and the United States. Unlike China, India's growth is driven more by the production of services than goods. But India is also the world's second-largest producer of farm products. In 2005, India's primary sector still employed 60 percent of its labor force while accounting for only 19 percent of total GDP. This meant that its secondary and tertiary sectors could still expand relative to the primary sector and thereby increase economy wide productivity. As with China before, India's embrace of the Global Shift requires large-scale movement of labor from the rural primary sector to the urban secondary and tertiary sectors. By 2018, India's primary sector's share of GDP had shrunk to 15 percent, while its tertiary sector had expanded to 60 percent.

India is ranked tenth in the world in output of manufactured goods. While its secondary sector employs only 15 percent of its labor force, it accounts for 25 percent of total GDP. As workers continued to move out of the relatively low-productivity primary sector into the secondary and tertiary sectors, overall productivity rose. India's manufacturing sector is growing at 8 percent annually. India is ranked fifteenth in the world in the production of services. This sector is growing by 9 percent annually, slightly outpacing the growth in manufacturing. India's service sector is also growing faster than the service sector of any other country in the world. It is in this sector that foreign demand plays the most significant role. Heavy Western investments in undersea fiber-optic cables has linked India and other parts of Asia to the West. Along with the Internet, personal computers, and trained English-speaking workers, India has become the leading country for business process outsourcing, BPO. This is India's fastest-growing sector, and India has transitioned from being the major BPO destination to a major exporter of BPO services, IT services, and software. The world's demand for electronic hardware was US$400 billion in 2018.

In 2015, forty-seven Indian companies were listed in the Forbes Global 2000 ranking. The highest-ranking Indian company was Reliance Industries, specializing in oil and gas. India's State Bank of India was its second-highest-ranked company in the Forbes list. India's highest-ranking IT company was TCS, coming in at number 485. India is a member of the G20 group. India's labor force is almost five hundred million and growing at 2.5 percent annually. With employment growth somewhat less, there will not be any overall excess demand for workers. This will keep Indian wage rates competitive. With casual labor accounting for 30 percent of all jobs, employers have greater flexibility in hiring part-time, temporary, and contract workers. Many workers currently classified as self-employed are willing to transition from the informal sector to formal steady employment.

In 2014, the Indian government led by Prime Minister Narendra Modi launched a Make in India program to boost production in India by both Indian and foreign companies. In 2015, India became the largest recipient of FDI, surpassing both China and the USA. In 2016, 2,500 international companies from 72 countries and 8,000 domestic companies attended the Make in India Week, a weeklong expo in Mumbai.

CHAPTER 7

How the Global Shift Made Indonesia the Third-Largest Economy in Asia after China and India and the Role Played by These Three Largest Asian Economies in Making the Twenty-First Century the Asian Century

I did not invent the term "Asian century," but I fully understand why the Chinese leader after Mao Zedong, Deng Xiaoping, in 1988, refuted the notion that the twenty-first century will be the Asian century, when Deng met with India's prime minister Rajiv Gandhi. What I invented was the term "Global Shift," and it's the Global Shift that will make the twenty-first century the Asian century. In 1988, neither the Chinese nor the Indian leader, nor any Western leader, could ever have imagined the revolutionary forces yet to be unleashed by the Global Shift. In fact, those who dared to imagine the Asian century in 1988 did so not because of the Global Shift but because of the rise of some Western-type free enterprise economies in Asia. These were the economies of Japan, South Korea, Taiwan, Singapore, and Hong Kong. These are not the economies of Asia that the Global Shift transformed. The Asian economies transformed by the Global Shift include China, India, Indonesia, Malaysia, Vietnam, Thailand, and the Philippines, among others. In 1988, these were still relatively poor Third World economies where large populations were still more of a liability than an asset. While the Global Shift had moved from Mexico to China by 1980, it had still been isolated largely in Shenzhen and Guangzhou as late as 1988. It had not reached India until 1991 and reached other Asian countries even later. In this chapter, we turn to these other Asian countries beginning with Indonesia.

China is the largest economy of Asia. India is the largest economy of South Asia. Indonesia is the largest economy of Southeast Asia. India is an ex-British colony. Indonesia is an ex-Dutch colony. China is an ex-colony of every Western imperial power, including Japan and Russia. All three countries are members of the G20. While both India and Indonesia, like China before Deng, were beginning to recognize the failures of their postindependence centrally planned economic models, it took a financial crisis in both India and Indonesia, and the visit of President Nixon in the case of China, for these countries to begin the process of dismantling their central planning institutions and move toward a market economy open to international trade and capital flows. We have explained the Chinese and Indian abandonments in previous chapters. Indonesia's abandonment began in 1998–2000 when, like India before, Indonesia was forced to stave off bankruptcy by seeking help from the IMF, which came with the usual strict financial restraints imposed by the IMF on all countries that it bails out.

Like India, before its financial crisis of 1991 and subsequent IMF bailout, Indonesia had begun to open its economy before its 1997 financial crisis, which was part of the wider Asian financial crisis. As a result of that opening up, Indonesia had experienced average annual growth rates of 7 percent between 1989 and 1997. But in 1998, Indonesia's economy, far from growing, declined by over 13 percent. Indonesia's recognition as a small global player dates back to the founding of ASEAN in 1967. This was a group of five Southeast Asian economies, Indonesia, Malaysia, Thailand, Singapore, and the Philippines. The group has since expanded to ten countries. Indonesia is the largest economy of the group. At the time, only Singapore could be considered what is now referred to as an emerging economy. However, the intent of this group was to generate rapid economic growth in Southeast Asia similar to what was being achieved in some Asian economies such as Japan, South Korea, Taiwan, and Hong Kong. Prior to the Asian financial crisis of 1997, Southeast Asia attracted a massive inflow of Western capital looking for higher interest rates. This boosted economic growth in the ASEAN countries, including Indonesia. The Asian economic crisis was caused by a flight of foreign capital from the region. All of the ASEAN countries were adversely affected. But Indonesia and Thailand were the two worst hit ASEAN countries. Since all this had very little to do with the Global Shift, we will date the Global Shift as arriving in Indonesia in 2000, almost a decade after reaching India and two decades after reaching China. We recognize the foundation provided for the Global Shift during the last decade of the twentieth century.

Prior to the Global Shift, Indonesia's economy also got a boost from the creation of the D-8 Organization for Economic Cooperation. This was a grouping of eight Muslim countries to develop their economies through trade and cooperation. It was founded in Turkey in 1997 around the same time that the Asian financial crisis hit Indonesia. Turkey is the most developed economy of this group, which includes Pakistan, Iran, Malaysia, Egypt, Nigeria, and Bangladesh, in addition to Indonesia. With the exception of India, these are the countries with the largest Muslim population, about 60 percent of the world's Muslims. Indonesia has the largest Muslim population of any country in the world.

As a result of the Global Shift, Indonesia's economy has grown much faster than Western economies. Since 2000, Indonesia's average annual growth has exceeded 5 percent and is the third highest of the G20 countries after China and India. In 1972, Indonesia's GDP was US$11,605 million compared with US$1,225,399 million for the United States, US$112, 160 million for China, and US$71, 128 million for India. China was ranked seventh in the world. India was ranked ninth in the world, and Indonesia was ranked twenty-ninth in the world. Japan was the largest Asian economy with a world ranking of second, after the United States. South Korea was the next largest Asian economy after Indonesia with a ranking of thirty-two. In 2000, China had moved up to sixth place, while Indonesia had moved up to twenty-seventh place. India had moved to thirteenth place, behind South Korea, which had moved up to twelfth place. Japan kept its second-place ranking after the United States. This is what we would expect because the Global Shift reached China before India and Indonesia. But we would expect all three to move up the ranking as the Global Shift took hold. That is precisely what happened. By 2016, China had moved up the global ranking to second place, replacing Japan as Asia's largest economy. Japan had fallen to third place in the world. India had moved up to seventh place, and Indonesia had moved up to sixteenth place. South Korea had moved to eleventh place. While the U.S. GDP was 106 times the GDP of Indonesia in 1972, it was only 20 times the GDP of Indonesia in 2016. In 2000, South Korea's GDP was over three times as large as Indonesia's. By 2016, South Korea's GDP was less than one and a half times that of Indonesia.

Using PPP instead of exchange rates, Indonesia ranked as the eighth-largest economy in 2016, while China ranked first, ahead of the United States, and India ranked third, after China and the United States. Using the PPP measure of GDP, China and India had overtaken Japan as the two largest Asian economies. Indonesia had overtaken South Korea as the largest Asian economy after China, India, and Japan. This is further proof of the miracle produced by the Global Shift. By 2020, Indonesia is expected to move up to seventh place using the PPP measure of GDP.

Thailand and the Global Shift

We now analyze the effect of the Global Shift on Thailand. Thailand is the largest Asian economy after China, India, Indonesia, Japan, and South Korea. Japan and South Korea developed before the Global Shift reached Asia. We therefore exclude them from our analysis of Asian economies. This means that Thailand is the largest Asian economy benefitting from the Global Shift after China, India, and Indonesia. Thailand is the second-largest economy in Southeast Asia after Indonesia. In 1972, Thailand had the thirty-ninth-largest economy in the world. It was well behind other Asian economies such as Japan, China, India, Indonesia, South Korea, and Pakistan. But it was ranked higher than some Asian economies such as the Philippines, Bangladesh, Hong Kong, and Malaysia. As it is difficult to identify precisely when the Global Shift reached Thailand, we will use the year 2000 as we did with Indonesia. In that year, Thailand had moved up the global ranking to number thirty-one. This is no surprise as Thailand, like Indonesia, was a founding member of ASEAN in 1967 and the second-largest economy of the group. Like Indonesia, Thailand had benefitted immensely from the capital inflow into Southeast Asia and was as severely damaged by the Asian financial crisis as Indonesia. While predating the Global Shift, membership in ASEAN laid a good foundation for Thailand to easily respond to the Global Shift as Indonesia had done.

In embracing the Global Shift, Thailand followed the example of China by establishing SEZs. Thailand also took advantage of China's early embrace of the Global Shift by creating a free trade agreement with China. As a result, China replaced the United States as Thailand's largest export market. This is another example of the Global Shift maturing in Asia with China upgrading from recipient of the Global Shift from the developed economies to the emerging economies, to playing a role in moving the Global Shift to all of Asia. Prior to the Asian financial crisis of 1997, Thailand had experienced annual rates of growth exceeding 7 percent as part of the Western obsession with Southeast Asia. In the post–Global Shift era, beginning in 2000, economic growth was more modest, around 5 percent, annually. Thailand was then hit hard by the December 2004 tsunami, especially its tourism sector. This was followed by a period of political instability. Nevertheless, Thailand continued to achieve annual economic growth averaging 5 percent. While lower than China, India, and Indonesia, it is twice as large as the Western economies.

Thailand will continue to play an important role in ASEAN and Southeast Asia. In 2016, the government unveiled a new growth strategy called 4.0 with the goal of increasing annual growth and transforming Thailand from a middle-income economy to a high-income economy. By 2017, Thailand's global ranking had moved up from number thirty-one in 2000 to number twenty-six, just behind the Western European economy of Belgium, ranked twenty-fifth. In 1965, when the Global Shift began on Mexico's border with the United States, Belgium was the world's sixteenth-largest economy, while Thailand was ranked at number thirty-six. Belgium's GDP of US$17,371 million was almost four times as large as Thailand's GDP of US$4,389 million. Belgium had been one of Western Europe's imperial powers with one of the largest colonies in Africa, the Belgian Congo.

The Philippines and the Global Shift

The next largest economy in Southeast Asia after Indonesia and Thailand is the Philippines. The Philippines was also a founding member of ASEAN in 1967. In 1972, its world economic ranking was forty, just behind Thailand at thirty-ninth place. As an American uncolony like Taiwan, South Korea, and Japan, it benefitted from its Cold War alliance with the United States against the Soviet Union. But it never achieved the high rates of economic growth achieved by America's other Asian Cold War prostitutes. In fact, it was at one time referred to as the sick man of Southeast Asia. That began to change with the influx of Western capital into Southeast Asia. In the decade preceding the 1997 Asian financial crash, economic growth averaged 5 percent and peaked at 6.75 percent in 1988. While this economic growth was lower than those achieved by the Asian tigers, South Korea, Taiwan, Singapore, and Hong Kong, it was high enough to gain the nickname of Tiger Cub, alongside its other two ASEAN partners, Indonesia and Thailand.

We will date the Global Shift reaching the Philippines at the same time as it reached Indonesia and Thailand, 2000. In 2000, the Philippines had fallen behind in the world ranking of economies by GDP, slipping from forty to forty-two. In the meantime, Thailand had moved up from thirty-nine to thirty-one. While Thailand copied China by creating SEZs, the Philippines copied India by setting up call centers and attracting the Western offshoring business, business processing outsourcing, BPO. Like India, the Philippines had a large supply of English-speaking educated workers who could provide these services to Western companies at a much lower wage rate than Western workers. In fact, the Philippines raced past India to become the world's largest host country for BPO in 2008.

In addition to attracting a large share of the offshoring business as a result of the Global Shift, the Philippines also benefitted from huge annual remittances from overseas Filipinos. These remittances accounted for 10 percent of the GDP of the Philippines. These two key factors returned the Philippines to the growth status of Tiger Cub achieved in the decade prior to the 1997 crash. In the two decades following the Global Shift, the Philippines achieved average annual growth rates exceeding 5 percent, peaking at 7.63 percent in 2010. Its growth rate is comparable to Indonesia and higher than Thailand. These three founding members and three largest economies of ASEAN play a key role in advancing economic growth in Southeast Asia. Together with China and India, they lead the Global Shift in Asia. By 2017, the Philippines had also improved its global ranking from number forty-two in 2000 to number thirty-four, just behind Hong Kong at number thirty-three. In 2000, Hong Kong, one of the four Asian Tigers, was ranked at number twenty-five. We now turn to another founding member of ASEAN, Malaysia.

Malaysia and the Global Shift

In 1972, Malaysia was ranked as the world's fiftieth-largest economy behind the other founding members of ASEAN, Indonesia, Thailand, and the Philippines. It is the fourth-largest economy in Southeast Asia. While Singapore was the sixth founding member of ASEAN, it was an emerging economy before the Global Shift and one of the four Asian Tigers. Malaysia, like India, is an ex-British colony. When the Global

Shift arrived in Malaysia in 2000, it had moved up the global ranking to number forty. This move up by Indonesia, Thailand, and Malaysia would be due to the same reason, which was the influx of Western capital into Southeast Asia in the years immediately preceding the crash of 1997. The West was of the view that these Southeast Asian economies would take off as the Asian Tigers had done earlier. In the two decades prior to the crash, Malaysia experienced average annual economic growth over 7 percent. After the crash, it was the Global Shift that would return their economies to high rates of growth.

Despite its larger percentage of English-speaking workers, Malaysia is following China more than India to the extent that the focus of the Global Shift in Malaysia is manufacturing. Malaysia is one of the largest exporters of electronics and semiconductors. Its semiconductor industry is 30 percent of its total manufacturing sector. The Global Shift pushed up the global ranking of Malaysia from number forty in 2000 to number thirty-six in 2017, just behind South Africa. In summary, the Asian economies that we have so far analyzed for the effect of the Global Shift have the following global ranking in 2017. China is ranked number two, India is ranked number six, Indonesia is ranked number fifteen, Thailand is ranked number twenty-six, the Philippines is ranked number thirty-four, and Malaysia is ranked number thirty-six. China has made the most gains because the Global Shift reached China almost two decades earlier, even though the Southeast Asian economies had a jump start on China prior to the Asian financial crisis of 1997. We will now look at how ASEAN as a group has been affected by the Global Shift.

ASEAN and the Global Shift

We have analyzed individually the effect of the Global Shift on each of the founding members of ASEAN except Singapore. However, by 2000, when the Global Shift reached the ASEAN economies, ASEAN had doubled its membership from the original five to ten. The later five members have economies smaller than the four we have analyzed individually. We will therefore look at how the Global Shift affected this enlarged group as a whole. As a group, ASEAN has an economy that would have a global ranking of number five. The goal of ASEAN is to behave as a group similar to the European Union. It is not yet as integrated as the EU as it began the process much later than the EU. It was not until 2007 that ASEAN agreed to a charter to form an EU-type community. Like the EU before, that charter referred to the underlying goal of bringing permanent peace to Southeast Asia just as the underlying goal of the EU is to bring permanent peace to Western Europe. Like the EU, ASEAN is focusing on common economic growth as the key weapon against military conflicts. It was not until 2015 that ASEAN followed the EU in creating a common market. It has begun to implement greater freedom for flows of labor starting with professionals. It is discussing the formation of a monetary union with a single currency like the majority of countries in the EU. The five countries that joined the group after 1967 are Vietnam, Cambodia, Laos, Myanmar, and Brunei. ASEAN includes all the countries in Southeast Asia except for Timor-Leste, which has a GDP much smaller than any of the member state of ASEAN. We can conclude that ASEAN speaks for all of Southeast Asia.

By 2000, the Global Shift had reached all the member countries of ASEAN. Once the United States had determined that it could work with China against the Soviet Union, the West also embraced the Communist countries in Indo-China, Vietnam, Cambodia, and Laos, which the United States had waged war on for decades. The United States, like the French empire before, lost that war. As a result, the United States turned to economic colonization as it had done elsewhere. Western capital flowed into ASEAN even before the Global Shift reached China. But that was a pre–Global Shift capital inflow similar to what had occurred in other Asian countries such Japan, South Korea, Taiwan, Hong Kong, and Singapore. It was the strategy the United States had used in Canada and Western Europe before. That inflow of Western capital into ASEAN ended abruptly in 1997. After 2000, it was the Global Shift that injected new growth into ASEAN. The world was moving in a direction no longer controlled by the United States even though it had the implicit blessing of the United States. No one truly understands the revolutionary nature of the Global Shift because they confuse it with old-fashioned *Globalization* and outsourcing. The latter was tightly controlled by the United States as the dominant player in the military, financial markets, capital flows, international trade, colonization, reserve currency, WTO, IMF, UN, and the World Bank.

The creation of a group called ASEAN Pus Three in 1997 is another indication of the United States losing its grip on Asia. The Plus Three countries are China, Japan, and South Korea. The latter two are longtime economic uncolonies of the American empire. That they would even contemplate forming a union that excludes their master is a sign of how the Global Shift is revolutionizing global hegemony. U.S. silence on this arrangement emboldened the group to move toward an expanded group of ASEAN Plus Six by adding India, Australia, and New Zealand. The latter two countries are not only longtime uncolonies of the American empire but also members of the English-speaking Anglo imperialism group of the United States, Britain, Canada, Australia, and New Zealand. The latter group is the most die-hard group of pro-imperialism military invaders the world has ever created. That two of their members, albeit the two weakest in terms of military might, are also located in Asia is another sign of how the Global Shift is replacing the American century with the Asian century. In 2009, ASEAN signed a free trade agreement with Australia and New Zealand. In 2010, a free trade agreement between ASEAN and China came into effect. ASEAN has also concluded free trade agreements with India, South Korea, and Japan. In 2013, the ASEAN Plus Six group began formal talks to create a regional economic partnership. This group produces over a third of the world's GDP.

Pakistan-China Integration and the Global Shift

As we explained in the previous chapter, British colonization of India had reduced India from a country richer than all of Europe to one of the most poverty-stricken countries on the planet. India's independence from Britain in 1947 came with the price of losing some of its territory and population to a newly created country called Pakistan. Like India, Pakistan was a poverty-stricken country where it was as cursed as India in having too many mouths to feed with too few resources. In 1972, India was the world's ninth-largest economy, while Pakistan was the world's thirty-fourth-largest economy. Since both countries had large populations, their per capita incomes were very low. The standard view of economists was that these densely populated countries were trapped into permanent poverty with no means of escape. Like India, Pakistan would refute the theory of the poverty trap after embracing the Global Shift in 2000. In addition to embracing the Global Shift, Pakistan has increased the integration of its economy with that of China. One of the important stumbling blocks to embracing the Global Shift is poor infrastructure.

The China-Pakistan post–Global Shift embrace is one of many examples of how the massive economic growth of China caused by the Global Shift has enabled China to have the wealth to assist many of the smaller Asian, African, and Latin American economies, such as Pakistan, build the infrastructure to facilitate the Global Shift in their countries.

Ever since Pakistan broke away from India, there have been military rivalry and border conflicts between the two countries. There has also been border conflicts between China and India. Economic integration between Pakistan and China is therefore motivated not only by the resulting economic gains but also for security concerns. This economic integration between China and Pakistan is best illustrated by the China-Pakistan Economic Corridor, CPEC, a project costing US$54 billion. The goal of CPEC is for China to pay for infrastructure modernization in Pakistan, which will benefit China's security as well as its economy. CPEC is China's largest foreign investment project as well as Pakistan's largest capital inflow project. It is the key to transforming Pakistan from a poor Third World country to an economic hub in South Asia. China showed an interest in creating an economic and transportation link to Pakistan's deepwater ports on the Arabian Sea long before the Global Shift. But it was the Global Shift in China that enabled China to have the funds for such an expensive project, and it was the Global Shift to both China and Pakistan that solidified the profitability of such an expensive undertaking for both countries. CPEC is seen as a win-win for both countries. Pakistan will modernize its relatively primitive infrastructure to accommodate the Global Shift, and China will get an alternative route for its needed imports of energy from the Middle East and much more.

A key part of the CPEC project is the development of Pakistan's three deepwater ports, Gwardar, Karachi, and Qasim, and providing the transportation infrastructure to link these ports to China as well as SEZs in Pakistan. This includes an 1,100-kilometer modern highway linking Pakistan's two major cities and industrial hubs, Karachi and Lahore. Karachi is Pakistan's largest city with a population of seventeen million. It is also Pakistan's primary financial and industrial center. Located on the Arabian Sea, it has Pakistan's two largest deepwater ports, the Port of Karachi and Port Qasim. Lahore is Pakistan's second-largest city with a population of eleven million. It is the capital city of Pakistan's Punjab Province located on the border of India's Punjab Province. Another important transportation project is the modernization of the Karakoram Highway from Pakistan's other two large cities, Islamabad and Rawalpindi, to the border of China. Islamabad is the capital city of Pakistan, and Rawalpindi is another large city in Pakistan's Punjab Province. Other transportation infrastructure includes fast trains from Pakistan to China and pipelines for oil and gas.

Construction of the deepwater Gwardar Port began in 2007. This port is close to Pakistan's border with Iran and 530 kilometers west of Karachi. It provides access to Iran, Afghanistan, Oman, the Persian Gulf, and the Central Asian Republics created after the fall of the Soviet Union. CPEC will improve transportation infrastructure from China to the Central Asian Republics via Pakistan's Gwardar Port. In 2015, the expansion of this port as well as the city of Gwardar became part of the CPEC project. The Gwardar SEZ is modeled after China's SEZs. Prior to CPEC, China's imports of energy from the Middle East came via the Sea of Malacca and the South China Sea. The security of this route is threatened by the United States. It is also a longer route than the one created by CPEC via Pakistan's deepwater Gwadar Port. CPEC not only modernized Pakistan's infrastructure but also linked Pakistan's Gwadar Port to China. China's Xinjiang Province is only three thousand kilometers from Gwadar Port. Xinjiang Province can act as a gateway to China's Western Economic Region, all the way to Tibet. In addition to bringing energy to China from the Middle East, China uses the port for its exports to West Asia and Africa. These exports began in 2016.

While Pakistan's GDP had risen significantly between 1972 and 2017, its global ranking had fallen from thirty-fourth place to forty-third place, behind the five largest ASEAN economies, Indonesia, Thailand, the Philippines, Malaysia, and Singapore. This was due both to its lack of infrastructure and political instability. CPEC is essential to Pakistan's future economic growth. The World Bank predicts GDP growth exceeding 5 percent as a result of CEPEC. Pakistan is becoming an increasingly attractive country for services offshoring. Like the Philippines, Pakistan receives remittances from overseas Pakistanis working in the Gulf States, Western Europe, and North America. As a Muslim majority country, Pakistan is a member of the D-8 Organization for Economic Cooperation, along with Indonesia and Malaysia.

Bangladesh and the Global Shift

In 1971, the territory of Pakistan, called East Pakistan, waged a successful war of independence with Pakistan to become the new country of Bangladesh. India aided East Pakistan in this war just as France had aided the United States in its war of independence. Bangladesh, like India and Pakistan, was another poverty-stricken country. In 1972, India had the world's ninth-largest economy, Pakistan had the World's thirty-fourth-largest economy, and Bangladesh had the world's forty-fifth-largest economy. Since all three countries had large populations, their per capita incomes were all very low. Bangladesh is also a member of the D-8 Organization for Economic Cooperation, along with Indonesia, Malaysia, and Pakistan.

After independence, Bangladesh followed a similar "planned" economic system like India. Economic growth was disappointing. After embracing the Global Shift, economic growth matched that of India, averaging over 6.5 percent annually. Bangladesh has the second-highest rate of economic growth among all the countries of South Asia, just slightly behind India. While India specialized in services, Bangladesh specialized in textiles. As a result, female employment opportunities have increased significantly. Bangladesh has become the world's second-largest exporter of textile products after China. The textiles are produced in SEZs similar to SEZs established in China. Political and economic relations between Bangladesh and Pakistan were strained because of the War of Independence. They improved after Pakistan's prime minister visited Bangladesh in 1974. Pakistan and Bangladesh have signed a free trade agreement to boost trade and economic cooperation.

In 2017, Bangladesh was ranked as the world's forty-fifth-largest economy, slightly behind Pakistan with a ranking of forty-third. However, its per capita GDP is somewhat higher. China has made an effort to cooperate with Bangladesh, Pakistan, and India with its Belt and Road Initiative. An important part of that massive project is BCIM, the Bangladesh-China-India-Myanmar Economic Corridor. This complements CPEC, which we discussed above as being important to the development of Pakistan. Since both of these infrastructure projects are led by China, they will help to integrate the South Asian economies and reduce conflicts among China, India, Pakistan, and Bangladesh.

This completes our analyses of the impact of the Global Shift on the major Asian countries China, India, and Indonesia, as well as its impact on two major groups of Asian countries, ASEAN and South Asia. The remainder of this chapter will look at how the Global Shift has combined with the pre–Global Shift advanced Asian economies such as Japan to make the twenty-first century the Asian century. While the notion of an Asian century replacing the American century began with Japan becoming the world's second-largest economy before China, our contention is that Asia would not have replaced the West as the dominant continent had it not been for the Global Shift. The Global Shift has made this happen for two reasons. First, it has added significant growth to the Asian economies of China, India, and Indonesia as well as Asian groups of economies such as ASEAN and in South Asia. This complements the pre–Global Shift high GDP Asian economies such as Japan, South Korea, Taiwan, Singapore, and Hong Kong. The second reason is the economic opportunities provided by post–Global Shift high GDP Asian economies to the pre–Global Shift high GDP Asian economies. We have seen how Hong Kong's economy was boosted by China's first SEZ in Shenzhen. This is only one example of how the pre–Global Shift high GDP Asian economies grabbed the economic opportunities presented to them by their close geographic proximity to the emerging Asian economies. Initially, they supplied the factories and entrepreneurship, just as the United States built the factories along the Mexican border in the maquiladoras. But as incomes rose and technology and infrastructure improved in the emerging economies, they became more equal trading partners much like the developed economies in Western Europe. We now turn to this analysis of the coming Asian century.

How the Global Shift Created the Asian Century

The American century was based on the fact that after Western European economies self-destructed during the Second World War, the United States became both the largest economy in the world and the dominant military power. It's sad that hegemony in the world has always been based on military might. Military might requires a significant economic base. The United States had the economic base and the military muscle after the Second World War to control the skies, the shipping lanes, global financial markets, the WTO, the World Bank, the IMF, the UN, and the reserve currency. It used its military might to threaten or induce most countries in the world to accept its dominance and leadership. Dissenters were either bombed back to the Stone Age or impoverished by economic sanctions. No dissent was tolerated. There was no freedom of speech, free media, genuine democracy, justice, or human development. American propaganda became sophisticated and all powerful. American culture was exported en masse to the many American uncolonies across the globe. After a while, these uncolonies did not question American leadership. It became the norm. Any and all non-American behavior was automatically deemed immoral, stupid, deranged, idiotic, unjust, undemocratic, unpatriotic, crazy, and insane. The media never questioned its subservience but embraced it with stupid splendor and devout ignorance. In time, they championed it.

As the U.S. share of the world's GDP shrinks because of the Global Shift, its ability to use its military power to coerce concessions and obedience from those it has ruled with an iron fist, as the Roman Empire had done, will shrink as well. Economic growth will also enable countries to grow their military, which will gradually erode the huge gap between the military might of the United States and those it rules. Some U.S. allies will begin to question the subservience required by the alliance and form new alliances among themselves or with the emerging economies. As U.S. domination and leadership wane, Asia will become more assertive. In particular, the United States made a huge mistake when it agreed to engage with China without insisting that China relinquish its independent military and political system. The United States had not agreed to that with any other country, including Japan, Germany, Saudi Arabia, South Korea, Canada, and the other countries of Western Europe. That mistake could not have been seen in 1980 when the Global Shift first reached China. In 1980, China was such a poor country relative to many of the U.S. staunchest allies, much less the United States itself, that the thought of China ever challenging the United States for hegemony was preposterous.

To understand how the Global Shift has replaced the American century with the Asian century, we will analyze relative changes in GDPs, military spending, reserve currencies, and new regional alliances in Asia such as China's Belt and Road Initiative, the Asian Infrastructure Investment Bank, AIIB, the Shanghai Cooperation Organization, SCO, and the South Asia Free Trade Agreement after 1979. We begin with

GDPs since we firmly believe that military, political, and financial domination of the world requires a massive GDP base.

In 1979, The GDP of the United States was US$2,544.5 million. By comparison, China's GDP was US$175.6 million, India's GDP was US$150.9 million, and Indonesia's GDP was US$55.1 million. We selected the latter three Asian economies because these are the three Asian economies among the many emerging economies of Asia that are leading the replacement of the American century by the Asian century. These figures show that the GDP of these three important Asian economies together constituted only 15 percent of the GDP of the United States in 1979. Fast forward to 2017, the GDP of the United States increased to US$19,417.1 billion, while the GDP of China increased to US$11,795.3 million, that of India increased to US$2,454.5 million, and that of Indonesia increased to US$1,020.5 million. As a result, the combined GDP of these three important Asian economies rose to 79 percent of the GDP of the United States. That is over five times as much as 1979.

The second part of our analysis of how the Global Shift is replacing the American century with the Asian century was that the pre–Global Shift Asian allies of the United States were entangling their economies with the emerging economies of Asia in their efforts to cash in on the Global Shift in Asia. These are the economies of Japan, South Korea, and Singapore. We have excluded Hong Kong since Hong Kong has since become part of China. We have also excluded Taiwan as it is a disputed province of China. In 1979, the GDP of Japan was US$1,007.2 million, the GDP of South Korea was US$65.6 million, and the GDP of Singapore was US$9.1 million. The combined GDP of these three American allies in Asia was US$1,081.9 million. By comparison, the combined GDP of the three important emerging economies in Asia, China, India, and Indonesia was only US$381.6 million. In 1979, not only did the GDP of the United States far exceed the combined GDP of the three important Asian economies leading the creation of the Asian Century, but also the GDP of American allies in Asia, excluding Taiwan and Hong Kong, also far exceeded the combined GDP of the three important emerging economies in Asia. Specifically, the combined GDP of the three U.S. allies was almost three times the combined GDP of the three emerging economies.

In 2017, the GDP of Japan had increased to US$4,841.2 million, the GDP of South Korea had increased to US$1,498.1 million, and the GDP of Singapore had increased to US$291.9 million. Their combined GDP in 2017 was US$6,631.2 million. This was now much *lower* than the combined GDP of US$15,270.3 million for the three emerging economies. At the same time, the economies of Hong Kong and Taiwan had largely switched over to China, while alliance of Japan, South Korea, and Singapore with the United States had weakened. In 2017, the GDP of the entire Asian continent was much larger than that of the United States. Even if we exclude the combined GDP of the three historical allies of the West, Japan, South Korea, and Singapore, the GDP of the rest of Asia exceeded that of the United States in 2017.

Prior to the Second World War, the United States had challenged Japan for imperial dominance in the Asia-Pacific region. This had led to war between the United States and Japan with the United States emerging as the winner and the United States' "colonization" of Japan and South Korea. The rise of China has not only replaced Japan with China as the new competitor with the United States for military, political, and economic dominance in the Asia-Pacific region but also strained the ability of the United States to keep Japan and South Korea as uncolonies of the American empire. Since Japan, South Korea, and Singapore were the first of the "Western" countries to fuel the move of their manufacturing factories from their home locations to China, it is natural to expect that they would be the first of many more to jump ship on a relatively declining superpower to the new emerging superpower. Another important difference between China and Japan is that Japan colonized Asia to become a Western imperial power like the United States, Britain, France, Germany, and Russia. China has always maintained its strong commitment to Asia first. It's a difference similar to France and Britain. When France and Britain competed for global dominance, Britain behaved like Japan, while France behaved like China. For France, it was always Europe first. For Britain, it was always empire first.

A Western G7 Compared to an Asian G7 during the American Century and the Asian Century

In the previous section, we compared the three leading emerging economies of Asia created by the Global Shift with the U.S. economy as well as with three of the five pre–Global Shift U.S. allies in Asia. Since we claim that the primary basis for expecting the American century to be replaced by the Asian century is the higher GDP growth created by the Global Shift in Asia compared with the West, we want to do a *broader* comparison of pre–Global Shift and post–Global Shift Western and Asian economies. We have decided on a total of seven economies because of the post–World War II dominance of the G7 Western economies. Note that this was increased to the G8 by adding Russia, but Russia was once again denounced and discarded by the West. Canada led that most recent chastising of Russia even though the Canadian state was built by stealing First Nations lands and resources. Western hypocrisy implies that building a nation on lands stolen by military force, as Canada and the United States did, is far more moral than if a country like Russia democratically reclaims a piece of territory as Russia did in Crimea in 2014.

Kicking Russia out of the G8 confirms our view that it's never clear which side Russia will be on. Likewise, Japan's permanent place in the G7 confirms our view that Japan has always chosen to be Western first and Asian second. This G7 group of economies had largely been developed and semicolonized by the United States after World War II. Prior to World War II, the United States was content to let the world be led by the dominant Western European empires as it consolidated its dominance in the Asia-Pacific region. But the destruction of the Western European empires during World War II led the United States to rebuild the Western European economies as well as Japan and Canada to form this powerful group of economies, the G7. While the U.S. share of the world's GDP declined after its high point following the Second World War, this was offset by growing the economies of its uncolonies, Canada, Germany, Japan, France, the UK, and Italy. It was a brilliant strategy to maintain its global dominance. Instead of having six global empires, the United States, the UK, Japan, Germany, France, and Italy, competing for global dominance, as they did before World War II, the United States would lead a combined G7 group against the rest. With opposition coming only from the Soviet Union, the West launched a massive propaganda war to demonize Communism. When that had limited success, the United States turned to China in 1972 to help it defeat its only threat to global domination, the Soviet Union. While the formation of the G7 was a brilliant strategic move by the United States, courting China on China's terms was a disaster. But in 1972, when the Global Shift was still largely confined to the Mexican maquiladoras, the United States was a superpower and tightly controlled the other six largest economies through its leadership of the G7. By contrast, China was a poverty-stricken, overpopulated, has-been imperial power whose only use to the United States was its ability to sway a few Communist countries against the Soviet Union.

An Asian post–Global Shift equivalent of the G7 would be the seven largest emerging economies in Asia, China, India, Indonesia, Thailand, the Philippines, Malaysia, and Pakistan. In 1979, the Western G7 was made up of the world's seven largest economies. These were the United States, Japan, Germany, France, the UK, Italy, and Canada. Their combined GDP in 1979 was US$6,047.5 million. In 1979, the combined GDP of the countries that we have included to create the post–Global Shift, Asian G-7, was a paltry US$477.8 million. This was less than 8 percent of the GDP of the G7 countries. By 2017, China's GDP had overtaken all the G7 countries except the United States. France had slipped from fourth place to sixth place, behind both China and India. Canada had slipped even more from seventh place to tenth place, behind China, India, and Brazil. In 2017, the combined GDP of the Western G7 countries was US$36,006.5 million. In 2017, the combined GDP of the Asian G7 was US$16,594.3 million. It had increased from 7.9 percent to 46 percent, almost six times as large. The relative economic decline of the Western G7 looks even worse if Japan and South Korea switch their alliance with the West to Asia. GDP can be measured by using exchange rates or purchasing power parity, PPP. The latter comparison used exchange rates to measure GDP. Using the PPP measure, the combined GDP for the G7 countries will fall to 28.73 percent of the world's GDP in 2020. By contrast, the combined GDP of an Asian G7 will rise to 34.30 percent of the world's GDP in 2020. This makes an Asian G7 a real threat to American hegemony.

The New Military Balance of Power Created by the Global Shift

In assessing how the Global Shift has undermined the military superiority of the American empire, a complicating factor is Russia. Russia, like Japan before, was often marginalized by the other Western imperial powers, the United States, Britain, France, and Germany. It's therefore never clear which side Russia is on. While in the pre–Global

Shift era, Russia switched sides between East and West and fought a long Cold War with the West; in the post–Global Shift era, the uncertainty is whether Russia will throw its immense military prowess with China or with the United States. During the Second World War, the United States was clever enough to understand that it could never defeat Germany without the aid of the Russian military. That is why it taught its children to think of Josef Stalin as their dearly beloved "Uncle Joe." Once there was no German threat, the West turned on Russia as it had done many times before. We will analyze the Global Shift in Russia in greater detail in the next chapter where we will return to this important question. In this chapter, we will focus more on the changing military prowess of the United States and its pre–Global Shift Asian allies, compared with China and the emerging economies of Asia. However, we cannot totally ignore Russia since Russia has made significant moves to mend relations with China after the fall of the Soviet Union. In 1972, the United States took advantage of strained relations between the Soviet Union and China to court China as an ally. But in the twenty-first century, the United States has underestimated the new leadership in Russia. Just as the Soviet Union thrived under Stalin and Khrushchev, Russia is thriving again under Putin. By foolishly demonizing Putin, the United States is unwittingly driving Russia into the arms of a rising and increasingly assertive Asia led by China, not the United States or its Asian allies, Japan and South Korea.

NATO versus the SCO

After the Second World War, the American empire created a military alliance, NATO, with the old Western European empires, to complement its G7 economic alliance, in its bid to dominate the post–World War II world and create the American century. The Asian century cannot become a reality unless Asia can match the military prowess of NATO. We therefore need to review NATO and its Asian counterpart. NATO was created in 1949 by the North Atlantic Treaty. Western propaganda called it a defensive treaty, but it was an offensive treaty designed to contain the Soviet Union and secure American hegemony. While the G7 largest seven economies provided the economic resources for American hegemony, NATO provided the military hardware to threaten, invade, destroy, and colonize any who dared to resist, challenge, or voice any disagreement with the new "Roman Empire," which is the American empire. Unlike the Roman Empire, which had a global reach limited by armies traveling over land, the NATO alliance had the most powerful planes and bombs, which could bomb, and did bomb, even the remotest corner of the globe, back to the Stone Age and create millions of refugees. Just as the Western European empires used sophisticated propaganda to justify their evil deeds for six centuries before World War II, NATO uses even more sophisticated propaganda to convince the great gullible majority that bombing and destroying poor defenseless countries is the best way to help the millions of refugees and bring Western democracy to their countries.

When NATO rejected a request by the Soviet Union to join the alliance in 1954, it sent an explicit message to the Soviet Union that NATO was an offensive military alliance intended to oppose any, including the Soviet Union, who would threaten American domination. In response, the Soviet Union created the Warsaw Pact to deter American-led Western aggression. The Warsaw Pact was a military alliance of the Soviet Union with countries in Eastern Europe. These Eastern European allies provided a buffer region between the Soviet Union and the American allies in Western Europe. The Warsaw Pact collapsed with the collapse of the Soviet Union. At the same time, the reunification of East and West Germany and the incorporation of the Eastern European allies of the Soviet Union into the EU and NATO expanded the economic and military power of NATO. During the period between the collapse of the Soviet Union in 1991 and before the creation of the Asian century later in this century, NATO reigned supreme and unchecked. It began a merciless bombing campaign of Muslim countries in the Middle East and North Africa using a newfound propaganda, *fighting terrorism,* to replace its old propaganda, *fighting Communism.* The world has never witnessed such wanton destruction of property and large-scale creation of refugees. When the American empire stole the First Nations lands in the New World, it *explicitly* claimed that "the only good Indian is a dead Indian." With the rise of political correctness after 1991, NATO could only *implicitly* claim that "the only good Muslim was a dead Muslim."

We have suggested above that the creation of the Asian century will require an Asian G7 to match the American G7 economic alliance. In like manner, the creation of the Asian century will require a military alliance to match NATO. This will be a challenge for Asia since the total military expenditure of NATO is 70 percent of the world's total. This brings us to the Shanghai Cooperation Organization, SCO. The SCO is the most likely candidate to provide an Asian military alliance capable of coming close to matching NATO. For this reason, we now turn to a description and analysis of SCO.

The SCO began modestly in 1996 as the Shanghai Five, made up of China, Russia, and three of the new Republics created after the fall of the Soviet Union, Kazakhstan, Tajikistan, and Kyrgyzstan. Its name was changed to the Shanghai Cooperation Organization in 2001 when another of the new Central Asian republics, Uzbekistan, was added. In some ways, the SCO can be seen as a Central Asian attempt to mirror the initial creation of the European Economic Community, EEC, in 1958 by West Germany, France, Italy, Holland, Belgium, and Luxembourg. The SCO, like the original EEC, would reduce the likelihood of border conflicts and wars while promoting trade and economic integration. Just as the EEC saw opportunities to expand its global clout by increasing its members, the SCO has followed suit. The SCO has a lot of catching up to do to match the twenty-eight-member European Union. It was not until 2017 that India and Pakistan became members of the SCO. Adding India is significant both because India is the second-largest emerging economy in Asia after China and because it will reduce military and border tensions between India and China. Adding Pakistan is also significant in reducing border and military tensions between India and Pakistan while adding another member of what we have identified as an Asian G7.

The eight-member SCO has a combined GDP comparable to that of the twenty-eight-member EU. The SCO has a larger population base because of its inclusion of the world's two most populous countries, China and India. Its military capabilities is comparable to that of the EU but falls short of matching that of NATO since NATO includes the United States, Turkey, and Canada. Its military capability is also highly dependent on its inclusion of Russia, which we will analyze in the next chapter from the point of view of the Global Shift. On the other side of the coin, we have indicated before that the two largest American allies in Asia, Japan and South Korea, may jump ship and align with China in the future. Turkey, an important member of NATO, may also jump ship and align with the SCO. Turkey, like Russia, is not fully accepted as an equal by the West. American domination of the world has been built on subservient allies such as Canada and members of the EU. Turkey, like

Russia, has refused to be a docile ally. Other possible countries likely to become future members of the SCO include Iran, Afghanistan, Belarus, Mongolia, Azerbaijan, Cambodia, Armenia, Sri Lanka, Nepal, Egypt, Bangladesh, Vietnam, Iraq, and Syria. These are all countries that have benefitted from the Global Shift. Many have had difficult relations with the West. Qingdao hosted the eighteenth summit of SCO in June 2018.

CHAPTER 8

The Global Shift and Russia

As we have explained above, it's unclear whether Russia views itself as an emerging economy created by the Global Shift, like China, India, and Indonesia, or a pre–Global Shift developed economy and one of the great powers like Britain, France, Germany, Japan, and the United States. Of course, Russia had not only been a great power for centuries but also led the Soviet Union as one of the only two superpowers after the Second World War. But the collapse of the Soviet Union in 1991 turned Russia into what the West deemed to be a developing economy on par with China, India, and Brazil, one of the four members of BRIC. The economy of the Soviet Union had been in relative decline since the late 1960s and collapsed under its last leader, Mikhail Gorbachev. The dissolution of the Soviet Union created a large number of newly independent countries, including Russia. The United States saw an opportunity to add these newly independent countries as subservient allies to its large existing list of subservient allies. It was able to do so with many Eastern European countries such as Poland and Hungary but not with Russia. Russia, like China, was determined not to relinquish its sovereignty as countries like Canada, Germany, Japan, and Britain had done. This did not sit well with the American empire nor with its subservient allies. As a result, Russia, and its intelligent leader Vladimir Putin, has been demonized by the West. Since the West has always turned truth on its head, demonization of any leader by the West is the surest indicator that such a leader is both wise and moral.

In 1991, Russia was playing a dangerous game, given the enormous economic, military, political, financial, and propaganda powers of the American empire, its G7 allies, and NATO. But with the unexpected rise of China as an independent Asian country willing and determined to lead Asia in the twenty-first century, Russia sees an opportunity to ally with Asia as an equal partner. Under the leadership of Putin, Russia has risen from the ashes of 1991 to claim its rightful place alongside China as two great powers willing and able to challenge the American empire and its long list of prostitutes such as Germany, France, Britain, Japan, and Canada. As the leader of the Soviet Union, Russia had been the country to aid weaker Third World countries threatened by the American empire and its subservient allies like Canada. It now has the opportunity to once again lead Asia and the Third World with support from countries like China and India. While it is still tied to its European heritage, it is being pushed by the West to favor its Asian heritage. Western threats and sanctions, far from turning Russia into another Western prostitute, is strengthening its geographic ties with Asia and its old Soviet Union ties with the Third World. Asia and the emerging economies desperately need the military muscle that Russia can add to the Global Shift. The bullying tactics of the West are making it easy for Russia to make the right moral choice. We devote a full chapter to Russia because the weaker link in the Global Shift replacing the West with the emerging economies is not the economy but the military. In terms of GDP, the emerging economies are on track to overtake the West. But their military is a long way from overtaking the military of NATO. If Russia throws its military might with NATO because of the Western threats and sanctions, the emerging economies will have the economic clout but not the military clout. The emerging economies would love the military might of both Russia and Turkey, two countries that are still unsure of their European allegiance. Both are being pushed into their Asian halves by the bullying tactics of their European brethren.

Russia straddles Asia and Europe. It has always had a foot in both continents. Never fully accepted by the West because of its Asian half, it has swung between supporting Europe and distancing itself from Europe. It is geographically the largest country in the world. Once the greatest empire of Eurasia, after the collapse of the Soviet Union in 1991, Russia was struggling for recognition as a great power worthy of consultation by the West in international affairs. Up until its leadership by Vladimir Putin, the West treated Russia with great disdain after 1991. Putin has had to project Russia's enormous military power explicitly for the West to take notice of Russia in the twenty-first century. Once regarded as a lightweight, especially by the most lightweight prostitute of the Western alliance, Canada, under Stephen Harper, Russia, under Putin, is increasingly treated by the weakened American empire, led by Presidents Obama and Trump, as its equal in dealing with Syria, Iran, Ukraine, and other international hot spots. Putin was even named Person of the Year by *Time* magazine in 2007. Putin also beat President Obama for the most powerful person on Forbes list for *four* years, 2013, 2014, 2015, and 2016.

Historical Overview of Russia

We feel the need to provide this historical overview of Russia to understand why Vladimir Putin and the Russian people who love him are at a loss to understand why the people and media of the West think of Russia as this primitive barbaric country without culture and civilization. It's unfortunate that new countries like Canada and the United States, built on lands stolen from the First Nations, pay only lip service to the long civilized history of old countries like Russia, China, and India. While pretending to honor the history and traditions of old countries, Canada and the United States constantly speak of their supposed superiority of language, culture, democracy, freedoms, human rights, and morality in ways that denigrate all others. Everything about them is deemed to be the best, superior to all others by far. They use foul language to denounce the leaders and the people of other countries, especially those they do not regard as Western. They attribute to themselves a morality that has no factual basis or substance but is ingrained in their DNA and oblivious to rational analyses or objective questioning.

Russia is a far older and more civilized country than either the United States or Canada. This large country began as a Slavic state with a center of power initially in Kiev and later in Moscow. Initially, Russia was more Asian than European and more receptive to Islam than Christianity. It has been pulled between East and West throughout its long history. But with the rise of the West after the industrial revolution, Russia turned westward to develop its economy and play the great game with Britain and the other great powers. Its rulers married into the royal families of Austria and France as was the custom of all the Western royal families. By this time, it had long embraced Christianity, albeit Greek Orthodox, not Roman Catholic, as its state religion, over Islam.

The initial Slavic Russian state located in Kiev owed its foundation to the Viking invasions of the ninth century. Intermarriage between Slavs and Vikings blurred the historical distinction between Slavs and Vikings. Like the Vikings before, the Russians converted to Christianity in the tenth century, during the reign of Prince Vladimir I. Vladimir was baptized in 988. As a result, 988 marks the birth of the Russian Orthodox Church. This conversion to Christianity increased Russia's engagement with the Eastern Roman/Byzantine Empire centered in

Constantinople. The Eastern Roman Empire had worked long and hard to convert the inhabitants of Russia and Ukraine to Christianity. Vladimir's desire to improve relations with the Byzantine Empire was sealed by his marriage to Princess Anna, the sister of the Byzantine emperor. It was common practice for a Western ruler to marry off their relations to get a military advantage. The Byzantine emperor received military support from Prince Vladimir to help him defend Constantinople. This marked the beginning of Russia's long struggle to be accepted by the West as an equal. At the same time, Russia continued to absorb Islamic influences from the Arabs and Persians.

Russia, therefore, has a long history with Eastern Europe and the Orthodox Christianity first embraced by the Roman emperor Constantine. In the century following Russia's conversion to Orthodox Christianity by Prince Vladimir, the schism between the Eastern Greek-Orthodox, Roman Empire, and the Western Latin-Catholic, Roman Empire, became much deeper. Russia was dragged into this historical religious conflict between Greek and Latin Christians. After the fall of the "second" Rome, Constantinople, to the Muslim Ottoman Empire, Russia argued for its recognition as the "third" Rome. But in the thirteenth century, Russia was invaded, conquered, and ruled by the Golden Horde for two centuries. The leaders of the Golden Horde had converted to Islam. Historically, Russia has been pulled by geography, conquests, and religion between Europe and Asia.

The Mongol rule led to the decline of Kiev as the center of Russia and its replacement by Moscow. Initially, Moscow was a tiny trading post within the larger principality of Vladimir-Suzdal. Moscow's ascendancy began under the rule of Prince Ivan I, 1325–1341. Ivan's father had married the sister of the ruling Mongol overlord, Uzbeg Khan, thereby cementing an alliance between Moscow and the Golden Horde. Ivan I achieved greater independence from Mongol rule when he aided the Mongols in putting down a rebellion in a competing principality, Tver, in 1327. By 1327, Moscow and Tver had emerged as the two most powerful principalities in all of Russia. They competed with other lesser principalities for the coveted title of Grand Prince of Vladimir, bestowed on a Russian prince by the Golden Horde. By aiding the Golden Horde in quelling the insurrection in Tver, Ivan I was rewarded with this title in 1328. This title gave Ivan I the right to collect taxes throughout Russia. It made Moscow the implicit center of Russia. By working cooperatively with Russia's Mongol overlord, Ivan I made Moscow the most wealthy and powerful Russian principality. Ivan I also convinced the Golden Horde to pass on the title of Grand Prince of Vladimir to his son. This set a precedent for the ruler of Moscow to inherit this title.

Ivan I and his dynasty expanded the territory of Moscow despite opposition from both Tver and Lithuania. Under the rule of Ivan the Great, Ivan III, 1462–1505, Moscow overthrew the Mongols, and Ivan the Great became the first tsar of all Russia. The title of tsar was the equivalent of Roman emperor, Mongol khan, and Ottoman sultan. Ivan also invaded and annexed the wealthy port city of Novgorod in 1478. Novgorod had been the main Russian port for centuries. Moscow was strategically located to expand territory in a way not matched until the birth of countries like the United States, Canada, and Australia. While Western Europe acquired colonies outside Europe after the voyages of da Gama and Columbus, Ivan the Great and his descendants expanded the Russian homeland much like the thirteen English colonies that became the independent United States expanded the territory of the United States by invading and conquering First Nations lands. Russia became a bigger and bigger country or unified nation state, like the United States, rather than a Western European imperial power like Portugal, Spain, Holland, France, or Britain. This expansion took place over a similar time as that of the United States, Canada, or Australia but began much earlier than the United States, Canada, and Australia. Another difference was that the original nonwhite inhabitants of the United States, Canada, and Australia were largely killed off and replaced by white Europeans. Not so in the case of the expansion of Russia. Russia was transformed into a truly multiethnic society of Slavs, Vikings, Mongols, Cossacks, and others. It was also multireligious embracing both Islam and Christianity.

The territorial expansion of Moscow from 20,000 square kilometers in 1300 to 5.4 million square kilometers in 1584 matched the pace of growth of the United States after its independence from Britain. See my *American Invasions*. This massive geographical growth, begun by Ivan I and continued under Ivan the Great, was enhanced even more under the rule of Ivan the Terrible, Ivan IV, 1533–1584. Ivan the Terrible continued to wage wars on the Mongols, defeating the khanates of Kazan and Astrakhan and adding their territory to Russia. Ivan IV then established international relations between Russia and the Ottoman Empire. Russia became an international player like the Ottoman, Habsburg, and Spanish empires. Ivan IV also forged trade relations with England. At the time, Moscow was a larger city than London. The English Muscovy Company, established in 1551, was allowed exclusive rights to trade with Russia through the port of Arkhangelsk in the White Sea. Ivan IV was eager to compete for European trade with the well-established Hanseatic League. English wool was exchanged for Russian furs. Russia established diplomatic relations with England in 1556. The monopoly rights to the Anglo-Russian trade was held by the Muscovy Company until 1698. After 1698, it continued to trade with Russia until the Russian revolution of 1917. It currently operates as a charity centered in Moscow. This is one of many important examples that should help the West today understand its long historical links with Russia and why Russia today denounces Western propaganda aimed at vilifying its current leader, Vladimir Putin, and treating him as some kind of uncivilized barbarian. The reality is that it is Western leaders like Canada's Steven Harper who are uncivilized barbarians. Following the decline of the Muscovy Company, the Dutch replaced England as the leading Western European nation trading with Russia.

The Christian Church survived Mongol rule, and in 1327, the center of the Russian Orthodox Church was moved from Vladimir to Moscow. Moscow benefitted from the growth and enrichment of the Orthodox Church centered in Moscow. While the Orthodox Church prospered in Russia, the Byzantine Empire came under increasing threat from the Ottoman Empire. When Constantinople fell to the Ottoman Empire in 1453, Russia became by default the leader of the Greek Orthodox Church. It was able to return to its pre-Mongol claim to establish the third Rome in Russia. Moscow was to replace Constantinople and become the third Rome as Constantinople had earlier replaced Rome to become the second Rome. As the power of the Russian empire grew under the rule of Ivan III and Ivan IV, it enhanced the power of the Russian Greek Orthodox Church.

The Romanov Tsars Including Peter the Great and Catherine the Great

Ivan IV died in 1584, and his son, Feodor, became the last tsar of the Rurikid dynasty. Feodor died in 1598 without an heir. Russia descended into chaos because of foreign invasions and civil wars. In addition, poor harvests caused famine, which killed a third of its population. The powerful Commonwealth of Poland and Lithuania took advantage of Russia's *Time of Troubles* to invade and occupy Russia. Russia desperately needed a new dynasty, and its Grand National Assembly convinced *Michael Romanov* to become the first Romanov tsar of Russia in 1613. The Romanovs were related to the Rurikids by marriage after Tsar Ivan IV married Anastasia Zakharyina, daughter of Roman Romanov, in 1547. Michael Romanov was succeeded by his son, Alexei, but it was his grandson, *Peter the Great,* who laid the foundations for a Russian empire that would rival the modern Western European empires of Britain and France from the eighteenth century.

Peter the Great became the tsar of Russia in 1682 and ruled Russia until his death in 1725. During his rule, he transformed Russia from a largely Eastern empire to a semi-Western, semi-European empire. Up until the advent of sea power in the fifteenth century, the Eastern empires had dominated the world. This was true of the Chinese empires, the Indian empires, the Persian empires, the Greek empire, the Roman Empire, the Arab/Muslim empires, and the Russian empires. But superior navies had made relatively small maritime powers like Portugal, Spain, Holland, France, and Britain the dominant empires by the eighteenth century. These were all Western empires. The balance of power had shifted from East to West after navies became more militarily powerful than armies. The Russian empire, like the Chinese, Ottoman, and Austro-Hungarian empires, failed to recognize this revolutionary change in military prowess until Peter the Great became the tsar of Russia.

Peter the Great traveled the Western European capitals to learn firsthand about their naval ascendancy. In the period following the rise of the Western European empires, a powerful navy was essential to becoming a great power. Unlike the Western European empires, Portugal, Spain, Holland, France, and Britain, Russia was largely landlocked. It would be useless to build a powerful navy without access to the oceans and seas. Russia desperately needed both a powerful navy and year-round access to deepwater ports. Peter the Great would deliver both to make Russia a great power of equal status to Britain and France. During his reign, Peter the Great depended heavily on Western European advisors to convert Russia from a purely land-based empire to a maritime power like Britain and France. Russia's options for access to the seas and oceans were via the Black Sea and the Baltic. At the time, the Baltic was controlled by Sweden, a powerful empire at the time. The Black Sea was controlled by an even more powerful empire, the Ottoman Empire.

Peter the Great attempted to capture the Turkish fortress of Azov to give Russia access to the Black Sea. He launched an overland campaign in 1695, which failed. Peter the Great realized that building a navy to capture Azov would achieve the simultaneous goals of getting access to the Black Sea and having a navy. Peter therefore built a fleet in 1696 before launching a second land and sea campaign to take Azov. This time, he succeeded. The Ottoman Empire, like the Russian empire before Peter the Great, was not a great naval power. Like all the long list of Eastern empires that had dominated the world before the Portuguese empire, the Ottoman Empire had built their military prowess on armies, not navies. Russia's victory over the Ottoman Empire in 1696 heralded the simultaneous rise of Russia as a great power that would replace the Ottoman Empire as the Eastern competitor to Western Europe. Russia could not do it without becoming a maritime power like Britain and France. Shortly after the successful conquest of Azov, the Russian Duma officially launched the building of the Imperial Russian Navy. This navy was the third largest in the world after the British and French. Much has been written about the Ottoman Empire becoming the "sick man" of Europe after the death of Suleiman the Magnificent. But it was Peter the Great's foresight in recognizing the importance of sea power in the post–Portuguese imperial age and the Ottoman Empire's failure to shift sufficient resources toward building an equally strong navy that clinched the replacement of the Ottomans by the Russians after the seventeenth century. Future threats to Russia would come less from the Ottomans and more from Japan and Germany.

Having secured Azov from the Ottoman Empire, Peter the Great turned his attention to the Baltic. Peter's goal had always been to secure Russia's access to the oceans from both the Black Sea and the Baltic. Azov had given Russia access to the oceans via the Black Sea only. As we said above, Russia's access to the Baltic was stymied by the then powerful Swedish empire. Having made a temporary peace with the Ottomans after conquering Azov, Peter the Great turned his attention to the Swedes. Peter declared war on the Swedish empire in 1700. During the Great Northern War of 1700–1721, the Russians built the Baltic Fleet. Peter built the city of St. Petersburg in 1703 on land conquered from the Swedish empire during this war, securing Russia's access to the Baltic. St. Petersburg is located on the Neva River with access to the Baltic. The Swedish empire was defeated by the Russian alliance with Denmark, Norway, Saxony, and Poland.

The Roman emperor Constantine had moved the capital of the Roman Empire eastward from Rome to Constantinople in recognition of the balance of power in the world residing in the East. By 1703, the balance of power had shifted to the West, and in recognition of that, Peter the Great shifted Russia's capital westward from Moscow to St. Petersburg in 1712. Apart from the years 1728-1732, St. Petersburg was the capital of the Russian empire, founded by Peter the Great, until the Russian revolution of 1917. These were the two centuries when Russia emphasized its European heritage over its Asian heritage and came closest to being accepted by the West as a Western empire. But like Japan, it was never fully accepted, despite the best efforts of Catherine the Great, the empress credited the most with modernizing Russia and embracing the Age of Enlightenment. But Catherine did succeed in consolidating Russia's ascent over the Ottomans as the leading empire to the East of the Western European empires. Despite the crusades and the many wars waged by the Christian West against the Muslim East, it was really the Russian empire that replaced the Muslim empires to the east of Spain. Russia denied its Muslim heritage to embrace Christianity only to find itself denied acceptance by the Christian West because the Christian West abandoned Greek-Orthodox Christianity for Roman-Catholic and Protestant Christianity. But the final nail in the coffin for Russia was its embrace of Communism after 1917. Communism provided the ideal propaganda weapon for the American empire to use against the Soviet Union.

Catherine the Great ruled the Russian empire from 1762 to 1796. This was the time period when Britain and France were waging wars against each other for imperial dominance in the New World, in India, and across the globe. Britain and France had seized maritime supremacy from Portugal, Spain, and Holland and were now duking it out for first place. While they were busy, Catherine the Great was taking over from the Ottomans and Austro-Hungarians in the East. She expanded the Russian empire westward into Central Europe and southward to the Black Sea. Odessa became a Russian port in the Black Sea. Catherine annexed the Crimea in *1783*, a fact that the West today is having a serious problem denying despite its powerful propaganda machine and brain-dead media. It was also during Catherine's reign that Russia incorporated most of Ukraine into its empire, another fact that the West is finding difficult to deny today.

Another factor in the rise of Russia had to do with the birth of the American empire during the reign of Catherine the Great. While

Russia had increased its westward expansion under Peter the Great and Catherine the Great, it had simultaneously moved development eastward into the vast expanse of Siberia and overland into Alaska and the western coast of North America. The discovery of America had not gone unnoticed by Russia. While the Western European empires had reached the New World by sailing across the Atlantic Ocean, Russia saw an opportunity to take its share of the booty by exploring westward across the north of Russia "overland" to North America and further south. The explorer that Russia chose to perform this task was Vitus Bering. Bering was a Danish explorer and cartographer who had served in the expanding navy built by Peter the Great. After serving in Peter's navy for twenty years, he was commissioned by the tsar to lead the *First Kamchatka Expedition* in December 1724, a month before the Tsar's death. The Tsar had left clear instructions for a three-year voyage of discovery prior to his death. This began a Russian colonization of North America, which grew with the important sea otter trade but ended with the sale of Alaska to the new American empire.

Bering's mission was to determine if Russia was linked continuously to North America by land and to map navigable routes to the New World to enable Russia to compete with Spain and Britain for territory and trade in the New World. While the British and Spanish had the advantage of early naval superiority and location advantage across the Atlantic to the eastern coasts of the New World, Russia clearly had a location advantage for conquests in the northwest. Bering began his first expedition from Russia's new capital, St. Petersburg, in February 1725, with thirty-four men. This initial three-year expedition was successful in determining that Russia was not linked continuously by land to North America but that Russians could reach North America directly from Northern Russia and conquer territory as the British and Spanish had done. Like Cabot and Columbus before, Bering led a second Russian voyage of discovery with more men and resources. This began in 1741. This led to Russia's discovery of Alaska and the Aleutian Islands. Bering died in December 1741, but the exploration continued under the new leadership of Sven Waxell.

After these two voyages of discovery, Russians began to move into North America in search of furs and other opportunities for trade with the New World. The Spanish and Portuguese had conquered all of South and Central America. The British and French had seized most of the eastern part of North America but were slow to penetrate overland to the West. The Russians saw an opportunity to conquer from the north southward down the Pacific coast, and this is what they did. The Spanish had found gold and silver. The British had found tobacco, furs, and sugar. The Russians found the sea otter. Sea otters have the thickest fur of any mammal. While the market for the beaver fur of the British Hudson Bay Company was in Europe, the market for the Russian sea otter fur was in China. The Russians began their hunt for the sea otters in the Kuril Islands. After Bering's expeditions, many Russians switched from hunting for sable skins in Siberia to hunting for the much more valuable sea otter pelts in North America. The Russians began their hunt for North American sea otters in the Commander Islands before moving to the Aleutian Islands. Under Catherine the Great, the Russian empire was expanding both eastward into Siberia and westward into North America. At the time when Britain and France were fighting the Seven Years' War for the eastern portion of North America, the Russians began to settle Alaska.

In 1799, Russia's tsar Paul I created the equivalent of the British Hudson Bay Company in the Russian-American Company. The Hudson Bay hunted for beaver pelts across North America, while the Russian-American Company hunted for sea otter pelts in Alaska and the Pacific. Like the Hudson Bay Company, the Russian-American Company was expected to trade and colonize. As with all the Western European nations, the fundamental goal was to colonize and steal while pretending to trade. At the same time, the Spanish were hunting the sea otters from the southern Pacific. The British joined the hunt after their captain James Cook discovered Vancouver Island in 1778. Russia began to establish settlements in Alaska in the 1780s as the British had done in the eastern parts of North America earlier. Russian settlements began on Kodiak Island and moved southward along the Pacific coast. The British had begun in Virginia in 1607 and had moved both north and south along the Atlantic coast. By the 1780s, the British had fought many wars with the French for control of this eastern part of North America. The British were now competing with the Russians for the western part of North America. Here the Russians had the advantage, having established settlements before the British had settled along the western coast in British Columbia and Oregon. In the end, it was the thirteen British colonies that became the independent United States in 1783 that would dominate over the Russians, the British, the French, the Spanish, the indigenous inhabitants, and the world at large.

With so many countries hunting the sea otters in what came to be called the Maritime Fur Trade, it was simply a matter of time before stocks were depleted. Without this valuable resource, it became difficult to attract the numbers of Russian settlers required for Russia to permanently steal the lands of the indigenous inhabitants of the New World as the Spanish, British, Americans, and Canadians had done. The Russian population in North America never exceeded nine hundred. Russia made the same mistake the French did. Fearful of the power of the British, the French had aided the thirteen British colonies in North America in their War of Independence from Britain. During that war, the British had asked Catherine the Great for military aid, twenty thousand troops, against the rebels. Catherine had declined in part to weaken the British Empire. In like manner, the Russian empire sold Alaska to the new American empire partly to prevent British expansion. At the time, the British had called the American empire a *puny* empire. What a mistake that was! By the time of the Russian sale in 1867, the Russians had settlements along the Pacific coast as far as Northern California. Fort Ross was a Russian fort in California between 1812 and 1841. The Russians had even established a fort in Hawaii between 1814 and 1817.

Russian Empire after Catherine the Great

One of the primary goals of both Peter the Great and Catherine the Great was to get the West to recognize Russia as an equal Western empire and great power as modern, "civilized," and sophisticated as the French and British empires. We saw how Peter the Great recognized the need for a strong navy in the age of maritime supremacy after the rise of Portugal and Spain. He made the Russian navy the fourth largest after Britain, France, and Spain. Russia also recognized the need to colonize parts of the New World and engage in voyages of discovery. Most importantly, Russia needed to industrialize as Britain, France, Germany, and the United States were doing. During Catherine's rule, Russia had waged wars against the Ottoman Empire to take over the leadership of the Eastern Roman Empire and protect the rights of Greek-Orthodox Christians. Russia expanded southward into the Crimea, westward into the Balkans and Poland, eastward into Siberia, and further west into the northwest of the New World.

Russia cemented its great power status when Tsar Nicholas Alexander I defeated Napoleon. When Napoleon's military genius threatened to enable France to dominate Europe, Russia allied with Britain and Austria to stop this threat. When Napoleon defeated the Russians and Austrians, Russia became a temporary ally in 1807. This alliance enabled Russia to expand territory in Finland and Turkey. But when Napoleon made the military blunder to invade Russia, as Hitler would later do, Russia not only defeated the invasion but also destroyed Napoleon's army. This enabled Russia to march into Western Europe all the way to Paris. Tsar Alexander I played as crucial a role in the peace treaty that ended the Napoleonic wars as Stalin later did in the peace treaty ending the Second World War. The year 1815 was a high point for the Russian empire. It stood as an equal to the British Empire in defeating Napoleon's France and bringing peace to the world. No one could question its great power status. But that status was not to last.

Russia failed to modernize its industry as much as its competitors did. Competition came from Britain, Germany, France, the United States, and Japan. Lagging behind in industrial development not only reduced economic growth but also meant outdated equipment for its armed forces. In addition, the other great powers were more than willing to gang up on Russia to keep it in check. The West has always used Russia when needed but was never willing to accord it equal status as a "civilized" great power. This was most evident during the Crimean War of 1853–1856, when the Christian empires of Britain, France, and Austria allied with the Muslim Ottoman Empire against the Greek-Orthodox Russian empire. To the West, Russia was backward and primitive. Western "civilization" is based on military prowess and successful warmongering. To prove that Russia was not "civilized," it had to be defeated in war by the "civilized" weapons of the West. The opportunity to do so presented itself during the Crimean War.

The Crimean War was simply another example of nations addicted to warmongering but using religion as an excuse to feed that addiction. The Ottoman Empire had long been the dominant empire in the area of the world previously occupied by the eastern half of the Roman Empire. But the Ottoman Empire had steadily declined after the rule of Suleiman the Magnificent. While all the other empires wanted to share the spoils of the Ottoman Empire, the Russian empire was best positioned to take most of it by conquest. But this did not sit well with the French, Austrian, and British empires. Despite the desire of the French empire to protect the rights of Catholic Christians in the Ottoman empire, it was willing to sacrifice that goal to prevent Russia from gaining territory by defeating the Ottoman Empire in the Crimean War. It's possible that the French preferred Islam to Russian Orthodox Christianity. In any case, imperial dominance trumped concern for Catholic Christians, and the French joined the British and Austrians on the side of the Muslims to prevent Russia from winning the war. France and Britain declared war on Russia on March 27, 1854.

The British and French navies sailed into the Black Sea in the summer of 1853. The allies attacked the Russians and laid seize to Sevastopol, the main port in the Crimean peninsula. The Russian navy was defeated, and the allies controlled the Black Sea. Russian defeats forced Russia to sue for peace. The Treaty of Paris ended the war on March 30, 1856. Russia no longer dominated the Black Sea until 1871. While Russia's defeat was largely caused by France, Britain, and Austria aiding the Ottoman Empire, that defeat also signaled to Russia that it had not kept pace with the modernization of industry that had taken place in Britain and France. If Russia wanted to maintain its great power status, it would have to increase its pace of modernization. Later threats would come from Britain and France as well as new great powers Germany, Japan, and the United States. The defeat of France by Prussia in 1871 signaled the rise of Germany as an even more modern great power than France. But French defeat provided the opportunity for Russia to renounce the Black Sea clauses of the 1856 Treaty of Paris and once again put its navy in the Black Sea.

The much-needed modernization of Russia began under Tsar Alexander II, who succeeded Nicholas I in 1855. Part of this modernization process was the freedom of twenty-five million serfs who could provide the labor force to fuel industrialization and urbanization. Reforms in education, culture, finance, government, and the military were other aspects of the modernization process. Tsar Alexander II was killed by a suicide bomber in 1881, and he was succeeded by his son, Alexander III. Unfortunately for Russia, Alexander III, rather than increasing the pace of modernization in Russia, retracted many of the reforms of his father. Russia began to isolate itself from Western Europe and would pay a heavy price for not keeping pace with the progress of the other great powers. Russia's first major defeat would come from one of the new great powers, Japan. But Alexander III would not live long enough to see that. He died at the age of forty-nine in 1894. He was succeeded by his son, Tsar Nicholas II, who was the last tsar of Russia.

At the beginning of the twentieth century, the Russian empire was one of the great powers competing with the British Empire, the American empire, the German empire, the Japanese empire, and the French empire for colonies and world domination. The Russian empire was a sixth of the world's landmass with a population close to 130 million. It had the largest standing army of any great power with 1.5 million men. Its Achilles heel was that it was still largely a rural economy dominated by agriculture. It had not industrialized and urbanized as much as the other great powers. This limited its ability to produce the most modern and "civilized" weapons for its army and navy.

Russia, like every imperial power, looked for opportunities to expand its empire and influence. Having consolidated its naval presence in the Black Sea after Prussia's defeat of France, Russia began to look to Asia and the Pacific. It could expand overland into a military weak China and compete with the great powers for the Pacific. China was seen by all the great powers as the "sick man of Asia" after losing the Opium Wars. Russia, like every great power, wanted a piece of China. A warm-water port with access to the Pacific Ocean would boost Russia's imperial reach. Port Arthur, in China's Liaodong Peninsula, would be such a port. But securing such a port from China would bring Russia into military conflict with the rising Asian power Japan.

The West had forcibly opened both China and Japan to free trade. Their ultimate goal was the colonization of both China and Japan. But Japan turned the tables on the West by using its forced exposure to the West to copy the West's modern militarization and become an empire as powerful as the Western empires of Britain, France, Germany, Russia, and the United States. After the Meiji Restoration of 1868, Japan transformed itself into an advanced industrial state. Of course, such a "civilized" boast had to be proven with successful warmongering and colonies. Japan's obvious targets for such proofs were its immediate neighbors China, Korea, and Taiwan. The latter two countries were vassal countries of China. Japan would therefore have to defeat China to colonize any or all of China, Korea, and Taiwan. While China had been soundly defeated by Western empires such as Britain and France, it was still recognized as the dominant Asian power. Just as Prussia had to defeat Austria to prove that Germany, not Austria, was the dominant Central European power, Japan would have to defeat China to prove that it was the dominant Asian power.

Japan began its warmongering with China by threatening to colonize China's vassal state, Korea. Japan had seen how the British had colonized parts of China by beginning to forcibly open China to trade. This was the strategy it pursued in Korea. While both China and Japan had been forcibly opened to trade with the West, Korea had resisted. The Japanese played the Western game of pretending to open Korea to trade with all nations. Such a move by Japan would not only secure it a colony to prove itself an empire but also prevent Korea from becoming a colony of one of the Western powers, such as Britain or Germany. Japan's move did not fool China. Just as China knew that the ultimate goal of the British was the colonization of China, China knew that the ultimate goal of Japan was the colonization of Korea. As with all colonies, Korea would not simply be a symbol of Japanese military prowess but provide Japan with valuable coal, iron ore, and agricultural products, which can be stolen by colonization rather than paid for by trade. Japan made its move in 1876 with its own "unequal treaty," forcing Korea to open its ports to foreign trade. Japan took advantage of the fact that some Koreans favored opening up Korea to westernization. That made them allies of Japan against the more traditional Koreans who supported Korea's historical ties with China and proud isolation. By 1876, China had demonstrated its military decline by losing both of the Opium Wars against Britain. Japan felt that it was ready to take on the Asian giant to prove its superiority to all Asians and simultaneously become a modern "Western" empire like Britain. Of course, the West would never fully recognize an Asian power as an equal. The West had even refused to recognize Russia as an equal because of Russia's Asian half. The German emperor Wilhelm II was very explicit in referring to Japan's imperial ambitions as the *Yellow Peril*. But like Russia, Japan has never given up on its desire to be accepted as an equal by the West, even at the detriment of losing leadership of Asia to China. It's like Britain, never content to be just a European power like France or Germany, Japan has never been content to be just an Asian power.

The Korean drought of 1882 presented another opportunity for Japan's colonization of Korea. The Korean military supported a popular uprising over food shortages and months of not being paid. Japan sent four war ships with troops to Seoul to protect its investments. China responded by sending its troops to Seoul. Japan was not only paid damages but also allowed to station troops in Seoul. This was the beginning of several incidents involving Japan and China in the internal affairs of Korea from food shortages to military coups. After 1876, Korea became a contest between Japan and China as to which country would colonize it. This was reminiscent of the earlier contest between England and France for North America. Just as the British and French ignored the claims of the First Nations whose lands and resources they wanted to steal, China and Japan ignored the rights of Koreans. In the wars between Britain and France in North America, the British prevailed. In Korea, the Japanese won. In what has since been called the *First Sino-Japanese War* of 1894–95, China under the Qing dynasty had become so military outdated that it was defeated by another Asian power. China's Beiyang Fleet was regarded at the time as the most powerful navy in Asia. But it was defeated by the Japanese navy in the *Battle of the Yalu River*, on September 17, 1894. This enabled the Japanese army to cross the Yalu River and invade Manchuria. The Japanese conquered the important port city of Port Arthur in the Liaodong Peninsula.

The Peace Treaty of Shimonoseki, signed by China and Japan in April 1895, transferred the Chinese territories of the Liaodong Peninsula, Taiwan, and the Penghu Islands to Japan. Korea was no longer a colony of China but designated an independent country. This was a tactic used by the American empire whenever it intervened on behalf of Spanish colonies. It would pretend to make the ex-Spanish colony independent to boost its claims to the right of self-determination. In reality, the ex-Spanish colony would become an American uncolony.

The Japanese victory over China did not sit well with the Western empires. Their initial goal in opening up China and Japan was to colonize both, not to enable Japan to gobble up parts of China or become an Asian empire. The British had been the first to declare war on China. Having colonized India and other parts of Asia, China was next on its list. It began its ultimate goal of colonizing China by forcing China to buy opium it produced in its colony of India. This provided the excuse for the First Opium War of 1840, which led to the *Unequal Treaty of Nanking* in 1842. Britain colonized Hong Kong and forced China to open the ports of Shanghai, Foochow, Amoy, and Ningpo in addition to Canton. Next, it was the American empire forcing China to sign the *Unequal Treaty of Wanghia* in 1844. This was followed by the Second Opium War of 1856. China's defeat forced it to make further concessions to the British and the Americans. Not to be outdone, France declared war on China in 1884 in its efforts to colonize Vietnam. Japan saw an opportunity to seize Korea and threatened to join France in its war with China. With Japan seen as the greater threat to China, China hurriedly made peace with France and surrendered Vietnam to France. France eventually colonized Vietnam, Cambodia, and Laos.

While the British, French, and Americans were happy over their military defeats of China, the Russians were not. Russia felt that Japan and Germany were colonizing parts of China that encroached on their strategic interests. As we saw above, Japan had colonized Manchuria. The Germans had colonized Qingdao, and Germany's East Asia Squadron was based in the port of Qingdao in Jiaozhou Bay. Russia was able to get Germany and France on its side against Japan. At the time, the German emperor Wilhelm II was the cousin of Tsar Nicholas II of Russia. In addition, Wilhelm II was the most outspoken racist among Western leaders. He was the most adamant not to allow Japan great power status. France came onside because Russia had supported France during its war with China to steal Vietnam. As a result of the Russian alliance with France and Germany, Japan was forced to return the Liaodong Peninsula it had secured with the Peace Treaty of Shimonoseki.

Russia moved quickly to secure a lease of the Liaodong Peninsula from China to establish a military base and secure a warm-water port at Port Arthur. Russia's Pacific fleet was based in Port Arthur. Russia also built a railway to link Port Arthur to the northern Chinese city of Harbin close to its border with China. Russia also intervened in Korea against Japan. It was clear that Russia's desire to join the other great powers to colonize China came at the expense of Japan. While Russia was the least liked of the Western great powers because of its Asian half, Japan was liked even less because it was fully Asian. Russia felt secure in its military ability to take on Japan and was certain that the Western powers would not aid Japan. While Japan's defeat of China had made Japan the dominant Asian power, it was still an Asian power. Russia, on the other hand, was thought of grudgingly by the West as a Western power. The Western powers had no doubt that if it came to war, Russia would defeat Japan. Such a defeat would enable the Western powers to gobble up Japan in the same way they had gobbled up China.

War with Japan came in 1904, and Russia was soundly defeated. Russia lost both its Pacific and Baltic fleets. This surprised the Western powers and for the first time suggested that Western naval superiority since the fifteenth century could be threatened by a resurging Asia. Fortunately for Russia, the American empire was determined not to see a rising Japan threaten its desire to colonize Asia and dominate the Pacific. Pres. Theodore Roosevelt was able to convince Japan that America had no imperial ambitions. He was accepted as a neutral arbitrator during the peace negotiations. Alas, the American empire has never been neutral or honest. Roosevelt ensured that Russia would win the peace, having lost the war. The Japanese delegation was outsmarted by Roosevelt. Roosevelt made sure that Russia would not pay indemnity to Japan. But Russia's defeat not only halted its imperial ambitions in Asia but also provided ammunition to its people who had long opposed tsarist rule. Russia's humiliation by an Asian power emboldened its armed forces to join with the poor and the serfs to riot across the country in 1905. This led to the disaster of *Bloody Sunday*. On January 22, 1905, unarmed protestors led by Fr. Georgy Gapon marched toward Russia's Winter Palace in St. Petersburg to present a petition to Tsar Nicholas II. They were fired on by the imperial guard. This was the impetus for factory workers to launch strikes across the country and force the tsar to make reforms. Bloody Sunday was the catalyst for the Russian Revolution of 1905. The revolution included strikes, peasant uprisings, and mutinies by the military. It culminated in the tsar creating the Russian duma or parliament, a Russian constitution, and political parties.

In the West, the defeat of Russia was of no great concern. In their view, Russia was not a full-blooded European power. Germany was accepted as the rising European power to replace Austria. The Ottoman Empire was in decline. Britain, France, and Germany would dominate Europe, while the Americans would take on the Japanese in the Pacific. The West would continue to dominate the world as it had done since the fifteenth century. Just as the British and French had replaced Portugal, Spain, and Holland, the Germans and Americans would replace the Austro-Hungarians. The new great powers would be Britain, France, Germany, and America. Russia would be ignored as backward. Japan would be allowed to take a share of China, but the American empire would constrain Japanese expansion. Britain and France would keep their colonial empires, and Germany would take what it could.

World War I, Communism, the Russian Revolution of 1917, and the Creation of the Soviet Union

The reforms forced on Tsar Nicholas II by the Russian Revolution of 1905 kept the tsar in power. Russia was largely ignored by the great powers until the outbreak of World War I in 1914. The First World

War led to the second Russian Revolution in 1917. This time, the tsar abdicated, and Russia established the *first* Communist state in the world. During Russia's confrontation with Japan, Russia received moral support from Germany. But when Austria invaded Serbia after the Austrian archduke Franz Ferdinand was shot dead in Sarajevo in June 1914, Germany allied with Austria against Russia. Since Germany was the new industrial powerhouse of Europe, there was no way that Russia could win a war against Germany. War also worsened the poor state of the Russian economy, creating more dissent and discontent among the people. The tsar was forced to abdicate in March 1917 after three years of war. This led to a civil war in Russia that lasted until 1922. During the Civil War, the United States, Britain, and France intervened to prevent Russia from forming a Communist state and to feed their insatiable appetite for warmongering. The First World War had ended in 1918, leaving the Russian Civil War as the only good opportunity for continued Western warmongering. The Western powers were unsuccessful in preventing Russia becoming a Communist state. The Russian Communist state was led by Vladimir Lenin until his death in 1924.

Russia had been disliked by the West because it was half Asian, because it was Greek-Orthodox, and because it was deemed backward. But it was hated even more after it became a Communist state. The American empire had justified its theft of First Nations lands by claiming private property rights over communal property. It could not ally itself with a state based on the moral superiority of communal property over private property. America led the Western charge to demonize Communism as evil, even though Communism was born in the West, based on the writings of Karl Marx and Friedrich Engels. The other Western empires supported the American empire because they feared the appeal of Communism to the poor masses in their countries. The West allowed labor unions to increase wages and working conditions for the growing numbers of industrial workers and moved from a purely free enterprise economy toward a mixed economy with a growing public sector. Such a public sector was really a Communist sector but could not be called such for propaganda purposes. Western demonization of Communism as ungodly and evil combined with labor unions and a growing public sector to reduce income inequality prevented Western states from falling prey to the mass popularity of Communism.

However, many countries in Eastern Europe and across the globe went with the Russian Communist model of managing the state, the economy, and the welfare of the larger segment of their societies. The world came to be divided between Communism and capitalism. The leader of the Communist group was Russia, and the leader of the capitalist group was America. While Germany, Britain, and France were still the major great powers, they were being sidelined by this growing confrontation between Russia and America. In a rather ironic twist, it was the Communist Revolution in Russia that promoted Russia to a world status exceeding that of Britain, France, or Germany. Russia consolidated this new global status by forming the *Soviet Union* in 1922. Initially this was a union of four *Socialist Republics,* Russia, Ukraine, Belarus, and Moldova. It later expanded to include Uzbekistan, Turkmenistan, Tajikistan, Kyrgyzstan, Armenia, Georgia, Azerbaijan, Kazakhstan, Lithuania, Latvia, and Estonia.

Russia was the first country to experiment with a centrally planned economy. Lenin was succeeded by Josef Stalin. Under Stalin, Russia's planned economy achieved surprisingly high rates of economic growth. This led to the West demonizing not only Communism but also Russia's leader Stalin. Russia was increasingly isolated by the West until the Second World War. During the Second World War, the West desperately needed Russia to help them defeat Germany. Under Adolf Hitler, Germany became the most advanced industrial state capable of launching a war machine that could conquer all of Europe, including Britain. Fearful of defeat by Germany, American propaganda miraculously transformed Russia's leader Josef Stalin from an evil dictator to *Uncle Joe.* Without Uncle Joe, the West could not have won the Second World War against Germany. Once the Second World War ended, the American empire formed a strong Western alliance with Britain, France, Germany, Japan, Italy, Spain, Greece, Canada, Australia, and others with the single-minded intent of destroying the Soviet Union.

We have not dealt in detail with the period when Russia led the Soviet Union since our focus in the Global Shift is on Russia, as an emerging economy, following the dissolution of the Soviet Union in 1991. The Soviet Union, led by Russia, had offered the strongest opposition to world domination by the West, led by the American empire. This Cold War between the West and the Soviet Union ended in 1991, and the West won. Capitalism, free enterprise, mixed economies, and sophisticated propaganda about freedom of the press and democracy had won over the ideals of communal property and the social good. The West was free to drop their bombs on whichever country they hated or even disagreed with. The most devastating bombings took place in Muslim countries in Afghanistan, Iraq, Lebanon, Syria, and North Africa. Over sixty million refugees were created. In our view, the only hope of any restraint on this immoral abuse of military power by the West is the rise of the emerging economies caused by the Global Shift. Russia is one of those emerging economies and a member of BRIC, the four leading emerging economies. We will now turn to the effect of the Global Shift on Russia after 1991.

Russia as an Emerging Economy

While China and India were happy to move up from developing economies to emerging economies, classifying Russia as an emerging economy was a big comedown from its status during the Cold War as one of only two superpowers, along with the United States. Russia had experienced massive economic growth under the leadership of Josef Stalin. This had enabled it to develop a military arsenal equal to that of the United States. But Russia's centrally planned system preformed less well after the death of Stalin and much worse after Nikita Khrushchev was ousted as first secretary in 1964. Russia was plagued by weak and incompetent leaders after Khrushchev. This led to slower economic growth, especially after 1973. Low economic growth combined with the cost of Russia's invasion of Afghanistan meant that Russia would lose its superpower status and leadership of the Soviet Union. After the dissolution of the Soviet Union in 1991, Russia attempted to transition from a centrally planned economy to a mixed economy, similar to the economies in Western Europe. During this transition, economic growth was *negative*. Russia became poorer. Its GDP fell 40 percent between 1991 and 1998.

The Global Shift reached Russia much later than China. But Russia is as important a member of the emerging economies created by the Global Shift, as China or India. This is not due to the size of the post–Global Shift Russian economy but because of the military might of Russia and its long history of befriending developing countries threatened by colonization from the West. Russia's military might is second only to the United States. In time, it's very likely that it will be overtaken by China. But in 2018, Russia was still second to the United States in terms of nuclear power, modern military equipment, and exports of arms.

Russia's president Vladimir Putin is also the world leader most willing to stand up to the United States, even more than the Chinese president.

It's important to note that when the term "BRIC" was coined by Jim O'Neill in 2001, it included Russia among the four dominant emerging economies, even though the Russian economy had stagnated until 1998. O'Neill had the foresight to see that Russia had the fundamentals to be transformed by the Global Shift. In addition to its recent historical role as one of only two superpowers, second-largest exporter of arms, and second most powerful military, Russia possessed about 30 percent of the world's natural resources. The rapid growth of China, India, and other emerging economies meant a rapid growth in the demand for Russia's natural resources such as oil, gas, and precious metals. The election of Vladimir Putin also meant that Russia had the strongest leader since Josef Stalin. The Global Shift, abundant natural resources, sophisticated arms production, and strong leadership returned Russia as a player on the global stage alongside the other members of the UN Security Council, China, Britain, France, and the United States.

The Russian economy registered a growth rate of 6.4 percent in 1999 and 10 percent in 2000. The latter was the highest in the world and the first year of Putin's leadership. It was not until 2006 that the BRIC countries met as a group. By that time, the Russian economy had recovered the loss of GDP it had suffered between 1991 and 1998. There was no question that China, India, and Brazil were happy to include Russia as a member of O'Neill's group of the four dominant emerging economies. This is proven by Russia hosting the first formal summit in 2009. Only the foreign ministers had met in 2006 and only at the margins of a UN General Assembly meeting. The 2009 meeting was the first exclusive BRIC summit, and it was the leaders of the four countries who met. The summit also supported Russia's demand to create a second reserve currency to reduce the monopoly of the U.S. dollar.

In 2010, Russia's GDP was the smallest of the four BRIC emerging economies. China had the largest GDP in the BRIC group, followed by Brazil and India. Among the developed economies, the GDP of the United States was larger than China. In addition, four allies of the American empire, Japan, Germany, France, and the UK, had GDPs larger than Brazil, India, and Russia. Russia had the eleventh-largest GDP in the world, behind the United States, China, Japan, Germany, France, the UK, Brazil, Italy, India, and Canada.

In 2017, China and India had made significant gains to their GDPs relative to the United States and its four major allies, Japan, Germany, France, and the UK. China had significantly narrowed the gap between its GDP and that of the United States. India had moved up from ninth-place ranking in the world, as measured by GDP, in 2010, to sixth place in 2017, overtaking Italy, Brazil, and France. It was on a clear path to overtake the UK within a year. But Russia and Brazil had stagnated. The decline in the price of oil, caused primarily by increased oil production in the United States, had negatively impacted both Russia and Brazil. Russia was also suffering from economic sanctions imposed by the West, while Brazil was plagued by internal political turmoil. However, Russia maintained its eleventh-place world ranking as measured by GDP. Brazil had slipped from seventh place in 2010 to eighth place in 2017. As we saw in the previous chapter, Indonesia will be the emerging economy that will likely challenge Russia and Brazil for third place among the largest emerging economies.

250

CHAPTER 9

The Global Shift to Brazil
and Latin America

Brazil is one of the four countries identified by Jim O'Neill in 2001 as a member of the BRIC group. We began our book with an early chapter on Mexico because we identified the Mexican maquiladoras as the origin of the Global Shift. That alone made Mexico deserving of an entire chapter. Next, we spent two full chapters on China because China is the largest beneficiary, by far, of the Global Shift. China is also a member of BRIC. The two chapters on China were followed by an entire chapter on India, both because India is a member of BRIC and because India is the second-largest beneficiary of the Global Shift, after China. Next, we analyzed the Global Shift to the other emerging economies in Asia. We then turned to Russia, also a member of BRIC. Russia is also deserving of a full chapter because of its modern military hardware, second only to the United States, and its prior role as leader of the Soviet Union, the world's only other superpower besides the United States. Now we turn to the last member of BRIC, Brazil, but do not give it a full chapter. Instead, we begin this chapter with Brazil but add the rest of the New World outside North America. Brazil was once a dominant country in the New World like Mexico and Argentina. But it suffered a relative decline, as did Mexico and Argentina, after the rise of the United States, as the largest economy and most powerful military empire not only in the New World but also in the entire world and throughout history. The Global Shift will rebalance these countries, as well as all the other countries of Latin America and the Caribbean, making the gap between them and the United States and Canada less extreme.

While the Global Shift began in 1965 in the Mexican maquiladoras, it took several decades to reach the other countries of Latin America and the Caribbean. In addition, when China began to create its special economic zones, SEZs, in 1980, it competed successfully with Latin America and the Caribbean as a cheap labor destination for Western factories. For these reasons, we date the Global Shift to Latin American and Caribbean countries, other than Mexico, as beginning after 1979.

In 1979, the GDP of Brazil was US$224,969 million. It was ranked as having the eighth-largest economy in the world. Brazil is the largest country in Latin America by geographical area and the fifth largest in the world with an area of 8,515,767 square kilometers. It is the only ex-colony of Portugal in Latin America and the only Latin American country that is a member of BRIC. Brazil also has the largest GDP, measured in both U.S. dollars and in PPP, of all countries in Latin America and the Caribbean, including Mexico. Finally, Brazil is the most populous country in Latin America and the Caribbean. Its total population of 210 million in 2017 accounted for 2.8 percent of the total population of the world. For all these reasons, Brazil deserves special attention with respect to the Global Shift.

Brazil was rediscovered by the original Western imperial power, Portugal, in 1500. Portugal is the tiny European country responsible for the *original* Global Shift of the fifteenth century, which made Western Europe change from *barbarian* to *civilized* by making naval military power superior to armies in imperial conquests. Portugal began the *Age of Discovery,* which shifted economic growth and imperial domination from its long historical roots in the East to the West. While Portugal's focus for imperial dominance was the west coast of Africa across the Indian Ocean to India and Asia, one of its explorers, Pedro Alvares Cabral, en route to Asia, stumbled on Brazil. Based on the papal division of the world between Portugal and Spain by the Papal Bull of 1493 and the subsequent Treaty of Tordesillas of 1494, Cabral's landing on the coast of Brazil happened to be on the Portuguese side of this dividing line. Despite the best military efforts of Spain, England, Holland, and France, Portugal was able to colonize, expand, and hold the largest country in South America.

Unlike the Spanish colonies, no gold or silver was initially found. But the stolen land produced valuable products beginning with brazilwood and then sugar and later tobacco, cattle, and cotton. Gold and diamonds were later found inland in Minas Gerais, enabling territorial expansion of the colony. Portugal initially granted the stolen lands making up its only colony in the New World to fifteen Portuguese noblemen, known as *captains,* each responsible for governing their respective *captaincy,* for their benefit and the benefit of Portugal. When thirteen of the fifteen captaincies failed, mostly because of resistance from the original inhabitants whose lands were being stolen by military force and infectious diseases, the Portuguese king John III sent a formidable fleet and the first governor general in 1549. King John's intent was to crush the indigenous rebels as well as deal with threats from the French, Dutch, and Spanish. A capital city was established in Salvador da Bahia in Northeastern Brazil. But Brazil was too huge to govern as a single colony. It was divided in two in 1621 for administrative purposes. After the discovery of gold and diamonds in Minas Gerais and the subsequent influx of Portuguese and other foreign fortune hunters, the capital was moved to Rio de Janeiro in 1763. Rio was closer to the gold and diamond mines. During the eighteenth century, half a million of Portugal's two-million population immigrated to its colony of Brazil.

Brazil became an independent country in 1822 and a republic in 1889. Since it failed to industrialize as the United States had done, it was destined to be a relatively poor Third World country like every other country in the New World except Canada and the United States. Only the Global Shift would transform Brazil into an emerging economy. As an emerging economy, it experienced rapid economic growth during the first decade of the twenty-first century. In 2012, Brazil overtook the UK as the sixth-largest economy in the world. This was an amazing achievement. However, Brazil, like Russia, has stagnated since, leading some to question the hopes of BRIC as a new dynamic group challenging the status quo. Both Brazil and Russia have maintained their memberships in BRIC and in the larger G20 group. Brazil's GDP grew from US$644,476 million in 2000 to US$2,088 million in 2010. In 2010, it was ranked as the seventh-largest economy in the world behind the UK. This rapid economic growth slowed after 2010. GDP increased marginally to US$2,140,940 million in 2017, but its GDP ranking in the world fell to ninth place. Within BRIC, its economy was larger than that of Russia but smaller than China and India in 2017. The four BRIC countries were still the largest of the emerging economies created by the Global Shift. In 2000, the combined GDP of the four BRIC countries was US$2,562,860 million. By 2010, the combined GDP of the BRIC countries had increased to US$11,177 million. This was 76.6 percent of the GDP of the United States in 2010. By 2017, this combined GDP had grown to US$17,951 million, which was 92.4 percent of the U.S. GDP in 2017. BRIC's share of the world's GDP had grown to 23 percent by 2017.

The Global Shift to Latin America and the Caribbean

Latin America and the Caribbean is made up of thirty-three independent or semi-independent countries in the New World, rediscovered by the Western European empires of Portugal, Spain, Holland, Britain, and France. It excludes the two largest countries in the New World, Canada and the United States. They were all classified as Third World countries prior to the Global Shift. This chapter examines the role of the Global Shift in transforming this region from Third World status to emerging economy status. We have already examined two of these countries, Mexico and Brazil. They are the two largest economies in this group. Together, Mexico and Brazil had a GDP of US$3,128,243 in 2017. This was larger than the combined GDP of the other thirty-one countries in the region. While our ultimate goal is to analyze the effect of the Global Shift on the group as a whole, we will continue the analysis by first providing a separate but brief overview of the next eight largest economies in the region.

After the ten largest economies, GDP falls significantly. This explains our choice of focusing on the ten largest. After Brazil and Mexico, the largest economies in this group are Argentina, Colombia, Venezuela, Chile, Peru, Ecuador, Dominican Republic, and Guatemala. This list excludes Cuba and Puerto Rico, which we will analyze separately because of their post–Spanish colonization by the American empire. In 2017, the GDP of these eight next largest economies in Latin America and the Caribbean ranged from the highest of US$628, 935 million for Argentina to the lowest of US$70,943 million for Guatemala. By contrast, the smallest economy in Latin America and the Caribbean, Dominica, had a GDP of only half a million U.S. dollars in 2017.

The American empire dominated this region after the Monroe Doctrine of 1823. This was America's backyard to use as its colonial possessions, its playground, and to feed its insatiable appetite for *warmongering*. Prior to the Global Shift, the GDP of the United States in 1979 was US$2,544.5 billion. By contrast, the total GDP of the ten largest economies in Latin America and the Caribbean was only US$565.5 billion, 22.22 percent of the GDP of the United States. The Global Shift narrowed this economic dominance of the United States. In 2010, the combined GDP of the ten largest economies had increased to US$4,682 billion. This represented 32.11 percent of the U.S. GDP of US$14,582 billion in 2010. However, economic growth slowed in some of the ten largest economies such as Brazil and Venezuela. As a result, the economic gap widened again. By 2017, the combined GDP of the ten had increased to US$5,317 billion, but the GDP of the United States had increased to US$19,417 billion, making the combined GDP of the ten only 27.38 percent.

The Global Shift to Argentina

We begin this section with Argentina because it is the economy with the largest GDP among the next eight largest economies in Latin America and the Caribbean. Argentina is the eighth-largest country in the world by geographical area, and the second largest in Latin America and the Caribbean, after Brazil. Its total area is 2,780,400 square kilometers. Argentina had a population of forty-five million in 2017. This represented about 0.6 percent of the world's population. Within the region of Latin America and the Caribbean, its total population was smaller than Brazil, Mexico, and Colombia. It therefore ranked fourth in population. Argentina has the third-largest economy in Latin America and the Caribbean after Brazil and Mexico. Prior to the Global Shift, Argentina was ranked the twenty-second-largest economy in the world by GDP, with a GDP of US$69,252 million in 1979. Brazil had the eighth-largest GDP in the world, and Mexico had the fourteenth-largest GDP in the world. These were relatively large economies even before the Global Shift. However, they were still considered as developing economies but would be transformed to emerging economies by the Global Shift. Argentina is unique in that it is the only ex-colonial economy in Latin America that achieved the status of a *developed* economy, like other ex-colonies such as Canada and Australia, only to lose that status and return to developing economy status.

While Argentina was colonized by Spain, Spain did not find silver and gold as it did in Peru and Mexico. The Spanish colony of Argentina was therefore much poorer than Mexico and Peru initially. However, after Britain lost its thirteen North American colonies to the independent United States, and after Britain allied with Spain against Napoleon, Argentina became a semi-British colony. This led to the development of its rich ranching lands. A large and growing export sector based on exports of cattle and sheep led to high rates of economic growth. Argentina became an independent country in 1810. Exports grew at an annual rate exceeding 6 percent between 1810 and 1870. During this period, Argentina became wealthier than Mexico and Peru by specializing in ranching rather than mining silver or gold. The British invested in the ranching industry, meat packing, and in railways. British investment increased after 1870 until the outbreak of the First World War. Other Western European countries such as France, Germany, and Belgium followed the British lead and increased their investments in Argentina as well. Western Europeans immigrated to Argentina because of its high economic growth. By the First World War, Argentina had one of the highest per capita GDP among developed economies in the world. It's GDP and per capita GDP were higher than other developed ex-colonies such as Canada and Australia. Its population also grew faster than Canada and Australia. During this period, its per capita GDP increased steadily and peaked at 80 percent of the per capita GDP of the United States. At the outbreak of the First World War, Argentina had the tenth-highest per capita GDP in the world. Its per capita GDP was even higher than the country that had colonized it, Spain.

Argentina's fortunes declined as a result of World War I. World War I had changed Britain from a creditor nation to a debtor nation. Britain was forced to borrow heavily from the United States to fight the war. As a result, its massive investments in Argentina dried up. Economic growth slowed in Argentina relative to countries that were industrializing after World War I. Its position in the global economy declined significantly. It fell behind other developed ex-colonies such as Canada and Australia. In 2000, Canada was ranked the eighth-largest economy, while Australia was ranked fourteenth. Argentina had fallen behind both to sixteenth place. Argentina's ranking in Latin America and the Caribbean had also fallen, with Brazil and Mexico moving up to first and second place, respectively. Argentina now has the second-smallest GDP in the G20 group, after South Africa.

It would take the Global Shift to reinvigorate the Argentine economy. In 2000, the GDP of Argentina had increased to US$284,204 million compared to US$644,475 million for Brazil and US$581, 426 million for Mexico. In 2000, Argentina's GDP rank in the world had moved up to sixteenth place, while Brazil was ranked as the ninth-largest economy, and Mexico was ranked as the tenth largest. Like many of the developing economies stimulated by the Global Shift, economic growth in Argentina reached heights of 10 percent in the first decade of the twenty-first century. Its industrial sector expanded, adding to its relatively large agricultural and service sectors. By 2017, Argentina's economy had a GDP of US$628,439 million. It had easily maintained its third-place ranking in Latin America and the Caribbean, with a GDP more than twice that of fourth-ranked Colombia. More importantly, its GDP per capita was still higher than both Brazil and Mexico. Per capita GDP in Argentina in 2017 was US$14, 267 compared with US$10,309 in Brazil and US$7,993 in Mexico. Its high per capita GDP achieved during the economic boom created with the help of British investments during the nineteenth century has served to offset the decline in the average standard of living of Argentinians in the period after World War I and before the Global Shift. The Global Shift of the twenty-first century will return Argentina to a high-income economy matching Western economies. Argentina, like Brazil and Mexico, is a member of the G20 group created after the Global Shift.

The Global Shift to Colombia, Venezuela, Chile, and Peru

Columbia is ranked the fourth-largest economy in Latin America and the Caribbean, but its GDP in 2017 is well behind third-ranked Argentina. The economies of Brazil, Mexico, and Argentina are much larger than the next four economies of Colombia, Venezuela, Chile, and Peru, which all have economies of similar size. This means that the total GDP of the three-largest economies exceeds by far the total GDP of the remaining thirty economies of Latin America and the Caribbean. We begin this section with Columbia because its economy in 2017 was slightly larger than the other three in this group.

Columbia is the twenty-sixth-largest country in the world by geographical area and the fifth largest in Latin America and the Caribbean, after Peru. Its total area is 1,197,411 square kilometers. Its total population in 2017 was fifty million. This was the third-largest population in Latin America and the Caribbean, accounting for 0.65 percent of the world's population. Prior to the Global Shift, its GDP in

1979 was US$27,939 million. It had the fifth-largest economy in Latin America and the Caribbean. In 1979, Venezuela was the fourth-largest economy in Latin America and the Caribbean. In 1979, Columbia was ranked as the thirty-fourth-largest economy in the world as measured by GDP. Like other Latin America economies, the Global Shift moved south from the U.S.-Mexican border to Colombia in South America. The Global Shift increased the GDP of Columbia from US$27,939 million in 1979 to US$83,779 million in 2000, to US$288,189 in 2010, to US$397.4 billion in 2017. In 2010, Venezuela's economy was still larger than that of Colombia. Columbia's GDP ranking in the global economy fell from thirty-fourth place in 1979 to forty-first place in 2000, but moved back up to thirty-eighth place in 2017, overtaking Venezuela to become the fourth-largest economy in Latin America and the Caribbean. In 2014, Columbia's economic growth was higher than any other country except China. In the decade between 2004 and 2014, economic growth averaged 5 percent annually. The Global Shift boosted its manufacturing sector, causing it to grow over 10 percent annually. Its IT sector became the fastest growing in the entire world. Colombia boasts the largest shipbuilding industry outside Asia.

The Global Shift to Venezuela

Venezuela is the thirty-third-largest country in the world by geographical area and the seventh largest in Latin America and the Caribbean, after Bolivia. Its total area is 912,050 square kilometers. Venezuela's population in 2017 was thirty-two million, making it the sixth most populous country in Latin America and the Caribbean, slightly smaller than Peru. Its total population in 2017 accounted for 0.42 percent of the world's population. In 1979, before the Global Shift, Venezuela was ranked ahead of Colombia in the global ranking by GDP. Venezuela was ranked twenty-seventh, while Columbia was ranked thirty-fourth. Venezuela's GDP in 1979 was US$55,750 million, significantly larger than Colombia's GDP of US$27,939 million. In 2000, Venezuela's GDP increased to US$117,148 million, but its GDP rank fell to thirty-fourth, while Colombia's fell to forty-first. In 2010, Venezuela's GDP rank had increased to twenty-fourth with a GDP of US$387,852. Columbia's GDP rank had also increased but only to thirty-third place. By 2017, Colombia replaced Venezuela as the fourth-largest economy in Latin America and the Caribbean. Venezuela's GDP had increased to US$550,226, but Colombia's GDP had increased to US$682,977. Venezuela slipped to fifth place and will likely slip further because of its economic decline after 2008. Initially, Venezuela did get a boost from the Global Shift and posted high rates of economic growth during the first decade of the twenty-first century. The fall in oil prices combined with political instability caused GDP to fall annually after 2008. With a shrinking economy, it's possible that by 2019, Venezuela will fall from the fifth-largest economy in Latin America and the Caribbean to the seventh, behind Chile and Peru.

The Global Shift to Chile

In 2017, Chile was the next largest economy in Latin America and the Caribbean, after Venezuela. Chile is the thirty-eighth-largest country in the world by geographical area and the eighth largest in Latin America and the Caribbean, after Venezuela. Its total area is 756,950 square kilometers. In 2017, Chile had a population of eighteen million, making it the seventh most populous country in Latin America and the Caribbean. Its population represented 0.24 percent of the world's population. Chile gained its independence from Spain in 1811. It is a relatively small country in South America lacking natural resources. In 1979, the economy of Chile was ranked forty-fourth largest in the world, well behind Venezuela and Colombia. Its GDP in 1979 was US$20,732 million. By 2000, Chile's ranking had moved up one spot to forty-third, still well behind Venezuela but closer to Colombia, whose ranking had fallen from thirty-fourth in 1979 to forty-first in 2000. Chile's GDP in 2000 had increased to US$75,775 million. In 2010, Venezuela was ranked twenty-fourth, Colombia was ranked thirty-third, and Chile was ranked forty-third. Chile's GDP had increased to US$203,443 million in 2010. While all three economies experienced rapid economic growth after the Global Shift, Venezuela's decline after 2008 led to Chile closing the GDP gap with Venezuela by 2017 and will likely overtake Venezuela after 2018. Since the Global Shift, Chile's economic growth has averaged 6 percent annually, one of the highest in Latin America and the Caribbean. In 2017, Chile's GDP was US$251,220 million compared to US$251,589 million for Venezuela and US$306,439 million for Colombia. These three economies are roughly equal in size but about half the size of the Argentinian economy and only one-seventh the size of the Brazilian economy in 2017. With Brazil facing political instability and low oil prices, the gap with Brazil will likely shrink with respect to Colombia and Chile.

Chile has a much higher per capita GDP than Brazil, Mexico, Colombia, and Venezuela. In 2017, Chile's per capita GDP was US$13,663. It was lower than Argentina's per capita GDP of US$14,267 but higher than Brazil's per capita GDP of US$10,309, Venezuela's per capita GDP of US$8,004, Mexico's per capita GDP of US$7,993, and Colombia's per capita GDP of US$6,217. Chile is ranked as a high-income economy by the World Bank. Chile became the first country in South America to become a member of the OECD, a thirty-four-member group of the wealthiest countries, which includes Mexico as the only other country in Latin America and the Caribbean. Chile became a member in 2010, while Mexico has been a member since 1994. However, Chile is ranked thirtieth by per capita GDP, while Mexico is ranked thirty-fourth. Chile has negotiated more free trade agreements than any other country in Latin America and the Caribbean. It has bilateral FTAs with the United States, China, the EU, Japan, India, South Korea, Australia, New Zealand, Malaysia, Singapore, Thailand, Vietnam, and Brunei. Foreign trade is very important to Chile's economic growth. Imports and exports account for over 30 percent of GDP, respectively. Exports of minerals such as copper account for half of total exports. Exports of industrial goods account for 30 percent of total exports.

The Global Shift to Peru

Peru had the smallest GDP in 2017 among the group of four largest economies in Latin America and the Caribbean, after Argentina. Peru is the twentieth-largest country in the world by geographical area and the fourth largest in Latin America and the Caribbean. It has a total area of 1,285,220 square kilometers. In 2017, Peru's total population was slightly larger than Venezuela's with just over thirty-two million. It was the fifth most populous country in Latin America and the Caribbean, accounting for 0.43 percent of the world's population.

Peru was Spain's richest colony in South America just as Mexico was its richest colony in North America. Spain's military conquest of both

Mexico and Peru was surprising, if not miraculous, with conquests of large indigenous forces by very small Spanish forces. In 1519, Hernando Cortez defeated an Aztec army, which had outnumbered his army by thirty to one, and conquered the Aztec Empire in Mexico for Spain. This amazing military feat was repeated just twelve years later when Francisco Pizarro defeated the Inca Empire and colonized Peru. Spain established the vice royalty of Peru in 1531 and stole the large quantities of silver and gold using the indigenous owners as slaves to mine the precious metals. Mexico and Peru became the two richest colonies in the New World. Despite the fact that the United States later stole half of Mexico with military force, today Mexico is still ranked as the sixteenth-largest economy by GDP. By contrast, Peru today has a GDP rank of only forty-eighth.

Peru did not regain its independence until 1821. During the War with Chile in 1879–1884, Peru lost the province of Arica to Chile. Prior to the Global Shift, Peru's GDP was US$15,543 million in 1979. It was ranked fifty-second in 1979 by GDP. Its GDP increased to US$53,290 million in 2000, and its GDP rank improved slightly to forty-ninth place. In 2010, Peru's GDP increased to US$153,845, but its GDP rank fell to fiftieth place. In 2017, Peru was the seventh-largest economy in Latin America. With a GDP of US$207.72 million, it was not far behind the economies of Colombia, Venezuela, and Chile and will possibly overtake Venezuela by 2020. Its GDP rank had moved back up one spot to forty-ninth in 2017, overtaking Greece.

The Global Shift to Ecuador, Dominican Republic, Guatemala, Costa Rica, Panama, and Uruguay

These are the last six of the thirteen largest economies in Latin America and the Caribbean. Like the previous group of four, these countries can be considered another group of six similar-sized economies, ranging from a GDP of US$97,362 million for Ecuador to a GDP of US$58,123 million for Uruguay in 2017. The next largest economy after this group is Bolivia with a much smaller GDP of US$39,267 million in 2017. For that reason, we will not analyze the other twenty economies in Latin America and the Caribbean separately.

Ecuador is the seventy-fourth-largest country in the world by geographical area. Its population in 2017 was seventeen million, 0.22 percent of the world's population. Prior to the Global Shift, its GDP in 1979 was US$9,589 million. Its GDP rank was fifty-sixth. By 2010, its GDP had increased to US$58,910 million, but its GDP rank had fallen to sixty-eighth place. In 2017, Ecuador was the eighth-largest economy in Latin America and the Caribbean. But its GDP was well behind seventh-place Peru, with a GDP of only US$97,362 million. Its GDP rank in the world had moved up to sixty-second place. Ecuador punched well above its global rank in 2012 when it granted diplomatic asylum to Julian Assange in its embassy in London, England. In doing so, it was fighting not only the United Kingdom but also the most powerful empire in the world, the American empire. Despite determined efforts by the British and the Americans, Assange was still holed up in the Ecuadorian embassy in 2018. For a relatively tiny country to fight for justice and freedom of the press shows how *corrupt* the West is and how *pathetic* are their claims to freedom of the press.

Ecuador was part of the viceroyalty of Peru. It was in Ecuador that Francisco Pizarro had landed in 1531 to defeat the powerful Inca Empire. Unlike Peru, there was no silver or gold for Spain to steal. Ecuador produced cacao, sugar, bananas, tobacco, and cattle. Later it manufactured cotton and woolen textiles. Spain established over five hundred encomiendas in Ecuador to steal the land and enslave the inhabitants. Ecuador gained its independence from Spain in 1830. Like most commodity producers, Ecuador was subjected to the volatility of international commodity prices. Oil and natural gas were discovered and exported in the late 1970s. Ecuador's manufacturing sector also expanded and got a boost from the Global Shift. Annual economic growth averaged 4.6 percent between 2000 and 2006. By 2010, economic growth had increased to 6.9 percent. Oil accounts for 40 percent of total exports. Ecuador is the largest exporter of bananas in the world.

The Global Shift to the Dominican Republic

The Dominican Republic is the ninth-largest economy in Latin America and the Caribbean and the largest economy in the Caribbean, except for Cuba and Puerto Rico, which are analyzed separately below because of their special respective status. The economy of the Dominican

Republic is about the same size as eighth-place Ecuador and tenth-place Guatemala. It has a geographical area of 48,730 square kilometers, making it the 129th-largest country in the world. In 2017, the population of the Dominican Republic was eleven million, 0.14 percent of the world's population. Prior to the Global Shift, it had a GDP of US$5,499 million in 1979, the sixty-sixth highest in the world. By 2010, the GDP of the Dominican Republic had increased to US$51,577 million, but its GDP rank had fallen to seventy-first place. In 2017, its GDP had grown to US$76,850 million, and its GDP rank had increased to sixty-ninth place.

The Dominican Republic is a classic example of using free trade zones after the Global Shift to move from developing economy status to emerging economy status. In the last twenty-five years, the Dominican Republic has had one of the highest average rates of growth in Latin America and the Caribbean. Its high growth rates were fueled both by its free trade zones and a booming tourism industry. In 2017, the per capita GDP of the Dominican Republic was close to US$7,000.

The Global Shift to Guatemala

Guatemala is the tenth-largest economy in Latin America and the Caribbean today. Prior to the Global Shift, its GDP in 1979 was only US$6,071 million. At that time, it was the ninth-largest economy in Latin America and the Caribbean, ahead of the Dominican Republic. Guatemala is the most populous country in Central America with a population of seventeen million in 2017. This accounts for 0.22 percent of the world's population. Guatemala has a total land area of 108,890 square kilometers, making is the 106th-largest country in the world. A thirty-six-year civil war hindered the economic development of Guatemala. In 1990, its GDP was only US$19,100 million. The war ended in 1996. The Global Shift to Guatemala was aided by the Korean *maquila* factories, which imitated the earlier American maquiladoras in Mexico. The creation of the Central American Free Trade Agreement, CAFTA, in 2006 boosted investment from the United States into Guatemala. In 2010, Guatemala had a GDP of US$41,190 million, with a GDP rank of seventy-eighth place. In 2017, its GDP had grown to US$70,943 million, making it the tenth-largest economy in Latin America and the Caribbean.

Summarizing the Global Shift to the Ten Largest Economies in Latin America and the Caribbean

There are simply too many independent economies in Latin America and the Caribbean to deal separately with all of them. Dealing separately with the many very small economies runs the risk of missing the forest for the trees. In this section, therefore, we summarize the effect of the Global Shift to this region by combining the ten largest economies. These are the economies of Brazil, Mexico, Argentina, Columbia, Venezuela, Chile, Peru, Ecuador, Dominican Republic, and Guatemala. In 1979, these ten economies had a total GDP of US$565.5 billion. In 2010, the combined GDP of these ten economies had grown to US$4,682 billion. More important than this massive absolute increase in their GDP was the fact that they had grown much faster than the United States, the dominant economy in both the New World and in the entire globe. In 1979, the combined GDP of these ten economies was 22.22 percent of the GDP of the United States. In 2010, this had increased to 32.11 percent. After 2010, growth slowed somewhat because of major problems in some of the ten economies, such as Brazil and Venezuela. As a result, the GDP of these ten economies had increased to US$5,317 billion in 2017. This was only 27.38 percent of the GDP of the United States. However, these ten economies are all members of the new class of economies referred to as emerging economies. Together, their GDP represents 6 percent of the world's GDP. The Global Shift to Latin America and the Caribbean represents a significant part of the total Global Shift.

While economic growth has slowed, the countries in Latin America and the Caribbean gained a significant degree of political and economic independence during the first three decades of the Global Shift. While some of this growing independence must be attributed to the Global Shift, some of it can be attributed to the engagement of the United States in the disastrous wars in the Middle East beginning with its invasion of Afghanistan in 2001. This diversion of U.S. attention to the Middle East took its eye off its own backyard, which had been its major focus since the Monroe Doctrine in 1823. In this way, America's *invented* war on terrorism has played into the hands of those pushing the long historical independence movement in Latin America and the Caribbean. America's continued global warmongering, despite the promise of candidate Trump to reign it in, will reduce not only its capacity to colonize Latin America and the Caribbean but also its capacity to colonize globally. As China moves to increase its trade and investments with Latin America, we can expect the Global Shift to the emerging economies in Asia to reinvigorate the Global Shift to Latin America and the Caribbean at the expense of the American empire.

The Global Shift to Cuba and Puerto Rico

Two large Caribbean economies we have ignored so far are Cuba and Puerto Rico. These two large Caribbean islands were colonized by the American empire after the United States defeated Spain in the Spanish-American War of 1898. The American empire wanted to keep both colonies just as it later attempted to colonize both North and South Korea. The resulting relationship between Cuba and Puerto Rico with the American empire is very similar to the relationship between North and South Korea with the American empire. Just as the American empire demonizes and embargoes North Korea, it demonizes and embargoes Cuba. While North Korea stands up almost alone to the American empire in Asia, Cuba stands up almost alone to the American empire in the New World. Just as North Korea today threatens the United States with its defensive nuclear program, so did Cuba threaten the United States during the 1960s with its defensive nukes supplied by the Soviet Union. While America's new invented war is its war on terrorism, it has not given up on its older invented war, its war on Communism. America is still fighting that old war in Cuba and North Korea.

While Cuba has been punished inhumanely by America's continued war on Communism, Puerto Rico has been showered with American generosity like South Korea. Much of this American generosity comes in the form of allowing Puerto Rico to engage in international trade, capital inflows, and participation in the global financial markets. One difference from South Korea is the large numbers of Puerto Ricans who have been allowed to immigrate into the United States. People who are born in Puerto Rico are U.S. citizens. Many Puerto Ricans immigrated into the United States after 1950. Puerto Rico's close geographic proximity to New York City made America's largest city the key destination for Puerto Ricans. While Puerto Rico is not a state of the Union, like Hawaii, it has a status not much different from that of a state. Puerto Rico is a territory of the United States. It became a U.S. territory in 1898, when it was stolen from Spain after the Spanish-American War. It is the most populous territory of the United States.

Puerto Rico's choice of semicolonial status with the United States, like South Korea, had made Puerto Rico a developed economy before the Global Shift. This is why we have not analyzed it as part of the Global Shift to Latin America and the Caribbean. It's the same reason we excluded South Korea in our analyses of the Global Shift to Asia. Until the Global Shift, Puerto Rico was the most developed economy in Latin America and the Caribbean. It was designated a high-income economy by the World Bank before the Global Shift.

Cubans chose not to be a semicolony of the American empire. For this, it was isolated by the United States and its allies and impoverished much like North Korea. Since it is still punished by the United States because Cubans refuse to change their political system, it has not benefitted from the Global Shift. This is our reason for omitting Cuba from our analyses of the Global Shift to Latin America and the Caribbean. It's the same reason we excluded North Korea from our analyses of the Global Shift to Asia. It's somewhat ironic that the United States agreed to engage with China without demanding that China renounce the same political system it has as Cuba. As I said before, the United States was willing to do that in return for China's help in bringing down the Soviet Union. The United States has continued its isolation of Cuba and North Korea because they had nothing to bargain with.

China in Latin America: The Global Shift Comes Full Circle

The Global Shift to China began with developed Asian economies Hong Kong, Taiwan, South Korea, and Japan loyal to the West, given the green light by the American empire that it was OK to engage with China. They jumped at the opportunity because their Western engine of economic growth had begun to stutter. The Global Shift had begun in Latin America, specifically in the maquiladoras of the Mexican-U.S. border. The American empire had kept China out of its backyard even more strictly than it had kept China out of its Asian economic colonies.

But the American empire had its hands full dealing with its "policing duties" in hot spots in the Middle East, North Africa, North Korea, Georgia, and Ukraine. It began to ease up on its tight control of its own backyard. The countries in Latin America and the Caribbean never took to the notion of welcoming the American empire after fighting the Western European empires. Now was their chance to push back even harder against American meddling in their internal affairs and reduce their economic dependence on the West.

At the time that Latin America and the Caribbean, led by countries such as Venezuela, Bolivia, Brazil, Argentina, Nicaragua, Peru, El Salvador, Paraguay, Uruguay, and Ecuador, which had elected pro-independence governments hostile to Western imperialism, were looking for a country like China, which would both assist their pro-independence struggle while reducing their economic dependence on the United States, China was looking for an offset to President Obama's pivot to Asia. China saw Asia as its backyard. If the United States was bent on meddling in China's backyard, China would meddle in the American backyard. China was also looking for other sources for commodities and energy to feed its rapid economic growth and provide new markets for its cheap manufactured goods. These would be the same reasons why China would take the Global Shift to Africa, as we explain in our last chapter. It's somewhat ironic that the Global Shift had begun in Latin America but slowed by China becoming an even cheaper source of labor than Latin America. As a result of the Global Shift moving from Latin America to China, it began to move from China to other Asian sources of cheap labor such as Vietnam, Bangladesh, India, Malaysia, and Indonesia. Latin America lost most of its competitive cheap labor edge. Now China and the other Asian emerging economies are using their new emerging economy status, created by the Global Shift, to reinvigorate growth in Latin America while simultaneously reducing the tight hold the West has had on this region since Columbus rediscovered the New World.

China had previously provided some economic and political support to Cuba because of Cuba's lone defiance of the West in Latin America and the Caribbean. Another historical link with the region was through its leadership role in the Non-Aligned Movement against Western imperialism and support for the pro-independence movement of Third World colonies of the West. After China was courted by President Nixon to help the United States fight the Soviet Union, Latin America began slowly to forge greater economic and political links with China. The region was geographically too remote to compete with Asian economies such as Hong Kong, Taiwan, South Korea, and Japan, which were the countries that were able to maximize the economic benefits of the American empire allowing engagement with China. No one could have foreseen that the Global Shift to China, initiated by Hong Kong, Taiwan, South Korea, and Japan, would have so quickly spread to Western Europe and the United States with the birth of container shipping and the building of massive container ports in China. With that total Western engagement of China, China grew at rates that astounded everyone. China switched from being the cheap labor target of the West to prime economic challenger of the leader of the West. In that new capacity, China is encroaching on the economic colonization that the West had practiced alongside its military and political colonizations. Like the West before, China will not restrict its new role as competitor to the West to any area but compete across the globe, including America's backyard.

Latin America wants to engage with China just like Hong Kong, Taiwan, South Korea, and Japan did in the 1980s. It's primarily about the gains to both parties from international trade. It's not about old-style Western colonization that is theft by military force. The West had opted for colonization over trade because they had the military advantage, wanted to steal rather than buy, wanted to enslave rather than pay for labor, wanted to dominate and be superior and Christian rather than be equal and respectful of all religions, and wanted to promote white racism and white hegemony. The Global Shift is about free trade and free capital flows for mutual benefits to both parties. Once the United States had engaged with China without requiring China to be an economic colony like Canada, Japan, Germany, or South Korea, Western imperialism was struck an important blow. But it was the massive growth of the new emerging economies like China and India that was the final nail in the coffin of colonization by military force. Much as some of us may dislike some of the negative aspects of free international trade and foreign investment, the latter is as revolutionary a change of the global order as night is to day. Imperialism is totally immoral. It has absolutely no saving graces despite rhetoric to the contrary. International trade and foreign investment, by contrast, are the only way to grow Third World economies and reduce global poverty. There is no other way.

China has engaged with Latin America since the beginning of this century, two decades after it first engaged with the West, to find new sources of raw materials to feed its massive economic growth unleashed by the Global Shift. Western countries had moved their factories to China to take advantage of cheap labor to feed the insatiable appetite of their consumers for cheap junk while shifting the pollution caused by heavy industries to China. The West had cleaned up after the first industrial revolution based on heavy industry. It had to shift dirty industries based on coal to China and India while maximizing the use of the cheap labor provided by billions of poor Asians. China and India agreed because they wanted to improve employment opportunities for their billions of poor citizens. But these Western factories need raw materials as well as labor. China and India had the cheap labor but not the cheap raw materials or sufficient energy supplies. That was the key reason for China to seek out sources of raw materials. It needed those raw materials to feed the Western factories located in China to produce the cheap manufactured goods for greedy Western consumers made addicted to consumerism by the *civilized* West. China accepted the role of "factory for the West" because it enabled China to grow its economy to a size that both enriches its citizens and opposes Western domination. As the dominant economy benefitting from the Global Shift, China also sees the opportunity to lead all emerging economies, just as the United States has led all developed economies. Latin America is simply part of the leadership role China is taking on.

Every country, including Canada, that has specialized on commodity exports has criticized the economic instability it brings and mourned the lack of value added. Some have even gone so far as to brand Canadians as hewers of wood and drawers of water. The reality is that these countries are simply observing Ricardo's law of comparative advantage, which gives them the greatest benefits from international trade, which, in turn, grows their GDP by the most. China's imports from Latin America are therefore predominantly commodities and from the extractive industries. Initially, China's appetite for these Latin American imports created what has been dubbed the "China boom." Other commodity exporters like Canada and Australia benefitted from this China-led demand. But commodity prices crashed after the 2008 financial crisis caused by the United States. Since this crash, China's economic growth has slowed, but China continues to import commodities from both Latin America and other countries. Just as prices rose enormously before 2008, prices collapsed after 2008. That's the nature of commodity exports throughout history. It's the instability that comes from reaping the gains from comparative advantage. China also continues its investment in the extractive industries in Latin America,

fuelling continued economic growth in Latin America. Exports from these
extractive industries continue to account for 50 percent of total exports
from Latin America. China continues to import 20 percent of these
exports. China is still the second-largest market for total exports from
Latin America, after the United States. This is remarkable considering the
long Western European colonial presence in Latin America. Moreover,
growing exports from Latin America's extractive industries to China comes
at the expense of falling exports to the United States.

The top-four Latin American exports to China are copper, soy
beans, iron ore, and oil. These four products account for 60 percent of
exports to China. Some 90 percent of total Latin American exports to
China are from only four countries, Argentina, Brazil, Peru, and Chile.
In the first decade of the twenty-first century, Latin American exports
to China increased tenfold. China is now the largest export market for
Chile, Brazil, and Peru and the second-largest export market for Cuba,
Costa Rica, and Argentina. One of the ironies of the expanding trade
relationship between Latin America and China is that China's primary
exports to Latin America are cheap manufactured goods. Initially, the
Global Shift made Latin America the cheap producer of manufactured
goods by Western factories destined for Western consumers. American
rapprochement with China robbed Latin America of that advantage,
moving the advantage to Asia. Now, China's exports of manufactured
goods can compete with manufactured goods even in Latin America's
home market. It's clear that the Global Shift to Asia has returned
Latin America to its more traditional exporter role of specialization in
commodities. Latin America and the Caribbean is now China's third-
largest market for its exports after the United States and the EU. If
Latin America wants to benefit the most from the theory of comparative
advantage, it has to accept this reversal and hope to use that benefit to
industrialize more slowly but become a high-income commodity exporter
like Canada and Australia.

The new reality is that Asian countries like China and India,
which initially imported the Global Shift from developed economies,
are increasingly using their new emerging economy status to compete
with the old developed economies by becoming exporters of the Global
Shift to Third World economies in Latin America and Africa. As China
and other Asian emerging economies pursue their economic interests
in Latin America, China will see Latin America as a strategic partner
in challenging Western dominance. Chinese president Xi Jinping

signaled China's strategic interest in Latin America and the Caribbean by proposing a China-Latin America and the Caribbean Summit. Such a summit was held in 2014, hosted by Brazil. President Xi attended the summit where he announced his vision of creating a partnership between China and Latin America and the Caribbean. President Xi announced a five-year plan to provide the region with six thousand scholarships, training programs in China for Latin Americans and those from the Caribbean, and increasing China's investments in the region to US$250 billion. These were among many promises made by President Xi under his proposed 2015–2019 plan for China-LAC cooperation. As President Trump withdraws from international trade with Latin America and Asia to pursue his "Make America Great Again" program, President Xi is expanding China's international trade with both Asia and Latin America. While China gained immensely from the last four decades of international trade, gains by the United States were very modest. While Ricardo's theory of comparative advantage proves that both sides gain from trade, it says nothing about which side will gain the most. The evidence is clear that the last four decades of international trade between the West and China added at least 7 percent to the annual economic growth of China, while adding a modest 1 percent or less to the economic growth of the United States and the EU. That is a *political reason,* not an economic one, for President Trump to withdraw and President Xi to engage more. International trade is not simply about economic gains. It's also about *political losses.* As international trade reduces the economic gap between China and the United States, the political and strategic gains to China increase relative to the United States and its allies. Unfortunately for President Trump, the horse bolted out of the gate after China established its first SEZ in 1980. Even if President Trump was supported by his allies and the Western media in his quest to put the genie of the Global Shift back in the bottle, it would have been a daunting task. With both the Western media and all Western leaders opposing President Trump in his quest, it's an impossible task. The fact that President Trump is the visionary and his opponents are dumb witted makes no difference.

CHAPTER 10

The Global Shift to Africa

We have often compared the revolutionary nature of the Global Shift with the birth of Western imperialism. In this regard, Western imperialism and enslaving of Africans began in Africa, with Portugal's colonizations along the West coast of Africa after Portugal's conquest of the North African city of Ceuta, in 1415. But this new revolution, the Global Shift, which will reverse the outcome of that first revolution, reached Africa last. After Portugal's African conquests, Africa was colonized by the Dutch, British, French, Italians, Belgians, and Germans. Africa was raped, pillaged, and invaded by the Western European empires, much as the New World was. Africans were enslaved, killed, and ethnic cleansed as much as the First Nations of the New World were. Western racism, barbarism, and brutality were meted out to Africans as much as they were meted out to the First Nations in the New World. Forcing Christianity on heathens was never civilizing. It was as barbaric then as it is today. That Western penchant for warmongering, military invasions, death, and destruction show no signs of letting up today. The incessant bombings, destructions, killings, and creation of sixty-five million refugees in the Middle East and North Africa today are incontrovertible evidence of this.

Africa, like the New World, had developed civilized societies long before the West arrived to colonize, steal, and rape. But the Western naval superiority enabled it to conquer and rape at will the advanced countries and empires in Africa as it did to the advanced countries and empires in the New World. Humanity was born in Africa. It should therefore come as no surprise that civilized societies began in Africa. Ancient African empires include the Egyptian empire, the Berber Empire, the Ethiopian Empire, the Mali Empire, the Nubian Empire, the Ashanti Empire, the Bantu Empire, and many more. These advanced civilized empires were older than the advanced civilized empires of the New World such as the Mayan, Inca, Aztec, Carib, Norte Chico, and many more. But the Western European empires used their superior naval power to decimate all these civilizations and make the remaining original inhabitants, the ones they did not kill or enslave, poor and primitive by stealing their wealth, destroying their languages and cultures, and preaching incessantly that the white man was superior to all nonwhites.

The one difference between Africa and the New World was that the African population remained larger than the whites who had come from Europe to settle on the lands they had stolen by military force from the Africans. In the New World, the Europeans had brought diseases to which the First Nations had no natural immunity. This killed off many more of the original inhabitants than were killed off in Africa. A second difference was that the Western European empires handed off the colonies to their children, enabling the rise of powerful countries such as the United States, Mexico, and Canada, where the First Nations had absolutely no chance of having their stolen lands returned. Matters took a different turn in Africa. The Western European empires were willing to go to war with each other to steal more of Africa than the other Western European empire. These constant wars in Africa, as in Asia and the New World, would often spill over into Western Europe, devastating their home economies. Up until the rise of Germany, these wars were costly but never disastrous. But the rise of Germany led to the self-destruction of these Western European empires during World War II. The Germans and Italians, on one side, waged the most disastrous war ever fought for colonies by the Western European empires, against Britain and France, on the other side.

While Western historians will continue to lie to you, the Second World War was never about freedom and equality. It was mostly about imperial dominance, primarily between Britain and Germany, and primarily over colonies in Africa. This was the war that allowed colonies in both Africa and Asia to wrest their independence after this war had destroyed the military superiority of the Western European empires. In this respect, it was similar to the U.S. Civil War leading to the abolition of slavery. Again, Western historians will continue to lie and say that President Lincoln waged the Civil War to abolish slavery. The truth is that he waged the Civil War to keep America as a more powerful empire. But he abolished slavery to help him achieve that goal. He needed the free blacks to help him win the war.

Germany was a latecomer to Western European imperialism. It had been predated by Portugal, Spain, Holland, France, Britain, Italy, and even Belgium, in the case of African colonizations. But after the rise of Prussia, following Prussia's military defeat of both Austria and France, Germany quickly became the new powerhouse of Europe, challenging

Britain for both European and imperial dominance, after the defeats of Austria and France. It was at the Berlin Conference of 1884–85 that Germany signaled to the other Western European colonizers in Africa that it would join the competition in what came to be called the Scramble for Africa. Germany's powerful chancellor Otto von Bismarck hosted and chaired this conference in Germany's capital city, Berlin. Germany's entry into the Scramble for Africa was the equivalent of the United States signaling its entry into the Scramble for Latin America and the Caribbean, with the Monroe Doctrine of 1823. While the United States succeeded in that equal quest to dominate Latin America and the Caribbean over all the older Western European empires, Germany would self-destruct in its quest to dominate Africa over all the other older Western European empires. But by simultaneously destroying all the other Western European empires, it provided the opportunity for African colonies to wrest independence. As a result of the successful bid of the United States to dominate Latin America and the Caribbean, the latter region had to wait for the Global Shift, diversion of U.S. focus to the Middle East wars, and the rise of China to secure its economic and political independence.

Global competition for colonies by Britain, France, and Italy as allies, against Germany, led to the First World War. When Germany lost that war, it was stripped of its African colonies. Most of those African colonies were taken by Britain and France. Italy felt cheated by Britain and France. Germany bided its time to rearm and take revenge on Britain and France for stealing its colonies in Africa and the Asia-Pacific and imposing punitive reparations. The First World War, like the hundreds of wars before among the Western European empires for colonies, had not destroyed the Western European empires. They would live to fight one last war that would destroy them. What surprised Britain and France was the speed at which Germany, under Adolf Hitler, industrialized and rearmed with technology far superior than theirs. Had it not been for Russia, Germany would have easily defeated Britain and France.

Italy had allied with Britain against Germany during the First World War. But it had been cheated out of the spoils by Britain and France. In particular, Italy was convinced that Britain and France were determined to keep both Germany and Italy from sharing in the Scramble for Africa. As a result, it felt as aggrieved as Germany. It therefore allied with Germany against Britain and France in the Second World War. The Second World War was as inevitable as all the previous wars fought among the Western European empires since Portugal began the colonization of Africa in 1415. Italy, led by Mussolini, made the first move against Britain and France in 1935 by colonizing Ethiopia. Italy took a page out of British hypocrisy by declaring Italian king Victor Emmanuel III emperor of Ethiopia. The British had made Queen Victoria empress of India. The following year, Italy merged its three African colonies, Ethiopia, Eritrea, and Italian Somaliland, into *Italian East Africa.* Italy had found itself a strong post–World War I leader in Benito Mussolini to challenge Britain and France in the Scramble for Africa. Britain and France had simultaneously handed Adolf Hitler an ally. Hitler supported Italian colonization in Africa in return for Mussolini's support of Hitler's goal of unifying Germany with Austria. The British underestimated the ability of Germany to ever threaten British hegemony after the punitive measures it had imposed on Germany following Germany's defeat in the First World War. Dominant empires have a bad habit of underestimating their competition. The American empire today underestimates the threat from the emerging economies caused by the Global Shift.

Africa played another pivotal role in cementing the alliance of Italy with Germany against Britain and France. Italy had attempted to colonize Tunisia before France. Italians had immigrated into Tunisia long before the nineteenth century. Many Italian Jews had settled in Tunisia since the seventeenth century. After the 1848 revolutions in Europe, many more Italians immigrated into Tunisia. But in 1881 Britain had supported French colonization of Tunisia in return for French support for Britain's colonization of Cyprus. Despite French colonization, Italian immigrants had continued to settle in Tunisia in large numbers, opposing French controls. France introduced policies in Tunisia to coerce Italians to become French citizens. In 1919, France prohibited Italian Tunisians from owning property. When Mussolini became prime minister of Italy in 1922, there were more Italians in Tunisia than French. French discrimination against Italian Tunisians prompted Mussolini to return to the question of Italian colonization of Tunisia. Conquest of Tunisia would provide Italy with a strategic base for expansion in the Mediterranean. But the British continued to support France. Britain's continued preferential treatment of France over Italy in the Scramble for Africa led to the military alliance between Mussolini and Hitler, signed on May 22, 1939.

Italy's entry into World War II began in North Africa. Italy declared war on Britain and France on June 10, 1940. Mussolini's key goal was to steal British and French colonies in Africa. He sought revenge on Britain and France for isolating Italy in the Scramble for Africa. Italy felt that it had a strategic advantage in using its powerful navy to dominate the Mediterranean and North Africa. The British felt secure in Egypt and responded to Italy's declaration of war by sending British forces based in Egypt to attack the Italian colony of Libya. Mussolini responded by sending his Tenth Army to invade Egypt in August. With the aid of troops from its colonies, the British defeated the Italians. This prompted Hitler to send his best general, *desert fox,* Erwin Rommel, to win the war in Africa. The Second World War in North Africa lasted from June 10, 1940 to May 13, 1943. This confirms my view that the Second World War was fought over colonies in Africa and Asia.

In both the First and Second World War, France and Britain were forced to use their colonists from their many worldwide colonies to defeat Germany. In doing so, they had made promises of independence much like President Lincoln's promise of freedom to blacks to help him win the Civil War. But Britain and France had reneged on those promises after the First World War and were still militarily powerful enough after the First World War to enforce continued colonization. But the Second World War had severely weakened the military power of Britain and France relative to their colonies. The colonies were willing to fight for their independence as the American colonies had done. This was as true in Africa as it was in Asia. The first colony that Britain was forced to give up was India. The independence of India in 1947 served to galvanize the independence movement in Africa. As usual, the American empire pretended to support independence for British and French colonies as it had done before with Spanish colonies. As with the ex-Spanish colonies, the goal of the American empire was to aid its own colonization, economically, politically, and militarily, of these ex-colonies of Britain and France. During the Cold War between the American empire and the Soviet Union, African colonies were courted by both the American empire and the Soviet Union.

African colonies gradually achieved independence or semi-independence from Britain and France in the post–World War II period. At first, many did relatively well and attempted to forge a New World Order with the newly independent countries in Asia and the Caribbean that were not aligned with either the American empire or the Soviet Union, the so-called Non-Aligned Movement. (See Mirza, *How the West Was Won and Lost,* pages 442–449.) The 1960s turned out to be the high point of leadership in African ex-colonies. It was followed by decades of wars, famines, dictatorships, corruption, and stagnant or declining economies. Poverty increased, and Africa became the continent that was unstable and dependent on Western handouts. Thanks to the Global Shift, Africa is now on a new growth path that will see many African countries join the growing group of emerging economies. While we have dated the Global Shift as beginning in 1980 when China created its first SEZ in Shenzhen, the Global Shift arrived in Africa about two decades later.

The Role of China in Bringing the Global Shift to Africa

By the time the Global Shift reached Africa after 2000, China had moved from emerging economy status to developed economy. Just as China was fortunate to be surrounded by the developed economies of Hong Kong, Taiwan, South Korea, Singapore, and Japan to jump start the Global Shift to China before the United States, Western Europe, Australia, and Canada joined the bandwagon to make the Global Shift to China a worldwide phenomenon, Africa is fortunate that China was now sufficiently developed to be an important contributor to the later Global Shift to Africa. As the birthplace of humanity, Africa made commercial contact with China long before the West. Humans have a long history of traveling great distances to engage in trade. As Africa developed in ancient times, it naturally expanded outward to Asia, making contact with China as early as the first century. History has also recorded the voyages of Chinese admiral Zheng He, who reached East Africa in 1415, the same year Portugal colonized the North African city of Ceuta.

Unlike Portugal, China abandoned its seafaring adventures and isolated itself from the world. It was not until the post–World War II period that China began to engage once more with Africa. However, the Western empires, especially Britain, had moved millions of Chinese workers to their colonies in Africa, establishing a Chinese diaspora that would help China's twenty-first-century efforts to compete with the West in Africa. Many Chinese also immigrated to Africa after the Communists defeated Chiang Kai Shek in the Civil War. The Chinese in the diaspora were excited at the prospect of reconnecting with their mother country while seizing new trade and commercial opportunities presented by China's growing investments and trade with Africa. It was a win-win for both sides, reminiscent of the Chinese in Hong Kong and Taiwan seizing new commercial and investment opportunities in China beginning with China's creation of its first SEZ in Shenzhen in 1980. There is an estimated one million Chinese living in Africa today.

In the late 1950s, China began to reengage with Africa by forging bilateral trade agreements with many African countries, including Egypt, Sudan, Algeria, Morocco, Somalia, and Guinea. China began to engage with many of the ex-colonies of the Western European empires in an attempt to work together against political and economic interference by the United States and Western Europe. China supported the independence movements across Africa and also supported black South Africans fighting apartheid. At the Bandung Conference in 1955, China showed its interest in leading the Third World countries and the Non-Aligned Movement. China helped African economies develop by investing in the infrastructure of many African countries. In return, African countries lobbied for China's seat in the Security Council of the UN to be removed from the ROC, Taiwan, and given to the PRC, China, its rightful owner. This was accomplished in 1971. When the Global Shift arrived in China in 1980, China's trade with Africa was only US$1billion. By 2000, China-Africa trade had increased tenfold to US$10 billion. That had laid the foundation for the massive growth that came after China transformed its economy from emerging to developed in the twenty-first century. By 2012, China-Africa trade had jumped to a staggering US$200 billion, becoming Africa's largest trading partner, surpassing both the United States and former colonial masters such as Britain and France.

Much more important than trade is China's capital investment in Africa. Just as China was transformed by the foreign investments flowing into China from Hong Kong, Taiwan, South Korea, Singapore, Australia, the United States, and Western Europe, China is aiding in the transformation of Africa in the twenty-first century by adding to the traditional sources of foreign investment in Africa. The traditional sources had long been the Western European empires. After the Second World War, the United States became another important investor in Africa. The United States had also become a leading trade partner with

Africa. Prior to the Global Shift, China had done some infrastructure investments in Africa such as building and financing the rail link between Zambia and Tanzania in the early 1970s. China had sent over fifty thousand workers, including engineers, to build that railway. China has over a thousand corporations operating in Africa today, investing in infrastructure, energy, banking, agriculture, and manufacturing. These investments create jobs, increase wages, and grow the economy. One railway project in Nigeria alone is estimated to have created two hundred thousand new jobs. Infrastructure investment is the key to transforming any economy from developing to emerging economy status. Container ports and railways are essential. No country has ever developed without foreign investment in infrastructure. This is a key area in which China is helping Africa to move forward and industrialize. Chinese banks are also helping to provide the complementary financial infrastructure needed to industrialize and provide loans to business.

China's relationship with Africa somewhat resembles that of Britain when Britain first industrialized in the second half of the eighteenth century. Like Britain then, China imports mostly raw materials, energy, and agricultural products and exports mostly cheap manufactured goods. Chinese who belong to the large Chinese diaspora in Africa are hungry for Western-style manufactured goods now produced much cheaper in China and exported to Africa. They lead the way, and African consumers follow. The difference, of course, was that Britain had colonized, using superior military force. Colonization can never be the same as free trade. China is engaged in trade, not colonization, in Africa. There is no military conquest or political governance, which Britain, France, and other Western European empires engaged in. One can argue that there may be a form of economic colonization, but that may be impossible to prevent and the necessary cost of economic development and poverty reduction. Many African countries still face massive starvation from droughts and wars. Economic colonization by China may be a small price to pay. Africa's abundance of minerals and raw materials attracted Western imperial powers. Today, African leaders are partnering with a new superpower, China, to use those same resources, oil, diamonds, bauxite, platinum, nickel, copper, timber, cobalt, silver, uranium, agricultural products, and cheap labour to provide greater economic benefits to its own citizens. China's fast-growing demand for these imports boosts both prices and wages, adding value to Africa's exports while increasing the incomes of African workers and consumers.

The value of both imports and exports between China and Africa is experiencing annual growth rates exceeding 20 percent. Africa has the largest mineral industries in the world. Africa produces 46 percent of the world's diamonds, 62 percent of the world's platinum, 21 percent of the world's gold, and 16 percent of the world's uranium. Africa also has 60 percent of the world's arable land but produces only 10 percent of the world's food. This implies massive business and investment opportunities in agriculture.

China has also been very generous to African countries with debt forgiveness and low-interest loans. In December 2015, Chinese president Xi Jinping pledged a cheap loan and aid package of US$60 billion to Africa. Today, China provides aid to more African countries than the United States. China was also helping generously in the medical area long before the Global Shift. China has sent more than fifteen thousand doctors to the many countries in Africa since 1960. Since the Global Shift, China has increased its aid for hospitals and fighting diseases in Africa, including malaria, AIDS, and tuberculosis. In many ways, China's new engagement with Africa is more similar to the post–Global Shift engagement of the West with China than with Britain's earlier engagement with colonies, or that of the French, Dutch, and Portuguese empires, or the post–World War II engagement of Africa by the American empire. As we have explained, this new post–Global Shift engagement with China and the Third World emphasizes trade and investment over military invasions and colonization. Using this later model of engagement implies that China will do the same in Africa as the West did in China. Just as China has maintained its political independence while embracing the Global Shift to grow its economy and reduce poverty, China's current engagement with Africa should allow African countries to maintain their political independence while embracing the Global Shift to grow their economies and reduce poverty.

The Global Shift has been of immense benefit to China. It has increased real wages so much that Chinese businesses, which initially partnered with the West to become Chinese-owned corporations in China, now look outside China for the cheap labor they initially found at home. That cheap Chinese labor gave them the competitive edge over Western corporations. Now those same businesses are reaching out to Africa to maintain that competitive edge. It was the same reason that Hong Kong and Taiwan businesses jumped headlong into China after President Nixon's visit. At the time, labor in China was far cheaper than labor in Hong Kong and Taiwan. New factories were set up in China to take advantage of that cheaper labor. Now, Chinese businesses are doing exactly the same in Africa. Many of these businesses would have begun their overseas search in Asian countries such as Vietnam, India, and Bangladesh. But Africa has opened a whole new front for them. It's an entire continent rich in cheap untapped labor. It would be natural for Chinese corporations to begin on the east coast of Africa just as Western corporations began on the south coast of China. But these Western corporations pushed north and west from China's southern and eastern coasts into the heartland of China to tap all its immense labor supply. In like manner, Chinese corporations will move inland from Africa's eastern coastline to tap all its immense labor supply. Africa's population today exceeds 1.25 billion. China has begun with countries like Kenya and Ethiopia and will push further west through the Congo and Zambia to Angola on the West African coast. It is reminiscent of Portugal's beginning along the West African coast in the fifteenth century. But it will not be based on the slave trade or ivory.

China and Chinese corporations will make mistakes in Africa. But they will be mistakes like those made by the West in the post–Global Shift era. These mistakes will occur because both Chinese corporations and local partners minimize wages and safe working conditions to maximize profits. They will be similar to those made by Apple and Foxconn in Shenzhen and the factory collapse in Bangladesh. Apple partnered with the Taiwan electronic manufacturing giant to produce its iPhones in China. In its pursuit of maximum profits, Apple allowed Foxconn to exploit Chinese workers in its massive Longhua factory in Shenzhen, nicknamed Foxconn City. Western journalists were able to penetrate Apple-Foxconn tight security measures to publicize the inhumane working condition. In 2010, Chinese employees began to commit suicide by jumping off their dorm high-rises rather than continue to work the forced long hours in dangerous working conditions. Apple's infamous founder, Steve Jobs, was unapologetic. In 2013, a garment factory, Rana Plaza, producing cheap clothing for Western retail outlets, including Canadian outlets, collapsed, killing 1,134 workers and injuring another 2,500. This was the most deadly garment factory collapse in history. Later investigation concluded that the factory owners had ignored a warning to evacuate the factory after cracks in the building were discovered a day before the collapse. As with Apple-Foxconn, it was the pursuit of maximum profits that made the owners risk worker safety. It's no different from disasters in the West such as the BP disaster in the Gulf of Mexico in 2010. The Deepwater Horizon oil spill killing American workers was the result of owners taking undue risks to maximize profits. Mistakes made by China and Chinese corporations in Africa will be caught by the Western press eager to prove that China is as evil as the Western empires have been. China will be held to a higher standard by Western journalists who begin from the presumption that China has a far worse record on human rights than Western countries, even though China never stole the lands of their First Nations like Canada and the Untied States did, nor enslaved Africans or First Nations, like the West did.

China has also increased arms sales to African countries, competing with the United States and Russia. China had begun selling arms to Africa in the 1980s. But the United States is still a much bigger arms exporter to Africa than China. In 2017, China established its first overseas military base in Djibouti, Africa. China has joined the UN peacekeeping missions in Africa. Wars in Africa continue to cause as much poverty as droughts. China has cooperated with the United States in military training and military supplies in some countries. China has established embassies in many African countries to aid communication between the governments and businesses in Africa with the government of China. Diplomatic relations are crucial to any political or economic relationship. They enable quick resolutions of disagreements and conflicts while promoting a good public image. China's public policy is referred to as "soft" diplomacy. No official copying of America's official "Big Stick" diplomacy, coined by Pres. Theodore Roosevelt, and used even today by the American empire.

In 2000, China and Africa established the Forum on China-Africa Cooperation, FOCAC. At its third summit in Beijing in 2006, China's president Hu Jintao promised US$5 billion in soft loans. The summit was attended by the heads of states of thirty-five African countries. The fourth summit in 2009 was attended by forty-nine heads of states of African countries. China promised to double its soft loans to US$10 billion. China also promised to write off the entire debts of the poorest African countries. China will provide scientific, medical, and technical training to Africans in China and build agricultural research centers in Africa. China will provide medical equipment to hospitals in Africa. The fifth summit held in Beijing on September 3–4, 2018, was the largest and most high-profile diplomatic event held in China. It was attended by over three thousand people from Africa, China, and international organizations.

Africa will be a key component of the massive New Silk Road investment project announced by Chinese president Xi Jinping in 2013. One component of this project is the construction of deepwater ports and railways across Africa. China has begun building deepwater ports and railways in many African countries linking the East African coast, across the continent, to ports located on the West African coast. Egypt, Kenya, Djibouti, Tanzania, Tunisia, Gabon, Senegal, Mozambique, and Ghana are some of the countries that will be linked and developed. Admiral Zheng He had crossed the Indian Ocean to Africa's east coast in 1415, but it was Portugal that capitalized on its explorations of the West African coast after colonizing Ceuta that same year. The West has explored, colonized, and built infrastructure in Africa since 1415. Today, it is China that has the bigger dream for Africa.

Just as colonization by Western empires led to Europeans moving to the colonies and colonists moving to the West, China's growing relationship with Africa has led to many Africans immigrating into China to find higher-paying employment. Some two hundred thousand Africans have immigrated to China since the Global Shift. The largest number is from Nigeria. The southern province of Guangzhou is the largest recipient of African immigrants. Somewhat ironic is the fact that Guangzhou, then Canton, was also the same province that China was forced by the West to initially open with the so-called unequal treaties. China today has to deal with illegal immigrants from Africa as the United States and Western Europe deal with illegals from Mexico or the Middle East countries they bomb. China will face criticism by the West for implementing relationships in Africa that bear some resemblance to the earlier Western Scramble for Africa. Just as the American empire became the world's most powerful and extensive empire in history while denying any imperial ambitions, China will face similar charges of imperialism. One important difference, so far, is that China has never invaded militarily or used military force to change the regime of the country. That alone is a vast difference from both the American empire and the Western European empires. The American empire has invaded militarily and regime changed with military force more countries than any other. (See Mirza, *American Invasions*.) Another difference is that both China and Africa see themselves as equal victims of five centuries of Western colonization and use of military force to plunder and steal, while destroying livelihoods, languages, cultures, and religions, and enslaving millions, while using all kinds of propaganda to justify their evil deeds.

One of the ironies of China's post–Global Shift engagement with Africa is Taiwan's competition with China in Africa today. As we have explained many times, Taiwan was second only to Hong Kong in initiating foreign investment in China, which began the Global Shift in China after President Nixon's visit had given the green light to Hong Kong and Taiwan. However, Taiwan has a historical connection with Africa as a "Western" country doing business in Africa as part of the Western alliance with the United States, Western Europe, Japan, and South Korea. Many African countries had followed the United States in recognizing the ROC, Taiwan, as the legitimate government of China. It was not until 1971 that the United States made the decision to switch its policy and recognize the PRC as the legitimate government of China in return for China's support in its Cold War with the Soviet Union. While most of the African countries followed the U.S. lead and switched to the PRC, a few clung to the ROC. One reason is that in 1971, Taiwan's economy was far more developed than China. At that time, Taiwan was much more able to assist African development and trade. By the 1990s, China's ability to aid African development had increased immensely because of the Global Shift. However, continued competition between China and Taiwan for trade and investment opportunities was seen by some African countries as healthy. While Taiwan's investment in Africa today has shrunk relative to China, less than one-tenth annually because of the massive growth of China's investments, continued Taiwanese investment in Africa is seen more as complementary and less as competitive.

The Role of India in Bringing the Global Shift to Africa

Among the emerging economies created by the Global Shift, India is second only to China in aiding the Global Shift to transform and develop Africa. In many respects, India's pre– and post–Global Shift presence in Africa mirrors that of China. First, Western European empires like Britain, France, and Holland brought as many, if not more, Indians as Chinese as indentured labor to work in their African colonies. As many as thirty-two thousand Indian workers were brought to Kenya to build the Mombasa-Uganda railway alone. As a result, there is as large an Indian diaspora as the Chinese diaspora in Africa. India's diaspora is dominant in East Africa and South Africa. In those areas, they tend to be more engaged with India than those in the Chinese diaspora are with China. All of us know that India's most famous son, Mahatma Gandhi, began his nonviolent movement in South Africa. During the British colonial era in African countries like Kenya, Uganda, and South Africa, Indians held prominent positions, aiding the British. Many had moved up the social ladder from indentured labor to professionals, politicians, trade union leaders, and successful entrepreneurs.

Second, both India and China supported the African independence movements after the Second World War. They were both leaders of the Non-Aligned Movement, perhaps India more so than China. They can both empathize with Western colonizations in Africa having been colonized themselves by the same Western empires. Third, both India and China achieved high rates of economic growth because of the Global Shift. China and India are the two most populous countries. Where once their massive populations was the primary cause of their poverty, it was their massive populations that attracted the Global Shift because of their plentiful supply of cheap labor. Both countries now have the resources and the desire to compete with the older Western European empires in developing Africa. Both countries now have the greatest market potential for imports from African growth. One difference is that China has many more state-owned enterprises operating in Africa than India. As a result, India's post–Global Shift engagement with Africa is more dependent on private initiative than on the Indian government.

Just as India is playing catch up with China in embracing the Global Shift, India is playing catch-up with China in playing a major role today in Africa's future economic growth. But number two is a phenomenal achievement, much like the silver medal at the Olympics. We saw that when the Global Shift reached Africa in 2000, China-Africa trade was US$10 billion. At that time, India-Africa trade was US$2.5 billion. In 2015, India's trade with Africa was valued at US$90 billion, compared to China's African trade of US$230 billion. While China is Africa's largest trading partner today, India ranks fourth behind China, the United States, and the EU. India's investment in Africa in 2014 was US$50 billion. China's investment in Africa is at least twice that of India. There are forty thousand African immigrants in India compared to two hundred thousand in China. India has created a number of specific institutions dedicated to increasing India's ties with Africa. These include the India-Africa Institute of Information Technology, the India-Africa Institute for Foreign Trade, and the India-Africa Institute of Educational Planning and Administration.

In many ways, India had a stronger trade relationship with Africa than China prior to Portugal's sea voyages to India following da Gama's first voyage in 1498. Africans had crossed the Indian Ocean using the monsoon winds since ancient times. Recorded trade between India and Africa goes back to the first century. Trade between Egypt and India via the Red Sea is also ancient. India's trade with Egypt expanded after Rome conquered Egypt. North Africans traded with India using the Mediterranean. During the Cold War, many African countries engaged with India to trade and aid their similar struggle for independence from Britain. These pre–Global Shift engagements led to India-Africa trade reaching US$3 billion in 2001. In the twenty-first century, India decided to use its post–Global Shift economic and political clout to take advantage of its strategic location across the Indian Ocean from the Horn of Africa to enhance trade and investment with Africa, while having a military presence in the Indian Ocean, at least equal to that of China. India will use that military presence to aid Africa with maritime security threats from nations and pirates. India also has a longer history of involvement with U.S. peacekeeping missions in Africa than China. India also has a long history of training Africa's militaries and peacekeepers.

India's African engagement today still remains primarily in East and South Africa where it has long historical ties and where most of the Indian diaspora lives. India's focus on this region of Africa is evidenced by the 2003 forum, which formalized the close relationship between India and the South African Development Community, SADC. This helps to explain India's decision to initiate the creation of a BRICS New Development Bank, NDB, which came into effect at the Seventh Summit of BRICS in July 2015. The NDB was proposed by India's prime minister Narendra Modi during the Fourth BRICS Summit held in India in 2012. Agreement was reached by the five member BRICS countries, Brazil, Russia, *India,* China, and *South Africa,* at the Fifth Summit in South Africa in 2013. This agreement was signed at the Sixth Summit in Brazil in 2014. The headquarters of the bank is in Shanghai, China. The five members of BRICS are equal partners in the NDB. In July 2016, the NDB signed an agreement with the Asian Development Bank, ADB, to cooperate on development projects. While 45 percent of the shares of ADB is owned by Japan, the United States, and the EU, China and India together own 13 percent of the shares. In September 2016, the NDB signed an agreement to cooperate with the World Bank on development projects. In 2016, the NDB announced seven investment development projects worth a total of US$1.5 billion. In 2017, the total value of development loans increased to US$2.5 billion.

In 2006, India provided US$125 million to construct a Pan-African e-Network. In 2008, India established the India-Africa Forum Summit, IAFS, to compete with China's older and more established FOCAC. The first summit was attended by heads of states from fourteen African countries. At the second IAFS Summit in 2011, India's prime minister Manmohan Singh announced a US$700 million package to aid education and training in Africa. Many Africans are also being trained and educated in India. The 2011 summit was attended by fifteen African heads of state. At the third summit in 2015 under India's new prime minister, Narendra Modi, attendance by African heads of state increased significantly to forty-one. A total of fifty-four African countries were represented. In 2017, India played host for the first time for the fifty-second annual meeting of the African Development Bank in an attempt to raise the international profile of the bank. India's lead in initiating the creation of the NDB can also be seen as India's response to the earlier initiative taken by China in 2009, at the Boao Forum for Asia, to create the Asian Infrastructure Investment Bank, AIIB. It was not until October 2013 that Pres. Xi Jinping formally launched the AIIB. In June 2014, a memorandum of agreement for the AIIB was signed by twenty-one countries, including India. A total of fifty founding members signed an agreement on June 29, 2015. While the AIIB is primarily China's response to Western domination of the World Bank, ADB, and IMF, India's NDB initiative should complement China's AIIB initiative.

The Global Shift to South Africa

We now turn to examining the Global Shift to the largest economies in Africa. We begin our analyses of the Global Shift to specific African countries with South Africa because it was added to the four-member BRIC countries to create the five-member BRICS countries, and because South Africa is the only African country in the G20 group, created after the Global Shift, to replace the outdated G7 group. In many ways,

South Africa is representative of what the Western imperial powers did to colonize all of Africa just as they colonized all of the New World. As I said above, the one key difference is that fewer of the indigenous African population were killed off with European arms and diseases, compared to the indigenous population of the New World. As a result, the Dutch colonial power in their colony of South Africa had to invent a governance system, commonly referred to as apartheid, to maintain white supremacy. Canada and the United States, by contrast, maintained white supremacy by killing off the majority of First Nations, importing large numbers of whites and severely restricting nonwhite immigrants, imposing a pretend democracy and acting superior to the Dutch in South Africa. The reality is that countries like Canada, the United States, Australia, and New Zealand were no more morally superior than apartheid South Africa but were able to use their hypocrisy to critique far less human abusers such as China and Russia and get away with it because of their control of the media and Western propaganda.

South Africa is also representative of how all the Western imperial powers initially traded with nonwhite countries in Africa, Asia, and the New World, until they were militarily powerful enough to colonize. Portugal had discovered the future Dutch colony of South Africa during its quest to colonize areas of West Africa and simultaneously find a sea route to India and China. Portugal had begun pushing further and further south along the West African coast with their famous caravels since their colonization of the Madeiras in 1418. Urged on by Prince Henry the Navigator, the Portuguese explorers had reached the Gambia River by 1455. They could now use their ill-gotten gains from capturing and selling Africans into slavery to finance their quest to find that sea route to the spices and silk of the orient. This would catapult Portugal into a dominant Western imperial power, enabling it to compete as a Christian power against the dominant Muslim power, the Ottoman Empire. It was Bartholomeu Dias who first rounded the Cape of Good Hope in 1488. Portugal did not colonize South Africa as its primary interest at the time was the spice trade with India.

It was the Dutch empire that first colonized South Africa. Naval power had made Portugal and Spain larger empires than Germany and France. It was the same naval power that enabled the tiny European country, Holland, to steal colonies, trade, and markets in Asia from the powerful Portuguese empire. Having stolen the rich spices of the Moluccas from the Portuguese thieves, Holland decided to add the colony of South Africa to its ill-gotten gains. Prior to the English East India Company, the Dutch East India Company was the richest and most powerful multinational corporation in the world. It needed a foothold in the southern tip of Africa to provide supplies to its merchant navy rounding the Cape of Good Hope en route to the spices of the Moluccas. The Portuguese empire had colonized the Moluccas after landing there in 1512. The later Dutch empire went to war with the Portuguese empire, beginning in 1602 and ending in 1663. The Dutch successfully conquered many of the Portuguese colonies in Asia, including the Spice Islands of the Moluccas.

Unlike the Portuguese, the Dutch were not content with South Africa being just a supply station for its ships to the East Indies. The Dutch East India Company established what came to be called the Dutch Cape Colony in South Africa by stealing land from the African inhabitants. Initially, the Dutch colony protected and served the provisioning needs of the Dutch East India Company for the long sea voyages of its ships to Asia. But the colony soon attracted retired employees of the Dutch East India Company as white settlers. White settlers stole more African land and expanded the geographic size of the colony. The white settlers also added to the population by importing slaves from Asia, Madagascar, and Mozambique to work their stolen African land. The Portuguese had begun an evil Western tradition of capturing slaves to sell for profit and to work stolen lands. This motivated them to use their superior military to steal more lands than they could farm without slaves. Slavery was an essential ingredient of their so-called civilized behavior.

The British stole the colony of South Africa from the Dutch and expanded its size by stealing more African land. The British imported more indentured labor from India to work the stolen land. The discovery of gold and diamonds only made the British more determined to keep South Africa a British colony by using superior military force. South Africa, like other British colonies, helped the British win the First and Second World Wars against its primary imperial rival, Germany. Post–World War II Britain was militarily weakened by the two world wars and unable to hold many of its colonies, including South Africa. The independent Republic of South Africa was established in 1960. In 1966, the UN imposed an economic embargo on South Africa because of its use of apartheid to exclude blacks from the government. This helped to end apartheid in 1991 and enable a democratically elected government in 1994. However, South Africa remains a country dominated by whites and a minority of blacks. The great majority of blacks still live in poverty, experiencing very high rates of unemployment.

The Global Shift has increased industrialization and the rate of growth of South Africa. It has transformed South Africa into one of the leading emerging economies. GDP increased from US$132.96 billion in 2000 to US$416.42 billion in 2011. South Africa has established itself as an outsourcing destination for call centers and business processing services. South Africa is the second-largest economy in Africa, after oil-rich Nigeria. South Africa is ranked as the forty-first-largest economy in the world today. In 2010, South Africa was added to the four-member BRIC group, changing the acronym to BRICS. The five-member BRICS group represents over 40 percent of the world's population, most of whom lived in dire poverty before the Global Shift. Today, this group accounts for about one-quarter of the world's GDP. The Fifth BRICS Summit was hosted by South Africa. However, South Africa remains the poorest of the five BRICS countries, its GDP falling to US$317.5 billion in 2017. Some have argued that such a low GDP makes South Africa ineligible for inclusion in BRICS. However, by including South Africa to represent Africa, BRICS signal that one of its goals is the removal of poverty in Third World economies. When the G20 group was created in 1999 to replace the older G7, South Africa was included as the only country from Africa. The G20 members, including the EU, produce 85 percent of the world's GDP. South Africa has the lowest GDP among the twenty members.

The Global Shift to Nigeria

Nigeria is the largest economy in Africa as measured by GDP. Nigeria's GDP overtook that of South Africa in 2014. Nigeria is also the most populous country in Africa, with a population of 180 million in 2017, representing one-quarter of the total population of Africa. While South Africa is famous for gold and diamonds, Nigeria's natural wealth is oil. Nigeria became a member of OPEC in 1971. Nigeria is the eighth-largest oil exporter in the world. Oil represents about 40 percent of Nigeria's GDP. During the 1970s, Nigeria borrowed heavily, using its oil reserves as collateral, to finance infrastructure. The fall in oil price during the 1980s made it difficult for Nigeria to service its debt. It was not until 2006 that Nigeria was able to repay its debt. The second-largest source of income, after oil, is remittances from the eighteen million Nigerians living in foreign countries such as the United States, Britain, France, Spain, Italy, China, and Canada.

Like South Africa, Nigeria was colonized by Britain for more than a century. Portugal had begun the slave trade in West Africa, and that misnamed "trade" reached Nigeria in the fifteenth century. By the eighteenth century, Britain had become the world's largest slave trading empire. Many British slave traders began to settle in Lagos, one of the thirty-six states of today's Federal Republic of Nigeria. The British also converted many of the primarily Muslim African population of Lagos to Christianity, creating a lasting conflict between Christian and Muslim Nigerians. It was a useful "divide and rule" tactic of the British. It was this "divide and rule" tactic that led to the creation of *Boko Haram,* a group the British now demonize as terrorists. The American empire later took a page from the British and created ISIS in the Middle East. The British steadily increased the area of land stolen from the African people using military force. The British also stole part of the German colony of Cameroon after defeating Germany, adding both to an ever-expanding colony of Nigeria. The other part of German Cameroon went to France, confirming our thesis that the two world wars were primarily about colonies and not Hitler. Nigeria gained its independence from Britain in 1960. The British had combined several of its African colonies to create what became the Federal Republic of Nigeria. Independence naturally brought civil wars and military rule.

By the time of the Global Shift in 2000, independent Nigeria had become a relatively stable African country, ready to be transformed to an emerging economy. Despite having to deal with the continuing conflict between the Nigerian government and Muslim-led Boko Haram, the Global Shift has led to increased development of Nigeria's manufacturing sector, producing cars, trucks, buses, and electronics. A manufacturing hub was established in Ogun state, which is located close to Nigeria's largest city and former capital, Lagos. By 2013, Nigeria had the largest manufacturing sector in Africa. Nigeria's GDP more than tripled between 2000 and 2014. In 2014, Nigeria was ranked as the twentieth-largest economy in the world, using the PPP measure. Nigeria is a member of a group called the Next Eleven, N-11. This is a group of eleven emerging economies identified by the same economist, Jim O'Neill, who coined the BRIC acronym. This new group was created by O'Neill to enlarge the five-member BRICS group to sixteen, BRICS plus N-11. In 2016, countries in the N-11 group had GDP's ranging from US$1,416.9 billion for South Korea to US$186 billion for Vietnam. If we exclude South Korea on the grounds that it was a developed economy before the Global Shift, Indonesia had the highest GDP at US$888.6 billion. Nigeria's 2016 GDP of US$573.6 billion was not far behind.

Nigeria, like South Africa, has attempted to play a leadership role for Africa. They are the two giants of Africa. In this regard, Nigeria was a founding member of the African Union. The African Union is made up of all fifty-five countries in Africa. It's the only example of an organization attempting to unify an entire continent. As such, it's both an overambitious and daunting task. It was created in 2001, just as the Global Shift was beginning to reach Africa. It replaced the older Organization for African Unity, OAU, in 2002. The OAU had been founded in 1963, when many African countries were still fighting for independence from their Western European masters, Britain, France, Italy, and others. The founding fathers of the OAU included two Nigerian leaders, Abubakar Balewa and Nnamdi Azikiwe. The OAU played an important role in removing white colonial rule in Africa. However, the ex-imperial masters continued to undermine the economic and political independence of their ex-colonies. Where once Britain, France, and Italy fought each other for African colonies, they were now united in their efforts to subjugate Africa. Where once their stated mission was to Christianize the heathens, their post–world war mission was to force democracy on them. In both periods, they hid their desire to steal, pillage, rape, and invade, with their powerful propaganda and hypocrisy. Nigeria continues to support the Non-Aligned Movement created by ex-colonies of the West. During the apartheid rule by whites in South Africa, Nigeria supported the efforts of the African National Congress to bring democracy to South Africa. South Africa became a member of the OAU in 1994. Nigeria contributes heavily to UN peacekeeping missions in Africa.

The Global Shift to West Africa

Rather than continuing to address the Global Shift to each of the fifty-five countries in Africa, it makes easier reading if we take advantage of the common groupings of African countries, such as the West African group. We begin with the West African group since Nigeria is one of the key members of this group. Nigeria has the largest economy in the group, and Nigeria's population of 180 million is slightly over half the total population of the group. West Africa is also where the Portuguese empire began the five centuries of Western colonizations, enslavement, rape, and pillage of the African people and their entire continent. After gaining their independence, fifteen countries in West Africa, Benin, Burkina Faso, Cape Verde, Côte d'Ivoire, the Gambia, Ghana, Guinea, Guinea-Bissau, Liberia, Mali, Niger, Nigeria, Senegal, Sierra Leone, and Togo created the Economic Community of West African States (ECOWAS) in 1975. They united to attempt to repair the damage done by centuries of Western colonization. The primary goal of ECOWAS is developing member economies through economic integration and trade. ECOWAS created the Bank for Investment and Development, EBID, to fund both public sector and private sector investments. The bank also finances interregional trade among member countries. As a result of colonizations by three different Western empires, Portugal, France, and Britain, ECOWAS has to be trilingual. There is also a division between the eight French-speaking countries and the seven English- and Portuguese-speaking countries.

A secondary goal of ECOWAS is promoting peace within the region. In 1990, the English-speaking countries in ECOWAS, led by Nigeria, created a military arm called the Economic Community of West African Monitoring Group, ECOMOG. The catalyst for this was the Civil War in Liberia. After the West had indicated that it would not intervene, Nigeria lobbied ECOWAS to intervene. The French-speaking members opposed intervention, but ECOMOG was created and intervened. The "peacekeepers" were made up of soldiers from the member countries in ECOWAS. The vast majority was from the Nigerian army. Nigeria also provided most of the funds for the intervention. ECOMOG later intervened in the Civil War in Sierra Leone in 1997–98 after ending its intervention in Liberia.

ECOWAS has little choice but to work with its old colonial masters if it is to attract the Global Shift to West Africa. Since those colonial masters had formed an Economic Union, EU, after granting independence to their West African colonies, ECOWAS partnered with the EU to trade and attract foreign investment. The EU is the group's largest trading partner, and West Africa is the primary destination of foreign investment by the EU into Africa. The eight-member French-speaking subgroup of ECOWAS uses a common currency tied to the euro. West Africa had an annual average of 6 percent increase in GDP since 2013, the second highest of any region in Africa, after East Africa. In 2016, the EU signed an Economic Partnership Agreement, EPA, with ECOWAS. One of the goals of the EPA is to assist West African countries attract foreign investment and boost their international trade.

The Global Shift to East Africa

Western colonization naturally reached East African countries later than West Africa because of its much further geographical location from the maritime imperial powers of Portugal, Holland, France, and Britain. However, its closer geographical location to China is a key reason for having the highest average rate of economic growth among all the regions of Africa, since the Global Shift. The East African Community, EAC, is made up of six countries, Kenya, Uganda, Tanzania, South Sudan, Rwanda, and Burundi. This is the region of Africa most easily accessed by China by sea across the Indian Ocean. The British had a lengthy and turbulent colonial history in Kenya, Uganda and Tanzania, importing much indentured labor from India and creating the current large Indian diaspora in East Africa. Now China is exploiting its maritime advantage by investing heavily in ports and railways to compete with the old Western European empires. China's massive container ports located in Southern China can cheaply link China's exports of manufactured goods and infrastructure supplies by sea to ports in East Africa built with Chinese capital. In return, China can import raw materials, oil and gas, from East Africa cheaply.

China is a key partner in the massive Lamu corridor infrastructure project involving Kenya, Uganda, South Sudan, and Ethiopia. This project will link East Africa to Sudan and Ethiopia to the north. The project includes the Lamu deepwater port, in Kenya, an oil pipeline connecting Lamu to South Sudan and Ethiopia, an oil refinery, a railway from Lamu to South Sudan and Ethiopia, a highway connecting Lamu to South Sudan and Ethiopia, three international airports, three holiday resort cities, and fiber optic cable. The booming Ethiopian economy now has access to China and the world via the Lamu deepwater port. Once the ancient powerhouse of Africa, Ethiopia is making a long-awaited comeback on the world stage, thanks to the Global Shift and China's major participation in the Global Shift.

China has also signaled its intention to increase its military presence in the region to defend its commercial interests and infrastructure projects. In this regard, China has built a naval base in Djibouti where the American and French empires have naval bases. Djibouti's location on the Bab el-Mandeb Straight between the Red Sea and the Gulf of Aden is also ideal for linking East Africa with the Middle East. These are the reasons why China chose Djibouti to locate its first overseas military base. Where once the American empire could outbid all others for prime real estate, China will be paying Djibouti an annual rent exceeding US$100 million compared to the US$67 million paid by the American empire. Djibouti is connected by rail to Ethiopia's capital city, Addis Ababa. Djibouti is strategically located in the Horn of Africa. A military base is useful to protect shipping using the important Suez Canal. China's military and economic presence in Djibouti revives two of the most powerful African empires, the Ethiopian and the Egyptian, historical allies and competitors. China wants center stage in reviving the fortunes of three ancient African giants, Egypt, Ethiopia, and Sudan, dependent on the waters of the Nile River, reminiscent of Britain's nineteenth-century role. While both Egypt and Sudan have built dams on the Nile, Ethiopia is now building the largest dam in Africa, the Grand Renaissance Dam, on the Blue Nile, twenty-five miles from its border with Sudan. This massive dam will give Ethiopia control of most of the waters of the Nile by controlling the Blue Nile Gorge. All of the economies in the East African group are dependent on the Nile.

The Global Shift to Southern Africa and the Common Market for Eastern and Southern Africa, COMESA

The Western European empires were maritime empires. It was natural that they would colonize the coastal areas before penetrating inland. Portugal had begun the colonization of Africa by pushing further and further south along the West African coast, from its own strategic location in southern Europe. Once reaching the southern tip of

Africa, Portugal's immediate priority was across the Indian Ocean to the western coast of India. At that time, spices were as valuable as African slaves. But it was not long before Western European empires continued to expand their colonization of Africa by turning north from the Cape colony in South Africa into all of Southern Africa and into East Africa. This colonization of Southern Africa and East Africa led to the merging and overlap of the African economies in Southern Africa with those in East Africa. As a result, there are three somewhat overlapping economic groupings, East Africa, Southern Africa, and COMESA.

The economies in the Southern Africa group are South Africa, Angola, the Democratic Republic of the Congo, DRC, Mozambique, Zimbabwe, Madagascar, Malawi, Zambia, seven other smaller economies, as well as Tanzania, a member of the East African community. Tanzania borders Mozambique, Malawi, and Zambia to the south, as well as the DRC to the west. It is the second most populous country in the group, after South Africa. The sixteen countries in Southern Africa created the Southern African Development Community, SADC, to integrate their economies to fight for an end to Western colonization and to enhance trade and economic development. It had to agree to operate in three official languages, English, French, and Portuguese, because of its past colonial status with Britain, France, and Portugal. It chose to locate the headquarters of SADC in one of the smaller members, Botswana. A free trade area, FTA, was created in 2008, not long after the Global Shift had begun to reach Africa, and China and India had begun to capitalize on their emerging economy status to compete with the Western imperial powers in Africa. Just as Nigeria is the African giant dominating the West Africa group, South Africa is the other African giant dominating the Southern Africa group. In 2017, South Africa's president Jacob Zuma became the chair of the group.

The economies in Eastern and Southern Africa created yet another group of African countries in 1994, COMESA. With nineteen member states, it is the largest regional economic group in Africa. The member countries are Kenya, Uganda, DRC, Zimbabwe, Zambia, Rwanda, Swaziland, Burundi, Egypt, Libya, Sudan, Madagascar, Malawi, Mauritius, Ethiopia, Eritrea, Djibouti, Seychelles, and Comoros. Its headquarters is in Lusaka, Zambia. It has three official languages, English, French, and Portuguese. Of note is how COMESA links the Southern African and East African economies to the economies in North Africa, Egypt, and Libya. It also links the historically powerful

African empires of Egypt, Sudan, and Ethiopia. Finally, it includes the strategically important economy of Djibouti, where China now has its first international military base to compete with the military bases of the American and French empires. Djibouti provides a strategic link between the Islamic African countries and the Islamic countries in the Middle East. The United States signed a Trade and Investment Framework Agreement, TIFA, with COMESA in 2001.

In an attempt to merge and further integrate the somewhat overlapping and conflicting allegiances of the three African regional groups, COMESA, SADC, and EAC, an African Free Trade Zone, AFTZ, was created in 2008 by leaders of these three groups. The AFTZ will eliminate duplicative memberships in the three groups. The AFTZ is made up of the twenty-six members of the three groups and creates a larger single group with a more diverse population of Africans, Indians, and Arabs. It has a population close to six hundred million and a GDP of US$700 billion. It covers an area beginning north in Libya and Egypt, through Sudan, Ethiopia, and the DRC, east into Uganda, Kenya, and Tanzania, and south into Zambia, Zimbabwe, Botswana, Mozambique, and South Africa.

The Global Shift to Central Africa and the African Economic Community, AEC

By the beginning of the First World War, the entire continent of Africa had been colonized by the Western European empires. By the time of the Global Shift, all these ex-colonies had become members of one or more African economic communities or FTAs. Those ex-colonies in the heart of the African continent formed the Economic Community for Central African States, ECCAS, in 1983. The ten countries creating this regional group are the Congo and surrounding areas. The Congo is made up of two countries separated by the Congo River, the larger DRC in the south and the smaller Republic of the Congo in the north. North of the Republic of Congo is the Central African Republic and Chad. Gabon is to the west of the Congo. Cameroon, Equatorial Guinea, Sao Tome, and Principe are west of the Central African Republic. All four countries have borders on the West African coast south of Nigeria. They are all countries in West Africa but are not members of ECOWAS. Angola is a large country southwest of the Congo, also having a border on the West African coast. The last of the ten-member community, Burundi, is northwest of the Congo.

Africa has a total of fifty-four independent countries, almost all having a long history of Western colonization, which stole their most valuable resources, enslaved many of their people, rearranged many of their borders, and impacted their cultures, religions, and languages. They have created several regional economic communities to work together to boost their postcolonial economic growth and to take advantage of the Global Shift, which transformed economies in Asia and Latin America. They have also attempted to create a single economic union of all fifty-four countries with the ultimate goal of creating an African Economic Community, AEC. The regional economic communities, RECs, are called *pillars* of the AEC. It's as if the AEC is a single building held up high by the RECs, acting as the pillars of a massive building. The most important pillars are the five RECs we have analyzed above, in the following order, ECOWAS, EAC, SADC, COMESA, and ECCAS. Memberships vary from twenty in COMESA to six in EAC, with some countries being members in more than one REC.

While the Global Shift reached Africa later than Asia and Latin America, in 2013, Africa was the fastest-growing continent and projected to grow at 5 percent annually over the next decade. In 2013, Africa had seven of the world's fastest-growing economies. In the decade before 2015, the GDP of Africa grew by 50 percent compared with 23 percent for the world as a whole. These statistics have led to the phenomenon referred to as "Africa Rising." As a latecomer to the Global Shift, Africa attracts foreign investment both from the developed economies and the emerging economies. Africa is in a good position to bargain with these two competing groups, the EU and the United States on one side, and China and India on the other side. Where once Africans were not welcomed as immigrants into the West, they are now welcomed by both the West and by China and India. The West finds itself in competition with many of its ex-colonies in Asia and Latin America in the new post–Global Shift Scramble for Africa. China's launch of its massive maritime Silk Road infrastructure project is seen as a challenge to Western dominance in both Asia and Africa.

BIBLIOGRAPHY AND REFERENCES

In addition to the books listed below, I have used the Internet extensively to do the necessary research for this book. As everyone knows, a web reference leads to many other references on the same topic. It becomes tedious and time consuming to list all the related references used. We have therefore listed a few key web references on the understanding that those checking these references will easily find related references. I have used these references only to check facts, not to use the authors' interpretation of those facts. It is my unique interpretation of the facts that is the purpose of this book. Hopefully, readers will find my interpretation of the facts objective and logical.

1. An Introduction to China's Largest Cities: China Guide: Best of China
2. Asia Research Centre: Capitalism with Chinese Characteristics: the Public, the Private and the International: Shaun Breslin, Warwick University: June 2004
3. Bartlett, Roger: A History of Russia, Palgrave Macmillan, New York, 2005
4. Beijing Review: An Inside Look at the Xiamen SEZ: Aug. 10, 2009
5. Beijing Review: Hainan Province-China's Largest SEZ: Feb. 3, 2010
6. Brazilian Journal of African Studies e-ISSN 2448-3923 | ISSN 2448-3915 | v.1, n.2, Jul./Dec. 2016 | p.118-130
7. Canadian Branch plant economies: Study Moose
8. Capitalism with Chinese Characteristics: Entrepreneurship and the State (2008) by Yasheng Huang
9. Challenges of Industrial Growth in the US-Mexico Border: Regional Updates: By Isobel Heathcote, University of Guelph
10. China Approves 12th Five-Year Plan for Western Regions: China Briefing, Feb. 27, 2012
11. China's Pearl River Delta overtakes Tokyo as world's largest megacity: the Guardian: Nick van Mead, January 2015
12. Ebrey, Patricia Buckley: The Cambridge Illustrated History of China, Cambridge University Press, London, 2000

13. Foster, Lynn V.: A Brief History of Mexico, Updated edition, Checkmark Books, New York, 2007
14. Hosking, Jeffrey: Russia and the Russians: A History, Harvard University Press, Cambridge, 2001
15. Insight Guides: The Silk Road, Apa Publications, UK, 2012
16. Evaluating China's Special Economic Zones: https://scholarship. law.berkeley.edu/cgi/viewcontent.cgi?referer=http://www.google.ca/ url?sa=t&rct=j&q=&esrc=s&source=web&cd=1&ved=2ahUKEwj k3tzK8_bcAhU2FjQIHTFrBQQQFjAAegQIARAC&url=http% 3A%2F%2Fscholarship.law.berkeley.edu%2Fcgi%2Fviewcontent. cgi%3Farticle%3D1025%26context%3Dbjil&usg=AOvVaw3pnK Z8EZihJ8toyuvOVtUN&httpsredir=1&article=1025&context=bjil
17. Development of the Shenzhen Special Economic Zone: Li Hao: Member of the Standing Committee, National People's Congress China
18. http://welcome.topuertorico.org/
19. https://en.wikipedia.org/wiki/Economy_of_Cuba
20. https://en.wikipedia.org/wiki/List_of_Caribbean_islands
21. https://en.wikipedia.org/wiki/Economy_of_Puerto_Rico
22. https://en.wikipedia.org/wiki/Economy_of_Costa_Rica
23. https://en.wikipedia.org/wiki/Economic_Community_of_West_African_States
24. http://www.ecowas.int/member-states/
25. https://en.wikipedia.org/wiki/MV_Xue_Long
26. https://www.reuters.com/article/us-china-arctic/china-unveils-vision-for-polar-silk-road-across-arctic-idUSKBN1FF0J8
27. https://en.wikipedia.org/wiki/Nordic_countries
28. https://thediplomat.com/2017/04/trump-makes-china-great-in-latin-america/
29. http://www.tribune242.com/news/2014/sep/10/136-adds-up-to-a-new-era-of-china-relationships/
30. https://thediplomat.com/2016/12/is-latin-america-of-strategic-importance-to-china/
31. https://thediplomat.com/2016/11/whats-new-about-xis-new-era-of-china-latin-america-relations/
32. https://en.wikipedia.org/wiki/Economic_Community_of_West_African_States
33. https://en.wikipedia.org/wiki/Economic_history_of_Africa
34. https://en.wikipedia.org/wiki/African_Economic_Community

35. https://en.wikipedia.org/wiki/Economy_of_Africa
36. https://en.wikipedia.org/wiki/African_Free_Trade_Zone
37. https://en.wikipedia.org/wiki/African_Economic_Outlook
38. https://www.eac.int/
39. https://en.wikipedia.org/wiki/Southern_African_Development_Community
40. https://en.wikipedia.org/wiki/Common_Market_for_Eastern_and_Southern_Africa
41. https://ustr.gov/countries-regions/africa/regional-economic-communities-rec/common-market-eastern-and-southern-africa-comesa
42. https://www.usaid.gov/west-africa-regiona/economic-growth-and-trade
43. https://en.wikipedia.org/wiki/Economic_Community_of_Central_African_States
44. https://en.wikipedia.org/wiki/Lamu_Port_and_Lamu-Southern_Sudan-Ethiopia_Transport_Corridor
45. http://www.horndiplomat.com/2016/07/05/why-many-nations-have-military-bases-in-djibouti/
46. https://www.bbc.com/news/world-africa-33115502
47. https://en.wikipedia.org/wiki/Nigeria
48. http://www.ecowas.int/
49. https://en.wikipedia.org/wiki/African_Union
50. https://en.wikipedia.org/wiki/Organisation_of_African_Unity
51. https://en.wikipedia.org/wiki/Emerging_and_growth-leading_economies
52. http://scalar.usc.edu/works/niger-delta-black-gold-blues/12-colonial-subjugation-of-people-land-and-nature-slave-trade-resource-extraction-palm-oil-and-the-invention-of-a-national-territory-kaitlyn
53. https://en.wikipedia.org/wiki/Economy_of_Nigeria
54. https://www.britannica.com/place/Moluccas
55. https://en.wikipedia.org/wiki/Dutch%E2%80%93Portuguese_War
56. https://en.wikipedia.org/wiki/Dutch_Cape_Colony
57. https://en.wikipedia.org/wiki/Economy_of_South_Africa
58. https://tradingeconomics.com/south-africa/gdp
59. https://en.wikipedia.org/wiki/BRICS
60. https://en.wikipedia.org/wiki/History_of_South_Africa

61. https://en.wikipedia.org/wiki/Africa%E2%80%93 India_relations
62. https://www.redanalysis.org/2017/01/30/chinese-new-silk-road-east-africa/
63. https://en.wikipedia.org/wiki/Africa%E2%80%93China_economic_relations
64. https://en.wikipedia.org/wiki/Africa%E2%80%93China_relations
65. https://en.wikipedia.org/wiki/New_Development_Bank
66. https://en.wikipedia.org/wiki/Asian_Infrastructure_Investment_Bank
67. https://en.wikipedia.org/wiki/Boao_Forum_for_Asia
68. https://thewire.in/diplomacy/the-india-africa-relationship-is-beyond-strategic-considerations
69. https://en.wikipedia.org/wiki/Foxconn
70. https://en.wikipedia.org/wiki/Deepwater_Horizon_oil_spill
71. https://en.wikipedia.org/wiki/2013_Savar_building_collapse
72. https://www.theguardian.com/technology/2017/jun/18/foxconn-life-death-forbidden-city-longhua-suicide-apple-iphone-brian-merchant-one-device-extract
73. https://en.wikipedia.org/wiki/North_African_Campaign
74. https://en.wikipedia.org/wiki/Mineral_industry_of_Africa
75. https://www.mondialisation.ca/africa-and-chinas-21ˢᵗ-century-maritime-silk-road/5440861
76. http://blackeconomics.co.uk/wp/the-impact-of-world-war-ii-on-africa/
77. https://www.google.ca/search?ei=jLZ1W8mkNuGt0PEPlNWRkA4&q=east+african+campaign+wwii&oq=East+African+Campaign&gs_l=psy-ab.1.4.0l3j0i22i30k1l7.6812.17122.0.26051.22.22.0.0.0.0.150.2384.0j21.22.0....0...1c.1.64.psy-ab..0.22.2458.6..35i39k1j0i131k1j0i67k1j0i131i67k1j0i20i263k1j0i10k1.101.ls-BR8g4HzE
78. https://en.wikipedia.org/wiki/Economy_of_Puerto_Rico
79. https://en.wikipedia.org/wiki/History_of_Brazil
80. https://en.wikipedia.org/wiki/Economy_of_Brazil
81. https://en.wikipedia.org/wiki/Economy_of_the_Dominican_Republic
82. https://en.wikipedia.org/wiki/Economy_of_Ecuador
83. https://en.wikipedia.org/wiki/Embassy_of_Ecuador,_London

303

84. https://en.wikipedia.org/wiki/Economy_of_Peru
85. https://en.wikipedia.org/wiki/Italian_Tunisians
86. https://en.wikipedia.org/wiki/Economy_of_Venezuela
87. https://en.wikipedia.org/wiki/Economy_of_Colombia
88. https://en.wikipedia.org/wiki/Economy_of_Chile
89. http://factsanddetails.com/russia/History/sub9_1c/entry-4939.html
90. https://en.wikipedia.org/wiki/Military_history_of_the_Russian_Empire
91. https://en.wikipedia.org/wiki/Catherine_the_Great
92. https://en.wikipedia.org/wiki/History_of_Russia_(1721%E2%80%9396)
93. https://en.wikipedia.org/wiki/Aleutian_Islands
94. https://en.wikipedia.org/wiki/Vitus_Bering
95. https://en.wikipedia.org/wiki/Russian_colonization_of_the_Americas
96. https://en.wikipedia.org/wiki/Maritime_fur_trade
97. https://en.wikipedia.org/wiki/History_of_Alaska
98. https://en.wikipedia.org/wiki/History_of_China
99. https://en.wikipedia.org/wiki/Asian_Century
100. https://en.wikipedia.org/wiki/D-8_Organization_for_Economic_Cooperation
101. https://en.wikipedia.org/wiki/Shanghai_Cooperation_Organisation
102. https://en.wikipedia.org/wiki/1997_Asian_financial_crisis
103. https://en.wikipedia.org/wiki/1991_Indian_economic_crisis
104. https://en.wikipedia.org/wiki/Economy_of_Bangladesh
105. https://en.wikipedia.org/wiki/Bangladesh%E2%80%93Pakistan_relations
106. https://en.wikipedia.org/wiki/Economy_of_Pakistan
107. https://en.wikipedia.org/wiki/China%E2%80%93Pakistan_Economic_Corridor
108. https://en.wikipedia.org/wiki/Gwadar_Port
109. https://en.wikipedia.org/wiki/Islamabad
110. https://en.wikipedia.org/wiki/Economy_of_the_Philippines
111. https://en.wikipedia.org/wiki/Association_of_Southeast_Asian_Nations
112. https://en.wikipedia.org/wiki/List_of_ASEAN_countries_by_GDP

113. https://en.wikipedia.org/wiki/Economy_of_Malaysia
114. https://en.wikipedia.org/wiki/Economy_of_Thailand
115. https://en.wikipedia.org/wiki/Fall_of_Suharto
116. https://en.wikipedia.org/wiki/Economy_of_Indonesia
117. https://www.indonesia-investments.com/finance/macroeconomic-indicators/gross-domestic-product-of-indonesia/item253?
118. https://en.wikipedia.org/wiki/Dharamshala
119. https://scholarship.law.cornell.edu/cgi/viewcontent.cgi?article=1764&context=cilj
120. http://greaterpacificcapital.com/archive/
121. https://en.wikipedia.org/wiki/Low-cost_country_sourcing
122. http://statisticstimes.com/economy/gdp-growth-of-india.php
123. https://en.wikipedia.org/wiki/Make_in_India
124. https://en.wikipedia.org/wiki/Economic_development_in_India
125. https://en.wikipedia.org/wiki/History_of_India
126. https://en.wikipedia.org/wiki/History_of_the_Republic_of_India
127. https://en.wikipedia.org/wiki/Economic_history_of_India
128. https://en.wikipedia.org/wiki/Economy_of_India
129. https://en.wikipedia.org/wiki/Economic_liberalisation_in_India
130. https://en.wikipedia.org/wiki/Silicon_Valley_of_India
131. https://en.wikipedia.org/wiki/Business_process_outsourcing_to_India
132. https://en.wikipedia.org/wiki/Offshoring
133. https://en.wikipedia.org/wiki/Call_centre
134. https://en.wikipedia.org/wiki/Pramod_Bhasin
135. http://shodhganga.inflibnet.ac.in/bitstream/10603/5435/7/07_chapter%202.pdf
136. https://en.wikipedia.org/wiki/Chinese_economic_reform
137. https://en.wikipedia.org/wiki/Special_economic_zones_of_China
138. https://en.wikipedia.org/wiki/Tibet_(1912%E2%80%931951)
139. https://en.wikipedia.org/wiki/Tibetan_sovereignty_debate
140. https://en.wikipedia.org/wiki/History_of_Tibet
141. https://en.wikipedia.org/wiki/Dalai_Lama
142. https://en.wikipedia.org/wiki/Qinghai%E2%80%93Tibet_railway
143. https://en.wikipedia.org/wiki/Shaanxi
144. https://en.wikipedia.org/wiki/Sichuan
145. https://en.wikipedia.org/wiki/Yangtze

146. https://en.wikipedia.org/wiki/Three_Gorges_Dam
147. https://en.wikipedia.org/wiki/Chengdu
148. https://en.wikipedia.org/wiki/Economy_of_Chongqing
149. https://en.wikipedia.org/wiki/Chongqing
150. https://en.wikipedia.org/wiki/Xinjiang
151. https://en.wikipedia.org/wiki/South_China
152. https://en.wikipedia.org/wiki/China%E2%80%93United_States_relations
153. https://www.scmp.com/comment/insight-opinion/article/1897065/how-economic-dynamism-yangtze-river-delta-flowing-inland
154. https://www.worldbank.org/content/dam/Worldbank/Event/Africa/Investing%20in%20Africa%20Forum/2015/investing-in-africa-forum-chinas-special-economic-zone.pdf
155. https://en.wikipedia.org/wiki/Port_of_Shenzhen
156. https://www.chinahighlights.com/travelguide/transportation/shenzhen-hong-kong-transportation.htm
157. https://en.wikipedia.org/wiki/Shenzhen
158. https://en.wikipedia.org/wiki/Nanjing
159. https://en.wikipedia.org/wiki/Jiangsu
160. https://en.wikipedia.org/wiki/Three_Gorges_Dam
161. https://en.wikipedia.org/wiki/Shanghai
162. https://en.wikipedia.org/wiki/Zhejiang
163. https://en.wikipedia.org/wiki/Hangzhou
164. https://en.wikipedia.org/wiki/Anhui
165. https://en.wikipedia.org/wiki/Yangtze
166. https://en.wikipedia.org/wiki/Xinhai_Revolution
167. https://en.wikipedia.org/wiki/Richard_Nixon%27s_1972_visit_to_China
168. https://en.wikipedia.org/wiki/Canton_System
169. https://en.wikipedia.org/wiki/First_Sino-Japanese_War
170. https://en.wikipedia.org/wiki/History_of_Macau
171. https://en.wikipedia.org/wiki/Guangzhou
172. https://en.wikipedia.org/wiki/Xiamen_Special_Economic_Zone
173. https://en.wikipedia.org/wiki/Canton_System
174. https://en.wikipedia.org/wiki/Political_status_of_Taiwan
175. https://en.wikipedia.org/wiki/Zhuhai
176. https://en.wikipedia.org/wiki/Haicang_District

177. https://en.wikipedia.org/wiki/China_Western_Development
178. https://en.wikipedia.org/wiki/Shantou
179. https://en.wikipedia.org/wiki/Economy_of_Taiwan
180. https://en.wikipedia.org/wiki/History_of_Taiwan
181. https://en.wikipedia.org/wiki/Kinmen
182. https://en.wikipedia.org/wiki/Taiwan_Strait
183. https://en.wikipedia.org/wiki/Sun_Yat-sen
184. https://en.wikipedia.org/wiki/Shenzhen
185. https://en.wikipedia.org/wiki/Economy_of_Hong_Kong
186. https://eh.net/encyclopedia/economic-history-of-hong-kong/
187. https://en.wikipedia.org/wiki/Socialism_with_Chinese_characteristics
188. https://en.wikipedia.org/wiki/Economic_history_of_China_before_1912
189. https://en.wikipedia.org/wiki/History_of_the_People%27s_Republic_of_China
190. https://en.wikipedia.org/wiki/Four_Asian_Tigers
191. https://en.wikipedia.org/wiki/Dongguan
192. https://en.wikipedia.org/wiki/Foshan
193. https://en.wikipedia.org/wiki/Fujian
194. https://en.wikipedia.org/wiki/Guangdong
195. https://en.wikipedia.org/wiki/Guangxi
196. https://en.wikipedia.org/wiki/Taiping_Rebellion
197. https://en.wikipedia.org/wiki/China_and_the_United_Nations
198. https://en.wikipedia.org/wiki/Hainan
199. https://en.wikipedia.org/wiki/Taipa
200. https://en.wikipedia.org/wiki/Economy_of_Singapore
201. https://en.wikipedia.org/wiki/Maquiladora
202. https://en.wikipedia.org/wiki/National_Policy
203. https://en.wikipedia.org/wiki/Canada%E2%80%93United_States_Free_Trade_Agreement
204. https://en.wikipedia.org/wiki/North_American_Free_Trade_Agreement
205. https://en.wikipedia.org/wiki/Canadian_nationalism
206. https://en.wikipedia.org/wiki/Canada%E2%80%93United_States_Automotive_Products_Agreement
207. https://en.wikipedia.org/wiki/Good_Neighbor_policy
208. https://en.wikipedia.org/wiki/Mexican_Revolution
209. https://en.wikipedia.org/wiki/Zimmermann_Telegram

210. https://en.wikipedia.org/wiki/United_States_involvement_in_the_Mexican_Revolution
211. https://en.wikipedia.org/wiki/Economy_of_Mexico
212. https://en.wikipedia.org/wiki/Bracero_program
213. https://en.wikipedia.org/wiki/Mexico%E2%80%93United_States_relations
214. https://en.wikipedia.org/wiki/Yangtze_River_Delta_Economic_Zone
215. https://en.wikipedia.org/wiki/Ningxia
216. https://en.wikipedia.org/wiki/Inner_Mongolia
217. https://en.wikipedia.org/wiki/West_Triangle_Economic_Zone
218. https://en.wikipedia.org/wiki/Western_China
219. https://en.wikipedia.org/wiki/Harbin
220. https://en.wikipedia.org/wiki/Jingjinji
221. https://en.wikipedia.org/wiki/2022_Winter_Olympics
222. https://en.wikipedia.org/wiki/Beijing
223. https://en.wikipedia.org/wiki/Tianjin
224. https://en.wikipedia.org/wiki/Economy_of_China
225. https://en.wikipedia.org/wiki/Manchukuo
226. https://en.wikipedia.org/wiki/North_China
227. https://en.wikipedia.org/wiki/Chinese_Eastern_Railway
228. https://en.wikipedia.org/wiki/Qinghai
229. https://en.wikipedia.org/wiki/Xinjiang
230. https://en.wikipedia.org/wiki/Xinjiang_conflict
231. https://en.wikipedia.org/wiki/Gansu
232. https://en.wikipedia.org/wiki/Guizhou
233. https://en.wikipedia.org/wiki/Yunnan
234. https://en.wikipedia.org/wiki/Port_of_Yingkou
235. https://en.wikipedia.org/wiki/Shandong
236. https://en.wikipedia.org/wiki/Bohai_Economic_Rim
237. https://en.wikipedia.org/wiki/Bohai_Sea
238. https://en.wikipedia.org/wiki/Suifenhe
239. https://en.wikipedia.org/wiki/Shenyang
240. https://en.wikipedia.org/wiki/Changchun
241. https://en.wikipedia.org/wiki/Hebei
242. https://en.wikipedia.org/wiki/Dalian
243. https://en.wikipedia.org/wiki/Grand_Canal_(China)
244. https://en.wikipedia.org/wiki/Port_of_Tianjin

245. https://en.wikipedia.org/wiki/List_of_cities_in_China_by_population_and_built-up_area

246. https://en.wikipedia.org/wiki/Uyghur_Khaganate

247. https://en.wikipedia.org/wiki/ASEAN%E2%80%93_China_Free_Trade_Area

248. https://en.wikipedia.org/wiki/Association_of_Southeast_Asian_Nations

249. http://dailypost.ng/2018/09/12/startimes-star-china-africa-cooperation-focac-summit/

250. International Trade: The Canadian Encyclopedia

251. Joint Communique of the US and PRC: "Shanghai Communique," Feb. 28, 1972

252. Maquiladora: Encyclopedia Britannica

253. Market Profiles on Chinese Cities and Provinces: hktdc.com

254. Misery of the maquiladoras: Socialistworker.org

255. Proximity and complementarity in Hong Kong-Shenzhen industrialization
    W Wu - Asian Survey, 1997 – JSTOR

256. Rapprochement with China, 1972: US Department of State: Milestones: 1969-1976

257. Socialism Today: China's hybrid economy. Socialist Party magazine, Issue 122, Oct. 2008

258. Taiwan and US-China Relations: Asia for Educators: Columbia University

259. The great leap upward: China's Pearl River Delta, then and now: The Guardian, May 2016

260. The Canada-US Auto Pact of 1965: An Experiment in Selective Trade Liberalization: National Bureau of Economic Research: June 1986

261. The Role of Maquiladoras in Mexico's Export Boom: Gordon H. Hanson

262. US-China Relations Since 1949: Asia for Educators: Columbia University

263. U.S.-China Trade, 1971–2012: Insights into the U.S.-China Relationship https://apjjf.org/2013/11/24/Dong-Wang/3958/article.html

FREE PREVIEW

Riots in France, Brexit, populism, discontent, Far Right politicians across Europe, growing income and wealth inequality in the West, loss of the American dream of upward mobility, and *President Trump*. What is the real cause of these phenomena? My answer: The Global Shift of economic, political and military power from the Western developed economies of Europe and North America to the Eastern emerging economies of China, India, Indonesia, Latin America, and Africa. This Global Shift is responsible for the loss of high-paying manufacturing jobs in the West and the demise of high-paying union jobs. While consumers have benefitted from the imports of cheap manufactured goods from the emerging economies, high-wage workers in the coal and steel industries, in manufacturing and construction, and in unionized blue-collar jobs have permanently lost their middle-class-income status by trading jobs paying forty dollars per hour for jobs paying ten dollars at Walmart and other retail outlets. These are the voters candidate Clinton called the "basket of deplorables" because they were invisible to her as they are invisible to establishment leaders like Trudeau, Macron, and Merkel.

Western leaders continue to behave as if the countries they lead, Germany, Britain, France, Italy, Canada, are as powerful economically, politically, and militarily as they were before the Global Shift. They continue to waste billions of taxpayer dollars on imperialism, military invasions, warmongering, and the creation of sixty-five million refugees, none of which provide any economic benefits to the majority of their voters. At the same time, they reduce expenditures on programs that support the middle class and lower middle class and squeeze unions to abandon benefits such as higher wages, pensions, and health care by blaming global competition. They simultaneously pretend to care about global warming and environmental degradation but favor increased *Globalization* to win votes by enhancing economic growth. They blatantly ignore the inherent contradiction between fostering ever greater consumption of junk to promote economic growth and environmental degradation. They focus only on the "recycle" parts of the 3Rs, ignoring "reduce" and "reuse," because of their addiction to economic growth.

President Nixon began to engage with China not for trade but for enhancing Western imperialism. President Nixon exploited the political, ideological, and border conflict between China and the Soviet Union to wean China away from the Soviet Union to help the West win the Cold War. China was allowed to keep its Communist political system and its independent military. President Nixon could not have foreseen any political, military, or economic threat from China since China was a "dirt poor" country when President Nixon visited China in 1972. It was not until 1980 that Nixon's 1972 visit led to the creation of China's first SEZ. At the time, the GDP of the United States was 12.7 times that of the GDP of China. China was ranked the tenth-largest economy, behind the United States and all its major allies, Japan, Germany, the UK, France, Italy, Spain, and Canada.

In 1972, no Western leader ever imagined that China's economy would one day overtake any of the major allies of the United States, much less all of them. However, by the time the Soviet Union collapsed in 1991, Western leaders could have seen some signs of this possibility, however remote. They could have acted by disengaging with China since the West had now won the Cold War. But Western leaders are not visionaries. In 1991, Western leaders reevaluated their engagement with China as *economic* rather than *political*. That was an irreversible mistake. China outgrew the Western economies by a ratio of 5:1. While the average annual growth rate in the West was about 2 percent, it was about 10 percent in China.

The continued economic engagement with China after 1991 had the following benefits to the West:

1. much lower price of imported manufactured goods for their voters
2. shift of dirty polluting factories from the West to emerging economies
3. a small bump in growth rates from increased international trade

But continued economic engagement had the following costs:

1. the emergence of China as the second-largest economy in the world
2. an ever-increasing group of non-Western emerging economies such as India, Indonesia, Vietnam, Brazil, Russia, Mexico, Nigeria, ASEAN, and others
3. relative loss of political, economic, and military dominance by the West in institutions such as the G7, the WTO, the

IMF, the World Bank, the UN, the reserve currency, the financial markets, the mainstream media, and social media, cybersecurity, and spying.

4. increased income and wealth inequality in the West
5. erosion of the size and income of the middle class
6. loss of high-wage manufacturing jobs and high-wage jobs in construction, steel, and coal
7. loss of the American dream of upward mobility and emergence of a new "Chinese dream"
8. the replacement of the American century by a new Asian century
9. expected demise of the West and reemergence of Eastern dominance

While President Trump and Far Right leaders are correct in their analysis that this Global Shift, which they erroneously call *Globalization*, must be abandoned to reassert Western dominance, they are too late to reverse course. Once Columbus had rediscovered the New World, it was impossible to prevent the rise of the West. In like manner, once the Global Shift was allowed to expand from the Mexican maquiladoras to the SEZs of China and to the call centers of India for four decades, it is now too late for any Western leader or leaders to halt it. It now has an unstoppable momentum of its own.

The only hope for the West is to cease its continued wasteful spending on defense, warmongering, regime changes, policing the globe, creation of millions of refugees with its bombings, invasions, and wanton destruction of property. The West must now focus on the economic needs of its own voters and form equal partnerships with non-Western countries. It can no longer dictate and use military or economic threats as the execution of those threats will harm it far more that those attacked.

Printed in the United States
By Bookmasters